Glory Be to the Father

Source Unknown, 2nd Century   GLORIA PATRI   Henry W. Greatorex, 1813-1858

Glo-ry be to the Fa-ther, and to the Son, and to the Ho-ly Ghost; As it was in the beginning, is now and ever shall be, world without end. A - men, A - men.

(Second Tune)   GLORIA PATRI   Charles Meineke, 1782-1850

Glo - ry be to the Fa-ther, and to the Son, and to the Ho - ly Ghost; As it was in the be-gin-ning, is now and ev-er shall be, world without end. A-men, A-men.

(Third Tune)   GLORIA PATRI   Old Scottish Chant

Glo-ry be to the Fa - ther, and to the Son, and to the Ho - ly Ghost;
As it was in the be-gin-ning, is now and ev - er shall be, world with-out end. A - men.

Presented to

Edgemere Christian
Church

In Memory of

Father: Mr. Charles White

by

Mrs. Evelyn Sauerwald

Worship and Service Hymnal

For

Church, School, and Home

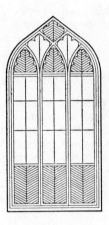

1967

Printed in U.S.A.

HOPE PUBLISHING COMPANY
Established 1892
5707 WEST LAKE STREET
CHICAGO

PREFACE

"Every good hymn learned and loved is another window through which the worshiping soul looks toward heaven."

Congregational singing should be the meaningful expression of every individual Christian—whether the hymn be one of praise or prayer, instruction or exhortation, and whether it be sung in a regular morning or evening service, a prayer hour, a church school assembly, or departmental service. The window embossed on the front cover of this "Worship and Service Hymnal" is a symbol of our hope and prayer that in all these ways and for whatever occasion, this hymnal may be one means of drawing the worshiping soul nearer to God.

The title, "Worship and Service Hymnal," was chosen to symbolize the broad use possible with this treasury of traditional and gospel hymnody and Scripture material: first, to meet the worship needs of the individual and the congregation; and second, to meet the service needs in all departments of the church, church school, the home, seminary, Bible institute, school and college.

We believe that there is a distinct relationship between a knowledge of our heritage in hymnody and better singing. The "Worship and Service Hymnal" provides a source book of the better historical hymns, which, though written in other centuries with differing cultural and scientific conceptions, still have a big place in the minds, hearts, and lives of Christians today. The hymnal includes many features which should bring more understanding and inspiration to every congregation, group, or person who sings from it.

The historic hymns written prior to the 16th Century, and translated from Greek or Latin, are listed in the Topical Index under "Ancient Hymns." Many German hymns of the Reformation are included; the most familiar are listed under "Chorales." Hymns taken from the Psalter or based on the Psalms will be found under "Metrical Psalms" and "Psalm Adaptations." The dates of authors, composers, and sources, as well as the tune names (when traditionally used) are placed on each music page. Whenever we were aware that a hymn is sung to two or more different tunes, we chose the most widely accepted one and listed the alternate tune reference at the bottom of the hymn.

The logical grouping of hymns by dominant thought will facilitate finding appropriate selections for most services. See Contents page 4. Where a special topic is required, however, a detailed Topical Index of 250 headings, beginning on page 499, will be invaluable in quickly locating an appropriate hymn. The Alphabetical and Metrical Tune Indexes, pages 489-492, include all tune names that are in use. A detailed Authors, Composers, and Sources Index will be found on pages 493-498.

Recognizing the increased emphasis on choir music in the church of today, this hymnal contains seventeen hymns set with descant arrangements in small notes for choral rendition. These hymns are listed in the Topical Index under "Descants." In addition, there are other hymns suitable for choir use listed in the Topical Index under "Choir" and "Chorales." There is a good variety of special Service Music material for the choir and congregation found on the front and back end sheets, and as hymn numbers 526 to 543. These include Opening Sentences, Doxologies, Glorias, Prayer Responses, Offertory Sentences, Responses to Scripture, and Closing Sentences, including Amens.

The 73 Scripture Readings, Nos. 544-616, have been carefully selected to meet every possible need throughout the entire year. These readings are alphabetically, scripturally, and topically indexed. They are rich in both Old and New Testament material and are in consecutive scriptural order. Each has multiple uses under as many as eleven different topics. An unusually helpful feature is the classification of these readings in the Subject Index, page 487, which follows in general the same order of classification as the hymns. All Scripture Readings are arranged for effective use as either Responsive or Unison Readings. Scriptural Calls to Worship and Benedictions follow the last Scripture Reading No. 616. They are numbered for easy reference for group use.

We have endeavored to trace the source of authorship and copyright ownership of all hymns. If any omissions have occurred, proper acknowledgement will be made in subsequent editions.

Grateful acknowledgement is made to the many pastors, musicians, and laymen, who, through questionnaires, counsel, and personal conferences, have made it possible to achieve in one book musical and scriptural material adequate to meet every hymnal need of the churches of all protestant bodies.

One of our contemporaries has said, "God gave His holy Word in the form of our Bible. Man has compiled a book to be a companion to the holy Word, namely the hymnbook. The Bible is God's expression to man, while the hymnbook is man's expression to God. The Bible presents truths and doctrines, and the hymnbook helps translate them to the masses. Good church music is not an end in itself. It is a means to the end that the lost may be saved and the redeemed may be brought closer to God."

May this hymnal go into all the world to do just that.

HOPE PUBLISHING COMPANY

CONTENTS

A Mighty Fortress Is Our God

1

EIN' FESTE BURG

Martin Luther, 1483-1546
Trans. by Frederick H. Hedge, 1805-1890

Martin Luther, 1483-1546

1. A might-y for-tress is our God, A bul-wark nev-er fail - ing;
2. Did we in our own strength confide, Our striv-ing would be los - ing,
3. And though this world, with dev-ils filled, Should threaten to un-do us,
4. That word a-bove all earth-ly powers—No thanks to them—a-bid - eth;

Our help-er He, a-mid the flood Of mor-tal ills pre-vail - ing.
Were not the right Man on our side, The Man of God's own choos - ing.
We will not fear, for God hath willed His truth to tri-umph through us.
The Spir-it and the gifts are ours Through Him who with us sid - eth.

For still our an-cient foe Doth seek to work us woe; His craft and power are
Dost ask who that may be? Christ Je-sus, it is He; Lord Sab-a-oth His
The prince of darkness grim—We trem-ble not for him; His rage we can en-
Let goods and kin-dred go, This mor-tal life al-so; The bod-y they may

great, And, armed with cru-el hate, On earth is not his e - qual.
name, From age to age the same, And He must win the bat - tle.
dure, For lo! his doom is sure, One lit-tle word shall fell him.
kill: God's truth a-bid-eth still, His King-dom is for-ev - er. A-MEN.

2 God Is Love; His Mercy Brightens

DULCETTA

John Bowring, 1792-1872

From Ludwig van Beethoven, 1770-1827

1. God is love; His mer-cy bright-ens All the path in which we rove;
2. Chance and change are bus-y ev-er; Man de-cays, and a-ges move;
3. E'en the hour that dark-est seem-eth, Will His change-less good-ness prove;
4. He with earth-ly cares en-twin-eth Hope and com-fort from a-bove;

Bliss He wakes and woe He light-ens; God is wis-dom, God is love.
But His mer-cy wan-eth nev-er; God is wis-dom, God is love.
From the gloom His brightness streameth; God is wis-dom, God is love.
Ev-ery-where His glo-ry shin-eth; God is wis-dom, God is love. A-MEN.

3 Forever

Effie Smith Ely, b. 1879

PLAGAL

Donald P. Hustad, b. 1918

1. We sigh for hu-man love, from which A whim or chance may sev-er,
2. We seek earth's peace in things that pass Like foam up-on the riv-er,
3. Man's help, for which we long, gives way, As trees in storm-winds quiv-er,
4. Turn un-to Thee our wav-'ring hearts, O Thou who fail-est nev-er;

And leave un-sought the love of God, Tho' God's love lasts for-ev-er.
While steadfast as the stars on high, God's peace a-bides for-ev-er.
But might-ier than all hu-man need God's help re-mains for-ev-er.
Give us Thy love and Thy great peace, And be our Help for-ev-er! A-MEN.

My God, How Wonderful Thou Art

4

ORTONVILLE

Frederick W. Faber, 1814-1863

Thomas Hastings, 1784-1872

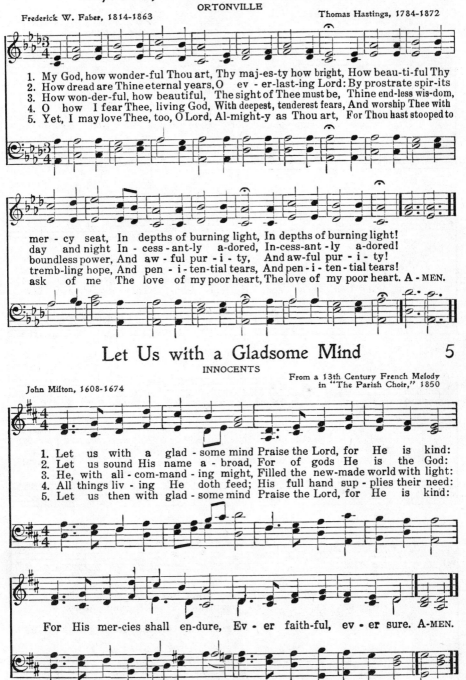

1. My God, how won-der-ful Thou art, Thy maj-es-ty how bright, How beau-ti-ful Thy
2. How dread are Thine eternal years, O ev - er-last-ing Lord: By prostrate spir-its
3. How won-der-ful, how beautiful, The sight of Thee must be, Thine end-less wis-dom,
4. O how I fear Thee, living God, With deepest, tenderest fears, And worship Thee with
5. Yet, I may love Thee, too, O Lord, Al-might-y as Thou art, For Thou hast stooped to

mer - cy seat, In depths of burning light, In depths of burning light!
day and night In - cess-ant-ly a-dored, In-cess-ant-ly a-dored!
boundless power, And aw - ful pur - i - ty, And aw-ful pur - i - ty!
trem-bling hope, And pen - i - ten-tial tears, And pen - i - ten-tial tears!
ask of me The love of my poor heart, The love of my poor heart. A - MEN.

Let Us with a Gladsome Mind

5

INNOCENTS

John Milton, 1608-1674

From a 13th Century French Melody in "The Parish Choir," 1850

1. Let us with a glad - some mind Praise the Lord, for He is kind:
2. Let us sound His name a - broad, For of gods He is the God:
3. He, with all - com-mand - ing might, Filled the new-made world with light:
4. All things liv - ing He doth feed; His full hand sup - plies their need:
5. Let us then with glad - some mind Praise the Lord, for He is kind:

For His mer-cies shall en-dure, Ev - er faith-ful, ev - er sure. A-MEN.

6 The God of Abraham Praise

LEONI (Yigdal)

Daniel ben Judah, 14th Century
Revised Version of "The Yigdal"
By Thomas Olivers, 1725-1799

From a Hebrew Melody
Arr. by Meyer Leoni, d. 1797

1. The God of A-braham praise, Who reigns en-throned a - bove;
2. The God of A-braham praise, At whose su - preme com - mand
3. He by Him - self hath sworn, I on His oath de - pend;
4. The whole tri - um - phant host Give thanks to God on high;

An - cient of ev - er - last - ing days, And God of love.
From earth I rise, and seek the joys At His right hand.
I shall, on ea - gles' wings up - borne, To heaven as - cend;
"Hail, Fa - ther, Son and Ho - ly Ghost!" They ev - er cry.

Je - ho - vah, great I AM, By earth and heaven con - fessed;
I all on earth for - sake, Its wis - dom, fame, and power;
I shall be - hold His face, I shall His power a - dore,
Hail, A-braham's God and mine! I join the heaven - ly lays;

I bow and bless the sa - cred Name, For - ev - er blest.
And Him my on - ly por - tion make, My shield and tower.
And sing the won - ders of His grace For - ev - er - more.
All might and maj - es - ty are Thine, And end - less praise. A - MEN.

Lead, Kindly Light

LUX BENIGNA

John H. Newman, 1801-1890

John B. Dykes, 1823-1876

1. Lead, kind-ly Light, a - mid th' en-cir-cling gloom, Lead Thou me on;
2. I was not ev - er thus, nor prayed that Thou Shouldst lead me on;
3. So long Thy power hath blest me, sure it still Will lead me on,

The night is dark, and I am far from home; Lead Thou me on:
I loved to choose and see my path; but now Lead Thou me on.
O'er moor and fen, o'er crag and tor - rent, till The night is gone;

Keep Thou my feet; I do not ask to see
I loved the gar - ish day, and, spite of fears,
And with the morn those an - gel fac - es smile,

The dis - tant scene—one step e - nough for me.
Pride ruled my will: re - mem - ber not past years.
Which I have loved long since, and lost a - while. A - MEN.

8 O God, Our Help in Ages Past

ST. ANNE

From Psalm 90
Isaac Watts, 1674-1748

Ascribed to William Croft, 1678-1727
"Supplement to the New Version," 1708

1. O God, our help in a - ges past, Our hope for years to come,
2. Un - der the shad - ow of Thy throne Still may we dwell se - cure;
3. Be - fore the hills in or - der stood, Or earth re - ceived her frame,
4. A thou - sand a - ges, in Thy sight, Are like an eve - ning gone;
5. O God, our help in a - ges past, Our hope for years to come,

Our shel - ter from the storm - y blast, And our e - ter - nal home!
Suf - fi - cient is Thine arm a - lone, And our de - fense is sure.
From ev - er - last - ing Thou art God, To end - less years the same.
Short as the watch that ends the night, Be - fore the ris - ing sun.
Be Thou our guide while life shall last, And our e - ter - nal home. A - MEN.

9 When All Thy Mercies, O My God

BELMONT

Joseph Addison, 1672-1719

William Gardiner's "Sacred Melodies," 1812

1. When all thy mer - cies, O my God, My ris - ing soul sur - veys,
2. Un - num - bered com - forts to my soul Thy ten - der care be - stowed,
3. When worn with sick - ness, oft hast Thou With health re - newed my face;
4. Thro' ev - ery pe - riod of my life Thy good - ness I'll pur - sue,

Trans - port - ed with the view, I'm lost In won - der, love and praise.
Be - fore my in - fant heart con - ceived From whom those com - forts flowed.
And, when in sins and sor - rows bowed, Re - vived my soul with grace.
And af - ter death, in dis - tant worlds, The glo - rious theme re - new. A - MEN.

Alternate tunes: MANOAH, No. 126; ST. PETER, No. 244

Praise Ye the Lord, the Almighty

LOBE DEN HERREN

Joachim Neander, 1650-1680
Trans. by Catherine Winkworth, 1829-1878

"Stralsund Gesangbuch," 1665
Arr. in "Praxis Pietatis Melica," 1668

1. Praise ye the Lord, the Al-might-y, the King of cre-a-tion! O my soul, praise Him, for He is thy health and sal-va- - tion! All ye who hear, Now to His tem-ple draw near; Join me in glad ad-o-ra - - - tion!

2. Praise ye the Lord, who o'er all things so won-drous-ly reign-eth, Shel-ters thee un-der His wings, yea, so gen-tly sus-tain - - eth! Hast thou not seen How thy de-sires e'er have been Grant-ed in what He or-dain - - - eth?

3. Praise ye the Lord, who with mar-vel-ous wis-dom hath made thee! Decked thee with health, and with lov-ing hand guid-ed and stayed thee; How oft in grief Hath not He brought thee re-lief, Spread-ing His wings for to shade . . . thee!

4. Praise ye the Lord! O let all that is in me a-dore Him! All that hath life and breath, come now with prais-es be-fore Him! Let the A-men Sound from His peo-ple a-gain: Glad-ly for aye we a-dore . . . Him. A-MEN.

Great Is Thy Faithfulness

Thomas O. Chisholm, b. 1866   William M. Runyan, b. 1870

1. "Great is Thy faith-ful-ness," O God my Fa-ther, There is no shad-ow of
2. Sum-mer and win-ter, and springtime and harvest, Sun, moon and stars in their
3. Par-don for sin and a peace that en-dur-eth, Thy own dear pres-ence to

turn-ing with Thee; Thou chang-est not, Thy com-pas-sions, they fail not;
cours-es a-bove, Join with all na-ture in man-i-fold wit-ness
cheer and to guide; Strength for to-day and bright hope for to-mor-row,

REFRAIN

As Thou hast been Thou for-ev-er wilt be.
To Thy great faith-ful-ness, mer-cy and love. "Great is Thy faith-ful-ness!
Bless-ings all mine, with ten thou-sand be-side!

Great is Thy faithfulness!" Morning by morning new mer-cies I see; All I have

need-ed Thy hand hath pro-vid-ed—"Great is Thy faithfulness," Lord, un-to me!

God Will Take Care of You

Civilla D. Martin, 1869-1948

W. Stillman Martin, 1862-1935

1. Be not dis-mayed what-e'er be-tide, God will take care of you;
2. Through days of toil when heart doth fail, God will take care of you;
3. All you may need He will pro-vide, God will take care of you;
4. No mat-ter what may be the test, God will take care of you;

Be-neath His wings of love a-bide, God will take care of you.
When dan-gers fierce your path as-sail, God will take care of you.
Noth-ing you ask will be de-nied, God will take care of you.
Lean, wea-ry one, up-on His breast, God will take care of you.

REFRAIN

God will take care of you, Through ev-ery day, O'er all the way;

He will take care of you, God will take care of you.........
take care of you.

The Lord Is My Shepherd

POLAND (Koschat)

Psalm 23
James Montgomery, 1771-1854

Thomas Koschat, 1845-1914
Arr. by Edwin O. Excell, 1851-1921

1. The Lord is my Shep-herd, no want shall I know; I feed in green
2. Through the val-ley and shad-ow of death though I stray, Since Thou art my
3. In the midst of af-flic-tion my ta-ble is spread; With bless-ings un-
4. Let good-ness and mer-cy, my boun-ti-ful God, Still fol-low my

pas-tures, safe-fold-ed I rest; He lead-eth my soul where the
Guard-ian, no e-vil I fear; Thy rod shall de-fend me, Thy
meas-ured my cup run-neth o'er; With per-fume and oil Thou a-
steps till I meet Thee a-bove: I seek by the path which my

still wa-ters flow, Re-stores me when wan-dering, re-deems when op-
staff be my stay; No harm can be-fall with my Com-fort-er
noint-est my head; O what shall I ask of Thy prov-i-dence
fore-fa-thers trod, Through the land of their so-journ, Thy king-dom of

pressed; Re-stores me when wan-dering, re-deems when op-pressed.
near; No harm can be-fall with my Com-fort-er near.
more? O what shall I ask of Thy prov-i-dence more?
love; Through the land of their so-journ, Thy king-dom of love. A-MEN.

The Lord's My Shepherd, I'll Not Want 14

CRIMOND

From Psalm 23
"Scottish Psalter"

Jessie Seymour Irvine, 1836-1887
Har. by David Grant, 19th Century

1. The Lord's my Shep - herd, I'll not want; He makes me down to lie
2. My soul He doth re - store a - gain; And me to walk doth make
3. Yea, though I walk through death's dark vale, Yet will I fear no ill;
4. My ta - ble Thou hast fur - nish - ed In pres - ence of my foes;
5. Good-ness and mer - cy all my life Shall sure - ly fol - low me;

In pas-tures green; He lead - eth me The qui - et wa - ters by.
With-in the paths of right-eous-ness, E'en for His own name's sake.
For Thou art with me, and Thy rod And staff me com - fort still.
My head Thou dost with oil a-noint, And my cup o - ver-flows.
And in God's house for - ev - er-more My dwell-ing place shall be. A-MEN.

Alternate tunes: MARTYRDOM, No. 64; BELMONT, No. 9

The King of Love My Shepherd Is 15

DOMINUS REGIT ME

From Psalm 23
Henry W. Baker, 1821-1877

John B. Dykes, 1823-1876

1. The King of love my Shep-herd is, Whose good - ness fail - eth nev - er;
2. Where streams of liv-ing wa - ter flow My ran - somed soul He lead - eth,
3. Per-verse and fool - ish oft I strayed, But yet in love He sought me.
4. In death's dark vale I fear no ill With Thee, dear Lord, be - side me;
5. And so through all the length of days Thy good - ness fail - eth nev - er:

I noth - ing lack if I am His And He is mine for-ev - er.
And, where the ver-dant pas-tures grow, With food ce - les - tial feed - eth.
And on His shoul-der gen - tly laid, And home re - joic-ing brought me.
Thy rod and staff my com - fort still, Thy cross be - fore to guide me.
Good Shep-herd, may I sing Thy praise With - in Thy house for-ev - er. A-MEN.

16 God Moves in a Mysterious Way

DUNDEE (French)

William Cowper, 1731-1800

"Scottish Psalter," 1615

1. God moves in a mys - te - rious way His won - ders to per - form;
2. Ye fear - ful saints, fresh cour - age take; The clouds ye so much dread
3. Judge not the Lord by fee - ble sense, But trust Him for His grace;
4. His pur - pos - es will ri - pen fast, Un - fold - ing ev - er - y hour:
5. Blind un - be - lief is sure to err, And scan His work in vain:

He plants His foot-steps in the sea, And rides up - on the storm.
Are big with mer - cy, and shall break In bless-ings on your head.
Be - hind a frown-ing prov - i - dence He hides a smil - ing face.
The bud may have a bit - ter taste, But sweet will be the flower.
God is His own in - ter - pre - ter, And He will make it plain. A-MEN.

Alternate tunes: MANOAH, No. 126; ST. ANNE, No. 8

17 How Gentle God's Commands

DENNIS

Phillip Doddridge, 1702-1751

Hans G. Nägeli, 1773-1836
Arr. by Lowell Mason, 1792-1872

1. How gen - tle God's com-mands! How kind His pre - cepts are!
2. Be - neath His watch - ful eye His saints se - cure - ly dwell;
3. Why should this anx - ious load Press down your wea - ry mind?
4. His good - ness stands ap - proved, Un - changed from day to day:

Come, cast your bur - dens on the Lord, And trust His con-stant care.
That Hand which bears all na - ture up Shall guard His chil-dren well.
Haste to your heavenly Fa-ther's throne, And sweet re - fresh-ment find.
I'll drop my bur - den at His feet, And bear a song a - way. A-MEN.

For the Beauty of the Earth

DIX

Folliott S. Pierpoint, 1835-1917

Arr. from Conrad Kocher, 1786-1872

1. For the beau-ty of the earth, For the glo-ry
of the skies, For the love which from our birth
O-ver and a-round us lies, Lord of all, to
Thee we raise This our hymn of grate-ful praise.

2. For the beau-ty of each hour Of the day and
of the night, Hill and vale, and tree, and flower,
Sun and moon, and stars of light, Lord of all, to
Thee we raise This our hymn of grate-ful praise.

3. For the joy of hu-man love, Broth-er, sis-ter,
par-ent, child, Friends on earth, and friends a-bove,
For all gen-tle thoughts and mild, Lord of all, to
Thee we raise This our hymn of grate-ful praise.

4. For Thy Church that ev-er-more Lift-eth ho-ly
hands a-bove, Of-fering up on ev-ery shore
Her pure sac-ri-fice of love, Lord of all, to
Thee we raise This our hymn of grate-ful praise. A-MEN.

19   I Sing the Mighty Power of God

ELLACOMBE

Isaac Watts, 1674-1748, alt.   "Gesangbuch der Herzogl," Württemberg, 1784

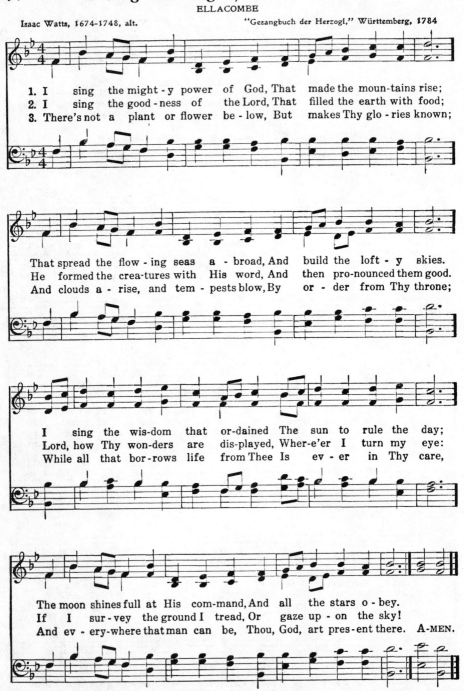

1. I sing the might-y power of God, That made the moun-tains rise;
2. I sing the good-ness of the Lord, That filled the earth with food;
3. There's not a plant or flower be-low, But makes Thy glo-ries known;

That spread the flow-ing seas a - broad, And build the loft-y skies.
He formed the crea-tures with His word, And then pro-nounced them good.
And clouds a - rise, and tem - pests blow, By or - der from Thy throne;

I sing the wis-dom that or-dained The sun to rule the day;
Lord, how Thy won-ders are dis-played, Wher-e'er I turn my eye:
While all that bor-rows life from Thee Is ev - er in Thy care,

The moon shines full at His com-mand, And all the stars o - bey.
If I sur-vey the ground I tread, Or gaze up - on the sky!
And ev - ery-where that man can be, Thou, God, art pres-ent there. A-MEN.

All Creatures of Our God and King

LASST UNS ERFREUEN

20

St. Francis of Assisi, 1182-1226
Trans. by William H. Draper, 1855-1933

Melody from "Geistliche Kirchengesäng," 1623

In unison

1. All crea-tures of our God and King, Lift up your voice and with us
2. Thou rush-ing wind that art so strong, Ye clouds that sail in heav'n a-
3. Dear moth-er earth, who day by day Un - fold - est bless-ings on our
4. And all ye men of ten-der heart, For - giv - ing oth - ers, take your
5. Let all things their Cre - a - tor bless, And wor - ship Him in hum - ble-
   Praise God from whom all bless - ings flow, Praise Him all crea - tures here be-

Harmony ... *Unison*

sing, Al-le - lu - ia! Al-le - lu - ia! Thou burn-ing sun with gold - en
long, O praise Him! Al-le - lu - ia! Thou ris - ing morn, in praise re-
way, O praise Him! Al-le - lu - ia! The flow'rs and fruits that in thee
part, O sing ye! Al-le - lu - ia! Ye who long pain and sor - row
ness. O praise Him! Al-le - lu - ia! Praise, praise the Fa-ther, praise the
low, Al - le - lu - ia! Al - le - lu - ia! Praise Him a - bove, ye heav'n-ly

beam, Thou sil - ver moon with soft - er gleam! O praise Him, O
joice, Ye lights of eve-ning, find a voice! O praise Him, O
grow, Let them His glo - ry al - so show! O praise Him, O
bear, Praise God and on Him cast your care! O praise Him, O
Son, And praise the Spir - it, Three in One! O praise Him, O
host, Praise Fa - ther, Son and Ho - ly Ghost, Al-le - lu - ia, Al-le-

Harmony

Unison

praise Him, Al-le - lu - ia! Al-le - lu - ia! Al-le - lu - ia! A-MEN.
lu - ia!

The Spacious Firmament

CREATION

Joseph Addison, 1672-1719   Franz Joseph Haydn, 1732-1809

1. The spa - cious fir - ma - ment on high, With all the
2. Soon as the eve - ning shades pre - vail, The moon takes
3. What though, in sol - emn si - lence, all Move round this

blue, e - the - real sky, And span - gled heavens, a shin - ing frame,
up the won - drous tale; And night - ly, to the lis - tening earth,
dark ter - res - trial ball? What though no re - al voice nor sound

Their great O - rig - i - nal pro - claim: Th' un-wea-ried sun, from
Re - peats the sto - ry of her birth; While all the stars that
A - mid their ra - diant orbs be found? In rea - son's ear they

day to day, Does his Cre - a - tor's power dis - play; And pub - lish -
round her burn, And all the plan - ets in their turn, Con - firm the
all re - joice, And ut - ter forth a glo - rious voice, For - ev - er

es to ev - ery land The work of an al-might-y hand.
ti - dings as they roll, And spread the truth from pole to pole.
sing - ing as they shine, "The hand that made us is di - vine." A-MEN.

This Is My Father's World

TERRA BEATA

Maltbie D. Babcock, 1858-1901   Franklin L. Sheppard, 1852-1930

1. This is my Fa-ther's world, And to my lis-tening ears All
2. This is my Fa-ther's world, The birds their car-ols raise, The
3. This is my Fa-ther's world, O let me ne'er for-get That

na-ture sings, and round me rings The mu-sic of the spheres.
morn-ing light, the lil-y white, De-clare their Mak-er's praise.
though the wrong seems oft so strong, God is the Rul-er yet.

This is my Fa-ther's world: I rest me in the thought Of
This is my Fa-ther's world: He shines in all that's fair; In the
This is my Fa-ther's world: The bat-tle is not done; Je-

rocks and trees, of skies and seas—His hand the won-ders wrought.
rus-tling grass I hear Him pass, He speaks to me ev-ery-where.
sus who died shall be sat-is-fied, And earth and heaven be one. A-MEN.

Joyful, Joyful, We Adore Thee

HYMN TO JOY

Henry van Dyke, 1852-1933

Ludwig van Beethoven, 1770-1827
Descant (small notes) William Lester, b. 1889

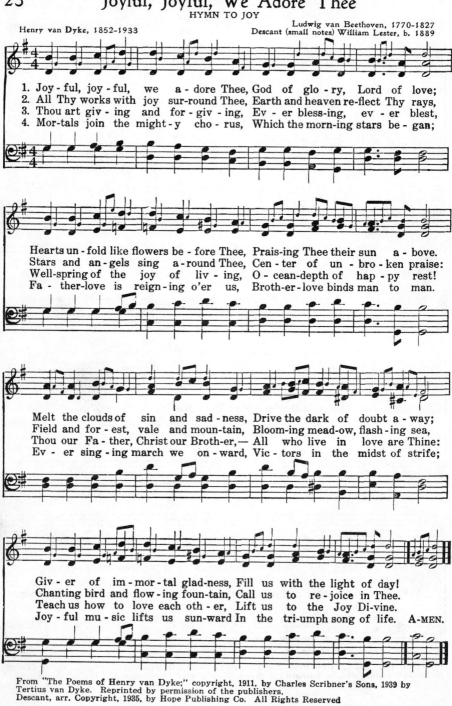

1. Joy - ful, joy - ful, we a - dore Thee, God of glo - ry, Lord of love;
2. All Thy works with joy sur-round Thee, Earth and heaven re-flect Thy rays,
3. Thou art giv - ing and for - giv - ing, Ev - er bless-ing, ev - er blest,
4. Mor-tals join the might - y cho - rus, Which the morn-ing stars be - gan;

Hearts un - fold like flowers be - fore Thee, Prais-ing Thee their sun a - bove.
Stars and an - gels sing a - round Thee, Cen - ter of un - bro - ken praise:
Well-spring of the joy of liv - ing, O - cean-depth of hap - py rest!
Fa - ther-love is reign-ing o'er us, Broth-er-love binds man to man.

Melt the clouds of sin and sad - ness, Drive the dark of doubt a - way;
Field and for - est, vale and moun-tain, Bloom-ing mead-ow, flash-ing sea,
Thou our Fa - ther, Christ our Broth-er,— All who live in love are Thine:
Ev - er sing-ing march we on - ward, Vic - tors in the midst of strife;

Giv - er of im - mor - tal glad-ness, Fill us with the light of day!
Chanting bird and flow-ing foun-tain, Call us to re - joice in Thee.
Teach us how to love each oth - er, Lift us to the Joy Di-vine.
Joy - ful mu - sic lifts us sun-ward In the tri-umph song of life. A-MEN.

O Come, O Come, Emmanuel

VENI EMMANUEL

Latin Hymn, c. 12th Century
Trans. by John M. Neale, 1818-1866

Ancient Plain Song

1. O come, O come, Em-man-u-el, And ran-som cap-tive
2. O come, Thou Rod of Jes-se, free Thine own from Sa-tan's
3. O come, Thou Day-spring, come and cheer Our spir-its by Thine
4. O come, Thou Key of Da-vid, come, And o-pen wide our

Is-ra-el, That mourns in lone-ly ex-ile here
tyr-an-ny; From depths of hell Thy peo-ple save
ad-vent here; And drive a-way the shades of night,
heaven-ly home; Make safe the way that leads on high,

Un-til the Son of God ap-pear. Re-joice! re-joice! Em-
And give them vic-tory o'er the grave. Re-joice! re-joice! Em-
And pierce the clouds and bring us light! Re-joice! re-joice! Em-
And close the path to mis-er-y. Re-joice! re-joice! Em-

man-u-el Shall come to thee, O Is-ra-el!
man-u-el Shall come to thee, O Is-ra-el!
man-u-el Shall come to thee, O Is-ra-el!
man-u-el Shall come to thee, O Is-ra-el! A-MEN.

25 Thou Didst Leave Thy Throne

MARGARET

Emily E. S. Elliott, 1836-1897   Timothy R. Matthews, 1826-1910

1. Thou didst leave Thy throne and Thy king - ly crown When Thou
2. Heav-en's arch - es rang when the an - gels sang, Pro-
3. Thou cam - est, O Lord, with the liv - ing Word That should
4. When the heav - ens shall ring, and the an - gels sing, At Thy

cam - est to earth for me; But in Beth - le - hem's home
claim - ing Thy roy - al de - gree; But in low - ly birth
set Thy peo - ple free; But with mock - ing scorn,
com - ing to vic - to - - ry, Let Thy voice call me home,

was there found no room For Thy ho - ly na - tiv - i - ty:
didst Thou come to earth, And in great hu - mil - i - ty:
and with crown of thorn, They bore Thee to Cal - va - ry:
say - ing, "Yet there is room, There is room at My side for thee:"

REFRAIN

1-3. O come to my heart, Lord Je-sus! There is room in my heart for Thee.
4. My heart shall rejoice, Lord Je-sus! When Thou comest and call-est for me. A-MEN.

Music used by permission of Novello & Co., Ltd.

Come, Thou Long-expected Jesus

HYFRYDOL

Charles Wesley, 1707-1788   Rowland H. Prichard, 1811-1887

1. Come, Thou long - ex - pect - ed Je - sus, Born to set Thy peo - ple free;
2. Born Thy peo - ple to de - liv - er, Born a child and yet a King.

From our fears and sins re - lease us; Let us find our rest in Thee.
Born to reign in us for - ev - er, Now Thy gra - cious king-dom bring.

Is-rael's Strength and Con - so - la - tion, Hope of all the earth Thou art;
By Thine own e - ter - nal Spir - it Rule in all our hearts a - lone;

Dear De - sire of ev - ery na - tion, Joy of ev - ery long-ing heart.
By Thine all - suf - fi - cient mer - it, Raise us to Thy glo-rious throne. A-MEN.

"Music from "The English Hymnal." Used by permission of the Oxford University Press, London."

27 Joy to the World!

ANTIOCH

From Psalm 98
Isaac Watts, 1674-1748

George F. Handel, 1685-1759

1. Joy to the world! the Lord is come; Let earth re-
2. Joy to the earth! the Sav - iour reigns; Let men their
3. No more let sins and sor - rows grow, Nor thorns in-
4. He rules the world with truth and grace, And makes the

ceive her King; Let ev - ery heart pre - pare Him room,
songs em - ploy; While fields and floods, rocks, hills, and plains,
fest the ground; He comes to make His bless - ings flow
na - tions prove The glo - ries of His right - eous - ness,

And heaven and na - ture sing, And heaven and na - ture
Re - peat the sound - ing joy, Re - peat the sound - ing
Far as the curse is found, Far as the curse is
And won - ders of His love, And won - ders of His

1. And heaven and na - ture sing,

1. And

sing, And heaven, and heaven and na - ture sing.
joy, Re - peat, re - peat the sound - ing joy.
found, Far as, far as the curse is found.
love, And won - ders, won - ders of His love. A-MEN.

heaven and na - ture sing,

As with Gladness, Men of Old

DIX

William C. Dix, 1837-1898

Arr. from Conrad Kocher, 1786-1872

1. As with glad - ness men of old Did the guid - ing
2. As with joy - ful steps they sped To that low - ly
3. As they of - fered gifts most rare At that man - ger
4. Ho - ly Je - sus, ev - 'ry day Keep us in the

star be - hold; As with joy they hailed its light,
man - ger - bed, There to bend the knee be - fore
rude and bare, So may we with ho - ly joy,
nar - row way; And, when earth - ly things are past,

Lead - ing on - ward, beam - ing bright, So, most gra - cious
Him Whom heav'n and earth a - dore, So may we with
Pure and free from sin's al - loy, All our cost - liest
Bring our ran - somed souls at last Where they need no

Lord, may we Ev - er - more be led to Thee.
will - ing feet Ev - er seek the mer - cy - seat.
treas - ures bring, Christ, to Thee our heav'n - ly King.
star to guide, Where no clouds Thy glo - ry hide. A-MEN.

29 O Little Town of Bethlehem

ST. LOUIS

Phillips Brooks, 1835-1893

Lewis H. Redner, 1831-1908

1. O lit-tle town of Beth-le-hem, How still we see thee lie! A-bove thy deep and
2. For Christ is born of Ma - ry, And gathered all a-bove, While mortals sleep, the
3. How si-lent-ly, how si-lent-ly, The wondrous gift is given! So God im-parts to
4. O ho-ly Child of Beth-le-hem! De-scend to us, we pray; Cast out our sin, and

dreamless sleep The si - lent stars go by. Yet in thy dark streets shineth The ev - er-
an - gels keep Their watch of wondering love. O morn-ing stars, to-geth-er Proclaim the
human hearts The blessings of His heaven. No ear may hear His com-ing, But in this
en - ter in; Be born in us to-day. We hear the Christmas an-gels The great glad

last-ing Light; The hopes and fears of all the years Are met in thee to-night.
ho - ly birth! And prais-es sing to God the King, And peace to men on earth.
world of sin, Where meek souls will receive Him still, The dear Christ enters in.
ti - dings tell; O come to us, a-bide with us, Our Lord Em-man-u - el. A-MEN.

30 While Shepherds Watched Their Flocks

CHRISTMAS

Nahum Tate, 1652-1715

George F. Handel, 1685-1759

1. While shepherds watched their flocks by night, All seat-ed on the ground, The an - gel
2. "Fear not!" said he; for might-y dread Had seized their troubled mind, "Glad ti-dings
3. "To you, in Dav-id's town this day, Is born of Da-vid's line, The Sav-iour
4. "The heavenly Babe you there shall find To hu-man view dis-played, All mean-ly
5. "All glo - ry be to God on high, And to the earth be peace: Good will hence-

While Shepherds Watched Their Flocks

of the Lord came down, And glo-ry shone a-round, And glo-ry shone a-round.
of great joy I bring To you and all man-kind, To you and all man-kind.
who is Christ, the Lord, And this shall be the sign: And this shall be the sign:
wrapped in swathing bands, And in a man-ger laid; And in a man-ger laid.
forth from heaven to men, Be-gin and nev-er cease, Be - gin and nev-er cease." A-MEN.

Angels, from the Realms of Glory

REGENT SQUARE

James Montgomery, 1771-1854   Henry Smart, 1813-1879

31

1. An - gels, from the realms of glo - ry, Wing your flight o'er all the earth;
2. Shep-herds, in the fields a - bid - ing, Watch-ing o'er your flocks by night,
3. Sa - ges, leave your con - tem-pla-tions, Bright-er vi - sions beam a - far;
4. Saints be-fore the al - tar bend-ing, Watch-ing long in hope and fear,

Ye who sang cre - a - tion's sto - ry, Now pro-claim Mes - si - ah's birth:
God with man is now re - sid - ing, Yon - der shines the in - fant Light:
Seek the great De - sire of na - tions, Ye have seen his na - tal star:
Sud - den - ly the Lord, de - scend-ing, In His tem - ple shall ap-pear:

Come and wor-ship, come and wor-ship, Worship Christ, the new-born King. A-MEN.

Hark, the Herald Angels Sing

MENDELSSOHN

Charles Wesley, 1707-1788

Felix Mendelssohn, 1809-1847
Arr. by William H. Cummings, 1831-1915

1. Hark! the her - ald an - gels sing, "Glo - ry · to the new - born King:
2. Christ, by high - est heaven a - dored; Christ, the Ev - er - last - ing Lord!
3. Hail the heaven-born Prince of Peace! Hail the Sun of Right-eous - ness!

Peace on earth, and mer - cy mild, God and sin - ners rec - on - ciled!"
Late in time be - hold Him come, Off - spring of the Vir - gin's womb:
Light and life to all He brings, Risen with heal - ing in His wings.

Joy - ful, all ye na - tions, rise, Join the tri - umph of the skies;
Veiled in flesh the God - head see; Hail th' In - car - nate De - i - ty,
Mild He lays His glo - ry by, Born that man no more may die,

With th' an - gel - ic host pro-claim, "Christ is born in Beth - le - hem!"
Pleased as man with men to dwell, Je - sus, our Em - man - u - el.
Born to raise the sons of earth, Born to give them sec - ond birth.

Hark! the her - ald an - gels sing, "Glo - ry to the new-born King." A-MEN.

Music used by permission of Novello & Co., Ltd.

Angels We Have Heard on High

GLORIA

Source Unknown

Old French Carol

1. An - gels we have heard on high, Sweet - ly sing - ing o'er the plains,
2. Shepherds, why this ju - bi - lee? Why your joy - ous strains pro - long?
3. Come to Beth - le - hem, and see Him whose birth the an - gels sing;
4. See with - in a man - ger laid Je - sus, Lord of heav'n and earth!

And the moun - tains in re - ply Ech - o back their joy - ous strains.
Say what may the ti - dings be, Which in - spire your heav'n - ly song?
Come, a - dore on bend - ed knee Christ the Lord, the new - born King.
Ma - ry, Jo - seph, lend your aid, With us sing our Sav - iour's birth.

REFRAIN

Glo - - - - - - - - - - - - - ri - a

in ex - cel - sis De - o, Glo - - - - - - -

- - - - - ri - a in ex - cel - sis De - o. A-MEN.

34 The First Noel, the Angel Did Say

THE FIRST NOEL

Old English Carol, 1833

Traditional Melody from
W. Sandy's "Christmas Carols," 1833

1. The first No - el, the an-gel did say, Was to cer-tain poor shepherds in fields as they lay; In fields where they lay keep-ing their sheep, On a cold win-ter's night that was so deep.

2. They look-ed up and saw a star Shin-ing in the east, be-yond them far, And to the earth it gave great light, And so it con-tin-ued both day and night.

3. And by the light of that same star, Three wise-men came from coun-try far; To seek for a king was their in - tent, And to fol-low the star wher-ev-er it went.

4. This star drew nigh to the north-west, O'er Beth - le - hem it took its rest, And there it did both stop and stay, Right o - ver the place where Je - sus lay.

5. Then en - tered in those wise-men three, Full rev - 'rent-ly up-on the knee, And of-fered there, in His pres-ence, Their gold, and myrrh, and frank - in-cense.

6. Then let us all with one ac-cord Sing prais-es to our heav'n - ly Lord, That hath made heav'n and earth of naught, And with His blood man - kind hath bought.

REFRAIN

No - el, No - el, No-el, No - el, Born is the King of Is - ra - el.

It Came Upon the Midnight Clear

CAROL

Edmund H. Sears, 1810-1876

Richard S. Willis, 1819-1900

1. It came up-on the mid-night clear, That glo-rious song of old,
2. Still through the clo-ven skies they come, With peace-ful wings un - furled,
3. And ye, be-neath life's crush-ing load, Whose forms are bend-ing low,
4. For lo, the days are has-tening on, By proph-et - bards fore - told,

From an - gels bend-ing near the earth To touch their harps of gold:
And still their heaven-ly mu - sic floats O'er all the wea - ry world:
Who toil a - long the climb-ing way With pain - ful steps and slow,
When, with the ev - er - cir - cling years, Comes round the age of gold:

"Peace on the earth, good-will to men, From heaven's all-gra-cious King": The
A - bove its sad and low - ly plains They bend on hov-ering wing: And
Look now! for glad and gold - en hours Come swift-ly on the wing; O
When peace shall o - ver all the earth Its an - cient splen-dors fling, And

world in sol - emn still - ness lay To hear the an - gels sing.
ev - er o'er its Ba - bel sounds The bless - ed an - gels sing.
rest be - side the wea - ry road, And hear the an - gels sing.
the whole world give back the song Which now the an - gels sing. A - MEN.

36 O Come, All Ye Faithful

ADESTE FIDELES

Latin Hymn, 18th Century
Trans. by Frederick Oakeley, 1802-1880

John F. Wade's "Cantus Diversi," 1751
Descant (small notes), William Lester, b. 1889

1. O come, all ye faith - ful, Joy - ful and tri - um - phant,
2. Sing, choirs of an - gels, Sing in ex - ul - ta - tion!
3. Yea, Lord, we greet Thee, Born this hap - py morn - ing,

O come ye, O come ye to Beth - le - hem!
O sing, all ye bright hosts of heaven a - bove;
Je - sus, to Thee be all glo - ry given;

Come and be - hold Him, Born the King of an - gels;
Glo - ry to God, all Glo - ry in the high - est;
Word of the Fa - ther, Now in flesh ap - pear - ing;

REFRAIN

O come, let us a - dore Him, O come, let us a - dore Him,

O come, let us a - dore Him, Christ the Lord. A - MEN.

For alternate Descant to same tune, see No. 279

There's a Song in the Air

CHRISTMAS SONG

Josiah G. Holland, 1819-1881

Karl P. Harrington, 1861-1953

1. There's a song in the air! There's a star in the sky!
2. There's a tu - mult of joy O'er the won - der - ful birth,
3. In the light of that star Lie the a - ges im - pearled,
4. We re - joice in the light, And we ech - o the song

There's a mo - ther's deep prayer, And a ba - by's low cry!
For the Vir - gin's sweet boy Is the Lord of the earth.
And that song from a - far Has swept o - ver the world.
That comes down through the night From the heav - en - ly throng.

And the star rains its fire while the beau - ti - ful sing,
Ay! the star rains its fire while the beau - ti - ful sing,
Ev - ery heart is a - flame, and the beau - ti - ful sing,
Ay! we shout to the love - ly e - van - gel they bring,

For the man - ger of Beth - le - hem cra - dles a King!
For the man - ger of Beth - le - hem cra - dles a King!
In the homes of the na - tions that Je - sus is King!
And we greet in His cra - dle our Sav - iour and King! A-MEN.

38 Silent Night! Holy Night!
STILLE NACHT

Joseph Mohr, 1792-1848 Franz Grüber, 1787-1863

1. Si - lent night! ho - ly night! All is calm, all is bright
2. Si - lent night! ho - ly night! Shep-herds quake at the sight,
3. Si - lent night! ho - ly night! Son of God, Love's pure light,
4. Si - lent night! ho - ly night! All is dark save the light

'Round yon vir - gin mo-ther and Child, Ho - ly In - fant so ten-der and mild,
Glo - ries stream from heav-en a - far, Heavenly hosts sing Al - le - lu - ia;
Ra - diant beams from Thy ho-ly face, With the dawn of re - deem-ing grace,
Yon - der, where they sweet vi - gils keep O'er the Babe who in si - lent sleep

Sleep in heav - en - ly peace, Sleep in heav - en - ly peace.
Christ the Sav - iour is born, Christ the Sav - iour is born.
Je - sus, Lord, at Thy birth, Je - sus, Lord, at Thy birth.
Rests in heav - en - ly peace, Rests in heav - en - ly peace. A-MEN.

39 Away in a Manger
MUELLER

Stanzas 1 and 2, Source Unknown James R. Murray, 1841-1905
Stanza 3, John Thomas McFarland, 1851-1913 Arr. by Donald P. Hustad, b. 1918

1. A - way in a man - ger, no crib for a bed, The lit - tle Lord
2. The cat - tle are low - ing, the Ba - by a - wakes, But lit - tle Lord
3. Be near me, Lord Je - sus, I ask Thee to stay Close by me for-

Away in a Manger

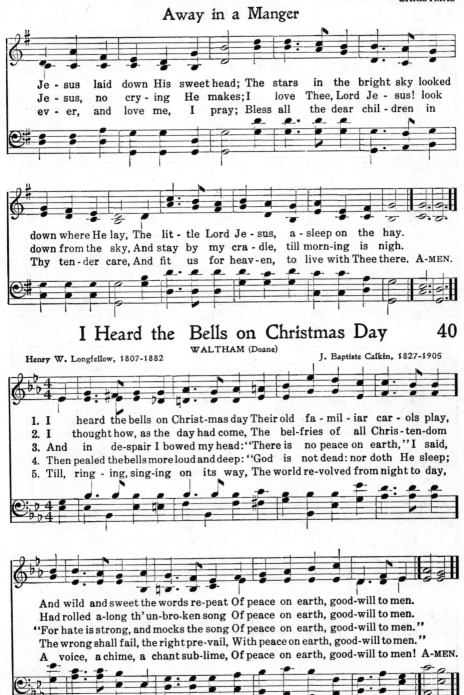

Je - sus laid down His sweet head; The stars in the bright sky looked
Je - sus, no cry - ing He makes; I love Thee, Lord Je - sus! look
ev - er, and love me, I pray; Bless all the dear chil - dren in

down where He lay, The lit - tle Lord Je - sus, a - sleep on the hay.
down from the sky, And stay by my cra - dle, till morn-ing is nigh.
Thy ten - der care, And fit us for heav - en, to live with Thee there. A-MEN.

I Heard the Bells on Christmas Day 40

WALTHAM (Doane)

Henry W. Longfellow, 1807-1882   J. Baptiste Calkin, 1827-1905

1. I   heard the bells on Christ-mas day Their old fa - mil - iar car - ols play,
2. I   thought how, as the day had come, The bel-fries of all Chris - ten-dom
3. And   in   de-spair I bowed my head: "There is   no peace on earth," I said,
4. Then pealed the bells more loud and deep: "God is not dead: nor doth He sleep;
5. Till, ring - ing, sing-ing on its way, The world re-volved from night to day,

And wild and sweet the words re-peat Of peace on earth, good-will to men.
Had rolled a-long th' un-bro-ken song Of peace on earth, good-will to men.
"For hate is strong, and mocks the song Of peace on earth, good-will to men."
The wrong shall fail, the right pre-vail, With peace on earth, good-will to men."
A voice, a chime, a chant sub-lime, Of peace on earth, good-will to men! A-MEN.

41   One Day!

J. Wilbur Chapman, 1859-1918   Charles H. Marsh, 1885-1956

1. One day when heav - en was filled with His prais - es, One day when
2. One day they led Him up Cal - va - ry's moun - tain, One day they
3. One day they left Him a - lone in the gar - den, One day He
4. One day the grave could con - ceal Him no lon - ger, One day the
5. One day the trum - pet will sound for His com - ing, One day the

sin was as black as could be, Je - sus came forth to be
nailed Him to die on the tree; Suf - fer - ing an - guish, de-
rest - ed, from suf - fer - ing free; An - gels came down o'er His
stone rolled a - way from the door; Then He a - rose, o - ver
skies with His glo - ry will shine; Won - der - ful day, my be-

born of a vir - gin, Dwelt a - mong men, my ex - am - ple is He!
spised and re - ject - ed, Bear - ing our sins, my Re - deem - er is He!
tomb to keep vig - il; Hope of the hope - less, my Sav - iour is He!
death He has con - quered; Now is as - cend - ed, my Lord ev - er - more!
lov - ed ones bring-ing; Glo - ri - ous Sav - iour, this Je - sus is mine!

REFRAIN

Liv - ing, He loved me; dy - ing, He saved me; Bur - ied, He

car - ried my sins far a - way; Ris - ing, He jus - ti - fied

One Day!

rit.

free - ly for - ev - er: One day He's com - ing—oh, glo - ri - ous day!

Who Is He in Yonder Stall?

42

Benjamin R. Hanby, 1833-1867

Benjamin R. Hanby, 1833-1867

1. Who is He in yon - der stall, At whose feet the shep-herds fall?
2. Who is He the peo - ple bless For His words of gen - tle - ness?
3. Who is He that stands and weeps At the grave where Laz - arus sleeps?
4. Lo! at mid - night, who is He Prays in dark Geth - se - ma - ne?
5. Who is He who from the grave Comes to suc - cour, help, and save?

Who is He in deep dis - tress, Fast - ing in the wil - der - ness?
Who is He to whom they bring, All the sick and sor - row - ing?
Who is He the gathering throng Greet with loud tri - um - phant song?
Who is He on yon - der tree Dies in grief and ag - o - ny?
Who is He who from His throne Rules through all the worlds a - lone?

REFRAIN

'Tis the Lord! oh won-drous sto - ry! 'Tis the Lord! the King of

glo - ry! At His feet we hum-bly fall, Crown Him! crown Him, Lord of all!

43 Tell Me the Story of Jesus

Fanny J. Crosby, 1820-1915

John R. Sweney, 1837-1899

1. Tell me the sto - ry of Je - sus, Write on my heart ev - ery word;
2. Fast-ing a - lone in the des - ert, Tell of the days that are past,
3. Tell of the cross where they nailed Him, Writh-ing in an-guish and pain;

REF.—*Tell me the sto - ry of Je - sus, Write on my heart ev - ery word;*

FINE

Tell me the sto - ry most pre - cious, Sweet-est that ev - er was heard.
How for our sins He was tempt-ed, Yet was tri - um-phant at last.
Tell of the grave where they laid Him, Tell how He liv - eth a - gain.

Tell me the sto - ry most pre - cious, Sweet-est that ev - er was heard.

Tell how the an - gels, in cho - rus, Sang as they wel-comed His birth,
Tell of the years of His la - bor, Tell of the sor - row He bore,
Love in that sto - ry so ten - der, Clear-er than ev - er I see:

D.C. for Refrain

"Glo - ry to God in the high - est! Peace and good ti - dings to earth."
He was de-spised and af - flict - ed, Home-less, re - ject-ed and poor.
Stay, let me weep while you whis - per, Love paid the ran-som for me.

That Beautiful Name

Jean Perry, 1865-1935, alt.

Mabel J. Camp, 1871-1937

1. I know of a Name, A beau-ti-ful Name, That an-gels brought
2. I know of a Name, A beau-ti-ful Name, That un-to a
3. The One of that Name, My Sav-iour be-came, My Sav-iour of
4. I love that blest Name, That won-der-ful Name, Made high-er than

down to earth; They whis-pered it low, One night long a-go,
Babe was given; The stars glit-tered bright Through-out that glad night,
Cal-va-ry; My sins nailed Him there, My bur-dens He bare,
all in heaven; 'Twas whis-pered, I know, In my heart long a-go—

To a maid-en of low-ly birth.
And an-gels praised God in heaven.
He suf-fered all this for me.
To Je-sus my life I've given.

REFRAIN

That beau-ti-ful Name, That

rit.

beau-ti-ful Name, From sin has power to free us! That beau-ti-ful

cres. *ad lib.*

Name, That won-der-ful Name, That match-less Name is Je - sus!

45 Footprints of Jesus

Mary B. C. Slade, 1826-1882

Asa B. Everett, 1828-1875

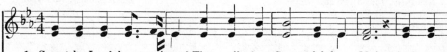

1. Sweet-ly, Lord, have we heard Thee call-ing, Come, fol-low Me! And we
2. Though they lead o'er the cold, dark mountains, Seek-ing His sheep; Or a-
3. If they lead through the tem-ple ho-ly, Preaching the Word; Or in
4. Then at last, when on high He sees us, Our jour-ney done, We will

REFRAIN

see where Thy footprints falling Lead us to Thee.
long by Si-lo-am's fountains, Help-ing the weak:
homes of the poor and low-ly, Serv-ing the Lord: Foot-prints of Je-sus, that
rest where the steps of Je-sus End at His throne.

make the pathway glow; We will fol-low the steps of Je-sus wher-e'er they go.

46 We May Not Climb the Heavenly Steeps

SERENITY

John G. Whittier, 1807-1892

William V. Wallace, 1814-1865

1. We may not climb the heaven-ly steeps To bring the Lord Christ down;
2. But warm, sweet, ten-der, e-ven yet A pres-ent help is He;
3. The heal-ing of His seam-less dress Is by our beds of pain;
4. Through Him the first fond prayers are said Our lips of child-hood frame;
5. O Lord and Mas-ter of us all, What-e'er our name or sign,

We May Not Climb the Heavenly Steeps

In vain we search the low-est deeps, For Him no depths can drown.
And faith has still its Ol - i - vet, And love its Gal - i - lee.
We touch Him in life's throng and press, And we are whole a - gain.
The last low whis-pers of our dead Are bur-dened with His name.
We own Thy sway, we hear Thy call, We test our lives by Thine! A - MEN.

Fairest Lord Jesus

CRUSADERS' HYMN

47

From the German, 17th Century
4th Verse Trans. by Joseph A. Seiss, 1823-1904

From "Schlesische Volkslieder," 1842
Arr. by Richard S. Willis, 1819-1900

1. Fair - est Lord Je - sus! Ru - ler of all na - ture,
2. Fair are the mead - ows, Fair - er still the wood - lands,
3. Fair is the sun - shine, Fair - er still the moon - light,
4. Beau - ti - ful Sav - iour! Lord of the na - tions!

O Thou of God and man the Son! Thee will I cher - ish,
Robed in the bloom - ing garb of spring: Je - sus is fair - er,
And all the twink - ling star - ry host: Je - sus shines bright-er,
Son of God and Son of Man! Glo - ry and hon - or,

Thee will I hon - or, Thou, my soul's Glo - ry, Joy, and Crown!
Je - sus is pur - er, Who makes the woe - ful heart to sing.
Je - sus shines pur - er, Than all the an - gels heaven can boast.
Praise, a - do - ra - tion, Now and for - ev - er-more be Thine! A-MEN.

48 Jesus, Thou Divine Companion

HYFRYDOL

Henry van Dyke, 1852-1933

Rowland H. Prichard, 1811-1887

1. Je - sus, Thou di - vine Com - pan - ion, By Thy low - ly hu - man birth
2. They who tread the path of la - bor Fol - low where Thy feet have trod;
3. Ev - ery task, how - ev - er sim - ple, Sets the soul that does it free;

Thou hast come to join the work-ers, Bur - den-bear - ers of the earth.
They who work with-out com - plain-ing Do the ho - ly will of God.
Ev - ery deed of love and kind-ness Done to man is done to Thee.

Thou, the Car - pen - ter of Naz-'reth, Toil - ing for Thy dai - ly food,
Thou, the Peace that pass-eth knowledge, Dwell-est in the dai - ly strife;
Je - sus, Thou di - vine Com - pan - ion, Help us all to work our best;

By Thy pa - tience and Thy cour - age, Thou hast taught us toil is good.
Thou, the Bread of heav'n, art bro - ken In the sa - cra - ment of life.
Bless us in our dai - ly la - bor, Lead us to our Sab-bath rest. A-MEN.

From "The Poems of Henry van Dyke;" copyright, 1911, by Charles Scribner's Sons; 1939, by Tertius van Dyke. Reprinted by permission of the publishers. "Music from "The English Hymnal." Used by permission of the Oxford University Press, London."
Alternate tune: BEECHER, No. 351

O for a Thousand Tongues

AZMON

Charles Wesley, 1707-1788

Carl G. Glaser, 1784-1829
Arr. by Lowell Mason, 1792-1872

1. O for a thou-sand tongues to sing My great Re-deem-er's praise,
2. My gra-cious Mas-ter and my God, As-sist me to pro-claim,
3. Je-sus! the name that charms our fears, That bids our sor-rows cease;
4. He breaks the power of can-celed sin, He sets the pris-oner free;
5. Hear Him, ye deaf; His praise, ye dumb, Your loos-ened tongues em-ploy;

The glo-ries of my God and King, The tri-umphs of His grace.
To spread through all the earth a-broad, The hon-ors of Thy name.
'Tis mu-sic in the sin-ner's ears, 'Tis life, and health, and peace.
His blood can make the foul-est clean; His blood a-vailed for me.
Ye blind, be-hold your Sav-iour come; And leap, ye lame, for joy. A-MEN.

This tune in lower key, No. 317

Jesus, the Very Thought of Thee

ST. AGNES

Bernard of Clairvaux, 1091-1153
Trans. by Edward Caswall, 1814-1878

John B. Dykes, 1823-1876

1. Je-sus, the ver-y thought of Thee With sweet-ness fills my breast;
2. Nor voice can sing, nor heart can frame, Nor can the mem-ory find
3. O Hope of ev-ery con-trite heart, O Joy of all the meek,
4. But what to those who find? Ah! this Nor tongue nor pen can show,

But sweet-er far Thy face to see, And in Thy pres-ence rest.
A sweet-er sound than Thy blest name, O Sav-iour of man-kind!
To those who fall, how kind Thou art! How good to those who seek!
The love of Je-sus, what it is None but His loved ones know. A-MEN.

This tune in lower key, No. 98

51 The Name of Jesus

W. C. Martin, 19th Century

Edmund S. Lorenz, 1854-1942

1. The name of Je - sus is so sweet, I love its mu - sic
2. I love the name of Him whose heart Knows all my griefs and
3. That name I fond - ly love to hear, It nev - er fails my
4. No word of man can ev - er tell How sweet the name I

to re - peat; It makes my joys full and com - plete, The pre-cious
bears a part; Who bids all anx - ious fears de - part— I love the
heart to cheer; Its mu - sic dries the fall - ing tear; Ex - alt the
love so well; Oh, let its prais - es ev - er swell, Oh, praise the
The

name of Je - sus! "Je - sus," oh, how sweet the name!
pre-cious name

REFRAIN

"Je - sus," ev - ery day the same; "Je - sus," let all

saints pro - claim Its wor - thy praise for - ev - er.
Its wor - thy praise

Oh, to Be Like Thee

Thomas O. Chisholm, b. 1866

William J. Kirkpatrick, 1838-1921

1. Oh, to be like Thee! bless-ed Re-deem-er, This is my con-stant
2. Oh, to be like Thee! full of com-pas-sion, Lov-ing, for-giv-ing,
3. Oh, to be like Thee! low-ly in spir-it, Ho-ly and harm-less,
4. Oh, to be like Thee! while I am plead-ing, Pour out Thy Spir-it,

long-ing and prayer. Glad-ly I'll for-feit all of earth's treas-ures,
ten-der and kind, Help-ing the help-less, cheer-ing the faint-ing,
pa-tient and brave; Meek-ly en-dur-ing cru-el re-proach-es,
fill with Thy love; Make me a tem-ple meet for Thy dwell-ing,

REFRAIN

Je-sus, Thy per-fect like-ness to wear.
Seek-ing the wan-dering sin-ner to find.
Will-ing to suf-fer oth-ers to save.
Fit me for life and heav-en a-bove.

Oh, to be like Thee!

Oh, to be like Thee, bless-ed Re-deem-er, pure as Thou art! Come in Thy

sweet-ness, come in Thy full-ness; Stamp Thine own im-age deep on my heart.

53 When, His Salvation Bringing

TOURS

John King, 1789-1858

Berthold Tours, 1838-1897

1. When, His sal - va - tion bring - ing, To Zi - on Je - sus came,
2. And since the Lord re - tain - eth His love for chil - dren still,
3. For should we fail pro - claim - ing Our great Re - deem - er's praise,

The chil - dren all stood sing - ing Ho - san - na to His name;
Though now as King He reign - eth On Zi - on's heaven-ly hill,
The stones, our si - lence sham - ing, Would their ho - san - nas raise.

Nor did their zeal of - fend Him, But, as He rode a - long,
We'll flock a - round His ban - ner Who sits up - on the throne,
But shall we on - ly ren - der The trib - ute of our words?

He bade them still at - tend Him, And smiled to hear their song.
And cry a - loud, "Ho - san - na To Da - vid's roy - al Son!"
No! while our hearts are ten - der, They, too, shall be the Lord's. A-MEN.

All Glory, Laud, and Honor
ST. THEODULPH

Theodulph of Orleans, 760-821
Trans. by John M. Neale, 1818-1866

Melchior Teschner, 1584-1635

ASCRIPTION

All glo - ry, laud, and hon - or To Thee, Re - deem - er, King,
To whom the lips of chil - dren Make sweet ho - san - nas ring.

1. Thou art the King of Is - rael, Thou, Da - vid's roy - al Son,
2. The com - pa - ny of an - gels Are prais - ing Thee on high,
3. The peo - ple of the He - brews With palms be - fore Thee went;
4. To Thee, be - fore Thy pas - sion, They sang their hymns of praise;
5. Thou didst ac - cept their prais - es; Ac - cept the prayers we bring,

Who in the Lord's name com - est, The King and Bless - ed One.
And mor - tal men, and all things Cre - at - ed, make re - ply.
Our praise and prayer and an - thems Be - fore Thee we pre - sent.
To Thee, now high ex - alt - ed, Our mel - o - dy we raise.
Who in all good de - light - est, Thou good and gra - cious King.

REFRAIN

D. S.

All glo - ry, laud, and hon - or To Thee, Re-deem-er, King,
To whom the lips of chil - dren Make sweet ho-san - nas ring. A - MEN.

55 Ride On! Ride On in Majesty

ST. DROSTANE

Henry Hart Milman, 1791-1868

John B. Dykes, 1823-1876

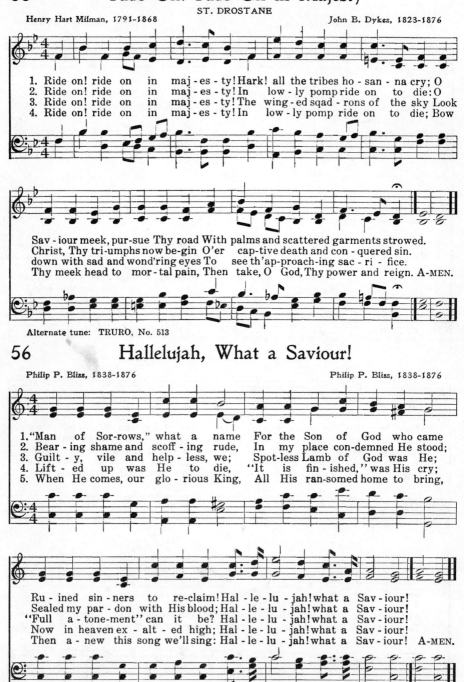

1. Ride on! ride on in maj - es - ty! Hark! all the tribes ho - san - na cry; O
2. Ride on! ride on in maj - es - ty! In low - ly pomp ride on to die: O
3. Ride on! ride on in maj - es - ty! The wing - ed sqad - rons of the sky Look
4. Ride on! ride on in maj - es - ty! In low - ly pomp ride on to die; Bow

Sav - iour meek, pur-sue Thy road With palms and scattered garments strowed.
Christ, Thy tri-umphs now be-gin O'er cap-tive death and con - quered sin.
down with sad and wond'ring eyes To see th'ap-proach-ing sac - ri - fice.
Thy meek head to mor-tal pain, Then take, O God, Thy power and reign. A-MEN.

Alternate tune: TRURO, No. 513

56 Hallelujah, What a Saviour!

Philip P. Bliss, 1838-1876

Philip P. Bliss, 1838-1876

1. "Man of Sor-rows," what a name For the Son of God who came
2. Bear - ing shame and scoff - ing rude, In my place con-demned He stood;
3. Guilt - y, vile and help - less, we; Spot-less Lamb of God was He;
4. Lift - ed up was He to die, "It is fin - ished," was His cry;
5. When He comes, our glo - rious King, All His ran-somed home to bring,

Ru - ined sin - ners to re-claim! Hal - le - lu - jah! what a Sav - iour!
Sealed my par - don with His blood; Hal - le - lu - jah! what a Sav - iour!
"Full a - tone-ment" can it be? Hal - le - lu - jah! what a Sav - iour!
Now in heaven ex - alt - ed high; Hal - le - lu - jah! what a Sav - iour!
Then a - new this song we'll sing: Hal - le - lu - jah! what a Sav - iour! A-MEN.

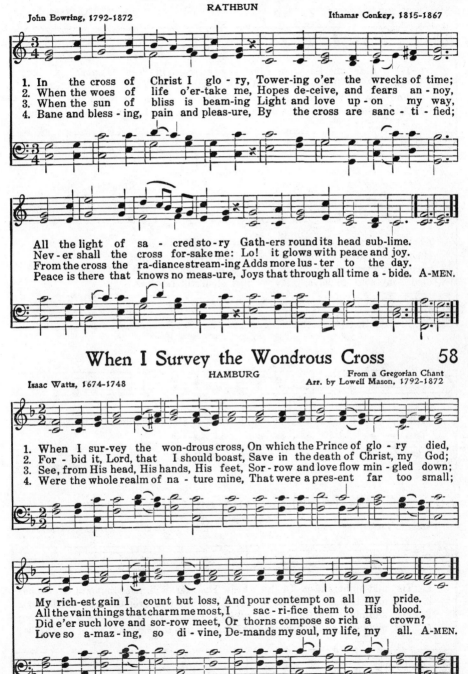

PASSION (ATONEMENT)

In the Cross of Christ

57

RATHBUN

John Bowring, 1792-1872

Ithamar Conkey, 1815-1867

1. In the cross of Christ I glo - ry, Tower-ing o'er the wrecks of time;
2. When the woes of life o'er-take me, Hopes de-ceive, and fears an - noy,
3. When the sun of bliss is beam-ing Light and love up - on my way,
4. Bane and bless - ing, pain and pleas-ure, By the cross are sanc - ti - fied;

All the light of sa - cred sto-ry Gath-ers round its head sub-lime.
Nev - er shall the cross for-sake me: Lo! it glows with peace and joy.
From the cross the ra-diance stream-ing Adds more lus - ter to the day.
Peace is there that knows no meas-ure, Joys that through all time a - bide. A-MEN.

When I Survey the Wondrous Cross

58

HAMBURG

Isaac Watts, 1674-1748

From a Gregorian Chant
Arr. by Lowell Mason, 1792-1872

1. When I sur-vey the won-drous cross, On which the Prince of glo - ry died,
2. For - bid it, Lord, that I should boast, Save in the death of Christ, my God;
3. See, from His head, His hands, His feet, Sor - row and love flow min - gled down;
4. Were the whole realm of na - ture mine, That were a pres-ent far too small;

My rich-est gain I count but loss, And pour contempt on all my pride.
All the vain things that charm me most, I sac - ri-fice them to His blood.
Did e'er such love and sor-row meet, Or thorns compose so rich a crown?
Love so a-maz - ing, so di - vine, De-mands my soul, my life, my all. A-MEN.

59 Jesus Paid It All

Elvina M. Hall, 1820-1889

John T. Grape, 1835-1915

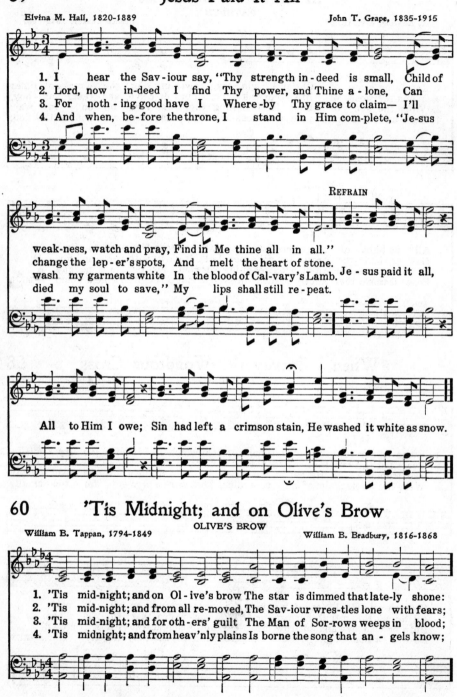

1. I hear the Sav-iour say, "Thy strength in-deed is small, Child of
2. Lord, now in-deed I find Thy power, and Thine a-lone, Can
3. For noth-ing good have I Where-by Thy grace to claim— I'll
4. And when, be-fore the throne, I stand in Him com-plete, "Je-sus

REFRAIN

weak-ness, watch and pray, Find in Me thine all in all."
change the lep-er's spots, And melt the heart of stone.
wash my garments white In the blood of Cal-vary's Lamb.
died my soul to save," My lips shall still re-peat.

Je - sus paid it all,

All to Him I owe; Sin had left a crimson stain, He washed it white as snow.

60 'Tis Midnight; and on Olive's Brow
OLIVE'S BROW

William B. Tappan, 1794-1849

William B. Bradbury, 1816-1868

1. 'Tis mid-night; and on Ol-ive's brow The star is dimmed that late-ly shone:
2. 'Tis mid-night; and from all re-moved, The Sav-iour wres-tles lone with fears;
3. 'Tis mid-night; and for oth-ers' guilt The Man of Sor-rows weeps in blood;
4. 'Tis midnight; and from heav'nly plains Is borne the song that an - gels know;

'Tis Midnight; and on Olive's Brow

'Tis mid-night; in the gar - den now, The suffering Sav-iour prays a-lone.
E'en that dis - ci - ple whom He loved Heeds not His Master's grief and tears.
Yet He that hath in an-guish knelt Is not for-sak-en by His God.
Un-heard by mor-tals are the strains That sweetly soothe the Saviour's woe. A-MEN.

Go to Dark Gethsemane 61
GETHSEMANE

James Montgomery, 1771-1854   Richard Redhead, 1820-1901

1. Go to dark Geth-sem-a-ne, Ye that feel the tempt-er's pow'r;
2. Fol-low to the judg-ment-hall; View the Lord of life ar-raigned.
3. Cal-v'ry's mourn-ful moun-tain climb; There, a-dor-ing at His feet,
4. Ear-ly has-ten to the tomb Where they laid His breath-less clay;

Your Re-deem-er's con-flict see; Watch with Him one bit-ter hour;
O the worm-wood and the gall! O the pangs His soul sus-tained!
Mark that mir-a-cle of time, God's own sac-ri-fice com-plete:
All is sol-i-tude and gloom, Who hath tak-en Him a-way?

Turn not from His griefs a-way; Learn of Je-sus Christ to pray.
Shun not suf-f'ring, shame, or loss; Learn of Him to bear the cross.
"It is fin-ished!"–hear the cry; Learn of Je-sus Christ to die.
Christ is ris'n! He meets our eyes. Sav-iour, teach us so to rise. A-MEN.

62 Hail, Thou Once-Despised Jesus!

AUTUMN

John Bakewell, 1721-1819

Arr. from François H. Barthélémon, 1741-1808

1. Hail! Thou once - de - spis - ed Je - sus! Hail, Thou Gal - i - le - an King!
2. Pas - chal Lamb, by God ap - point - ed, All our sins on Thee were laid;
3. Je - sus, hail! en - throned in glo - ry, There for - ev - er to a - bide;
4. Wor - ship, hon - or, power and bless - ing Thou art wor - thy to re - ceive;

Thou didst suf - fer to re - lease us; Thou didst free sal - va - tion bring.
By al - might - y love a - noint - ed, Thou hast full a - tone-ment made.
All the heaven - ly hosts a - dore Thee, Seat - ed at Thy Fa - ther's side.
Loud - est prais - es, with - out ceas - ing, Meet it is for us to give.

Hail, Thou ag - o - niz - ing Sav - iour, Bear - er of our sin and shame!
All Thy peo - ple are for - giv - en, Through the vir - tue of Thy blood;
There for sin - ners Thou art plead - ing, There Thou dost our place pre - pare,
Help, ye bright an - gel - ic spir - its, Bring your sweet-est, no - blest lays;

By Thy mer - its we find fa - vor; Life is giv - en through Thy name.
O - pened is the gate of heav - en, Peace is made 'twixt man and God.
Ev - er for us in - ter - ced - ing Till in glo - ry we ap - pear.
Help to sing our Sav - iour's mer - its, Help to chant Im-man-uel's praise! A-MEN.

The Old Rugged Cross

George Bennard, b. 1873

George Bennard, b. 1873

1. On a hill far a - way stood an old rug-ged cross, The em-blem of
2. Oh, that old rug-ged cross, so de-spised by the world, Has a won-drous at-
3. In the old rug-ged cross, stained with blood so di - vine, A won - drous
4. To the old rug-ged cross I will ev - er be true, Its shame and re-

suf-fering and shame; And I love that old cross where the dear-est and best
trac - tion for me; For the dear Lamb of God left His glo - ry a - bove
beau - ty I see; For 'twas on that old cross Je - sus suf-fered and died
proach glad-ly bear; Then He'll call me some day to my home far a - way,

For a world of lost sin - ners was slain.
To bear it to dark Cal - va - ry.
To par - don and sanc - ti - fy me.
Where His glo-ry for - ev - er I'll share.

REFRAIN

So I'll cher-ish the old rug-ged
cross, the

cross,........ Till my tro-phies at last I lay down; I will cling to the
old rug-ged cross,

old rug-ged cross,......... And ex-change it some day for a crown.
cross, the old rug-ged cross,

64 Alas! and Did My Saviour Bleed?

MARTYRDOM (Avon)

Isaac Watts, 1674-1748

Hugh Wilson, 1764-1824

1. A - las! and did my Sav-iour bleed? And did my Sov-ereign die? Would
2. Was it for crimes that I have done He groaned up-on the tree? A-
3. Well might the sun in dark-ness hide, And shut his glo-ries in, When
4. But drops of grief can ne'er re-pay The debt of love I owe; Here,

He de-vote that sa-cred head For such a worm as I?
maz-ing pit-y! grace un-known! And love be-yond de-gree!
Christ, the might-y Mak-er, died For man, the crea-ture's sin.
Lord, I give my-self a-way—'Tis all that I can do. A - MEN.

Alternate tune with Refrain: No. 66 on opposite page

65 Majestic Sweetness Sits Enthroned

ORTONVILLE

Samuel Stennett, 1727-1795

Thomas Hastings, 1784-1872

1. Ma - jes-tic sweetness sits enthroned Up-on the Sav-iour's brow; His head with
2. No mor-tal can with Him compare, A-mong the sons of men; Fair-er is
3. He saw me plunged in deep distress, He flew to my re-lief; For me He
4. To Him I owe my life and breath, And all the joys I have; 'He makes me
5. Since from His bounty I re-ceive Such proofs of love di-vine, Had I a

radiant glories crowned, His lips with grace o'erflow, His lips with grace o'erflow.
He than all the fair That fill the heavenly train, That fill the heavenly train.
bore the shameful cross And car-ried all my grief, And carried all my grief.
triumph o-ver death, And saves me from the grave, And saves me from the grave.
thousand hearts to give, Lord, they should all be Thine, Lord, they should all be Thine. AMEN.

At the Cross

Isaac Watts, 1674-1748
Refrain, Ralph E. Hudson, 1843-1901

Ralph E. Hudson, 1843-1901

1. A - las, and did my Sav - iour bleed? And did my Sov-'reign die?
2. Was it for crimes that I have done, He groaned up - on the tree?
3. Well might the sun in dark-ness hide, And shut his glo - ries in,
4. But drops of grief can ne'er re - pay The debt of love I owe:

Would He de-vote that sa - cred head For such a worm as I?
A - maz - ing pit - y! grace un-known! And love be - yond de - gree!
When Christ, the might - y Mak - er, died For man the crea-ture's sin.
Here, Lord, I give my - self a - way, 'Tis all that I can do!

REFRAIN

At the cross, at the cross where I first saw the light, And the
bur-den of my heart rolled a - way, (rolled a-way,) It was there by faith
I re - ceived my sight, And now I am hap-py all the day!

Alternate tune without Refrain: MARTYRDOM, No. 64 on opposite page

67 Jesus, Thy Blood and Righteousness

GERMANY

Nicolaus L. Zinzendorf, 1700-1760
Trans. by John Wesley, 1703-1791

William Gardiner's "Sacred Melodies," 1815

1. Je - sus, Thy blood and right-eous-ness My beau-ty are, my glo - rious dress;
2. Bold shall I stand in Thy great day, For who aught to my charge shall lay?
3. Lord, I be-lieve Thy precious blood, Which, at the mer-cy seat of God,
4. Lord, I be-lieve were sin - ners more Than sands up-on the o - cean shore,

'Midst flaming worlds, in these arrayed, With joy shall I lift up my head.
Ful - ly ab-solved through these I am, From sin and fear, from guilt and shame.
For - ev - er doth for sin-ners plead, For me, e'en for my soul, was shed.
Thou hast for all a ran - som paid, For all a full a-tone-ment made. A-MEN.

Alternate tunes: OMBERSLEY, No. 393; QUEBEC, No. 508

68 I Am Not Skilled to Understand

Dora Greenwell, 1821-1882

William J. Kirkpatrick, 1838-1921

1. I am not skilled to un-der-stand What God hath willed, what God hath planned;
2. I take Him at His word indeed: "Christ died for sin - ners," this I read;
3. That He should leave His place on high And come for sin - ful man to die,
4. And oh, that He ful - filled may see The tra-vail of His soul in me,
5. Yes, liv - ing, dy - ing, let me bring My strength, my sol - ace from this Spring;

I on - ly know at His right hand Is One who is my Sav-iour!
For in my heart I find a need Of Him to be my Sav-iour!
You count it strange? so once did I, Be - fore I knew my Sav-iour!
And with His work con - tent-ed be, As I with my dear Sav-iour!
That He who lives to be my King Once died to be my Sav-iour! A-MEN.

Ivory Palaces

Henry Barraclough, b. 1891

Henry Barraclough, b. 1891
Arr. by Donald P. Hustad, b. 1918

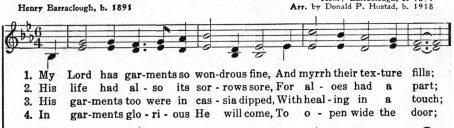

1. My Lord has gar-ments so won-drous fine, And myrrh their tex-ture fills;
2. His life had al - so its sor - rows sore, For al - oes had a part;
3. His gar-ments too were in cas - sia dipped, With heal - ing in a touch;
4. In gar-ments glo - ri - ous He will come, To o - pen wide the door;

Its fra-grance reached to this heart of mine, With joy my be - ing thrills.
And when I think of the cross He bore, My eyes with tear-drops start.
Each time my feet in some sin have slipped, He took me from its clutch.
And I shall en - ter my heaven-ly home, To dwell for - ev - er - more.

mf REFRAIN

Out of the i - vo - ry pal - a - ces, In - to a world of woe,

p

On - ly His great, e - ter - nal love Made my Sav-iour go.

mf

70   O Sacred Head, Now Wounded

PASSION CHORALE

Ascribed to Bernard of Clairvaux, 1091-1153
Trans.(into German) by Paul Gerhardt, 1607-1676   Hans L. Hassler, 1564-1612
Trans.(from the German) by James W. Alexander, 1804-1859   Har. by Johann S. Bach, 1685-1750

1. O sa - cred Head, now wound - ed, With grief and shame weighed down;
2. What Thou, my Lord, hast suf - fered Was all for sin - ners' gain:
3. What lan - guage shall I bor - row To thank Thee, dear - est Friend:

Now scorn-ful - ly sur - round - ed With thorns, Thine on - ly crown;
Mine, mine was the trans - gres - sion, But Thine the dead - ly pain.
For this Thy dy - ing sor - row, Thy pit - y with-out end?

O sa - cred Head, what glo - ry, What bliss till now was Thine!
Lo, here I fall, my Sav - iour! 'Tis I de - serve Thy place;
O make me Thine for - ev - er; And should I faint - ing be,

Yet, though de-spised and go - ry, I joy to call Thee mine.
Look on me with Thy fa - vor, Vouch-safe to me Thy grace.
Lord, let me nev - er, nev - er Out - live my love to Thee. A-MEN.

Alternate tune: MUNICH, No. 160

There Is a Green Hill Far Away

GREEN HILL

Cecil F. Alexander, 1818-1895

George C. Stebbins, 1846-1945

1. There is   a green hill far   a-way, With-out   a   cit-y   wall,
2. We   may   not know, we can-not tell   What pains He had   to   bear;
3. He   died that we might be   for-given, He died   to make   us   good,
4. There was   no oth-er good   e-nough   To   pay   the price   of   sin;

Where the dear Lord was cru-ci-fied, Who died   to   save   us   all.
But   we be-lieve   it was, for   us   He hung and   suf-fered there.
That   we might go   at last   to heaven, Saved by   His pre-cious blood.
He   on-ly could un-lock   the gate   Of heaven and   let   us   in.

REFRAIN

Oh, dear-ly, dear-ly has   He loved, And we   must love Him, too;

And trust in His   re-deem-ing blood, And try   His works to   do.

Alternate tunes without Refrain: MARTYRDOM, No. 64;   MEDITATION, No. 370

72 The Strife Is O'er

VICTORY

Latin, pub. Cologne, c. 1695
Trans. by Francis Pott, 1832-1909

Giovanni P. da Palestrina, 1525-1594
Adapted by W. H. Monk, 1823-1889

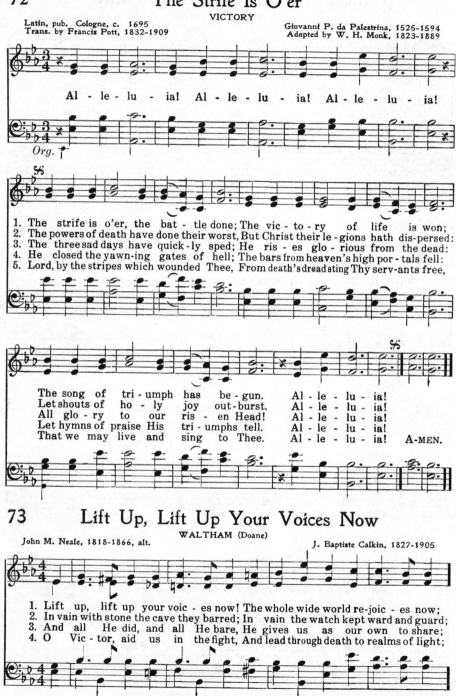

Al - le - lu - ia! Al - le - lu - ia! Al - le - lu - ia!

1. The strife is o'er, the bat - tle done; The vic - to - ry of life is won;
2. The powers of death have done their worst, But Christ their le - gions hath dis-persed:
3. The three sad days have quick-ly sped; He ris - es glo - rious from the dead:
4. He closed the yawn-ing gates of hell; The bars from heaven's high por - tals fell:
5. Lord, by the stripes which wounded Thee, From death's dread sting Thy serv-ants free,

The song of tri - umph has be - gun.   Al - le - lu - ia!
Let shouts of ho - ly joy out-burst.   Al - le - lu - ia!
All glo - ry to our ris - en Head!   Al - le - lu - ia!
Let hymns of praise His tri - umphs tell.   Al - le - lu - ia!
That we may live and sing to Thee.   Al - le - lu - ia! A-MEN.

73 Lift Up, Lift Up Your Voices Now

WALTHAM (Doane)

John M. Neale, 1818-1866, alt.

J. Baptiste Calkin, 1827-1905

1. Lift up, lift up your voic - es now! The whole wide world re-joic - es now;
2. In vain with stone the cave they barred; In vain the watch kept ward and guard;
3. And all He did, and all He bare, He gives us as our own to share;
4. O Vic - tor, aid us in the fight, And lead through death to realms of light;

Lift Up, Lift Up Your Voices Now

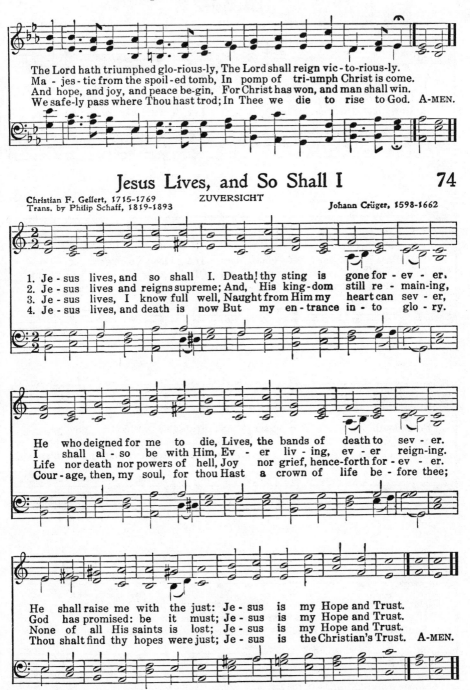

The Lord hath triumphed glo-rious-ly, The Lord shall reign vic-to-rious-ly.
Ma - jes - tic from the spoil-ed tomb, In pomp of tri-umph Christ is come.
And hope, and joy, and peace be-gin, For Christ has won, and man shall win.
We safe-ly pass where Thou hast trod; In Thee we die to rise to God. A-MEN.

Jesus Lives, and So Shall I 74

Christian F. Gellert, 1715-1769
Trans. by Philip Schaff, 1819-1893
ZUVERSICHT
Johann Crüger, 1598-1662

1. Je - sus lives, and so shall I. Death! thy sting is gone for - ev - er.
2. Je - sus lives and reigns supreme; And, His king-dom still re - main-ing,
3. Je - sus lives, I know full well, Naught from Him my heart can sev - er.
4. Je - sus lives, and death is now But my en - trance in - to glo - ry.

He who deigned for me to die, Lives, the bands of death to sev - er.
I shall al - so be with Him, Ev - er liv - ing, ev - er reign-ing.
Life nor death nor powers of hell, Joy nor grief, hence-forth for - ev - er.
Cour - age, then, my soul, for thou Hast a crown of life be - fore thee;

He shall raise me with the just: Je - sus is my Hope and Trust.
God has promised: be it must; Je - sus is my Hope and Trust.
None of all His saints is lost; Je - sus is my Hope and Trust.
Thou shalt find thy hopes were just; Je - sus is the Christian's Trust. A-MEN.

The Day of Resurrection
LANCASHIRE

John of Damascus, c.700-c.754
Trans. by John M. Neale, 1818-1866

Henry Smart, 1813-1879

1. The day of res - ur - rec - tion, Earth, tell it out a - broad,
2. Our hearts be pure from e - vil, That we may see a - right
3. Now let the heav'ns be joy - ful, Let earth her song be - gin,

The Pass - o - ver of glad - ness, The Pass - o - ver of God.
The Lord in rays e - ter - nal Of res - ur - rec - tion light;
Let the round world keep tri - umph And all that is there - in;

From death to life e - ter - nal, From this world to the sky,
And, lis - t'ning to His ac - cents, May hear, so calm and plain,
Let all things seen and un - seen Their notes in glad - ness blend;

Our Christ hath brought us o - ver With hymns of vic - to - ry.
His own "All hail!" and, hear - ing, May raise the vic - tor-strain.
For Christ the Lord hath ris - en, Our Joy that hath no end. A-MEN.

Alternate tune: GREENLAND, No. 135

I Know that My Redeemer Liveth 76

Jessie B. Pounds, 1861-1921   James H. Fillmore. 1849-1936

1. I know that my Redeemer liv - eth, And on the earth a-gain shall stand;
2. I know His promise never fail - eth, The word He speaks, it can-not die;
3. I know my mansion He pre-par - eth, That where He is there I may be;

1. And on the earth again shall stand;

I know e - ter-nal life He giv - eth, That grace and pow'r are in His hand.
Tho' cru-el death my flesh as-sail - eth, Yet I shall see Him by and by.
O won-drous tho't, for me He careth, And He at last will come for me.

1. That grace and pow'r are in His hand.

REFRAIN

I know, I know that Je - sus liv - eth, And on the
I know, I know

earth a - gain shall stand; I know, I know
And on the earth   I know, I know

that life He giv - eth, That grace and pow'r are in His hand.
That grace and pow'r

77 Christ the Lord Is Risen Today

EASTER HYMN (Worgan)

Charles Wesley, 1707-1788

Arr. from "Lyra Davidica," 1708

1. Christ the Lord is risen to - day, Al - - - - le - lu - ia!
2. Love's re - deem - ing work is done, Al - - - - le - lu - ia!
3. Lives a - gain our glo - rious King; Al - - - - le - lu - ia!
4. Soar we now where Christ has led, Al - - - - le - le - ia!

Sons of men and an - gels say: Al - - - - le - lu - ia!
Fought the fight, the bat - tle won; Al - - - - le - lu - ia!
Where, O death, is now thy sting? Al - - - - le - lu - ia!
Fol - lowing our ex - alt - ed Head; Al - - - - le - lu - ia!

Raise your joys and tri - umphs high, Al - - - - le - lu - ia!
Death in vain for - bids Him rise; Al - - - - le - lu - ia!
Dy - ing once, He all doth save: Al - - - - le - lu - ia!
Made like Him, like Him we rise; Al - - - - le - lu - ia!

Sing, ye heavens, and earth re - ply, Al - - - - le - lu - ia!
Christ has o - pened Par - a - dise. Al - - - - le - lu - ia!
Where thy vic - to - ry, O grave? Al - - - - le - lu - ia!
Ours the cross, the grave, the skies. Al - - - - le - lu - ia! A-MEN.

Alternate tune: LLANFAIR, No. 73 on opposite page

Christ the Lord Is Risen Again
LLANFAIR

Michael Weisse, c.1480-1534
Trans. by Catherine Winkworth, 1829-1878

Robert Williams, c.1781-1821
Descant arr. by William Lester, b. 1889

1. Christ the Lord is risen again, Al - - - le - lu - ia! Christ has bro-ken

1. Christ the Lord is risen a - gain, Al - - le - lu - ia! Christ has bro-ken
2. He who gave for us His life, Al - - le - lu - ia! Who for us en-
3. He who slumbered in the grave, Al - - le - lu - ia! Is ex - alt - ed
4. Now He bids us tell man-kind Al - - 'le - lu - ia! How all may sal-

death's strong chain, Al - le - lu - ia! Hark, the angels shout for joy, Al - - le-

death's strong chain, Al - le - lu - ia! Hark, the angels shout for joy, Al - - le-
dured the strife, Al - le - lu - ia! Is our Pas-chal Lamb to-day, Al - - le-
now to save; Al - le - lu - ia! Now through Christendom it rings, Al - - le-
va - tion find, Al - le - lu - ia! How poor sinners are forgiven, Al - - le-

lu - ia! Sing-ing ev - er-more on high: Al - - le - lu - ia! A - MEN.

lu - ia! Sing-ing ev - er-more on high: Al - - le - lu - ia!
lu - ia! We, too, sing for joy, and say: Al - - le - lu - ia!
lu - ia! That the Lamb is King of kings! Al - - le - lu - ia!
lu - ia! And through faith may enter heaven: Al - - le - lu - ia! A - MEN.

Alternate tune: EASTER HYMN, No. 77 on opposite page

Christ Arose

Robert Lowry, 1826-1899   Robert Lowry, 1826-1899

1. Low in the grave He lay— Je - sus my Sav - iour! Wait - ing the
2. Vain - ly they watch His bed— Je - sus my Sav - iour! Vain - ly they
3. Death can-not keep his prey— Je - sus my Sav - iour! He tore the

REFRAIN

com - ing day— Je - sus my Lord! Up from the grave He a - rose,
seal the dead— Je - sus my Lord!
bars a - way— Je - sus my Lord! He a - rose,

With a might - y tri-umph o'er His foes; He a - rose a
He a - rose!

Vic - tor from the dark do-main, And He lives for - ev - er with His saints to reign.

He a - rose! He a - rose! Hal - le - lu - jah! Christ a-rose!
He a - rose! He a - rose!

Come Ye Faithful, Raise the Strain

ST. KEVIN

80

John of Damascus, c. 700-c. 754
Trans. by John M. Neale, 1818-1866

Arthur S. Sullivan, 1842-1900
Descant (small notes), William Lester, b. 1889

1. Come, ye faith-ful, raise the strain Of tri - um - phant glad - ness;
2. 'Tis the spring of souls to - day, Christ hath burst His pris - on,
3. Now the queen of sea - sons, bright With the day of splen - dor,
4. "Hal - le - lu - jah!" now we cry To our King Im - mor - tal,

God hath brought His Is - ra - el In - to joy from sad - ness.
And from three day's sleep in death As a sun hath ris - en.
With the roy - al feast of feasts, Comes its joy to ren - der;
Who, tri - um - phant, burst the bars Of the tomb's dark por - tal;

Loosed from Pha - raoh's bit - ter yoke Ja - cob's sons and daugh - ters,
All the win - ter of our sins, Long and dark, is fly - ing
Comes to glad Je - ru - sa - lem, Who with true af - fec - tion
"Hal - le - lu - jah!" with the Son, God the Fa - ther prais - ing;

Led them with un - mois-tened foot Through the Red Sea wa - ters.
From His light, to whom we give Laud and praise un - dy - ing.
Wel-comes in un - wea-ried strains Je - sus' res - ur - rec - tion.
"Hal - le - lu - jah!" yet a - gain To the Spir - it rais - ing. A-MEN.

81 Look, Ye Saints! the Sight Is Glorious

CORONÆ

Thomas Kelly, 1769-1854   William H. Monk, 1823-1889

1. Look, ye saints! The sight is glo - rious: See the Man of
2. Crown the Sav - iour! An - gels, crown Him! Rich the tro - phies
3. Sin - ners in de - ri - sion crowned Him, Mock - ing thus the
4. Hark, those bursts of ac - cla - ma - tion! Hark, those loud tri-

Sor - rows now; From the fight re - turned vic - to - rious,
Je - sus brings; In the seat of power en - throne Him;
Sav - iour's claim; Saints and an - gels crowd a - round Him,
um - phant chords! Je - sus takes the high - est sta - tion;

Ev - ery knee to Him shall bow: Crown Him! Crown Him!
While the vault of heav - en rings: Crown Him! Crown Him!
Own His ti - tle, praise His name: Crown Him! Crown Him!
O what joy the sight af - fords! Crown Him! Crown Him!

Crowns be - come the Vic - tor's brow.
Crown the Sav - iour King of kings.
Spread a - broad the Vic - tor's fame.
King of kings, and Lord of lords! A - MEN.

Alternate tunes (both require some repetition in last phrases): REGENT SQUARE, No. 31;
CWM RHONDDA, No. 401

Golden Harps Are Sounding

HERMAS

Frances R. Havergal, 1836-1879

Frances R. Havergal, 1836-1879

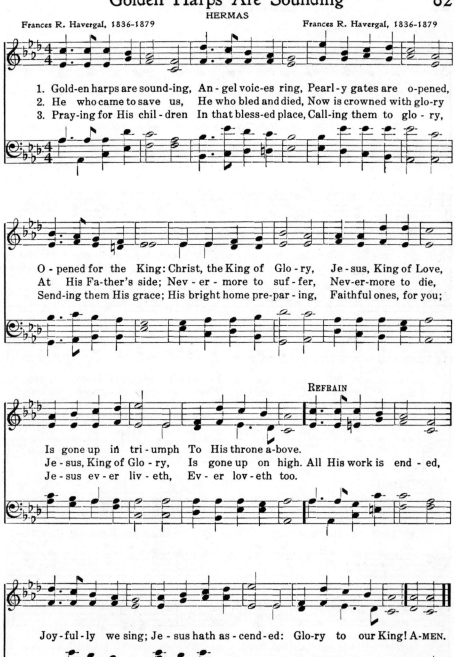

1. Gold-en harps are sound-ing, An - gel voic-es ring, Pearl - y gates are o-pened,
2. He who came to save us, He who bled and died, Now is crowned with glo-ry
3. Pray-ing for His chil - dren In that bless-ed place, Call-ing them to glo - ry,

O - pened for the King: Christ, the King of Glo - ry, Je - sus, King of Love,
At His Fa-ther's side; Nev - er - more to suf - fer, Nev-er-more to die,
Send-ing them His grace; His bright home pre-par - ing, Faithful ones, for you;

REFRAIN

Is gone up in tri - umph To His throne a-bove.
Je - sus, King of Glo - ry, Is gone up on high. All His work is end - ed,
Je - sus ev - er liv - eth, Ev - er lov - eth too.

Joy-ful - ly we sing; Je - sus hath as - cend-ed: Glo-ry to our King! A-MEN.

Christ Returneth

H. L. Turner, 19th Century

James McGranahan, 1840-1907

1. It may be at morn, when the day is a-wak-ing, When sun-light through darkness and shad-ow is break-ing, That Je-sus will come in the full-ness of glo-ry, To re-ceive from the world "His own."

2. It may be at mid-day, it may be at twi-light, It may be, per-chance, that the black-ness of mid-night Will burst in-to light in the blaze of His glo-ry, When Je-sus re-ceives "His own."

3. While its hosts cry Ho-san-na, from heav-en de-scend-ing, With glo-ri-fied saints and the an-gels at-tend-ing, With grace on His brow, like a ha-lo of glo-ry, Will Je-sus re-ceive "His own."

4. Oh, joy! oh, de-light! should we go with-out dy-ing, No sick-ness, no sad-ness, no dread and no cry-ing, Caught up through the clouds with our Lord in-to glo-ry, When Je-sus re-ceives "His own."

REFRAIN

O Lord Je-sus, how long, how long Ere we shout the glad song, Christ re-turn-eth! Hal-le-lu-jah! hal-le-lu-jah! A-men, Hal-le-lu-jah! A-men.

rit.

Lo! He Comes

SICILIAN MARINERS' HYMN

John Cennick, 1718-1755, and
Charles Wesley, 1707-1788, alt.

Arr. from a Sicilian Melody, 1794

1. Lo! He comes, with clouds de - scend-ing, Once for our sal-
2. Ev - ery eye shall now be - hold Him, Robed in dread - ful
3. Yea, A - men! let all a - dore Thee, High on Thine e-

va - tion slain; Thou - sand thou - sand saints at - tend - ing,
maj - es - ty; Those who set at naught and sold Him,
ter - nal throne; Sav - iour, take the power and glo - ry;

Swell the tri - umph of His train: Hal - le - lu - jah!
Pierced and nailed Him to the tree, Deep - ly wail - ing,
Claim the king - dom for Thine own: O come quick - ly,

Hal - le - lu - jah! God ap - pears on earth to reign.
deep - ly wail - ing, Shall the true Mes - si - ah see.
O come quick - ly, Hal - le - lu - jah! Come, Lord, come. A - MEN.

Alternate tune: REGENT SQUARE. No. 31

85 Will Jesus Find Us Watching?

Fanny J. Crosby, 1820-1915   William H. Doane, 1832-1915

1. When Je - sus comes to re - ward His serv-ants, Wheth-er it be
2. If, at the dawn of the ear - ly morn-ing, He shall call us
3. Have we been true to the trust He left us? Do we seek to
4. Bless - ed are those whom the Lord finds watch-ing, In His glo - ry

noon or night, Faith-ful to Him will He find us watch-ing,
one by one, When to the Lord we re - store our tal - ents,
do our best? If in our hearts there is naught con-demns us,
they shall share; If He shall come at the dawn or mid-night,

REFRAIN

With our lamps all trimmed and bright?
Will He an - swer thee—"Well done"? Oh, can we say we are
We shall have a glo - rious rest.
Will He find us watch - ing there?

read - y, broth - er? Read - y for the soul's bright home? Say, will He

find you and me still watch-ing, Wait-ing, wait-ing when the Lord shall come?

Is It the Crowning Day?

Henry Ostrom, 19th Century

Charles H. Marsh, 1885-1956

1. Je - sus may come to - day, Glad day! Glad day! And I would
2. I may go home to - day, Glad day! Glad day! Seem-eth I
3. Why should I anx - ious be? Glad day! Glad day! Lights ap-pear
4. Faithful I'll be to - day, Glad day! Glad day! And I will

see my Friend; Dan - gers and trou - bles would end If
hear their song; Hail to the ra - di - ant throng! If
on the shore, Storms will af - fright nev - er - more, For
free - ly tell Why I should love Him so well, For

REFRAIN

Je - sus should come to - day.
I should go home to - day.
He is "at hand" to - day.
He is my all to - day.

Glad day! Glad day! Is it the crown-ing

day? I'll live for to - day, nor anx - ious be, Je - sus, my Lord, I

soon shall see; Glad day! Glad day! Is it the crown - ing day?

87 What if It Were Today?

Lelia N. Morris, 1862-1929   Lelia N. Morris, 1862-1929

1. Je - sus is com-ing to earth a - gain, What if it were to - day?
2. Sa - tan's do - min-ion will soon be o'er, Oh, that it were to - day!
3. Faith-ful and true would He find us here, If He should come to - day?

Com-ing in pow - er and love to reign, What if it were to - day?
Sor - row and sigh-ing shall be no more, Oh, that it were to - day!
Watch-ing in glad-ness and not in fear, If He should come to - day?

Com-ing to claim His cho-sen Bride, All the re - deemed and pu - ri - fied,
Then shall the dead in Christ a - rise, Caught up to meet Him in the skies,
Signs of His com - ing mul - ti - ply, Morning light breaks in east-ern sky,

rit.   *a tempo*

O - ver this whole earth scat-tered wide, What if it were to - day?
When shall these glo - ries meet our eyes? What if it were to - day?
Watch, for that time is draw-ing nigh, What if it were to - day?

REFRAIN

Glo - ry, glo - ry! Joy to my heart 'twill bring;
Joy to my heart 'twill bring;

What if It Were Today?

Glo - ry, glo - ry! When we shall crown Him King;
When we shall crown Him King;

Glo - ry, glo - ry! Haste to pre-pare the way;
Haste to pre-pare the way;

rit.

Glo - ry, glo - ry! Je - sus will come some day.

The King Shall Come When Morning Dawns 88

Based on the Greek
Trans. by John Brownlie, 1859-1925

ST. STEPHEN

William Jones, 1726-1800

1. The King shall come when morn-ing dawns, And light tri - um - phant breaks;
2. Not as of old a lit - tle child To bear, and fight, and die,
3. O bright-er than the ris - ing morn When He, vic - to - rious, rose,
4. O bright-er than that glo-rious morn Shall this fair morn-ing be,
5. The King shall come when morn-ing dawns, And light and beau-ty brings:

When beau - ty gilds the east - ern hills, And life to joy a - wakes.
But crowned with glo - ry like the sun That lights the morn-ing sky.
And left the lone-some place of death, De - spite the rage of foes—
When Christ, our King, in beau - ty comes, And we His face shall see!
Hail, Christ the Lord! Thy peo - ple pray, Come quick-ly, King of kings! A-MEN.

Words from "Hymns of the Russian Church." Used by permission of the Oxford University Press

89 He Is Coming Again

Mabel Johnston Camp, 1871-1937   Mabel Johnston Camp, 1871-1937

1. Lift   up your heads, pil-grims a-wea-ry, See day's approach now crim-son the sky;
2. Dark was the night, sin warred against us; Heav-y the load   of sor-row we bore;
3. O   bless-ed hope! O bliss-ful prom-ise! Fill-ing our hearts with rap-ture di-vine;
4. E - ven so come, pre-cious Lord Jesus; Cre-a-tion waits re-demp-tion to see;

Night shadows flee, and your Be-lov-ed, A-waited with longing, at last draweth nigh.
But   now we see signs of His com-ing; Our hearts glow within us, joy's cup runneth o'er!
O   day of days! hail Thy ap-pear-ing! Thy tran-scendent glo-ry for-ev-er shall shine!
Caught up in clouds, soon we shall meet Thee; O bless-ed as-sur-ance, for-ev-er with Thee!

REFRAIN

He is com-ing a-gain, He is com-ing a-gain, The ver-y same

Je-sus, re-ject-ed of men; He is com-ing a-gain, He is com-ing a-gain,

With pow'r and great glo-ry, He is com-ing a-gain!
                                          is com-ing a-gain!

Hark! Ten Thousand Harps and Voices   90

HARWELL

Thomas Kelly, 1769-1854   Lowell Mason, 1792-1872

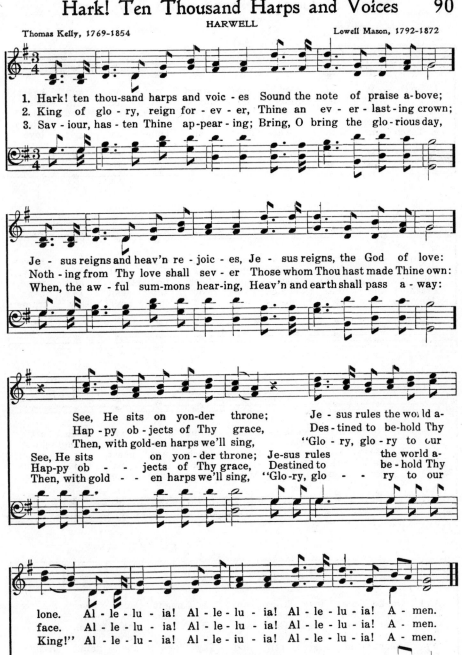

1. Hark! ten thou-sand harps and voic - es Sound the note of praise a-bove;
2. King of glo - ry, reign for - ev - er, Thine an ev - er - last-ing crown;
3. Sav - iour, has - ten Thine ap-pear - ing; Bring, O bring the glo - rious day,

Je - sus reigns and heav'n re - joic - es, Je - sus reigns, the God of love:
Noth - ing from Thy love shall sev - er Those whom Thou hast made Thine own:
When, the aw - ful sum-mons hear-ing, Heav'n and earth shall pass a - way:

See, He sits on yon-der throne; Je - sus rules the world a-
Hap - py ob - jects of Thy grace, Des - tined to be-hold Thy
Then, with gold-en harps we'll sing, "Glo - ry, glo - ry to our

See, He sits on yon - der throne; Je-sus rules the world a-
Hap-py ob - jects of Thy grace, Destined to be-hold Thy
Then, with gold - en harps we'll sing, "Glo-ry, glo - ry to our

lone. Al - le - lu - ia! Al - le - lu - ia! Al - le - lu - ia! A - men.
face. Al - le - lu - ia! Al - le - lu - ia! Al - le - lu - ia! A - men.
King!" Al - le - lu - ia! Al - le - lu - ia! Al - le - lu - ia! A - men.

91 Spirit of God, Descend upon My Heart

MORECAMBE

George Croly, 1780-1860   Frederick C. Atkinson, 1841-1897

1. Spir - it of God, de - scend up - on my heart;
2. I ask no dream, no proph - et ec - sta - sies,
3. Hast Thou not bid us love Thee, God and King?
4. Teach me to feel that Thou art al - ways nigh;
5. Teach me to love Thee as Thine an - gels love,

Wean it from earth, through all its puls - es move;
No sud - den rend - ing of the veil of clay,
All, all Thine own, soul, heart and strength and mind.
Teach me the strug - gles of the soul to bear,
One ho - ly pas - sion fill - ing all my frame;

Stoop to my weak - ness, might - y as Thou art,
No an - gel vis - it - ant, no o - pening skies;
I see Thy cross— there teach my heart to cling;
To check the ris - ing doubt, the reb - el sigh;
The bap - tism of the heaven - de - scend - ed Dove,

And make me love Thee as I ought to love.
But take the dim - ness of my soul a - way.
O let me seek Thee, and O let me find.
Teach me the pa - tience of un - an - swered prayer.
My heart an al - tar, and Thy love the flame. A-MEN.

O Breath of Life

SPIRITUS VITÆ

Bessie P. Head, 1850-1936

Mary J. Hammond, b. 1878

1. O Breath of Life, come sweeping through us, Re-vive Thy church with life and pow'r;
2. O Wind of God, come bend us, break us, Till hum-bly we con-fess our need;
3. O Breath of Love, come breathe with-in us, Re-new-ing thought and will and heart;
4. O Heart of Christ, once bro-ken for us, 'Tis there we find our strength and rest;
5. Re - vive us, Lord! Is zeal a - ba - ting While harvest fields are vast and white?

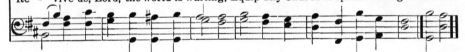

O Breath of Life, come, cleanse, renew us, And fit Thy Church to meet this hour.
Then in Thy ten-der-ness re-make us, Re-vive, re-store, for this we plead.
Come, Love of Christ, a-fresh to win us, Re-vive Thy Church in ev-ery part.
Our bro-ken con-trite hearts now solace, And let Thy wait-ing Church be blest.
Re - vive us, Lord, the world is waiting, Equip Thy Church to spread the light. A-MEN.

Thy Holy Spirit, Lord, Alone

93

Henrietta E. Blair, 19th Century

William J. Kirkpatrick, 1838-1921

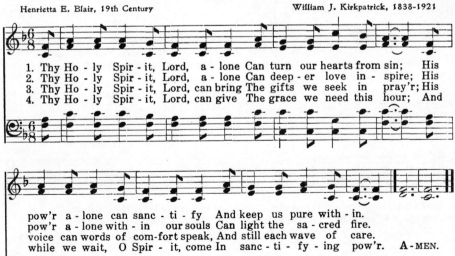

1. Thy Ho - ly Spir - it, Lord, a - lone Can turn our hearts from sin; His
2. Thy Ho - ly Spir - it, Lord, a - lone Can deep - er love in - spire; His
3. Thy Ho - ly Spir - it, Lord, can bring The gifts we seek in pray'r; His
4. Thy Ho - ly Spir - it, Lord, can give The grace we need this hour; And

pow'r a - lone can sanc - ti - fy And keep us pure with - in.
pow'r a - lone with - in our souls Can light the sa - cred fire.
voice can words of com-fort speak, And still each wave of care.
while we wait, O Spir - it, come In sanc - ti - fy - ing pow'r. A-MEN.

Holy Spirit, Faithful Guide

FAITHFUL GUIDE

Marcus M. Wells, 1815-1895

Marcus M. Wells, 1815-1895
Arr. by Donald P. Hustad, b. 1918

1. Ho - ly Spir - it, faith-ful Guide, Ev - er near the Chris-tian's side;
2. Ev - er pres - ent, tru - est Friend, Ev - er near Thine aid to lend,
3. When our days of toil shall cease, Wait-ing still for sweet re-lease,

Gen - tly lead us by the hand, Pil - grims in a des - ert land;
Leave us not to doubt and fear, Grop-ing on in dark - ness drear;
Noth - ing left but heav'n and prayer, Know-ing that our names are there;

Wea - ry souls for - e'er re - joice, While they hear that sweet-est voice
When the storms are rag - ing sore, Hearts grow faint, and hopes give o'er,
Wad - ing deep the dis - mal flood, Plead - ing naught but Je - sus' blood,

Whis-p'ring soft-ly, "Wand'rer, come! Fol - low Me, I'll guide thee home."
Whis-per soft-ly, "Wand'rer, come! Fol - low Me, I'll guide thee home."
Whis-per soft-ly, "Wand'rer, come! Fol - low Me, I'll guide thee home." A-MEN.

Breathe on Me, Breath of God

95

TRENTHAM

Edwin Hatch, 1835-1889

Robert Jackson, 1842-1914

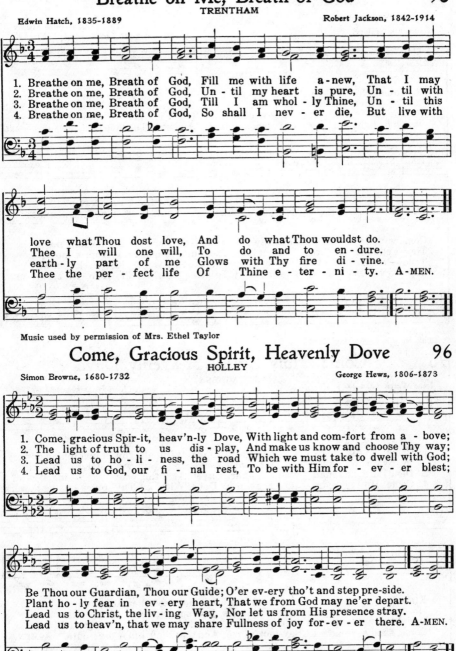

1. Breathe on me, Breath of God, Fill me with life a-new, That I may
2. Breathe on me, Breath of God, Un-til my heart is pure, Un-til with
3. Breathe on me, Breath of God, Till I am whol-ly Thine, Un-til this
4. Breathe on me, Breath of God, So shall I nev-er die, But live with

love what Thou dost love, And do what Thou wouldst do.
Thee I will one will, To do and to en-dure.
earth-ly part of me Glows with Thy fire di-vine.
Thee the per-fect life Of Thine e-ter-ni-ty. A-MEN.

Music used by permission of Mrs. Ethel Taylor

Come, Gracious Spirit, Heavenly Dove

96

HOLLEY

Simon Browne, 1680-1732

George Hews, 1806-1873

1. Come, gracious Spir-it, heav'n-ly Dove, With light and com-fort from a-bove;
2. The light of truth to us dis-play, And make us know and choose Thy way;
3. Lead us to ho-li-ness, the road Which we must take to dwell with God;
4. Lead us to God, our fi-nal rest, To be with Him for-ev-er blest;

Be Thou our Guardian, Thou our Guide; O'er ev-ery tho't and step pre-side.
Plant ho-ly fear in ev-ery heart, That we from God may ne'er depart.
Lead us to Christ, the liv-ing Way, Nor let us from His presence stray.
Lead us to heav'n, that we may share Fullness of joy for-ev-er there. A-MEN.

Alternate tune: FEDERAL STREET, No. 194

97 Come, Holy Ghost, Creator Blest

MENDON

Latin, 9th Century

Traditional German Melody
Arr. by Samuel Dyer, 1785-1835

1. Come, Ho - ly Ghost, Cre - a - tor blest, Vouchsafe within our souls to rest;
2. To Thee, the Com - fort - er, we cry; To Thee, the Gift of God most high;
3. The sev'n-fold gifts of grace are thine, O Fin - ger of the Hand Di-vine;
4. Thy light to ev - ery sense im-part, And shed Thy love in ev - ery heart;

Come with Thy grace and heav'nly aid, And fill the hearts which Thou hast made.
The Fount of life, the Fire of love, The soul's A-noint-ing from a-bove.
True Prom-ise of the Fa-ther Thou, Who dost the tongue with speech endow.
Thy own un-fail-ing might supply To strengthen our in-firm-i-ty. A-MEN.

This tune in higher key, No. 462

98 Come, Holy Spirit, Heavenly Dove

ST. AGNES

Isaac Watts, 1674-1748

John B. Dykes, 1823-1876

1. Come, Ho - ly Spir - it, heaven-ly Dove, With all Thy quick-ening powers;
2. In vain we tune our for - mal songs, In vain we strive to rise;
3. Dear Lord, and shall we ev - er live At this poor dy - ing rate?
4. Come, Ho - ly Spir - it, heaven-ly Dove, With all Thy quick - ening powers;

Kin - dle a flame of sa - cred love In these cold hearts of ours.
Ho - san - nas lan - guish on our tongues, And our de - vo - tion dies.
Our love so faint, so cold to Thee, And Thine to us so great!
Come, shed a-broad a Sav-iour's love, And that shall kin - dle ours. A-MEN.

This tune in higher key, No. 50. Alternate tune: AZMON, No. 49

Blessed Quietness

Manie P. Ferguson, 19th Century

W. S. Marshall, 19th Century
Arr. by James M. Kirk, 19th Century

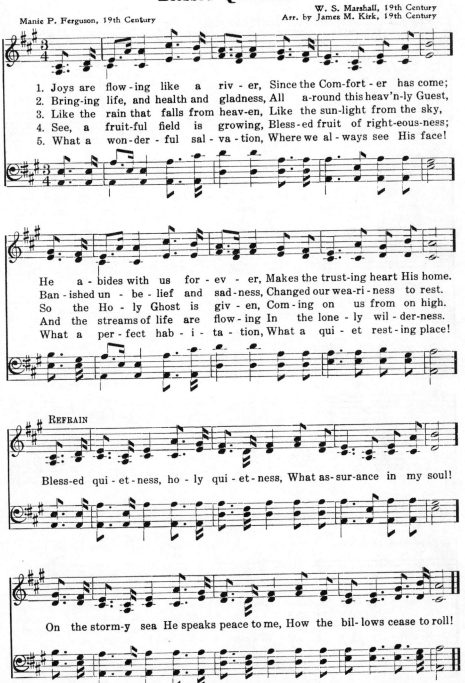

1. Joys are flow-ing like a riv-er, Since the Com-fort-er has come;
2. Bring-ing life, and health and gladness, All a-round this heav'n-ly Guest,
3. Like the rain that falls from heav-en, Like the sun-light from the sky,
4. See, a fruit-ful field is growing, Bless-ed fruit of right-eous-ness;
5. What a won-der-ful sal-va-tion, Where we al-ways see His face!

He a-bides with us for-ev-er, Makes the trust-ing heart His home.
Ban-ished un-be-lief and sad-ness, Changed our wea-ri-ness to rest.
So the Ho-ly Ghost is giv-en, Com-ing on us from on high.
And the streams of life are flow-ing In the lone-ly wil-der-ness.
What a per-fect hab-i-ta-tion, What a qui-et rest-ing place!

REFRAIN

Bless-ed qui-et-ness, ho-ly qui-et-ness, What as-sur-ance in my soul!

On the storm-y sea He speaks peace to me, How the bil-lows cease to roll!

100 Fill Me Now

Elwood H. Stokes, 1815-1895

John R. Sweney, 1837-1899

1. Hov - er o'er me, Ho - ly Spir - it, Bathe my trem-bling heart and brow;
2. Thou canst fill me, gra - cious Spir - it, Though I can - not tell Thee how;
3. I am weak-ness, full of weak-ness, At Thy sa - cred feet I bow;
4. Cleanse and com-fort, bless and save me, Bathe, O bathe my heart and brow;

Fill me with Thy hal - lowed pres-ence, Come, O come and fill me now.
But I need Thee, great - ly need Thee, Come, O come and fill me now.
Blest, di - vine, e - ter - nal Spir - it, Fill with power, and fill me now.
Thou art com - fort-ing and sav - ing, Thou art sweet - ly fill - ing now.

REFRAIN

Fill me now, fill me now, Je - sus, come and fill me now;

Fill me with Thy hal - lowed pres-ence, Come, O come and fill me now.

101 Holy Ghost, with Light Divine
MERCY

Andrew Reed, 1787-1862

Louis M. Gottschalk, 1829-1869
Arr. by Edwin P. Parker, 1836-1925

1. Ho - ly Ghost, with light di - vine Shine up - on this heart of mine;
2. Ho - ly Ghost, with power di - vine Cleanse this guilt - y heart of mine;
3. Ho - ly Ghost, with joy di - vine Cheer this sad-dened heart of mine;
4. Ho - ly Spir - it, all di - vine, Dwell with - in this heart of mine;

Holy Ghost, with Light Divine

Chase the shades of night a - way, Turn my dark-ness in - to day.
Long hath sin, with-out con-trol, Held do - min - ion o'er my soul.
Bid my man - y woes de - part, Heal my wound-ed, bleed-ing heart.
Cast down ev - ery i - dol-throne, Reign su - preme, and reign a-lone. A-MEN.

Old-Time Power

102

Paul Rader, 1879-1938

Paul Rader, 1879-1938

1. We are gath-ered for Thy bless-ing, We will wait up - on our God;
2. We will glo - ry in Thy pow-er, We will sing of won-drous grace;
3. Bring us low in prayer be - fore Thee, And with faith our souls in - spire,

We will trust in Him who loved us, And who bought us with His blood.
In our midst, as Thou hast prom-ised, Come, O come, and take Thy place.
Till we claim, by faith, the prom-ise Of the Ho - ly Ghost and fire.

REFRAIN

Spir - it, now melt and move All of our hearts with love,

Breathe on us from a - bove With old - time pow'r. A-MEN.

The Comforter Has Come

Frank Bottome, 1823-1894

William J. Kirkpatrick, 1838-1921

1. O spread the ti-dings 'round, wher-ev-er man is found, Wher-ev-er hu-man
2. The long, long night is past, the morn-ing breaks at last, And hushed the dreadful
3. Lo, the great King of kings, with heal-ing in His wings, To ev-'ry cap-tive
4. O bound-less love di-vine! how shall this tongue of mine To wond'ring mor-tals

hearts and hu-man woes a-bound; Let ev-'ry Christian tongue pro-claim the joy-ful
wail and fu-ry of the blast, As o'er the gold-en hills the day ad-vanc-es
soul a full de-liv'rance brings; And thro' the va-cant cells the song of tri-umph
tell the matchless grace di-vine—That I, a child of hell, should in His im-age

REFRAIN

sound: The Com-fort-er has come!
fast! The Com-fort-er has come!
rings; The Com-fort-er has come! The Com-fort-er has come, the Com-fort-er has
shine! The Com-fort-er has come!

come! The Ho-ly Ghost from Heav'n, the Fa-ther's promise giv'n; O spread the

ti-dings 'round, wher-ev-er man is found—The Com-fort-er has come!

Come, Thou Fount

NETTLETON

Robert Robinson, 1735-1790

John Wyeth, 1770-1858

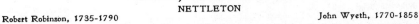

1. Come, Thou Fount of ev-ery bless-ing, Tune my heart to sing Thy grace;
2. Here I raise mine Eb-en-e-zer; Hith-er by Thy help I'm come;
3. O to grace how great a debt-or Dai-ly I'm con-strained to be!

Streams of mer-cy, nev-er ceas-ing, Call for songs of loud-est praise.
And I hope, by Thy good pleas-ure, Safe-ly to ar-rive at home.
Let Thy good-ness, like a fet-ter, Bind my wan-dering heart to Thee:

Teach me some me-lo-dious son-net, Sung by flam-ing tongues a-bove;
Je-sus sought me when a stran-ger, Wan-dering from the fold of God;
Prone to wan-der, Lord, I feel it, Prone to leave the God I love;

Praise the mount—I'm fixed up-on it—Mount of Thy re-deem-ing love.
He, to res-cue me from dan-ger, In-ter-posed His pre-cious blood.
Here's my heart, O take and seal it; Seal it for Thy courts a-bove. A-MEN.

105

Holy, Holy, Holy

NICÆA

Reginald Heber, 1783-1826

John B. Dykes, 1823-1876

1. Ho - ly, Ho - ly, Ho - ly! Lord God Al-might - y! Ear - ly in the
2. Ho - ly, Ho - ly, Ho - ly! All the saints a - dore Thee, Cast-ing down their
3. Ho - ly, Ho - ly, Ho - ly! Tho' the darkness hide Thee, Tho' the eye of
4. Ho - ly, Ho - ly, Ho - ly! Lord God Al-might - y! All Thy works shall

morn - ing our song shall rise to Thee; Ho - ly, Ho - ly, Ho - ly!
gold - en crowns a-round the glass-y sea; Cher - u - bim and ser-a-phim
sin - ful man Thy glo - ry may not see, On - ly Thou art ho - ly;
praise Thy name, in earth, and sky, and sea; Ho - ly, Ho - ly, Ho - ly!

Mer - ci - ful and Might-y! God in Three Per-sons, bless-ed Trin-i - ty!
fall-ing down be-fore Thee, Which wert and art, and ev-er-more shalt be.
there is none be-side Thee Per - fect in power, in love, and pu - ri - ty.
Mer - ci - ful and Might-y! God in Three Per-sons, bless-ed Trin-i - ty! A-MEN.

106

Lord of All Being

LOUVAN

Oliver W. Holmes, 1809-1894

Virgil C. Taylor, 1817-1891

1. Lord of all be - ing, throned a-far, Thy glo - ry flames from sun and star;
2. Sun of our life, Thy quickening ray Sheds on our path the glow of day;
3. Our mid-night is Thy smile withdrawn; Our noon-tide is Thy gra-cious dawn;
4. Grant us Thy truth to make us free, And kin-dling hearts that burn for Thee;

Alternate tune: Maryton, No. 454

Lord of All Being

Cen - ter and soul of ev - ery sphere, Yet to each lov-ing heart how near!
Star of our hope, Thy softened light Cheers the long watches of the night.
Our rain-bow arch, Thy mercy's sign; All, save the clouds of sin, are Thine.
Till all Thy liv - ing al - tars claim One ho - ly light, one heavenly flame. A-MEN.

O Worship the King   107

LYONS

From Psalm 104
Robert Grant, c. 1779-1838

Adapted from J. Michael Haydn, 1737-1806

1. O wor - ship the King, all - glo - rious a - bove, O grate-ful - ly
2. O tell of His might, O sing of His grace, Whose robe is the
3. Thy boun - ti - ful care what tongue can re - cite? It breathes in the
4. Frail chil - dren of dust, and fee - ble as frail, In Thee do we

sing His power and His love; Our Shield and De-fend - er, the An - cient of
light, whose can - o - py space. His char - iots of wrath the deep thun-der-clouds
air, it shines in the light, It streams from the hills, it de-scends to the
trust, nor find Thee to fail; Thy mer - cies how ten-der! how firm to the

Days, Pa - vil - ioned in splen-dor, and gird - ed with praise.
form, And dark is His path on the wings of the storm.
plain, And sweet-ly dis - tills in the dew and the rain.
end! Our Mak - er, De - fend - er, Re - deem - er and Friend. A - MEN.

108 We Sing the Boundless Praise
BOUNDLESS PRAISE

Joseph C. Macaulay, b. 1900   Harry Dixon Loes, b. 1892

1. We sing the bound-less praise Of Him who reigns on high,
2. Thy pre-cious blood a-lone, O Christ, has brought us near;
3. All hail! Re-deem-er, King, Thou Lamb of Cal-va-ry!

And of His glo-rious Son, the Lamb Who brought sal-va-tion nigh.
No long-er stran-gers, God in love Calls us His chil-dren dear.
Let ran-somed sin-ners sing Thy name Thro' all e-ter-ni-ty.

Thine ev-er-last-ing pow'r And maj-es-ty we sing,
The ti-tle of the Lamb Thou bear-est still in heav'n,
When stand the ran-somed throng Be-fore the great I Am,

But with our songs of sov-'reign grace We'll make heav'n's arch-es ring.
Me-mo-rial of Thy sac-ri-fice, And love to sin-ners giv'n.
This shall their end-less an-them be, "All wor-thy is the Lamb!" A-MEN.

Join All the Glorious Names

DARWALL

Isaac Watts, 1674-1748

John Darwall, 1731-1789

1. Join all the glo - rious names Of wis - dom, love, and power,
2. Great Pro - phet of my God, My tongue would bless Thy name:
3. Je - sus, my great High Priest, Of - fered His blood, and died;
4. Thou art my Coun - sel - lor, My Pat - tern, and my Guide,
5. My Sav - iour and my Lord, My Con - quer'r and my King,

That ev - er mor - tals knew, That an - gels
By Thee the joy - ful news Of our sal-
My guilt - y con - science seeks No sac - ri-
And Thou my Shep - herd art; Oh, keep me
Thy scep - tre and Thy sword, Thy reign - ing

ev - er bore: All are too poor to speak His worth,
va - tion came, The joy - ful news of sins for - giv'n,
fice be - side: His pow'r - ful blood did once a - tone
near Thy side; Nor let my feet e'er turn a - stray,
grace I sing: Thine is the pow'r; be - hold I sit

Too poor to set my Sav - iour forth.
Of hell sub - dued and peace with heav'n.
And now it pleads be - fore the throne.
To wan - der in the crook - ed way.
In will - ing bonds be - neath Thy feet. A - MEN.

110 Jesus, Priceless Treasure

JESU, MEINE FREUDE

Johann Franck, 1618-1677
Trans. by Catherine Winkworth, 1829-1878

Johann Crüger, 1598-1662
Descant arr. by William Lester, b. 1889

Slowly

1. Je - sus, priceless Treas-ure, Source of pur-est pleas - ure, Tru-est Friend to
2. In Thine arms I rest me, Foes who would mo-lest me Can-not reach me
3. Wealth, I will not heed thee, Wherefore should I need thee? Je - sus is my
4. Hence, all fears and sad-ness! For the Lord of glad - ness, Je - sus, en - ters

me! Long my heart hath pant - ed, Till it well-nigh faint - ed,
here; Though the earth be shak - ing, Ev - ery heart be quak - ing,
joy! Hon - ors, ye may glis - ten But I shall not lis - ten,
in; Those who love the Fa - ther, Though the storms may gath - er,

Thirsting aft-er Thee! Thine I am, O spot-less Lamb! I will suf-fer
Je - sus calms my fear; Sin and hell, in con-flict fell, With their heaviest
Ye the soul de-stroy! Want or loss or shame or cross Ne'er to leave my
Still have peace within; Yea, what-e'er I here must bear, Still in Thee lies

naught to hide Thee, Ask for naught be - side Thee.
storms as - sail me, Je - sus will not fail me.
Lord shall move me, Since He deigns to love me.
pur - est pleas - ure, Je - sus, price-less Treas - ure! A - MEN.

All Hail the Power

CORONATION

Edward Perronet, 1726-1792
Alt. by John Rippon, 1751-1836

Oliver Holden, 1765-1844

1. All hail the power of Je - sus' name! Let an - gels pros-trate fall;
2. Ye cho - sen seed of Is - rael's race, Ye ran-somed from the fall,
3. Let ev - ery kin - dred, ev - ery tribe, On this ter - res - trial ball,
4. O that with yon - der sa - cred throng We at His feet may fall!

Bring forth the roy - al di - a - dem, And crown Him Lord of all;
Hail Him who saves you by His grace, And crown Him Lord of all;
To Him all maj - es - ty as - cribe, And crown Him Lord of all;
We'll join the ev - er - last - ing song, And crown Him Lord of all;

Bring forth the roy - al di - a - dem, And crown Him Lord of all!
Hail Him who saves you by His grace, And crown Him Lord of all!
To Him all maj - es - ty as - cribe, And crown Him Lord of all!
We'll join the ev - er - last - ing song, And crown Him Lord of all! A-MEN.

(Second Tune)   MILES LANE   William Shrubsole, 1760-1806

1. All hail the power of Je-sus' name! Let angels prostrate fall; Bring forth the roy-al

di - a - dem, And crown Him, crown Him, crown Him, Crown Him Lord of all! A-MEN.

112 Light of the World, We Hail Thee

SALVE DOMINE

John S. B. Monsell, 1811-1875

Lawrence W. Watson, 1860-1925

1. Light of the world, we hail Thee, Flush-ing the east-ern skies;
2. Light of the world, Thy beau-ty Steals in-to ev-ery heart,
3. Light of the world, il-lu-mine This dark-ened earth of Thine,

Nev-er shall dark-ness veil Thee A-gain from hu-man eyes;
And glo-ri-fies with du-ty Life's poor-est, hum-blest part;
Till ev-ery-thing that's hu-man Be filled with what's di-vine;

Too long, a-las, with-hold-en, Now spread from shore to shore;
Thou rob-est in Thy splen-dor The sim-ple ways of men,
Till ev-ery tongue and na-tion, From sin's do-min-ion free,

Thy light, so glad and gold-en, Shall set on earth no more.
And help-est them to ren-der Light back to Thee a-gain.
Rise in the new cre-a-tion Which springs from love and Thee. A-MEN.

Music used by permission of Mrs. Sigrid Watson

Jesus! Jesus! Jesus!

LLANTHONY

Source Unknown

Abbey Hymns

1. Je - sus! Je - sus! Je - sus! Sing a - loud the Name;
2. Je - sus! Name of cleans - ing, Wash - ing all our stains;
3. Je - sus! Name of bold - ness, Mak - ing cow - ards brave;
4. Je - sus! Name of beau - ty, Beau - ty far too bright
5. Je - sus! be our joy - note In this vale of tears;

Till it soft - ly, slow - ly, Sets all hearts a - flame.
Je - sus! Name of heal - ing, Balm for all our pains.
Name! that in the bat - tle, Cer - tain - ly must save.
For our earth-born fan - cy, For our mor - tal sight.
Till we reach the home-land, And th'e - ter - nal years. A-MEN.

O Splendor of God's Glory Bright   114

SOLEMNIS HAEC FESTIVITAS

Ambrose of Milan, 340-397
Trans. by John Chandler, 1806-1876
and Louis F. Benson, 1855-1930

Angers Church Melody
Arr. by Donald P. Hustad. b. 1918

1. O splen-dor of God's glo -ry bright, From light e - ter - nal bring-ing light; Thou
2. Come, ver-y Sun of heaven's love, In last - ing ra-diance from a - bove, And
3. Con-firm our will to do the right, And keep our hearts from envy's blight; Let
4. O joy - ful be the pass - ing day With thoughts as clear as morn-ing's ray, With
5. Dawn's glory gilds the earth and skies; Do thou, our perfect Morn, a - rise; The

Light of life, light's liv-ing Spring, True Day, all days il - lu - min-ing.
pour the Ho - ly Spir-it's ray On all we think or do to-day.
faith her ea - ger fires re -new, And hate the false, and love the true.
faith like noon-tide shin-ing bright, Our souls un-shad-ow'd by the night.
Fa - ther's help his chil-dren claim, And sing the Fa-ther's glo-rious name. A-MEN.

115 Ancient of Days

ANCIENT OF DAYS

William C. Doane, 1832-1913

J. Albert Jeffery, 1854-1929

1. An - cient of Days, who sit - test throned in glo - ry, To Thee all knees are
2. O Ho - ly Fa - ther, who hast led Thy chil-dren, In all the a - ges,
3. O Ho - ly Je - sus, Prince of Peace and Sav-iour, To Thee we owe the
4. O Ho - ly Ghost, the Lord and the Life - giv - er, Thine is the quick- ening
5. O Tri - une God, with heart and voice a - dor - ing, Praise we the good - ness

bent, all voic - es pray; Thy love hast blest the wide world's won-drous sto-ry
with the fire and cloud, Through seas dry-shod, through wea-ry wastes be-wil-dering;
peace that still pre-vails, Still - ing the rude wills of men's wild be - hav - ior,
power that gives increase; From Thee have flowed, as from a pleas-ant riv - er,
that doth crown our days; Pray we that Thou wilt hear us, still im - plor - ing

With light and life since E - den's dawn - ing day.
To Thee, in rev - erent love, our hearts are bowed.
And calm - ing pas - sion's fierce and storm - y gales.
Our plen - ty, wealth, pros - per - i - ty and peace.
Thy love and fa - vor, kept to us al - ways. A-MEN.

116 O Jesus, King Most Wonderful!

SERENITY

Bernard of Clairvaux, 1091-1153
Trans. by Edward Caswall, 1814-1878

William V. Wallace, 1814-1865

1. O Je - sus, King most won - der - ful! Thou Con - quer - or re-nowned!
2. When once Thou vis - it - est the heart, Then truth be - gins to shine,
3. O Je - sus! Light of all be - low, Thou Fount of life and fire!
4. Thy won-drous mer - cies are un - told, Through each re - turn-ing day;
5. Thee may our tongues for - ev - er bless; Thee may we love a - lone;

O Jesus, King Most Wonderful

Thou Sweetness most in - ef - fa - ble, In Whom all joys are found!
Then earth - ly van - i - ties de - part, Then kin - dles love di - vine.
Sur - pass - ing all the joys we know, All that we can de - sire.
Thy love ex - ceeds a thou-sand fold, What-ev - er we can say.
And ev - er in our lives ex-press The im - age of Thine Own. A-MEN.

Ye Servants of God, Your Master Proclaim 117
HANOVER

Charles Wesley, 1707-1788

William Croft, 1678-1727

1. Ye serv - ants of God, your Mas - ter pro - claim, And pub - lish a-
2. God rul - eth on high, al - might - y to save; And still He is
3. "Sal - va - tion to God, who sits on the throne," Let all cry a-
4. Then let us a - dore, and give Him His right, All glo - ry and

broad His won - der - ful name; The name all vic - to - rious of
nigh— His pres - ence we have; The great con - gre - ga - tion His
loud, and hon - or the Son; The prais - es of Je - sus the
power, all wis - dom and might; All hon - or and bless - ing, with

Je - sus ex - tol; His King-dom is glo-rious, He rules o - ver all.
triumph shall sing, As - crib-ing sal - va - tion to Je - sus our King.
an - gels pro-claim, Fall down on their fa - ces, and wor-ship the Lamb.
an - gels a - bove, And thanks nev-er ceas - ing, and in - fi - nite love. A-MEN.

Alternate tune: LYONS, No. 107

118 Rejoice, Ye Pure in Heart

MARION

Edward H. Plumptre, 1821-1891   Arthur H. Messiter, 1834-1916

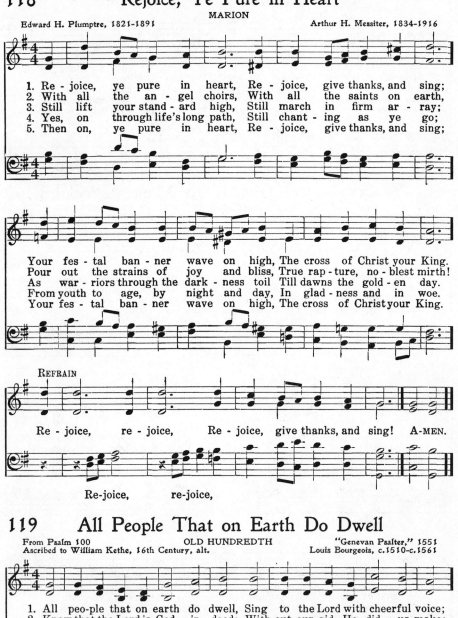

1. Re - joice, ye pure in heart, Re - joice, give thanks, and sing;
2. With all the an - gel choirs, With all the saints on earth,
3. Still lift your stand - ard high, Still march in firm ar - ray;
4. Yes, on through life's long path, Still chant - ing as ye go;
5. Then on, ye pure in heart, Re - joice, give thanks, and sing;

Your fes - tal ban - ner wave on high, The cross of Christ your King.
Pour out the strains of joy and bliss, True rap - ture, no - blest mirth!
As war - riors through the dark - ness toil Till dawns the gold - en day.
From youth to age, by night and day, In glad - ness and in woe.
Your fes - tal ban - ner wave on high, The cross of Christ your King.

REFRAIN

Re - joice, re - joice, Re - joice, give thanks, and sing! A-MEN.

Re-joice, re - joice,

119 All People That on Earth Do Dwell

From Psalm 100   OLD HUNDREDTH   "Genevan Psalter," 1551
Ascribed to William Kethe, 16th Century, alt.   Louis Bourgeois, c.1510-c.1561

1. All peo-ple that on earth do dwell, Sing to the Lord with cheerful voice;
2. Know that the Lord is God in - deed; With-out our aid He did us make;
3. O en - ter then His gates with praise, Ap-proach with joy His courts un - to;
4. For why? the Lord our God is good, His mer-cy is for - ev - er sure;

All People That on Earth Do Dwell

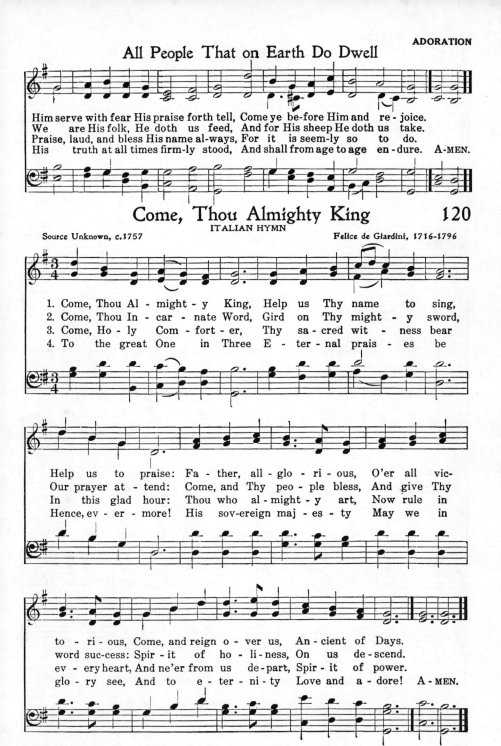

Him serve with fear His praise forth tell, Come ye be-fore Him and re - joice.
We are His folk, He doth us feed, And for His sheep He doth us take.
Praise, laud, and bless His name al-ways, For it is seem-ly so to do.
His truth at all times firm-ly stood, And shall from age to age en - dure. A-MEN.

Come, Thou Almighty King 120

ITALIAN HYMN

Source Unknown, c.1757 Felice de Giardini, 1716-1796

1. Come, Thou Al - might - y King, Help us Thy name to sing,
2. Come, Thou In - car - nate Word, Gird on Thy might - y sword,
3. Come, Ho - ly Com - fort - er, Thy sa - cred wit - ness bear
4. To the great One in Three E - ter - nal prais - es be

Help us to praise: Fa - ther, all - glo - ri - ous, O'er all vic-
Our prayer at - tend: Come, and Thy peo - ple bless, And give Thy
In this glad hour: Thou who al - might - y art, Now rule in
Hence, ev - er - more! His sov-ereign maj - es - ty May we in

to - ri - ous, Come, and reign o - ver us, An - cient of Days.
word suc-cess: Spir - it of ho - li - ness, On us de - scend.
ev - ery heart, And ne'er from us de-part, Spir - it of power.
glo - ry see, And to e - ter - ni - ty Love and a - dore! A - MEN.

121 Our Great Saviour

HYFRYDOL

J. Wilbur Chapman, 1859-1918

Rowland H. Prichard, 1811-1887
Arr. by Robert Harkness, b. 1880

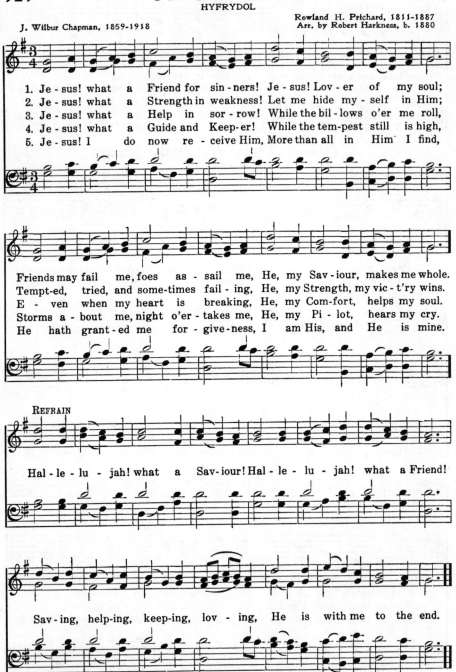

1. Je - sus! what a Friend for sin-ners! Je - sus! Lov - er of my soul;
2. Je - sus! what a Strength in weakness! Let me hide my - self in Him;
3. Je - sus! what a Help in sor - row! While the bil-lows o'er me roll,
4. Je - sus! what a Guide and Keep-er! While the tem-pest still is high,
5. Je - sus! I do now re - ceive Him, More than all in Him I find,

Friends may fail me, foes as - sail me, He, my Sav - iour, makes me whole.
Tempt-ed, tried, and some-times fail - ing, He, my Strength, my vic - t'ry wins.
E - ven when my heart is breaking, He, my Com-fort, helps my soul.
Storms a - bout me, night o'er - takes me, He, my Pi - lot, hears my cry.
He hath grant-ed me for - give-ness, I am His, and He is mine.

REFRAIN

Hal - le - lu - jah! what a Sav-iour! Hal - le - lu - jah! what a Friend!

Sav - ing, help-ing, keep-ing, lov - ing, He is with me to the end.

Crown Him with Many Crowns

DIADEMATA

Matthew Bridges, 1800-1894, and
Godfrey Thring, 1823-1903

George J. Elvey, 1816-1893

1. Crown Him with man - y crowns, The Lamb up - on His throne;
2. Crown Him the Son of God Be - fore the worlds be - gan,
3. Crown Him the Lord of life, Who tri - umphed o'er the grave,
4. Crown Him the Lord of love! Be - hold His hands and side,

Hark! how the heaven-ly an - them drowns All mu - sic but its own!
And ye, who tread where He hath trod, Crown Him the Son of man;
And rose vic - to - rious in the strife For those He came to save;
Rich wounds, yet vis - i - ble a - bove, In beau - ty glo - ri - fied:

A - wake, my soul, and sing Of Him who died for thee,
Who ev - ery grief hath known That wrings the hu - man breast,
His glo - ries now we sing Who died, and rose on high,
All hail, Re - deem - er, hail! For Thou hast died for me:

And hail Him as thy matchless King Through all e - ter - ni - ty.
And takes and bears them for His own, That all in Him may rest.
Who died, e - ter - nal life to bring, And lives that death may die.
Thy praise shall nev-er, nev - er fail Throughout e - ter - ni - ty. A-MEN.

For Descant arrangement, see No. 417

123 Sing Praise to God Who Reigns Above

MIT FREUDEN ZART

Johann J. Schütz, 1640-1690
Trans. by Frances E. Cox, 1812-1897

From the Bohemian Brethren's
"Gesangbuch," 1566

1. Sing praise to God who reigns a-bove, The God of all cre-a-tion, The God of power, the God of love, The God of our sal-va-tion; With heal-ing balm my soul He fills, And ev-ery faith-less mur-mur stills: To God all praise and glo-ry.

2. What God's al-might-y pow'r hath made, His gra-cious mer-cy keep-eth; By morn-ing glow or eve-ning shade His watch-ful eye ne'er sleep-eth; With-in the king-dom of His might, Lo! all is just and all is right: To God all praise and glo-ry.

3. The Lord is nev-er far a-way, But, through all grief dis-tress-ing, An ev-er-pres-ent help and stay, Our peace, and joy, and bless-ing; As with a moth-er's ten-der hand, He leads His own, His cho-sen band: To God all praise and glo-ry.

4. Thus, all my toil-some way a-long, I sing a-loud Thy prais-es, That men may hear the grate-ful song My voice un-wea-ried rais-es, Be joy-ful in the Lord, my heart, Both soul and bod-y bear your part: To God all praise and glo-ry. A-MEN.

Oh, It Is Wonderful!

Charles H. Gabriel, 1856-1932

Charles H. Gabriel, 1856-1932
Arr. by Donald P. Hustad, b. 1918

1. I stand all a-mazed at the love Je-sus of-fers me, Con-fused at the
2. I mar-vel that He would de-scend from His throne di-vine, To res-cue a
3. I think of His hands pierced and bleeding to pay the debt! Such mer-cy, such

grace that so ful-ly He prof-fers me; I trem-ble to know that for me He was
soul so re-bel-lious and proud as mine; That He should extend His great love un-to
love and de-vo-tion can I for-get? No, no! I will praise and a-dore at the

cru-ci-fied—That for me, a sin-ner, He suf-fered, He bled, and died.
such as I; Suf-fi-cient to own, to re-deem, and to jus-ti-fy.
mer-cy-seat, Un-til at the glo-ri-fied throne I kneel at His feet.

REFRAIN

Oh, it is won-der-ful that He should care for me, E-nough to

die for me! Oh, it is won-der-ful, won-der-ful to me!

125 Holy God, We Praise Thy Name

GROSSER GOTT, WIR LOBEN DICH

Te Deum, c.4th Century
Trans. by Clarence Walworth, 1820-1900

"Katholisches Gesangbuch," Vienna, 1774

1. Ho - ly God, we praise Thy name; Lord of all, we bow be - fore Thee;
2. Hark, the loud ce - les - tial hymn An - gel choirs a - bove are rais - ing;
3. Lo! the ap - os - tol - ic train Joins Thy sa - cred name to hal - low;
4. Ho - ly Fa - ther, Ho - ly Son, Ho - ly Spir - it, Three we name Thee;

All on earth Thy scep - ter claim, All in heav'n a - bove a - dore Thee.
Cher - u - bim and Ser - a-phim, In un - ceas - ing cho - rus prais-ing,
Proph-ets swell the glad re-frain, And the white-robed mar - tyrs fol - low;
While in es - sence on - ly One, Un - di - vid - ed God we claim Thee,

In - fi - nite Thy vast do-main, Ev - er - last - ing is Thy reign.
Fill the heav'ns with sweet ac-cord: Ho - ly, ho - ly, ho - ly Lord.
And, from morn to set of sun, Through the Church the song goes on.
And a - dor - ing bend the knee, While we sing our praise to Thee. A-MEN.

126 Begin, My Tongue, Some Heavenly Theme

MANOAH

Isaac Watts, 1674-1748

From "Henry W. Greatorex's Collection," 1851

1. Be - gin, my tongue, some heavenly theme, And speak some bound-less thing,
2. Tell of His won-drous faith-ful-ness, And sound His power a - broad;
3. His ver - y word of grace is strong As that which built the skies;
4. O might I hear Thy heaven-ly tongue But whis-per, "Thou art Mine,"

Begin, My Tongue, Some Heavenly Theme

The might-y works or might-ier Name Of our e - ter-nal King.
Sing the sweet prom-ise of His grace, The love and truth of God.
The voice that rolls the stars a - long Speaks all the prom-is - es.
Those gen - tle words should raise my song To notes al - most di - vine. A-MEN.

Rejoice, the Lord Is King   127

DARWALL

Charles Wesley, 1707-1788   John Darwall, 1731-1789

1. Re - joice, the Lord is King: Your Lord and King a - dore!
2. Je - sus, the Sav - iour, reigns, The God of truth and love;
3. His King-dom can - not fail, He rules o'er earth and heav'n;
4. Re - joice, in glo - rious hope! Our Lord the Judge shall come,

Re-joice, give thanks, and sing, And tri-umph ev - er - more: Lift up your heart,
When He had purged our stains, He took His seat a - bove: Lift up your heart,
The keys of death and hell Are to our Je - sus giv'n: Lift up your heart,
And take his ser-vants up To their e - ter - nal home. Lift up your heart,

lift up your voice! Re - joice, a - gain I say, re - joice!
lift up your voice! Re - joice, a - gain I say, re - joice!
lift up your voice! Re - joice, a - gain I say, re - joice!
lift up your voice! Re - joice, a - gain I say, re - joice! A-MEN.

128 Praise Ye the Triune God!

FLEMMING

Source Unknown

Friedrich F. Flemming, 1778-1813

1. Praise ye the Fa - ther! for His lov - ing kind - ness, Ten - der - ly
2. Praise ye the Sav - iour! great is His com-pas - sion, Gra - cious - ly
3. Praise ye the Spir - it! Com-fort - er of Is - rael, Sent of the

cares He for His err - ing chil - dren; Praise Him, ye an - gels,
cares He for His cho - sen peo - ple; Young men and maid - ens,
Fa - ther and the Son to bless us; Praise ye the Fa - ther,

praise Him in the heav - ens, Praise ye Je - ho - vah!
ye old men and chil - dren, Praise ye the Sav - iour!
Son and Ho - ly Spir - it, Praise ye the Tri - une God! A - MEN.

129 Jesus, Thou Joy of Loving Hearts

QUEBEC (Hesperus)

Bernard of Clairvaux, 1091-1153
Trans. by Ray Palmer, 1808-1887

Henry Baker, 1835-1910

1. Je - sus, Thou Joy of lov - ing hearts, Thou Fount of life, Thou Light of men,
2. Thy truth unchanged hath ev - er stood; Thou sav - est those that on Thee call;
3. We taste Thee, O Thou liv - ing Bread, And long to feast up - on Thee still;
4. Our rest-less spir - its yearn for Thee, Where'er our changeful lot is cast;
5. O Je - sus, ev - er with us stay, Make all our moments calm and bright;

Music copyright by W. Garret Horder. Used by permission
Alternate tune: FEDERAL STREET, No. 194

Jesus, Thou Joy of Loving Hearts

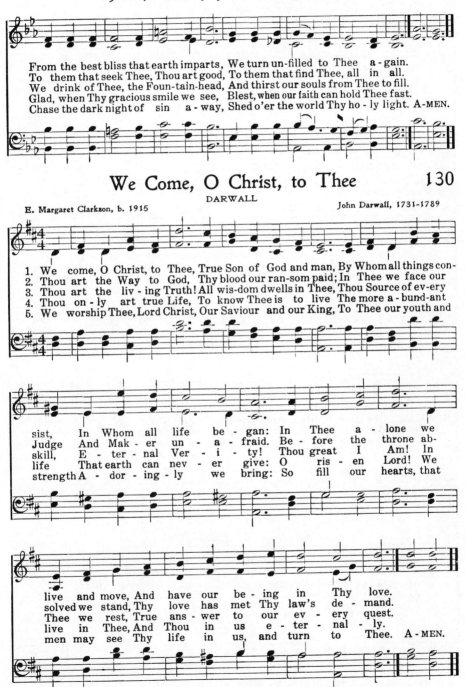

From the best bliss that earth imparts, We turn un-filled to Thee a-gain.
To them that seek Thee, Thou art good, To them that find Thee, all in all.
We drink of Thee, the Foun-tain-head, And thirst our souls from Thee to fill.
Glad, when Thy gracious smile we see, Blest, when our faith can hold Thee fast.
Chase the dark night of sin a-way, Shed o'er the world Thy ho-ly light. A-MEN.

We Come, O Christ, to Thee   130
DARWALL

E. Margaret Clarkson, b. 1915   John Darwall, 1731-1789

1. We come, O Christ, to Thee, True Son of God and man, By Whom all things con-
2. Thou art the Way to God, Thy blood our ran-som paid; In Thee we face our
3. Thou art the liv-ing Truth! All wis-dom dwells in Thee, Thou Source of ev-ery
4. Thou on-ly art true Life, To know Thee is to live The more a-bund-ant
5. We worship Thee, Lord Christ, Our Saviour and our King, To Thee our youth and

sist, In Whom all life be-gan: In Thee a-lone we
Judge And Mak-er un-a-fraid. Be-fore the throne ab-
skill, E-ter-nal Ver-i-ty! Thou great I Am! In
life That earth can nev-er give: O ris-en Lord! We
strength A-dor-ing-ly we bring: So fill our hearts, that

live and move, And have our be-ing in Thy love.
solved we stand, Thy love has met Thy law's de-mand.
Thee we rest, True ans-wer to our ev-ery quest.
live in Thee, And Thou in us e-ter-nal-ly.
men may see Thy life in us, and turn to Thee. A-MEN.

Words copyright by Inter-Varsity Christian Fellowship. Used by permission

131 Praise, My Soul, the King of Heaven

LAUDA ANIMA (Benedic Anima Mea)

From Psalm 103
Henry F. Lyte, 1793-1847

John Goss, 1800-1880

1. Praise, my soul, the King of heav - en, To His feet thy
2. Praise Him for His grace and fa - vor To our fa - thers
3. Fa - ther - like, He tends and spares us; Well our fee - ble
4. An - gels, help us to a - dore Him, Ye be - hold Him

trib - ute bring; Ran - somed, healed, re - stored, for - giv - en,
in dis - tress; Praise Him, still the same for - ev - er,
frame He knows, In His hands He gen - tly bears us,
face to face; Sun and moon, bow down be - fore Him;

Who, like me, His praise should sing? Al - le - lu - ia!
Slow to chide, and swift to bless. Al - le - lu - ia!
Res - cues us from all our foes. Al - le - lu - ia!
Dwell - ers all in time and space, Al - le - lu - ia!

Al - le - lu - ia! Praise the Ev - er - last - ing King!
Al - le - lu - ia! Glo - rious in His faith - ful - ness!
Al - le - lu - ia! Wide - ly as His mer - cy flows!
Al - le - lu - ia! Praise with us the God of grace! A - MEN.

Alternate tune: REGENT SQUARE, No. 31

Blessed Be the Name

W. H. Clark, 19th Century
Refrain, Ralph E. Hudson, 1843-1901

Ralph E. Hudson, 1843-1901
Arr. by William J. Kirkpatrick, 1838-1921

1. All praise to Him who reigns a - bove In maj - es - ty su - preme,
2. His name a - bove all names shall stand, Ex - alt - ed more and more,
3. Re - deem - er, Sav - iour, Friend of man Once ru - ined by the fall,
4. His name shall be the Coun - sel - or, The might - y Prince of Peace,

Who gave His Son for man to die, That He might man re - deem!
At God the Fa - ther's own right hand, Where an - gel - hosts a - dore.
Thou hast de - vised sal - va - tion's plan, For Thou hast died for all.
Of all earth's king - doms Con - quer - or, Whose reign shall nev - er cease.

REFRAIN

Bless-ed be the name, bless-ed be the name, Bless-ed be the name of the Lord;

Bless-ed be the name, bless-ed be the name, Bless-ed be the name of the Lord.

133 Praise the Lord! Ye Heavens, Adore Him

From Psalm 148
"Foundling Hospital Collection," 1796
Edward Osler, 1798-1863, stanza 3

FABEN

John H. Willcox, 1827-1875

1. Praise the Lord! ye heavens, a-dore Him; Praise Him, an-gels in the height;
2. Praise the Lord! for He is glo-rious; Nev-er shall His prom-ise fail:
3. Wor-ship, hon-or, glo-ry, bless-ing, Lord, we of-fer un-to Thee;

Sun and moon, re-joice be-fore Him, Praise Him, all ye stars of light.
God hath made His saints vic-to-rious; Sin and death shall not pre-vail.
Young and old, Thy praise ex-press-ing, In glad hom-age bend the knee.

Praise the Lord! for He hath spo-ken; Worlds His might-y voice o-beyed;
Praise the God of our sal-va-tion! Hosts on high, His power pro-claim;
All the saints in heaven a-dore Thee; We would bow be-fore Thy throne:

Laws which nev-er shall be bro-ken For their guid-ance He hath made.
Heaven, and earth, and all cre-a-tion, Laud and mag-ni-fy His name.
As Thine an-gels serve be-fore Thee, So on earth Thy will be done. A-MEN.

Alternate tunes: HYFRYDOL, No. 48; AUSTRIAN HYMN, No. 171

What a Wonderful Saviour!

Elisha A. Hoffman, 1839-1929

Elisha A. Hoffman, 1839-1929

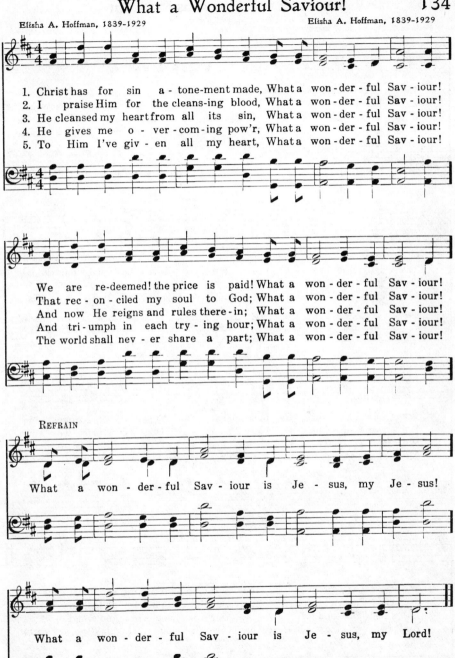

1. Christ has for sin a - tone-ment made, What a won-der-ful Sav-iour!
2. I praise Him for the cleans-ing blood, What a won-der-ful Sav-iour!
3. He cleansed my heart from all its sin, What a won-der-ful Sav-iour!
4. He gives me o - ver-com-ing pow'r, What a won-der-ful Sav-iour!
5. To Him I've giv - en all my heart, What a won-der-ful Sav-iour!

We are re-deemed! the price is paid! What a won-der-ful Sav-iour!
That rec - on - ciled my soul to God; What a won-der-ful Sav-iour!
And now He reigns and rules there-in; What a won-der-ful Sav-iour!
And tri-umph in each try-ing hour; What a won-der-ful Sav-iour!
The world shall nev - er share a part; What a won-der-ful Sav-iour!

REFRAIN

What a won-der-ful Sav-iour is Je-sus, my Je-sus!

What a won-der-ful Sav-iour is Je-sus, my Lord!

135 O Saviour, Precious Saviour

GREENLAND

Frances R. Havergal, 1836-1879

Arr. from J. Michael Haydn, 1737-1806

1. O Sav-iour, pre-cious Sav-iour, Whom yet un-seen we love,
2. O bring-er of sal-va-tion, Who won-drous-ly hast wrought,
3. In Thee all ful-ness dwell-eth, All grace and power di-vine;
4. O grant the con-sum-ma-tion Of this our song a-bove,

O Name of might and fa-vor, All oth-er names a-bove!
Thy-self the rev-e-la-tion Of love be-yond our thought,
The glo-ry that ex-cel-leth, O Son of God, is Thine;
In end-less ad-o-ra-tion, And ev-er-last-ing love;

We wor-ship Thee, we bless Thee, To Thee, O Christ, we sing;
We wor-ship Thee, we bless Thee, To Thee, O Christ, we sing;
We wor-ship Thee, we bless Thee, To Thee, O Christ, we sing;
Then shall we praise and bless Thee, Where per-fect prais-es ring,

We praise Thee, and con-fess Thee, Our ho-ly Lord and King.
We praise Thee, and con-fess Thee, Our gra-cious Lord and King.
We praise Thee, and con-fess Thee, Our glo-rious Lord and King.
And ev-er-more con-fess Thee, Our Sav-iour and our King. A-MEN.

Alternate tunes: ANGEL'S STORY No. 331; LANCASHIRE. No. 415

Safely through Another Week

SABBATH

John Newton, 1725-1807

Lowell Mason, 1792-1872

1. Safe - ly through an - oth - er week God has brought us on our way;
2. While we pray for par-doning grace, Through the dear Re-deem-er's name,
3. Here we come Thy name to praise, Let us feel Thy pres-ence near;
4. May Thy gos - pel's joy - ful sound Con - quer sin - ners, com-fort saints;

Let us now a bless - ing seek, Wait - ing in His courts to - day;
Show Thy rec - on - cil - ed face; Take a - way our sin and shame:
May Thy glo - ry meet our eyes, While we in Thy house ap - pear:
Make the fruits of grace a - bound, Bring re - lief for all com-plaints:

Day of all the week the best, Em - blem of e - ter - nal rest:
From our world - ly cares set free, May we rest this day in Thee:
Here af - ford us, Lord, a taste Of our ev - er - last - ing feast:
Thus may all our Sab-baths prove, Till we join the Church a - bove:

Day of all the week the best, Em-blem of e - ter - nal rest.
From our world - ly cares set free, May we rest this day in Thee.
Here af - ford us, Lord, a taste Of our ev - er - last - ing feast.
Thus may all our Sab-baths prove, Till we join the Church a - bove. A - MEN.

137 O Day of Rest and Gladness

MENDEBRAS

Christopher Wordsworth, 1807-1885

Old German Melody
Arr. by Lowell Mason, 1792-1872

1. O day of rest and glad-ness, O day of joy and light,
2. On thee, at the cre - a - tion, The light first had its birth;
3. To - day on wea-ry na - tions The heaven-ly man-na falls;
4. New grac - es ev - er gain-ing From this our day of rest,

O balm of care and sad-ness, Most beau-ti - ful, most bright;
On thee, for our sal - va - tion, Christ rose from depths of earth;
To ho - ly con-vo - ca - tions The sil - ver trump-et calls,
We reach the rest re - main-ing To spir - its of the blest;

On thee the high and low - ly, Through a - ges joined in tune, Sing
On thee our Lord vic - to - rious The Spir - it sent from heaven; And
Where gos - pel light is glow-ing With pure and ra - diant beams, And
To Ho - ly Ghost be prais - es, To Fa - ther and to Son; The

"Ho - ly, ho - ly, ho - ly," To the great God Tri - une.
thus on thee most glo - rious A tri - ple light was given.
liv - ing wa - ter flow-ing With soul-re - fresh-ing streams.
Church her voice up - rais - es To Thee, blest Three in One. A - MEN.

New Every Morning Is the Love

MELCOMBE

John Keble, 1792-1866

Samuel Webbe, 1740-1816

1. New ev-ery morn-ing is the love Our wak-ening and up-ris-ing prove;
2. New mer-cies each re-turn-ing day Hov-er a-round us while we pray;
3. If, on our dai-ly course, our mind Be set to hal-low all we find,
4. The triv-ial round, the com-mon task, Will fur-nish all we ought to ask;
5. On-ly, O Lord, in Thy dear love, Fit us for per-fect rest a-bove,

Through sleep and darkness safely brought, Restored to life and power and thought.
New per-ils past, new sins for-giv'n, New thoughts of God, new hopes of heav'n.
New treas-ures still, of countless price, God will provide for sac-ri-fice.
Room to de-ny our-selves, a road To bring us dai-ly near-er God.
And help us this and ev-ery day, To live more near-ly as we pray. A-MEN.

Alternate tune: CANONBURY. No. 338

This Is the Day of Light

SWABIA

139

John Ellerton, 1826-1893

Johann M. Spiess, c.1715-1772

1. This is the day of light: Let there be light to-day;
2. This is the day of rest: Our fail-ing strength re-new;
3. This is the day of peace: Thy peace our spir-its fill;
4. This is the day of prayer: Let earth to heaven draw near;
5. This is the first of days: Send forth Thy quick-ening breath,

O Day-spring, rise up-on our night And chase its gloom a-way.
On wea-ry brain and trou-bled breast Shed Thou Thy fresh-ening dew.
Bid Thou the blasts of dis-cord cease, The waves of strife be still.
Lift up our hearts to seek Thee there; Come down to meet us here.
And wake dead souls to love and praise, O Van-quish-er of death. A-MEN.

Alternate tune: ST. THOMAS, No. 247

140 When Morning Gilds the Skies

LAUDES DOMINI

From the German, 19th Century
Trans. by Edward Caswall, 1814-1878

Joseph Barnby, 1838-1896

1. When morn-ing gilds the skies, My heart a-wak-ing cries:
2. Does sad-ness fill my mind, A sol-ace here I find:
3. In heaven's e-ter-nal bliss The love-liest strain is this,
4. Be this, while life is mine, My can-ti-cle di-vine,

May Je-sus Christ be praised; A-like at work or prayer
May Je-sus Christ be praised; Or fades my earth-ly bliss,
May Je-sus Christ be praised; The powers of dark-ness fear,
May Je-sus Christ be praised; Be this th'e-ter-nal song,

To Je-sus I re-pair: May Je-sus Christ be praised.
My com-fort still is this: May Je-sus Christ be praised.
When this sweet chant they hear: May Je-sus Christ be praised.
Through all the a-ges long: May Je-sus Christ be praised. AMEN.

141 Awake, My Soul, and with the Sun

MORNING HYMN

Thomas Ken, 1637-1711

Francois H. Barthélémon, 1741-1808

1. A-wake, my soul, and with the sun Thy dai-ly stage of du-ty run;
2. Wake, and lift up thy-self, my heart, And with the an-gels bear thy part,
3. All praise to Thee, who safe hast kept, And hast re-freshed me while I slept:
4. Di-rect, con-trol, sug-gest, this day, All I de-sign, or do, or say;

Awake, My Soul, and with the Sun

Shake off dull sloth, and joy-ful rise To pay thy morn-ing sac-ri-fice.
Who all night long un-wear-ied sing High praise to the E-ter-nal King.
Grant, Lord, when I from death shall wake, I may of end-less life par-take.
That all my powers, with all their might, In Thy sole glo-ry may u-nite. A-MEN.

Still, Still with Thee 142

CONSOLATION

Harriet Beecher Stowe, 1812-1896   Felix Mendelssohn, 1809-1847

1. Still, still with Thee, when pur-ple morn-ing break-eth, When the bird
2. A-lone with Thee, a-mid the mys-tic shad-ows, The sol-emn
3. When sinks the soul, sub-dued by toil, to slum-ber, Its clos-ing
4. So shall it be at last, in that bright morn-ing When the soul

wak-eth, and the shad-ows flee; Fair-er than morn-ing, love-lier than the
hush of na-ture new-ly born; A-lone with Thee in breath-less ad-o-
eyes look up to Thee in prayer; Sweet the re-pose be-neath Thy wings o'er-
wak-eth, and life's shad-ows flee; Oh, in that hour, fair-er than day-light

day-light, Dawns the sweet con-scious-ness, I am with Thee.
ra-tion, In the calm dew and fresh-ness of the morn.
shad-ing, But sweet-er still to wake and find Thee there.
dawn-ing, Shall rise the glo-rious thought—I am with Thee. A-MEN.

143 Softly Now the Light of Day

SEYMOUR

George W. Doane, 1799-1859

Carl M. von Weber, 1786-1826

1. Soft - ly now the light of day Fades up - on my sight a - way;
2. Thou, whose all - per - vad - ing eye Naught es-capes, with - out, with - in,
3. Soon for me the light of day Shall for - ev - er pass a - way;
4. Thou who, sin - less, yet hast known All of man's in - firm - i - ty;

Free from care, from la - bor free, Lord, I would com-mune with Thee.
Par - don each in - firm - i - ty, O - pen fault, and se - cret sin.
Then, from sin and sor - row free, Take me, Lord, to dwell with Thee.
Then, from Thine e - ter - nal throne, Je - sus, look with pity - ing eye. A-MEN.

Alternate tune: MERCY. No. 101

144 Sun of My Soul

HURSLEY

John Keble, 1792-1866

Adapted from "Katholisches Gesangbuch," c. 1774

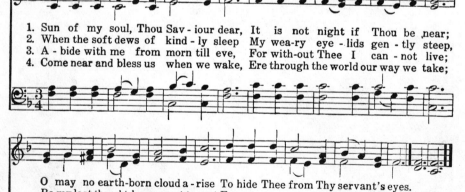

1. Sun of my soul, Thou Sav - iour dear, It is not night if Thou be near;
2. When the soft dews of kind - ly sleep My wea-ry eye - lids gen - tly steep,
3. A - bide with me from morn till eve, For with-out Thee I can - not live;
4. Come near and bless us when we wake, Ere through the world our way we take;

O may no earth-born cloud a - rise To hide Thee from Thy servant's eyes.
Be my last thought, how sweet to rest For-ev - er on my Sav-iour's breast.
A-bide with me when night is nigh, For with-out Thee I dare not die.
Till, in the o - cean of Thy love, We lose our-selves in heaven a-bove. A-MEN.

Saviour, Breathe an Evening Blessing   145
EVENING PRAYER

James Edmeston, 1791-1867

George C. Stebbins, 1846-1945

1. Sav - iour, breathe an eve-ning bless-ing, Ere re - pose our spir - its seal;
2. Though de-struc-tion walk a - round us, Though the ar - rows past us fly;
3. Though the night be dark and drear - y, Dark-ness can - not hide from Thee;
4. Should swift death this night o'ertake us, And our couch be - come our tomb,

Sin and want we come con-fess - ing, Thou canst save, and Thou canst heal.
An - gel-guards from Thee surround us, We are safe if Thou art nigh.
Thou art He who, nev-er wea - ry, Watch-est where Thy peo-ple be.
May the morn in heaven a-wake us, Clad in light and deathless bloom. A-MEN.

Now the Day Is Over   146
MERRIAL

Sabine Baring-Gould, 1834-1924

Joseph Barnby, 1838-1896

1. Now the day is o - ver, Night is draw - ing nigh,
2. Je - sus, give the wea - ry Calm and sweet re - pose;
3. Grant to lit - tle chil - dren Vi - sions bright of Thee;
4. Through the long night watch - es, May Thine an - gels spread
5. When the morn - ing wak - ens, Then may I a - rise

Shad - ows of the eve - ning Steal a - cross the sky.
With Thy ten-derest bless - ing May our eye - lids close.
Guard the sail - ors toss - ing On the deep blue sea.
Their white wings a - bove me, Watch-ing 'round my bed.
Pure and fresh and sin - less In Thy ho - ly eyes. A-MEN.

Words copyright, by J. Curwen & Sons, Ltd. Used by permission

147 God, That Madest Earth and Heaven

Reginald Heber, 1783-1826
Frederick L. Hosmer, 1840-1929, stanza 2
Richard Whately, 1787-1863, stanza 3

AR HYD Y NOS

Welsh Traditional Melody
Har. by L. O. Emerson, 1820-1915
Descant (small notes), William Lester, b. 1889

1. God, that mad-est earth and heav-en, Dark-ness and light;
2. When the con-stant sun re-turn-ing Un-seals our eyes,
3. Guard us wak-ing, guard us sleep-ing, And when we die,

Who the day for toil hast giv-en, For rest the night;
May we, born a-new like morn-ing, To la-bor rise;
May we in Thy might-y keep-ing All peace-ful lie;

May Thine an-gel guards de-fend us, Slum-ber sweet Thy mer-cy send us;
Gird us for the task that calls us, Let not ease and self en-thrall us,
When the last dread call shall wake us, Do not Thou, our God, for-sake us,

Ho-ly dreams and hopes at-tend us, This live-long night.
Strong through Thee what-e'er be-fall us, O God most wise!
But to reign in glo-ry take us With Thee on high. A-MEN.

Abide with Me

EVENTIDE

Henry F. Lyte, 1793-1847   William H. Monk, 1823-1889

1. A - bide with me: fast falls the e - ven - tide;
2. Swift to its close ebbs out life's lit - tle day;
3. I need Thy pres - ence ev - ery pass - ing hour;
4. I fear no foe, with Thee at hand to bless;
5. Hold Thou Thy cross be - fore my clos - ing eyes;

The dark - ness deep - ens; Lord, with me a - bide!
Earth's joys grow dim, its glo - ries pass a - way;
What but Thy grace can foil the tempt - er's power?
Ills have no weight, and tears no bit - ter - ness.
Shine through the gloom and point me to the skies:

When oth - er help - ers fail, and com - forts flee,
Change and de - cay in all a - round I see.
Who, like Thy - self, my guide and stay can be?
Where is death's sting? Where, grave, thy vic - to - ry?
Heaven's morn - ing breaks, and earth's vain shad - ows flee;

Help of the help - less, O a - bide with me.
O Thou, who chang - est not, a - bide with me.
Through cloud and sun - shine, Lord, a - bide with me.
I tri - umph still, if Thou a - bide with me.
In life, in death, O Lord, a - bide with me. A - MEN.

149 The Shadows of the Evening Hours

ST. LEONARD

Adelaide A. Procter, 1825-1864

Henry Hiles, 1826-1904

1. The shad-ows of the eve-ning hours Fall from the dark-ening sky;
2. The sor-rows of Thy serv-ants, Lord, O do not Thou de-spise,
3. Let peace, O Lord, Thy peace, O God, Up-on our souls de-scend;

Up-on the fra-grance of the flowers The dews of eve-ning lie;
But let the in-cense of our prayers Be-fore Thy mer-cy rise.
From mid-night fears and per-ils, Thou Our trem-bling hearts de-fend;

Be-fore Thy throne, O Lord of heaven, We kneel at close of day;
The bright-ness of the com-ing night Up-on the dark-ness rolls;
Give us a res-pite from our toil, Calm and sub-due our woes;

Look on Thy chil-dren from on high, And hear us while we pray.
With hopes of fu-ture glo-ry, chase The shad-ows from our souls.
Through the long day we la-bor, Lord, O give us now re-pose. A-MEN.

Day Is Dying in the West

CHAUTAUQUA

Mary A. Lathbury, 1841-1913

William F. Sherwin, 1826-1888

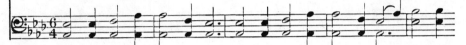

1. Day is dy-ing in the west, Heaven is touch-ing earth with rest; Wait and
2. Lord of life, be-neath the dome Of the u-ni-verse, Thy home, Gath-er
3. While the deepening shadows fall, Heart of Love, en-fold-ing all, Through the
4. When for-ev-er from our sight Pass the stars, the day, the night, Lord of

wor-ship while the night Sets her evening lamps a-light Through all the sky.
us, who seek Thy face, To the fold of Thy embrace, For Thou art nigh.
glo-ry and the grace Of the stars that veil Thy face, Our hearts as-cend.
an-gels, on our eyes Let e-ter-nal morn-ing rise, And shad-ows end.

REFRAIN

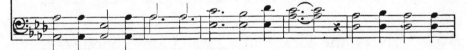

Ho-ly, ho-ly, ho-ly, Lord God of Hosts! Heaven and earth are

full of Thee! Heaven and earth are praising Thee, O Lord most high! A-MEN.

151 Lord, Dismiss Us with Thy Blessing

SICILIAN MARINERS' HYMN

Ascribed to John Fawcett, 1740-1817
Alt. by Godfrey Thring, 1823-1903

Arr. from a Sicilian Melody, 1794

1. Lord, dis - miss us   with Thy bless-ing;   Fill our hearts with joy   and peace;
2. Thanks we give and   ad - o - ra - tion   For Thy gos - pel's joy - ful sound;
3. So   that when Thy love shall call   us,   Sav-iour, from the world a - way,

Let   us   each, Thy love pos - sess - ing, Tri-umph in   re - deem - ing grace:
May the fruits of   Thy sal - va - tion   In   our hearts and lives   a - bound:
Let   no   fear of   death ap - pall us,   Glad Thy sum - mons to   o - bey:

O   re-fresh us,   O   re-fresh us,   Traveling through this wil-der - ness.
Ev - er faith-ful, Ev - er faith-ful   To   the truth may we   be found;
May we ev - er,   May we ev - er   Reign with Thee in   end-less day. A-MEN.

152 May the Grace of Christ Our Saviour

SARDIS

John Newton, 1725-1807

Arr. from Ludwig van Beethoven, 1770-1827

1. May the grace   of Christ our Sav - iour, And the   Fa-ther's boundless love,
2. Thus may we   a - bide in   un - ion   With each oth - er and the Lord,

May the Grace of Christ Our Saviour

With the Ho - ly Spir - it's fa - vor, Rest up - on us from a - bove.
And pos-sess, in sweet com-mun-ion, Joys which earth can-not af - ford. A-MEN.

Saviour, Again to Thy Dear Name 153
ELLERS

John Ellerton, 1826-1893

Edward J. Hopkins, 1818-1901

1. Sav - iour, a - gain   to   Thy dear name we raise   With one ac-
2. Grant us Thy peace up - on our home-ward way; With Thee be-
3. Grant us Thy peace, Lord, through the com-ing night, Turn Thou for
4. Grant us Thy peace through-out our earth - ly life, Our balm in

cord our part - ing hymn of praise; We stand to bless Thee ere our
gan, with Thee shall end the day; Guard Thou the lips from sin, the
us its dark-ness in - to light; From harm and dan - ger keep Thy
sor - row, and our stay in strife; Then, when Thy voice shall bid our

wor - ship cease; Then, low - ly kneel - ing, wait Thy word of peace.
hearts from shame, That in this house have called up - on Thy name.
chil - dren free, For dark and light are both a - like to Thee.
con - flict cease, Call us, O Lord, to Thine e - ter - nal peace. A-MEN.

154 God Be with You

FAREWELL

Jeremiah E. Rankin, 1828-1904

William G. Tomer, 1833-1896

1. God be with you till we meet a - gain; By His coun-sels guide, up-hold you,
2. God be with you till we meet a - gain; 'Neath His wings protecting hide you,
3. God be with you till we meet a - gain; When life's perils thick confound you,
4. God be with you till we meet a - gain; Keep love's banner floating o'er you,

With His sheep se-cure - ly fold you; God be with you till we meet a - gain.
Dai - ly man-na still pro-vide you; God be with you till we meet a - gain.
Put His arms un - fail-ing round you; God be with you till we meet a - gain.
Smite death's threatening wave before you; God be with you till we meet a - gain.

REFRAIN

Till we meet,...... till we meet, Till we meet at Je - sus' feet;
Till we meet, till we meet, till we meet;

Till we meet,...... till we meet, God be with you till we meet a - gain.
Till we meet, till we meet,

Can be sung omitting Refrain

The Spirit Breathes Upon the Word 155

MANOAH

William Cowper, 1731-1800

From Henry W. Greatorex's "Collection," 1851

1. The Spir - it breathes up-on the Word, And brings the truth to sight;
2. A glo - ry gilds the sa - cred page, Ma - jes - tic like the sun,
3. The hand that gave it still sup-plies The gra-cious light and heat;
4. Let ev - er-last - ing thanks be Thine For such a bright dis - play,
5. My soul re-joic - es to pur -sue The steps of Him I love,

Pre - cepts and prom-is - es af - ford A sanc-ti - fy - ing light.
It gives a light to ev - ery age; It gives, but bor-rows none.
His truths up - on the na - tions rise: They rise, but nev - er set.
As makes a world of dark-ness shine With beams of heaven-ly day.
Till glo - ry breaks up-on my view In bright-er worlds a - bove. A-MEN.

Holy Bible, Book Divine 156

ALETTA

John Burton, 1773-1822

William B. Bradbury, 1816-1868

1. Ho - ly Bi - ble, book di - vine, Pre - cious treas - ure, thou art mine;
2. Mine to chide me when I rove; Mine to show a Sav - iour's love;
3. Mine to com-fort in dis - tress, Suf-fering in this wil - der-ness;
4. Mine to tell of joys to come, And the reb - el sin - ner's doom;

Mine to tell me whence I came; Mine to teach me what I am;
Mine thou art to guide and guard; Mine to pun - ish or re - ward;
Mine to show, by liv - ing faith, Man can tri - umph o - ver death;
O thou ho - ly book di - vine, Pre-cious trea-sure, thou art mine. A-MEN.

157 The Divine Gift

CHARTERHOUSE

Sarah E. Taylor, 1883-1954

David Evans, 1874-1948

In unison

1. O God of Light, Thy Word, a lamp un - fail - ing, Shines through the
2. From days of old, through swift-ly roll - ing a - ges, Thou hast re-
3. Un - dimmed by time, the Word is still re - veal - ing To sin - ful
4. To all the world the mes-sage Thou art send - ing, To ev - ery

dark - ness of our earth-ly way, O'er fear and doubt, o'er black de-
vealed Thy will to mor - tal men, Speak-ing to saints, to proph-ets,
men Thy jus-tice and Thy grace; And quest-ing hearts that long for
land, to ev - ery race and clan; And myr - iad tongues, in one great

spair pre-vail - ing, Guid-ing our steps to Thine e - ter - nal day.
kings, and sa - ges, Who wrote the mes-sage with im - mor - tal pen.
peace and heal - ing See Thy com-pas - sion in the Sav - iour's face.
an - them blend-ing, Ac - claim with joy Thy won-drous gift to man. A-MEN.

Words from "Ten New Hymns on the Bible," copyright, 1952, by The Hymn Society of America.
Music controlled by Oxford University Press, London. Used by permission
Alternate tune: ANCIENT OF DAYS, No. 115

158 The Heavens Declare Thy Glory

UXBRIDGE

From Psalm 19
Isaac Watts, 1674-1748

Lowell Mason, 1792-1872

1. The heavens declare Thy glo-ry, Lord, In ev - ery star Thy wis - dom shines;
2. The roll-ing sun, the chang-ing light, And nights and days, Thy power con-fess;
3. Great Sun of Right-eous-ness, a - rise, Bless the dark world with heavenly light;
4. Thy no-blest won-ders here we view In souls re - newed, and sins for - giv'n;

The Heavens Declare Thy Glory

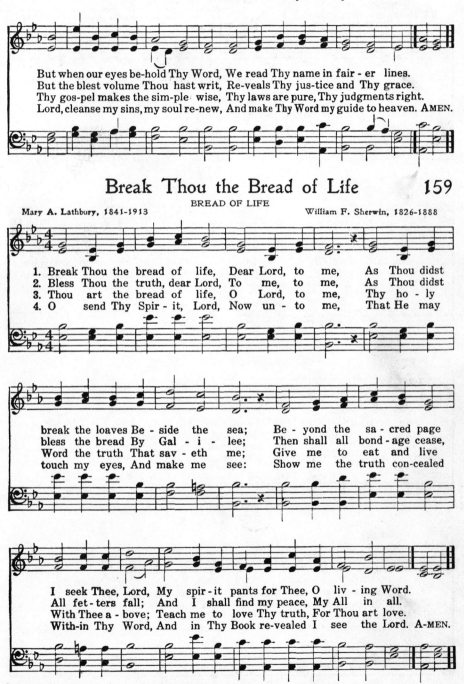

But when our eyes be-hold Thy Word, We read Thy name in fair - er lines.
But the blest volume Thou hast writ, Re-veals Thy jus-tice and Thy grace.
Thy gos-pel makes the sim-ple wise, Thy laws are pure, Thy judgments right.
Lord, cleanse my sins, my soul re-new, And make Thy Word my guide to heaven. AMEN.

Break Thou the Bread of Life   159

BREAD OF LIFE

Mary A. Lathbury, 1841-1913

William F. Sherwin, 1826-1888

1. Break Thou the bread of life, Dear Lord, to me, As Thou didst
2. Bless Thou the truth, dear Lord, To me, to me, As Thou didst
3. Thou art the bread of life, O Lord, to me, Thy ho - ly
4. O send Thy Spir - it, Lord, Now un - to me, That He may

break the loaves Be - side the sea; Be - yond the sa - cred page
bless the bread By Gal - i - lee; Then shall all bond - age cease,
Word the truth That sav - eth me; Give me to eat and live
touch my eyes, And make me see: Show me the truth con-cealed

I seek Thee, Lord, My spir - it pants for Thee, O liv - ing Word.
All fet - ters fall; And I shall find my peace, My All in all.
With Thee a - bove; Teach me to love Thy truth, For Thou art love.
With-in Thy Word, And in Thy Book re-vealed I see the Lord. A-MEN.

Used by permission of the Chautauqua Institution, Chautauqua, New York

160 O Word of God Incarnate

MUNICH

"Neuvermehrtes Meiningisches Gesangbuch," 1693

William W. How, 1823-1897

Har. by Felix Mendelssohn, 1809-1847

1. O Word of God in - car - nate, O Wis - dom from on high,
2. The Church from her dear Mas - ter Re - ceived the gift di - vine,
3. It float - eth like a ban - ner Be - fore God's host un-furled;
4. O make Thy Church, dear Sav - iour, A lamp of pur - est gold,

O Truth un-changed, un - chang - ing, O Light of our dark sky;
And still that light she lift - eth O'er all the earth to shine.
It shin - eth like a bea - con A - bove the dark - ling world.
To bear be - fore the na - tions Thy true light, as of old.

We praise Thee for the ra - diance That from the hal - lowed page,
It is the gold - en cas - ket, Where gems of truth are stored;
It is the chart and com - pass That o'er life's surg - ing sea,
O teach Thy wan-dering pil - grims By this their path to trace,

A lan - tern to our foot-steps, Shines on from age to age.
It is the heaven-drawn pic-ture Of Christ, the liv - ing Word.
'Mid mists and rocks and quick-sands, Still guides, O Christ, to Thee.
Till, clouds and dark-ness end - ed, They see Thee face to face. A-MEN.

Alternate tune: AURELIA, No. 164

Standing on the Promises

R. Kelso Carter, 1849-1928   R. Kelso Carter, 1849-1928

1. Stand-ing on the prom-is-es of Christ my King, Through e-ter-nal a-ges
2. Stand-ing on the prom-is-es that can-not fail, When the howl-ing storms of
3. Stand-ing on the prom-is-es of Christ the Lord, Bound to Him e-ter-nal-
4. Stand-ing on the prom-is-es I can-not fall, Lis-tening ev-ery mo-ment

let His prais-es ring; Glo-ry in the high-est, I will shout and sing,
doubt and fear as-sail, By the liv-ing word of God I shall pre-vail,
ly by love's strong cord, O-ver-com-ing dai-ly with the Spir-it's sword,
to the Spir-it's call, Rest-ing in my Sav-iour as my all in all,

REFRAIN

Stand-ing on the prom-is-es of God. Stand - - ing, stand - - ing,
Standing on the promises, standing on the promises,

Stand-ing on the prom-is-es of God my Sav-iour; Stand - - ing,
Standing on the prom-is-es,

stand - - - ing, I'm stand-ing on the prom-is-es of God.
stand-ing on the prom-is-es,

162 Thy Word Have I Hid in My Heart

From Psalm 119
Adapted by Ernest O. Sellers, 1869-1952

Ernest O. Sellers, 1869-1952

1. Thy Word is a lamp to my feet, A light to my path al - way,
2. For - ev - er, O Lord, is Thy Word Es - tab-lished and fixed on high;
3. At morn - ing, at noon, and at night I ev - er will give Thee praise;
4. Thro' Him whom Thy Word hath foretold, The Sav-iour and Morn-ing Star,

To guide and to save me from sin, And show me the heav'n-ly way.
Thy faith-ful-ness un - to all men A - bid - eth for - ev - er nigh.
For Thou art my por - tion, O Lord, And shall be thro' all my days!
Sal - va - tion and peace have been bro't To those who have strayed a - far.

REFRAIN

Thy Word have I hid in my heart (in my heart), That I might not

sin a-gainst Thee (a - gainst Thee); That I might not sin, that

I might not sin, Thy Word have I hid in my heart.

Thy Word Is Like a Garden, Lord 163

SERAPH (Bethlehem)

Edwin Hodder, 1837-1904   Gottfried W. Fink, 1783-1846

1. Thy Word is like a gar - den, Lord, With flow - ers bright and fair;
2. Thy Word is like a star - ry host: A thou - sand rays of light
3. O may I love Thy pre - cious Word, May I ex - plore the mine,

And ev - ery one who seeks may pluck A love - ly clus - ter there.
Are seen to guide the trav - el - er, And make his path-way bright.
May I its fra-grant flow - ers glean, May light up - on me shine.

Thy Word is like a deep, deep mine; And jew - els rich and rare
Thy Word is like an ar - mor - y, Where sol-diers may re - pair,
O may I find my ar - mor there, Thy Word my trust - y sword;

Are hid - den in its might - y depths For ev - ery search-er there.
And find, for life's long bat - tle-day, All need-ful weap-ons there.
I'll learn to fight with ev - ery foe The bat - tle of the Lord. A-MEN.

164 The Church's One Foundation

AURELIA

Samuel J. Stone, 1839-1900

Samuel S. Wesley, 1810-1876

1. The Church's one Foun - da - tion Is Je - sus Christ her Lord;
2. E - lect from ev - ery na - tion, Yet one o'er all the earth,
3. 'Mid toil and trib - u - la - tion, And tu - mult of her war,
4. Yet she on earth hath un - ion With God the Three in One,

She is His new cre - a - tion, By wa - ter and the word:
Her char - ter of sal - va - tion, One Lord, one faith, one birth;
She waits the con - sum - ma - tion Of peace for - ev - er - more;
And mys - tic sweet com - mun - ion With those whose rest is won:

From heaven He came and sought her To be His ho - ly bride;
One ho - ly name she bless - es, Par-takes one ho - ly food,
Till with the vi - sion glo - rious Her long - ing eyes are blest,
O hap - py ones and ho - ly! Lord, give us grace that we,

With His own blood He bought her, And for her life He died.
And to one hope she press - es, With ev - ery grace en - dued.
And the great Church vic - to - rious Shall be the Church at rest.
Like them, the meek and low - ly, On high may dwell with Thee. A-MEN.

I Love Thy Kingdom, Lord 165

ST. THOMAS

Timothy Dwight, 1752-1817

Aaron Williams, 1731-1776
Descant (small notes), William Lester, b. 1889

1. I love Thy king - dom, Lord, The house of Thine a - bode, The
2. I love Thy Church, O God! Her walls be - fore Thee stand, Dear
3. For her my tears shall fall; For her my prayers as - cend; To
4. Be - yond my high - est joy I prize her heaven-ly ways, Her
5. Sure as Thy truth shall last, To Zi - on shall be given The

Church our blest Re - deem - er saved With His own pre - cious blood.
as the ap - ple of Thine eye, And grav - en on Thy hand.
her my cares and toils be given, Till toils and cares shall end.
sweet com - mun - ion, sol - emn vows, Her hymns of love and praise.
bright-est glo - ries earth can yield, And bright-er bliss of heaven. A-MEN.

Descant arr. Copyright, 1935, by Hope Publishing Co., owner. All Rights Reserved
For arrangement without Descant, see No. 247

O Where Are Kings and Empires Now 166

ST. ANNE

A. Cleveland Coxe, 1818-1896

Ascribed to William Croft, 1678-1727
"Supplement to the New Version," 1708

1. O where are kings and em - pires now Of old that went and came?
2. We mark her good - ly bat - tle - ments, And her foun - da - tions strong;
3. For not like king - doms of the world Thy ho - ly Church, O God;
4. Un - shak - en as e - ter - nal hills, Im - mov - a - ble she stands,

But, Lord, Thy Church is pray - ing yet, A thou-sand years the same.
We hear with - in the sol - emn voice Of her un - end - ing song.
Though earthquake shocks are threatening her, And tem-pests are a - broad;
A moun-tain that shall fill the earth, A house not made with hands. A-MEN.

167 Lord of Our Life, and God of Our Salvation

FLEMMING

Matthaus von Loewenstern, 1594-1649
Trans. by Philip Pusey, 1799-1855

Friedrich F. Flemming, 1778-1813

1. Lord of our life, and God of our sal - va - tion, Star of our
2. Lord, Thou canst help when earth-ly ar - mor fail - eth; Lord, Thou canst
3. Peace in our hearts, our e - vil thoughts as-suag - ing; Peace in Thy
4. Grant us Thy help till back-ward they are driv - en; Grant them Thy

night, and hope of ev - ery na - tion, Hear and re - ceive Thy
save when dead - ly sin as - sail - eth; Lord, o'er Thy rock nor
Church, where brothers are en - gag - ing; Peace, when the world its
truth, that they may be for - giv - en; Grant peace on earth, or,

Church's sup - pli - ca - tion, Lord God Al - might - y.
death nor hell pre - vail - eth: Grant us Thy peace, Lord:
bus - y war is wag - ing: Calm Thy foes' rag - ing.
af - ter we have striv - en, Peace in Thy heav - en. A-MEN.

168 Blest Be the Tie

DENNIS

John Fawcett, 1740-1817

Hans G. Nägeli, 1773-1836
Arr. by Lowell Mason, 1792-1872

1. Blest be the tie that binds Our hearts in Chris - tian love;
2. Be - fore our Fa - ther's throne We pour our ar - dent prayers;
3. We share our mu - tual woes, Our mu - tual bur - dens bear;
4. When we a - sun - der part, It gives us in - ward pain;

Blest Be the Tie

The fel - low - ship of kin - dred minds Is like to that a - bove.
Our fears, our hopes, our aims are one, Our com - forts and our cares.
And oft - en for each oth - er flows The sym - pa - thiz - ing tear.
But we shall still be joined in heart, And hope to meet a - gain. A-MEN.

Faith of Our Fathers!   169

ST. CATHERINE

Frederick W. Faber, 1814-1863

Henri F. Hemy, 1818-1888
Alt. by James G. Walton, 1821-1905

1. Faith of our fa - thers! liv - ing still In spite of dun - geon, fire and sword:
2. Our fa - thers, chained in pris - ons dark, Were still in heart and conscience free:
3. Faith of our fa - thers! we will strive To win all na - tions un - to thee,
4. Faith of our fa - thers! we will love Both friend and foe in all our strife:

O how our hearts beat high with joy When-e'er we hear that glo - rious word!
How sweet would be their chil - dren's fate, If they, like them, could die for thee!
And through the truth that comes from God Mankind shall then be tru - ly free.
And preach thee, too, as love knows how, By kind - ly words and vir - tuous life:

Faith of our fa - thers, ho - ly faith! We will be true to thee till death!
Faith of our fa - thers, ho - ly faith! We will be true to thee till death!
Faith of our fa - thers, ho - ly faith! We will be true to thee till death!
Faith of our fa - thers, ho - ly faith! We will be true to thee till death! A-MEN.

170 Onward, Christian Soldiers

ST. GERTRUDE

Sabine Baring-Gould, 1834-1924　　　　　　　Arthur S. Sullivan, 1842-1900

1. On-ward, Christian sol-diers, March-ing as to war, With the cross of Je - sus
2. Like a might-y ar - my Moves the Church of God; Brothers, we are tread-ing
3. Crowns and thrones may perish, Kingdoms rise and wane, But the Church of Je - sus
4. On-ward, then, ye peo - ple, Join our hap-py throng, Blend with ours your voic-es

Go - ing on be - fore: Christ the roy-al Mas - ter Leads a-gainst the foe;
Where the saints have trod; We are not di - vid - ed, All one bod - y we,
Con-stant will re - main; Gates of hell can nev - er 'Gainst that Church prevail;
In the tri-umph song; Glo - ry, laud, and hon - or Un - to Christ the King;

REFRAIN

For-ward in - to bat - tle, See, His banners go.
One in hope and doc - trine, One in char - i - ty.　Onward, Christian sol - diers,
We have Christ's own promise, And that cannot fail.
This through countless a - ges Men and an-gels sing.

March-ing as to war, With the cross of Je - sus Go - ing on be - fore. A-MEN.

Glorious Things of Thee Are Spoken   171

AUSTRIAN HYMN

John Newton, 1725-1807

Franz Joseph Haydn, 1732-1809

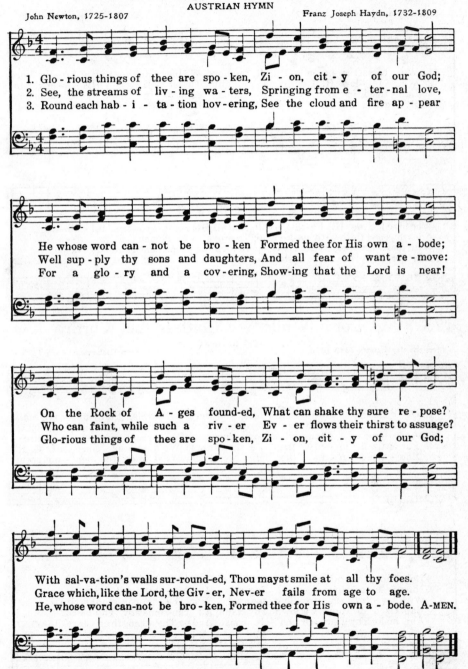

1. Glo - rious things of thee are spo - ken, Zi - on, cit - y of our God;
2. See, the streams of liv - ing wa - ters, Springing from e - ter - nal love,
3. Round each hab - i - ta - tion hov - ering, See the cloud and fire ap - pear

He whose word can - not be bro - ken Formed thee for His own a - bode;
Well sup - ply thy sons and daughters, And all fear of want re - move:
For a glo - ry and a cov - ering, Show-ing that the Lord is near!

On the Rock of A - ges found-ed, What can shake thy sure re - pose?
Who can faint, while such a riv - er Ev - er flows their thirst to assuage?
Glo-rious things of thee are spo - ken, Zi - on, cit - y of our God;

With sal-va-tion's walls sur-round-ed, Thou mayst smile at all thy foes.
Grace which, like the Lord, the Giv - er, Nev-er fails from age to age.
He, whose word can-not be bro - ken, Formed thee for His own a - bode. A-MEN.

172 We Bless the Name of Christ, the Lord

RETREAT

Samuel Frederick Coffman, b. 1872

Thomas Hastings, 1784-1872

1. We bless the name of Christ, the Lord, We bless Him for His ho - ly Word,
2. We fol - low Him with pure de-light To sanc - ti - fy His sa - cred rite;
3. Bap - tized in God—the Fa-ther, Son, And Ho - ly Spir - it—Three in One,
4. By grace we "Ab - ba, Fa - ther" cry; By grace the Com-fort-er comes nigh;

Who loved to do His Fa-ther's will, And all His right-eous-ness ful - fill.
And thus our faith with wa-ter seal, To prove o - be -dience that we feel.
With conscience free, we rest in God, In love and peace, through Je-sus' blood.
And for Thy grace our love shall be For-ev- er, on - ly, Lord, for Thee. A-MEN.

173 O Lord, While We Confess the Worth

ST. BERNARD

Mary Bowley Peters, 1813-1856

John Richardson, 1816-1879

1. O Lord, while we con - fess the worth Of this, the out - ward seal,
2. Death to the world we here a - vow, Death to each flesh - ly lust;
3. And we, O Lord, who now par-take Of res - ur - rec - tion life,
4. Bap - tized in - to the Fa-ther's name, We'd walk as sons of God;
5. Bap - tized in - to the Ho - ly Ghost, We'd keep His tem - ple pure;

Do Thou, the truths here-in set forth, To ev - 'ry heart re - veal.
New-ness of life our call - ing now, A ris - en Lord our trust.
With ev - 'ry sin, for Thy dear sake, Would be at con-stant strife.
Bap-tized in Thine, we own Thy claim, As ran-somed by Thy blood.
And make Thy grace our on - ly boast, And by Thy strength en-dure. A-MEN.

See Israel's Gentle Shepherd Stand 174

SERENITY

Philip Doddridge, 1702-1751

William V. Wallace, 1814-1865

1. See Is - rael's gen - tle Shep - herd stand With all - en - gag -ing charms;
2. "Per - mit them to ap-proach," He cries, "Nor scorn their hum - ble name;
3. We bring them, Lord, in thank - ful hands, And yield them up to Thee;

Hark, how He calls the ten - der lambs, And folds them in His arms!
For 'twas to bless such souls as these The Lord of an-gels came."
Joy - ful that we our-selves are Thine, Thine let our off-spring be. A - MEN.

Saviour, Who Thy Flock Art Feeding 175

BROCKLESBURY

William A. Muhlenberg, 1796-1877

Charlotte A. Barnard, 1830-1869

1. Sav - iour, who Thy flock art feed - ing With the shep-herd's kind - est care,
2. Now, these lit - tle ones re - ceiv - ing, Fold them in Thy gra-cious arm;
3. Nev - er, from Thy pas - ture rov - ing, Let them be the li - on's prey;
4. Then, with - in Thy fold e - ter - nal, Let them find a rest - ing place,

All the fee - ble gen - tly lead - ing, While the lambs Thy bos - om share;
There, we know, Thy word be - liev - ing, On - ly there se - cure from harm.
Let Thy ten - der - ness, so lov - ing, Keep them through life's dangerous way.
Feed in pas-tures ev - er ver-nal, Drink the riv - ers of Thy grace. A-MEN.

176 According to Thy Gracious Word

MARTYRDOM (Avon)

James Montgomery, 1771-1854

Hugh Wilson, 1764-1824

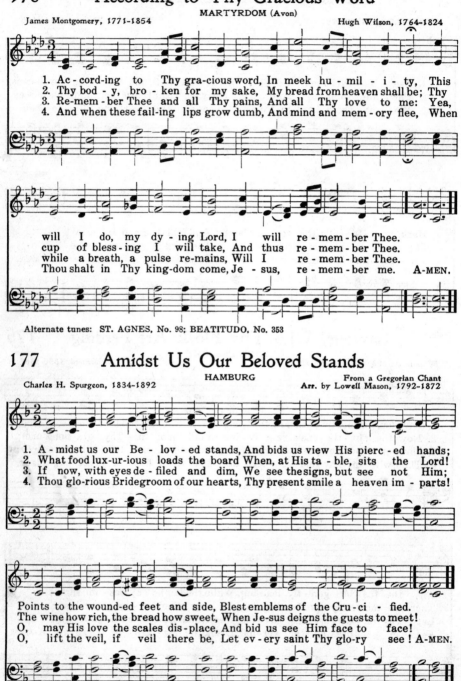

1. Ac - cord-ing to Thy gra-cious word, In meek hu - mil - i - ty, This
2. Thy bod - y, bro - ken for my sake, My bread from heaven shall be; Thy
3. Re-mem - ber Thee and all Thy pains, And all Thy love to me: Yea,
4. And when these fail-ing lips grow dumb, And mind and mem - ory flee, When

will I do, my dy - ing Lord, I will re - mem - ber Thee.
cup of bless - ing I will take, And thus re - mem - ber Thee.
while a breath, a pulse re-mains, Will I re - mem - ber Thee.
Thou shalt in Thy king-dom come, Je - sus, re - mem - ber me. A-MEN.

Alternate tunes: ST. AGNES, No. 98; BEATITUDO, No. 353

177 Amidst Us Our Beloved Stands

HAMBURG

Charles H. Spurgeon, 1834-1892

From a Gregorian Chant
Arr. by Lowell Mason, 1792-1872

1. A - midst us our Be - lov - ed stands, And bids us view His pierc - ed hands;
2. What food lux-ur-ious loads the board When, at His ta - ble, sits the Lord!
3. If now, with eyes de - filed and dim, We see the signs, but see not Him;
4. Thou glo-rious Bridegroom of our hearts, Thy present smile a heaven im - parts!

Points to the wound-ed feet and side, Blest emblems of the Cru - ci - fied.
The wine how rich, the bread how sweet, When Je-sus deigns the guests to meet!
O, may His love the scales dis - place, And bid us see Him face to face!
O, lift the veil, if veil there be, Let ev - ery saint Thy glo-ry see ! A-MEN.

Here, O My Lord, I See Thee Face to Face 178

PENITENTIA

Horatius Bonar, 1808-1889   Edward Dearle, 1806-1891

1. Here, O my Lord, I see Thee face to face;
Here would I touch and han - dle things un - seen;
Here, grasp with firm - er hand e - ter - nal grace,
And all my wea - ri - ness up - on Thee lean.

2. Here would I feed up - on the bread of God,
Here drink with Thee the roy - al wine of heav'n,
Here would I lay a - side each earth - ly load,
Here taste a - fresh the calm of sin for - giv'n.

3. I have no help but Thine, nor do I need
An - oth - er arm save Thine to lean up - on;
It is e - nough, my Lord, e - nough in - deed;
My strength is in Thy might, Thy might a - lone.

4. Mine is the sin, but Thine the right - eous - ness;
Mine is the guilt, but Thine the cleans - ing blood;
Here is my robe, my ref - uge, and my peace,
Thy blood, Thy right - eous - ness, O Lord, my God.

5. Too soon we rise; the sym - bols dis - ap - pear;
The feast, though not the love, is past and gone;
It is e - nough, my Lord, if Thou art near;
My strength is in Thy love, Thy love a - lone. A - MEN.

Alternate tunes: MORECAMBE, No. 91; CONSOLATION, No. 142

179 No, Not Despairingly

KEDRON

Horatius Bonar, 1808-1889

Ann B. Spratt, b. 1829

1. No, not de - spair - ing - ly Come I to Thee; No, not dis-
2. Ah! mine in - i - qui - ty Crim - son has been, In - fi - nite,
3. Lord, I con - fess to Thee Sad - ly my sin; All I am
4. Faith - ful and just art Thou For - giv - ing all; Lov - ing and
5. Then all is peace and light This soul with - in; Thus shall I

trust - ing - ly Bend I the knee: Sin hath gone o - ver me,
in - fi - nite Sin up - on sin; Sin of not lov - ing Thee,
tell I Thee, All I have been: Purge Thou my sin a - way,
kind art Thou When poor ones call: Lord, let the cleans - ing blood,
walk with Thee The loved Un - seen; Lean - ing on Thee, my God,

Yet is this still my plea, Je - sus hath died.
Sin of not trust - ing Thee, In - fi - nite sin.
Wash Thou my soul this day; Lord, make me clean.
Blood of the Lamb of God, Pass o'er my soul.
Guid - ed a - long the road, Noth - ing be - tween. A - MEN.

180 Depth of Mercy

SEYMOUR

Charles Wesley, 1707-1788

Carl M. von Weber, 1786-1826

1. Depth of mer - cy! can there be Mer - cy still re - served for me?
2. I have long with-stood His grace, Long pro - voked Him to His face,
3. Now in - cline me to re - pent; Let me now my sins la - ment;
4. There for me the Sav - iour stands, Hold - ing forth His wound - ed hands;

Alternate tune: ALETTA, No. 156

Depth of Mercy

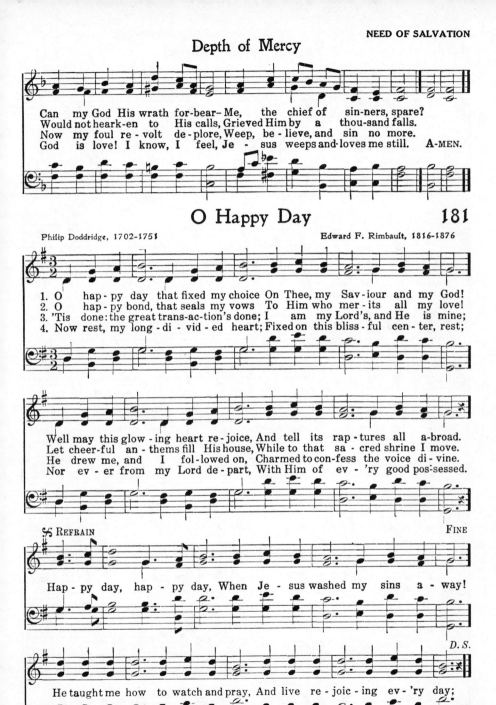

Can my God His wrath for-bear– Me, the chief of sin-ners, spare?
Would not heark-en to His calls, Grieved Him by a thou-sand falls.
Now my foul re - volt de - plore, Weep, be - lieve, and sin no more.
God is love! I know, I feel, Je - sus weeps and- loves me still. A-MEN.

O Happy Day   181

Philip Doddridge, 1702-1751   Edward F. Rimbault, 1816-1876

1. O hap - py day that fixed my choice On Thee, my Sav-iour and my God!
2. O hap - py bond, that seals my vows To Him who mer-its all my love!
3. 'Tis done: the great trans-ac-tion's done; I am my Lord's, and He is mine;
4. Now rest, my long - di - vid - ed heart; Fixed on this bliss-ful cen - ter, rest;

Well may this glow - ing heart re - joice, And tell its rap - tures all a-broad.
Let cheer-ful an - thems fill His house, While to that sa - cred shrine I move.
He drew me, and I fol-lowed on, Charmed to con-fess the voice di - vine.
Nor ev - er from my Lord de - part, With Him of ev - 'ry good pos-sessed.

REFRAIN   FINE

Hap - py day, hap - py day, When Je - sus washed my sins a - way!

D. S.

He taught me how to watch and pray, And live re - joic - ing ev - 'ry day;

Alternate tune without Refrain: HAMBURG, No. 177

Saved by the Blood

S. J. Henderson, 19th Century

Daniel B. Towner, 1850-1919

1. Saved by the blood of the Cru - ci - fied One! Now ran-somed from
2. Saved by the blood of the Cru - ci - fied One! The an - gels re-
3. Saved by the blood of the Cru - ci - fied One! The Fa - ther He
4. Saved by the blood of the Cru - ci - fied One! All hail to the

sin and a new work be - gun, Sing praise to the Fa - ther and
joic - ing be - cause it lis done; A child of the Fa - ther, joint-
spake, and His will it was done; Great price of my par - don, His
Fa - ther, all hail to the Son, All hail to the Spir - it, the

praise to the Son, Saved by the blood of the Cru - ci - fied One!
heir with the Son, Saved by the blood of the Cru - ci - fied One!
own pre-cious Son; Saved by the blood of the Cru - ci - fied One!
great Three in One! Saved by the blood of the Cru - ci - fied One!

REFRAIN

Saved! saved! My sins are all par-doned, my guilt is all gone!
Glo-ry, I'm saved! glo-ry, I'm saved!

Saved! saved! I am saved by the blood of the Cru-ci-fied One!
Glo-ry, I'm saved! glo-ry, I'm saved!

Jesus! Engrave It on My Heart 183

ST. CRISPIN

Samuel Medley, 1738-1799

George J. Elvey, 1816-1893

1. Je - sus! en-grave it on my heart, That Thou the One thing need-ful art:
2. Need - ful is Thy most pre-cious blood, To re-con-cile my soul to God;
3. Need-ful Thy pres-ence, dear-est Lord! True peace and comfort to af-ford;
4. Need-ful art Thou, my Guide! my Stay! Thro' all life's dark and wear-y way;
5. Then need-ful still my God! my King! Thy Name e-ter-nal-ly I'll sing:

I could from all things part-ed be, But nev-er, nev-er, Lord, from Thee!
Need-ful is Thy in-dul-gent care; Need-ful Thy all - pre-vail-ing prayer.
Need-ful Thy promise, to im-part Fresh life and vig-or to my heart.
Nor less in death Thou'lt need-ful be, To bring my spir-it home to Thee.
Glo-ry and praise be ev - er His, The One Thing needful, Je-sus is! A-MEN.

Not What These Hands Have Done 184

ST. ANDREW

Horatius Bonar, 1808-1889

Joseph Barnby, 1838-1896

1. Not what these hands have done Can save this guilt-y soul; Not
2. Not what I feel or do Can give me peace with God; Not
3. Thy work a-lone, O Christ, Can ease this weight of sin; Thy
4. Thy love to me, O God, Not mine, O Lord, to Thee, Can
5. Thy grace a-lone, O God, To me can par-don speak; Thy
6. I bless the Christ of God; I rest on love di-vine; And,

what this toil-ing flesh has borne Can make my spir-it whole.
all my prayers and sighs and tears Can bear my aw-ful load.
blood a-lone, O Lamb of God, Can give me peace with-in.
rid me of this dark un-rest, And set my spir-it free.
power a-lone, O Son of God, Can this sore bon-dage break.
with un-fal-tering lip and heart, I call this Sav-iour mine. A-MEN.

Nor Silver Nor Gold

James M. Gray, 1851-1935

Daniel B. Towner, 1850-1919

1. Nor sil - ver nor gold hath ob-tained my re-demp-tion, Nor rich - es of
2. Nor sil - ver nor gold hath ob-tained my re-demp-tion, The guilt on my
3. Nor sil - ver nor gold hath ob-tained my re-demp-tion, The ho - ly com-
4. Nor sil - ver nor gold hath ob-tained my re-demp-tion, The way in - to

earth could have saved my poor soul; The blood of the cross is my
con - science too heav - y had grown; The blood of the cross is my
mand-ment for - bade me draw near; The blood of the cross is my
heav - en could not thus be bought; The blood of the cross is my

on - ly foun-da - tion, The death of my Sav-iour now mak - eth me whole.
on - ly foun-da - tion, The death of my Sav-iour could on - ly a - tone.
on - ly foun-da - tion, The death of my Sav-iour re - mov - eth my fear.
on - ly foun-da - tion, The death of my Sav-iour re-demption hath wrought.

REFRAIN

I am re - deemed, but not with sil - ver;
I am re-deemed, I am re-deemed, but not with sil-ver;

I am bought, but not with gold; Bought with a
I am bought, I am bought, but not with gold;

Nor Silver Nor Gold

price— the blood of Je - sus, Pre-cious price of love un-told.
Bought with a price— the precious blood of Je-sus,

Grace! 'Tis a Charming Sound 186

Philip Doddridge, 1702-1751; 1, 3
A. M. Toplady, 1740-1778; 2, 4, 5

Ira D. Sankey, 1840-1908

1. Grace! 'tis a charm-ing sound, Har - mo - nious to the ear; Heav'n
2. 'Twas grace that wrote my name In life's e - ter - nal book; 'Twas
3. Grace taught my wand'ring feet To tread the heav'n-ly road; And
4. Grace taught my soul to pray, And made mine eyes o'er - flow; 'Twas
5. O let Thy grace in - spire My soul with strength di - vine: May

with the ech - o shall re - sound, And all the earth shall hear.
grace that gave me to the Lamb, Who all my sor - rows took.
new sup - plies each hour I meet, While press-ing on to God.
grace which kept me to this day, And will not let me go.
all my pow'rs to Thee as - pire, And all my days be Thine.

REFRAIN

Saved by grace a - lone! This is all my plea:

Je - sus died for all man - kind, And Je - sus died for me.

Once for All

Philip P. Bliss, 1838-1876

Philip P. Bliss, 1838-1876

1. Free from the law, O hap-py con-di-tion, Je-sus hath
2. Now are we free—there's no con-dem-na-tion, Je-sus pro-
3. "Chil-dren of God," O glo-ri-ous call-ing, Sure-ly His

bled, and there is re-mis-sion; Cursed by the law and bruised by the
vides a per-fect sal-va-tion; "Come un-to Me," O hear His sweet-
grace will keep us from fall-ing; Pass-ing from death to life at His

REFRAIN

fall, Grace hath redeemed us once for all.
call, Come, and He saves us once for all.
call, Bless-ed sal-va-tion once for all.   Once for all, O sin-ner, re-

ceive it; Once for all, O broth-er, be-lieve it; Cling to the

cross, the bur-den will fall, Christ hath re-deemed us once for all.

Tell Me the Old, Old Story

A. Catherine Hankey, 1834-1911   William H. Doane, 1832-1915

1. Tell me the old, old sto-ry Of un-seen things a - bove, Of Je-sus
2. Tell me the sto-ry slow-ly, That I may take it in— That won-der-
3. Tell me the sto-ry soft-ly, With ear-nest tones and grave; Re-mem-ber,
4. Tell me the same old sto-ry When you have cause to fear That this world's

and His glo-ry, Of Je-sus and His love. Tell me the sto-ry
ful re-demp-tion, God's rem-e-dy for sin. Tell me the sto-ry
I'm the sin-ner Whom Je-sus came to save. Tell me the sto-ry
emp-ty glo-ry Is cost-ing me too dear. Yes, and when that world's

sim-ply, As to a lit-tle child, For I am weak and wea-ry,
oft-en, For I for-get so soon; The "ear-ly dew" of morn-ing
al-ways, If you would real-ly be, In an-y time of troub-le,
glo-ry Is dawn-ing on my soul, Tell me the old, old sto-ry:

REFRAIN

And help-less and de-filed.
Has passed a-way at noon.   Tell me the old, old sto-ry, Tell me the
A com-fort-er to me.
"Christ Je-sus makes thee whole."

old, old sto-ry, Tell me the old, old sto-ry Of Je-sus and His love.

Words used by permission of Sybil Tremellen

189 There Is Power in the Blood

Lewis E. Jones, 1865-1936

Lewis E. Jones, 1865-1936

1. Would you be free from the bur-den of sin? There's pow'r in the blood,
2. Would you be free from your pas-sion and pride? There's pow'r in the blood,
3. Would you be whit-er, much whit-er than snow? There's pow'r in the blood,
4. Would you do serv-ice for Je-sus your King? There's pow'r in the blood,

pow'r in the blood; Would you o'er e-vil a vic-to-ry win? There's
pow'r in the blood; Come for a cleans-ing to Cal-va-ry's tide; There's
pow'r in the blood; Sin-stains are lost in its life-giv-ing flow; There's
pow'r in the blood; Would you live dai-ly His prais-es to sing? There's

REFRAIN

won-der-ful pow'r in the blood. There is pow'r, pow'r, Wonder-working pow'r
there is

In the blood of the Lamb; There is pow'r, pow'r,
In the blood of the Lamb; there is

Won-der-work-ing pow'r In the pre-cious blood of the Lamb.

Ye Must Be Born Again

William T. Sleeper, 1819-1904

George C. Stebbins, 1846-1945

1. A rul-er once came to Je-sus by night To ask Him the way of sal-va-tion and light; The Mas-ter made an-swer in words true and plain, "Ye must be born a-gain."
2. Ye chil-dren of men, at-tend to the word So sol-emn-ly ut-tered by Je-sus the Lord; And let not this mes-sage to you be in vain, "Ye must be born a-gain."
3. O ye who would en-ter that glo-ri-ous rest, And sing with the ran-somed the song of the blest; The life ev-er-last-ing if ye would ob-tain, "Ye must be born a-gain."
4. A dear one in heav-en thy heart yearns to see, At the beau-ti-ful gate may be watching for thee; Then list to the note of this sol-emn re-frain, "Ye must be born a-gain."

REFRAIN

"Ye must be born a-gain." a-gain. "Ye must be born a-gain, a-gain, Ye must be born a-gain; a-gain; I ver-i-ly, ver-i-ly say un-to thee, Ye must be born a-gain." a-gain.

191 **Complete in Thee**

Aaron R. Wolfe, 1821-1902
Refrain, James M. Gray, 1851-1935

Talmadge J. Bittikofer, b. 1892

1. Com-plete in Thee! no work of mine May take, dear Lord, the place of Thine;
2. Com-plete in Thee! no more shall sin, Thy grace hath conquered, reign within;
3. Com-plete in Thee—each want supplied, And no good thing to me de-nied;
4. Dear Sav-iour! when be-fore Thy bar All tribes and tongues as-sem-bled are,

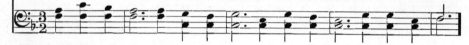

Thy blood hath par - don bought for me, And I am now com-plete in Thee.
Thy voice shall bid the tempt-er flee, And I shall stand com-plete in Thee.
Since Thou my por - tion, Lord, wilt be, I ask no more, com-plete in Thee.
A - mong Thy cho - sen will I be, At Thy right hand, com-plete in Thee.

REFRAIN

Yea, jus - ti - fied! O bless-ed thought! And sanc-ti - fied! Sal-va-tion wrought!

Thy blood hath par - don bought for me, And glo - ri - fied, I too, shall be!

There Is a Fountain

CLEANSING FOUNTAIN

William Cowper, 1731-1800

Early American Melody
Arr. from Lowell Mason, 1792-1872

1. There is a foun-tain filled with blood Drawn from Im - man-uel's veins;
2. The dy - ing thief re - joiced to see That foun-tain in his day;
3. Dear dy - ing Lamb, Thy pre-cious blood Shall nev - er lose its power,
4. E'er since by faith I saw the stream Thy flow - ing wounds sup-ply,
5. When this poor lisp-ing, stammering tongue Lies si - lent in the grave,

And sin-ners, plunged be - neath that flood, Lose all their guilt - y stains:
And there may I, though vile as he, Wash all my sins a - way:
Till all the ran-somed Church of God Be saved, to sin no more:
Re - deem-ing love has been my theme, And shall be till I die:
Then in a no - bler, sweet - er song, I'll sing Thy power to save:

Lose all their guilt - y stains, Lose all their guilt-y stains; And
Wash all my sins a - way, Wash all my sins a - way; And
Be saved, to sin no more, Be saved, to sin no more; Till
And shall be till I die, And shall be till I die; Re-
I'll sing Thy power to save, I'll sing Thy power to save; Then

sin - ners, plunged be-neath that flood, Lose all their guilt - y stains.
there may I, though vile as he, Wash all my sins a - way.
all the ran-somed Church of God Be saved, to sin no more.
deem-ing love has been my theme, And shall be till I die.
in a no - bler, sweet - er song I'll sing Thy power to save. A-MEN.

193 There Shall Be Showers of Blessing

Daniel W. Whittle, 1840-1901

James McGranahan, 1840-1907

1. "There shall be show-ers of bless-ing:" This is the prom-ise of love;
2. "There shall be show-ers of bless-ing"—Pre-cious re-viv-ing a-gain;
3. "There shall be show-ers of bless-ing:" Send them up-on us, O Lord;
4. "There shall be show-ers of bless-ing:" Oh, that to-day they might fall,

There shall be sea-sons re-fresh-ing, Sent from the Sav-iour a-bove.
O-ver the hills and the val-leys, Sound of a-bun-dance of rain.
Grant to us now a re-fresh-ing, Come, and now hon-or Thy Word.
Now as to God we're con-fess-ing, Now, as on Je-sus we call!

REFRAIN

Show - - ers of bless-ing, Show-ers of bless-ing we need:
Show-ers, show-ers of bless-ing,

Mer - cy-drops 'round us are fall-ing, But for the show-ers we plead.

194 God Calling Yet

FEDERAL STREET

Gerhard Tersteegen, 1697-1769
Trans. by Jane L. Borthwick, 1813-1897

Henry K. Oliver, 1800-1885

1. God call-ing yet! shall I not hear? Earth's pleasures shall I still hold dear?
2. God call-ing yet! shall I not rise? Can I His lov-ing voice de-spise,
3. God call-ing yet! and shall He knock And I my heart the clos-er lock?
4. God call-ing yet! I can-not stay; My heart I yield with-out de-lay;

Alternate tune: WOODWORTH, No. 198

God Calling Yet

Shall life's swift passing years all fly, And still my soul in slum-ber lie?
And base-ly His kind care re-pay? He calls me still; can I de-lay?
He still is wait-ing to receive, And shall I dare His Spir-it grieve?
Vain world, farewell! from thee I part; The voice of God hath reached my heart! A-MEN.

Wonderful Words of Life 195

Philip P. Bliss, 1838-1876

Philip P. Bliss, 1838-1876

1. Sing them o - ver a - gain to me, Won-der - ful words of Life;
2. Christ, the bless - ed One, gives to all Won-der - ful words of Life;
3. Sweet-ly ech - o the gos - pel call, Won-der - ful words of Life;

Let me more of their beau - ty see, Won-der - ful words of Life.
Sin - ner, list to the lov - ing call, Won-der - ful words of Life.
Of - fer par - don and peace to all, Won-der - ful words of Life.

Words of life and beau - ty, Teach me faith and du - ty:
All so free - ly giv - en, Woo - ing us to Heav - en:
Je - sus, on - ly Sav - iour, Sanc - ti - fy for - ev - er:

REFRAIN

Beau-ti-ful words, won-der-ful words, Wonderful words of Life. Life.

196 The Light of the World Is Jesus

Philip P. Bliss, 1838-1876   Philip P. Bliss, 1838-1876

1. The whole world was lost in the dark-ness of sin; The Light of the
2. No dark-ness have we who in Je - sus a - bide, The Light of the
3. Ye dwell-ers in dark-ness with sin-blind-ed eyes, The Light of the
4. No need of the sun-light in heav-en, we're told, The Light of the

world is Je - sus; Like sun-shine at noon-day His glo-ry shone in,
world is Je - sus; We walk in the Light when we fol-low our Guide,
world is Je - sus; Go, wash at His bid-ding, and light will a - rise,
world is Je - sus; The Lamb is the Light in the Cit - y of Gold,

REFRAIN

The Light of the world is Je - sus. Come to the Light, 'tis

shin - ing for thee; Sweet-ly the Light has dawned up - on me;

Once I was blind, but now I can see; The Light of the world is Je - sus.

Grace Greater Than Our Sin

Julia H. Johnston, 1849-1919

Daniel B. Towner, 1850-1919

1. Mar - vel - ous grace of our lov - ing Lord, Grace that ex - ceeds our
2. Sin and de - spair like the sea waves cold, Threat - en the soul with
3. Dark is the stain that we can - not hide, What can a - vail to
4. Mar - vel - ous, in - fi - nite, match-less grace, Free - ly be-stowed on

sin and our guilt, Yon - der on Cal - va - ry's mount out-poured,
in - fi - nite loss; Grace that is great - er, yes, grace un - told,
wash it a - way? Look! there is flow - ing a crim - son tide;
all who be - lieve; You that are long - ing to see His face,

REFRAIN

There where the blood of the Lamb was spilt.
Points to the Ref - uge, the might - y Cross. Grace, grace,
Whit - er than snow you may be to - day.
Will you this mo - ment His grace re - ceive? Mar - vel - ous grace,

God's grace, Grace that will par - don and cleanse with - in; Grace,
in - fi - nite grace, Mar - vel - ous

grace, God's grace, Grace that is great - er than all our sin.
grace, in - fi - nite grace.

198 Just As I Am, Without One Plea

WOODWORTH

Charlotte Elliott, 1789-1871

William B. Bradbury, 1816-1868

1. Just as I am, with-out one plea, But that Thy blood was shed for me, And
2. Just as I am, and wait-ing not To rid my soul of one dark blot, To
3. Just as I am, though tossed about With many a con-flict, many a doubt, Fight-
4. Just as I am, poor, wretched, blind; Sight, rich-es, heal-ing of the mind, Yea,
5. Just as I am, Thou wilt re-ceive, Wilt welcome, pardon, cleanse, relieve; Be-

that Thou bidd'st me come to Thee, O Lamb of God, I come! I come!
Thee whose blood can cleanse each spot, O Lamb of God, I come! I come!
ings and fears with-in, with-out, O Lamb of God, I come! I come!
all I need, in Thee I find, O Lamb of God, I come! I come!
cause Thy prom-ise I be-lieve, O Lamb of God, I come! I come! A-MEN.

199 Only Trust Him

MINERVA

John H. Stockton, 1813-1877

John H. Stockton, 1813-1877

1. Come, ev-ery soul by sin op-pressed, There's mer-cy with the Lord,
2. For Je-sus shed His pre-cious blood, Rich bless-ings to be-stow;
3. Yes, Je-sus is the Truth, the Way, That leads you in-to rest:
4. Come, then, and join this ho-ly band, And on to glo-ry go,

And He will sure-ly give you rest By trust-ing in His word.
Plunge now in-to the crim-son flood That wash-es white as snow.
Be-lieve in Him with-out de-lay, And you are ful-ly blest.
To dwell in that ce-les-tial land, Where joys im-mor-tal flow.

Only Trust Him

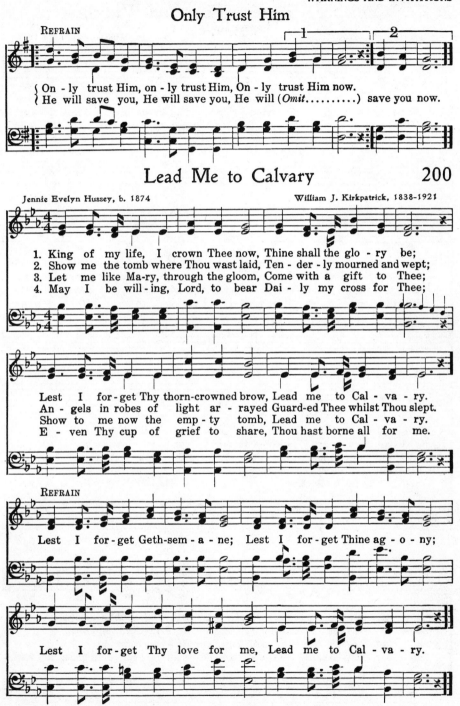

REFRAIN

On - ly trust Him, on - ly trust Him, On - ly trust Him now.
He will save you, He will save you, He will (*Omit* ....) save you now.

Lead Me to Calvary   200

Jennie Evelyn Hussey, b. 1874   William J. Kirkpatrick, 1838-1921

1. King of my life, I crown Thee now, Thine shall the glo - ry be;
2. Show me the tomb where Thou wast laid, Ten - der - ly mourned and wept;
3. Let me like Ma-ry, through the gloom, Come with a gift to Thee;
4. May I be will-ing, Lord, to bear Dai - ly my cross for Thee;

Lest I for - get Thy thorn-crowned brow, Lead me to Cal - va - ry.
An - gels in robes of light ar - rayed Guard-ed Thee whilst Thou slept.
Show to me now the emp - ty tomb, Lead me to Cal - va - ry.
E - ven Thy cup of grief to share, Thou hast borne all for me.

REFRAIN

Lest I for - get Geth-sem - a - ne; Lest I for - get Thine ag - o - ny;

Lest I for - get Thy love for me, Lead me to Cal - va - ry.

201 Come, Ye Sinners, Poor and Wretched

BRYN CALFARIA

Joseph Hart, 1712-1768

William Owen, 1814-1893

1. Come, ye sin - ners, poor and wretch-ed, Weak and wound-ed, sick and sore;
2. Come, ye need - y, come, and wel-come; God's free boun-ty glo - ri - fy;
3. Come, ye wea - ry, heav - y la - den, Bruised and brok-en by the fall;
4. Lo! th'in-car-nate God, as - cend - ed, Pleads the mer - it of His blood;

Je - sus read - y stands to save you, Full of pit - y, joined with power:
True be - lief and true re - pent-ance, Ev - ery grace that brings us nigh,
If you tar - ry till you're bet-ter, You will nev - er come at all:
Ven - ture on Him, ven-ture whol - ly; Let no oth - er trust in-trude:

He is a - ble, He is a - ble, He is a - ble,
With-out mon - ey, with - out mon - ey, with - out mon - ey,
Not the right - eous, not the right - eous, not the right - eous,
None but Je - sus, none but Je - sus, none but Je - sus, ·
  1. He is a - ble, He is a - ble, He is a - ble,

He is will-ing, doubt no more; He is will - ing, doubt no more.
Come to Je - sus Christ and buy; Come to Je - sus Christ and buy.
Sin - ners Je - sus came to call; Sin - ners Je - sus came to call.
Can do help-less sin - ners good; Can do help-less sin - ners good. A - MEN.

Softly and Tenderly Jesus Is Calling

Will L. Thompson, 1847-1909　　　　　　　　　Will L. Thompson, 1847-1909

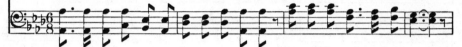

1. Soft - ly and ten-der-ly Je-sus is call-ing, Call-ing for you and for me;
2. Why should we tarry when Je-sus is pleading, Pleading for you and for me?
3. Time is now fleeting, the moments are passing, Passing from you and from me;
4. Oh,　for the won-der-ful love He has promised, Promised for you and for me!

See,　on the portals He's waiting and watching, Watching for you and for me.
Why should we linger and heed not His mercies, Mercies for you and for me?
Shadows are gath-er-ing, death-beds are coming, Coming for you and for me.
Though we have sinned, He has mercy and par-don, Par-don for you and for me.

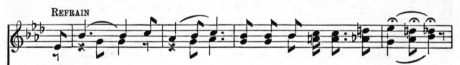

REFRAIN

Come home,　　　come home,　　　Ye who are wea-ry, come home;
Come home,　　　come home,

Ear-nest-ly, ten-der-ly, Je - sus is call-ing, Call-ing, O sin-ner, come home!

203 Look to the Lamb of God

H. G. Jackson, 19th Century

James M. Black, 1856-1938

1. If you from sin are long-ing to be free, Look to the Lamb of God;
2. When Satan tempts, and doubts and fears assail, Look to the Lamb of God;
3. Are you a-wea - ry, does the way seem long? Look to the Lamb of God;
4. Fear not when shad-ows on your path-way fall, Look to the Lamb of God;

He, to re-deem you, died on Cal - va - ry, Look to the Lamb of God.
You in His strength shall o - ver all pre-vail, Look to the Lamb of God.
His love will cheer and fill your heart with song, Look to the Lamb of God.
In joy or sor-row Christ is all in all, Look to the Lamb of God.

REFRAIN

Look to the Lamb of God, Look to the Lamb of God,
the Lamb of God, the Lamb of God,

For He a-lone is a - ble to save you, Look to the Lamb of God.

204 Art Thou Weary, Heavy Laden?

STEPHANOS

John M. Neale, 1818-1866. Based on an early
Greek hymn of Stephen the Sabaite, 725-794

Henry W. Baker, 1821-1877

1. Art thou wea - ry, heav - y lad - en, Art thou sore dis - trest?
2. Hath He marks to lead me to Him, If He be my Guide?
3. Is there di - a - dem, as Mon - arch, That His brow a - dorns?
4. If I still hold close - ly to Him, What hath He at last?
5. If I ask Him to re - ceive me, Will He say me nay?
6. Find-ing, follow-ing, keep - ing, strug-gling, Is He sure to bless?

Alternate tune: BULLINGER, No. 282

Art Thou Weary, Heavy Laden

"Come to Me," saith One, "and, com - ing, Be at rest."
"In His feet and hands are wound-prints, And His side."
"Yea, a crown, in ver - y sure - ty, But of thorns."
"Sor - row van-quished, la - bor end - ed, Jor - dan passed."
"Not till earth and not till heav - en Pass a - way."
"Saints, a - post - les, pro - phets, mar - tyrs, An - swer, 'Yes.'" A-MEN.

Have You Any Room for Jesus? 205

Source Unknown
Arr. by Daniel W. Whittle, 1840-1901

C. C. Williams, 19th Century

1. Have you an - y room for Je - sus, He who bore your load of sin?
2. Room for pleas-ure, room for busi - ness, But for Christ the Cru - ci - fied,
3. Have you an - y room for Je - sus, As in grace He calls a - gain?
4. Room and time now give to Je - sus, Soon will pass God's day of grace;

As He knocks and asks ad - mis - sion, Sin - ner, will you let Him in?
Not a place that He can en - ter, In the heart for which He died?
O, to - day is time ac - cept - ed, To-mor - row you may call in vain.
Soon thy heart left cold and si - lent, And thy Sav-iour's pleading cease.

REFRAIN

Room for Je - sus, King of glo - ry! Has - ten now, His word o - bey;

Swing the heart's door wide-ly o - pen, Bid Him en - ter while you may.

206 Lord, I'm Coming Home

William J. Kirkpatrick, 1838-1921

William J. Kirkpatrick, 1838-1921

1. I've wan-dered far a-way from God, Now I'm com-ing home;
2. I've wast-ed man-y pre-cious years, Now I'm com-ing home;
3. I've tired of sin and stray-ing, Lord, Now I'm com-ing home;
4. My soul is sick, my heart is sore, Now I'm com-ing home;

FINE

The paths of sin too long I've trod, Lord, I'm com-ing home.
I now re-pent with bit-ter tears, Lord, I'm com-ing home.
I'll trust Thy love, be-lieve Thy word, Lord, I'm com-ing home.
My strength re-new, my hope re-store, Lord, I'm com-ing home.

D. S.—O-pen wide Thine arms of love, Lord, I'm com-ing home.

REFRAIN

D. S

Com-ing home, com-ing home, Nev-er-more to roam,

207 Behold a Stranger at the Door

Joseph Grigg, c.1720-1768

BERA

John E. Gould, 1822-1875

1. Be-hold a Stran-ger at the door! He gen-tly knocks, has knocked be-fore,
2. O love-ly at-ti-tude! He stands With melting heart and la-den hands:
3. But will He prove a friend in-deed? He will; the ver-y friend you need;
4. Rise, touched with grat-i-tude di-vine; Turn out His en-e-my and thine,

Alternate tune: FEDERAL STREET, No. 194

Behold a Stranger at the Door

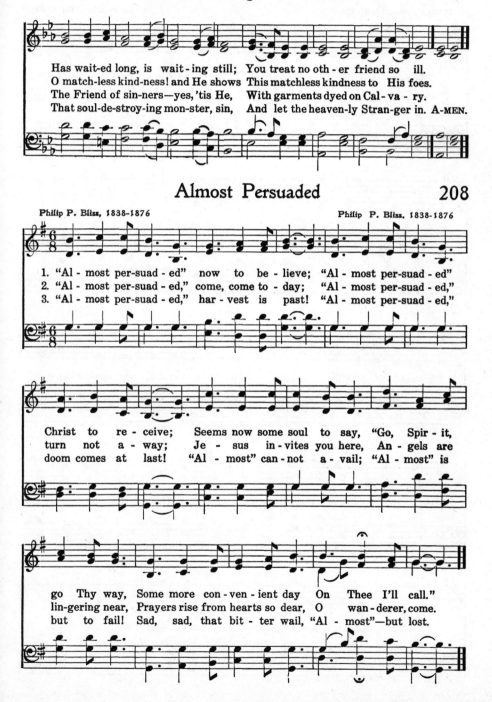

Has wait-ed long, is wait-ing still; You treat no oth-er friend so ill.
O match-less kind-ness! and He shows This matchless kindness to His foes.
The Friend of sin-ners—yes, 'tis He, With garments dyed on Cal-va-ry.
That soul-de-stroy-ing mon-ster, sin, And let the heaven-ly Stran-ger in. A-MEN.

Almost Persuaded

208

Philip P. Bliss, 1838-1876

Philip P. Bliss. 1838-1876

1. "Al - most per-suad - ed" now to be - lieve; "Al - most per-suad - ed"
2. "Al - most per-suad - ed," come, come to - day; "Al - most per-suad - ed,"
3. "Al - most per-suad - ed," har - vest is past! "Al - most per-suad - ed,"

Christ to re - ceive; Seems now some soul to say, "Go, Spir - it,
turn not a - way; Je - sus in - vites you here, An - gels are
doom comes at last! "Al - most" can - not a - vail; "Al - most" is

go Thy way, Some more con - ven - ient day On Thee I'll call."
lin-gering near, Prayers rise from hearts so dear, O wan - derer, come.
but to fail! Sad, sad, that bit - ter wail, "Al - most"—but lost.

"Whosoever Will"

Philip P. Bliss, 1838-1876   Philip P. Bliss, 1838-1876

1. "Who-so-ev-er hear-eth," shout, shout the sound! Spread the bless-ed ti-dings
2. Who-so-ev-er com-eth, need not de-lay, Now the door is o-pen,
3. "Who-so-ev-er will," the prom-ise is se-cure; "Who-so-ev-er will," for-

all the world a-round; Tell the joy-ful news wher-ev-er man is found,
en-ter while you may; Je-sus is the true, the on-ly Liv-ing Way:
ev-er must en-dure; "Who-so-ev-er will," 'tis life for-ev-er-more;

REFRAIN

"Who-so-ev-er will may come." "Who-so-ev-er will, who-so-ev-er will!"

Send the proc-la-ma-tion o-ver vale and hill; 'Tis a lov-ing

Fa-ther calls the wan-derer home: "Who-so-ev-er will may come."

Christ Receiveth Sinful Men

Erdmann Neumeister, 1671-1756
Trans. by Emma F. Bevan, 1827-1909

James McGranahan, 1840-1907

1. Sin - ners Je - sus will re - ceive; Sound this word of grace to all
2. Come, and He will give you rest; Trust Him, for His word is plain;
3. Now my heart con-demns me not, Pure be - fore the law I stand;
4. Christ re - ceiv - eth sin - ful men, E - ven me with all my sin;

Who the heaven-ly path - way leave, All who lin - ger, all who fall.
He will take the sin - ful - est; Christ re - ceiv - eth sin - ful men.
He who cleansed me from all spot, Sat - is - fied its last de - mand.
Purged from ev - ery spot and stain, Heaven with Him I en - ter in.

REFRAIN

Sing it o'er and o'er a - gain; Christ re-
Sing it o'er a-gain, sing it o'er a - gain; Christ re-

ceiv - - eth sin - ful men; Make the mes - - sage
ceiv-eth sin-ful men, Christ re-ceiv-eth sin-ful men; Make the message plain,

clear and plain: Christ re - ceiv - eth sin - ful men.
make the message plain:

Jesus Is Calling

Fanny J. Crosby, 1820-1915

George C. Stebbins, 1846-1945

1. Je - sus is ten - der - ly call - ing thee home—Call - ing to - day,
2. Je - sus is call - ing the wea - ry to rest— Call - ing to - day,
3. Je - sus is wait - ing; O come to Him now— Wait - ing to - day,
4. Je - sus is plead - ing; O list to His voice: Hear Him to - day,

call - ing to - day; Why from the sun - shine of love wilt thou roam
call - ing to - day; Bring Him thy bur - den and thou shalt be blest:
wait - ing to - day; Come with thy sins; at His feet low - ly bow;
hear Him to - day; They who be - lieve on His name shall re - joice;

REFRAIN

Far - ther and far - ther a - way? Call - - ing to - day,
He will not turn thee a - way.
Come, and no lon - ger de - lay.
Quick - ly a - rise and a - way. Call - ing, call - ing to - day, to - day,

Call - - ing to - day, Je - - sus is
Call - ing, call - ing to - day, to - day, Je - sus is ten - der - ly

call - - - ing, Is ten - der - ly call - ing to - day.
call - ing to - day,

Why Not Now?

Daniel W. Whittle, 1840-1901

Charles C. Case, 1843-1918

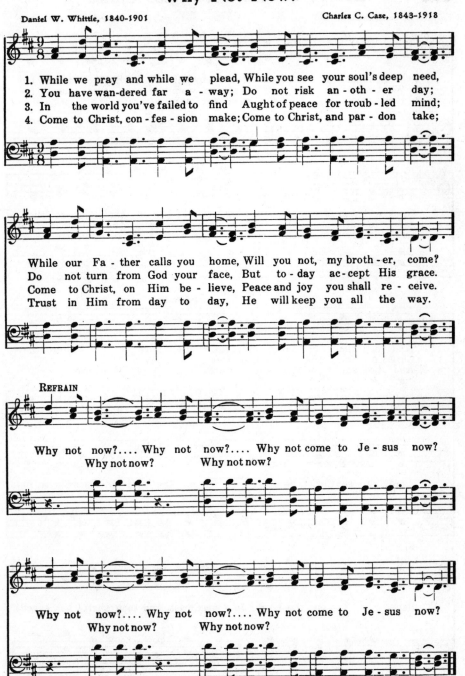

1. While we pray and while we plead, While you see your soul's deep need,
2. You have wan-dered far a - way; Do not risk an - oth - er day;
3. In the world you've failed to find Aught of peace for troub - led mind;
4. Come to Christ, con - fes - sion make; Come to Christ, and par - don take;

While our Fa - ther calls you home, Will you not, my broth - er, come?
Do not turn from God your face, But to - day ac - cept His grace.
Come to Christ, on Him be - lieve, Peace and joy you shall re - ceive.
Trust in Him from day to day, He will keep you all the way.

REFRAIN

Why not now?.... Why not now?.... Why not come to Je - sus now?
Why not now? Why not now?

Why not now?.... Why not now?.... Why not come to Je - sus now?
Why not now? Why not now?

213 Believe on the Lord Jesus Christ

Avis B. Christiansen, b. 1895

Harry D. Clarke, b. 1888

1. "What must I do?" the trem-bling jail - or cried, When dazed by
2. What must I do! O wea - ry, trem-bling soul, Just turn to-
3. His blood is all thy plea for sav - ing grace, The pre - cious

fear and won-der; "Be - lieve on Christ!" was all that Paul re-plied,
day to Je - sus; He will re - ceive, for - give and make thee whole —
fount of cleans-ing! O come, ac - cept His love, be - hold His face,

REFRAIN

"And thou shalt be saved from sin." Be - lieve on the
Christ a - lone can set thee free.
And be saved for - ev - er - more. Be - lieve

Lord Je - sus Christ, Be-lieve on the Lord Je - sus Christ, Be-
Be - lieve

lieve on the Lord Je - sus Christ, And thou shalt be saved!
Be - lieve

Give Me Thy Heart

Eliza E. Hewitt, 1851-1920 William J. Kirkpatrick, 1838-1921

1. "Give Me thy heart," says the Fa-ther a-bove, No gift so pre-cious to
2. "Give Me thy heart," says the Sav-iour of men, Call-ing in mer-cy a-
3. "Give Me thy heart," says the Spir-it di-vine, "All that thou hast, to My

Him as our love; Soft-ly He whis-pers, wher-ev-er thou art,
gain and a-gain; "Turn now from sin, and from e-vil de-part,
keep-ing re-sign; Grace more a-bound-ing is Mine to im-part,

REFRAIN

"Grate-ful-ly trust Me, and give Me thy heart."
Have I not died for thee? give Me thy heart." "Give Me thy heart,
Make full sur-ren-der and give Me thy heart."

give Me thy heart," Hear the soft whis-per, wher-ev-er thou art: From this dark

world He would draw thee a-part; Speak-ing so ten-der-ly, "Give Me thy heart."

215 O Jesus, Thou Art Standing

ST. HILDA

William W. How, 1823-1897

Justin H. Knecht, 1752-1817
Edward Husband, 1843-1908

1. O Je-sus, Thou art standing Out-side the fast-closed door, In low - ly pa-tience
2. O Je-sus, Thou art knocking; And lo! that hand is scarred, And thorns Thy brow en-
3. O Je-sus, Thou art pleading In ac-cents meek and low, "I died for you, My

wait - ing To pass the thresh-old o'er: Shame on us, Christian brothers, His Name and
cir - cle, And tears Thy face have marred: O love that passeth knowledge, So pa - tient-
chil-dren, And will ye treat Me so?" O Lord, with shame and sorrow We o - pen

sign who bear, O shame, thrice shame up-on us, To keep Him standing there!
ly to wait! O sin that hath no e - qual, So fast to bar the gate!
now the door; Dear Saviour, en - ter, en - ter, And leave us nev-er-more! A-MEN.

216 I Am Coming to the Cross

William McDonald, 1820-1901

William G. Fischer, 1835-1912

1. I am com - ing to the cross; I am poor and weak and blind;
2. Long my heart has sighed for Thee; Long has e - vil reigned with-in;
3. Here I give my all to Thee, Friends and time, and earth - ly store;
4. In the prom - is - es i trust; Now I feel the blood ap-plied;
5. Je - sus comes! He fills my soul! Per-fect - ed in Him I am;

REF. I am trust - ing, Lord, in Thee, Blest Lamb of Cal - va - ry;

I Am Coming to the Cross

D.C. for Refrain

I am count - ing all but dross; I shall full sal - va - tion find.
Je - sus sweet - ly speaks to me— "I will cleanse you from all sin."
Soul and bod - y Thine to be, Whol - ly Thine for - ev - er - more.
I am pros - trate in the dust; I with Christ am cru - ci - fied.
I am ev - ery whit made whole: Glo - ry, glo - ry to the Lamb!

Hum - bly at Thy cross I bow, Save me, Je - sus, save me now.

I Am Coming, Lord   217

Lewis Hartsough, 1828-1919   Lewis Hartsough, 1828-1919

1. I hear Thy welcome voice, That calls me, Lord, to Thee For cleans-ing in Thy
2. Though coming weak and vile, Thou dost my strength assure; Thou dost my vile-ness
3. 'Tis Je - sus calls me on To per-fect faith and love, To per-fect hope, and

REFRAIN

pre - cious blood That flowed on Cal - va - ry.
ful - ly cleanse, Till spot - less all and pure.   I am com - ing, Lord!
peace, and trust, For earth and heaven a - bove.

Com-ing now to Thee! Wash me, cleanse me in the blood That flowed on Cal-va-ry.

218 Let Jesus Come into Your Heart

Lelia N. Morris, 1862-1929

Lelia N. Morris, 1862-1929

1. If you are tired of the load of your sin, Let Je-sus come
2. If 'tis for pu-ri-ty now that you sigh, Let Je-sus come
3. If there's a tem-pest your voice can-not still, Let Je-sus come
4. If you would join the glad songs of the blest, Let Je-sus come

in-to your heart; If you de-sire a new life to be-gin,
in-to your heart; Foun-tains for cleans-ing are flow-ing near by,
in-to your heart; If there's a void this world nev-er can fill,
in-to your heart; If you would en-ter the man-sions of rest,

REFRAIN

Let Je-sus come in-to your heart. Just now, your

doubt-ings give o'er; Just now, re-ject Him no more; Just now, throw

o-pen the door; Let Je-sus come in-to your heart.

When I See the Blood

John Foote, 19th Century

J. G. Foote, 19th Century

1. Christ our Re-deem - er died on the cross, Died for the sin - ner,
2. Chief - est of sin - ners, Je - sus will save; All He has prom - ised,
3. Judg-ment is com - ing, all will be there, Each one re - ceiv - ing
4. O great com-pas - sion! O bound-less love! O lov - ing kind - ness,

paid all his due; Sprin - kle your soul with the blood of the Lamb,
that He will do; Wash in the foun - tain o - pened for sin,
just - ly his due; Hide in the sav - ing, sin - cleans - ing blood,
faith - ful and true! Find peace and shel - ter, un - der the blood,

REFRAIN

And I will pass, will pass o - ver you. When I see the
When I

blood, When I see the blood, When I see the
see the blood, When I see the blood, When I

blood, I will pass, I will pass o - ver you.
see the blood, o - ver you.

220 Turn Your Eyes upon Jesus

Helen H. Lemmel, b. 1864

Helen H. Lemmel, b. 1864

1. O soul, are you wea - ry and troub - led? No light in the
2. Thro' death in - to life ev - er - last - ing He passed, and we
3. His word shall not fail you— He prom - ised; Be - lieve Him, and

dark - ness you see? There's light for a look at the Sav - iour,
fol - low Him there; O - ver us sin no more hath do - min - ion—
all will be well: Then go to a world that is dy - ing,

And life more a - bun - dant and free!
For more than con - qu'rors we are!
His per - fect sal - va - tion to tell!

REFRAIN

Turn your eyes up - on Je -

sus, Look full in His won - der - ful face; And the things of

earth will grow strange - ly dim In the light of His glo - ry and grace.

Jesus, I Come

William T. Sleeper, 1819-1904

George C. Stebbins, 1846-1945

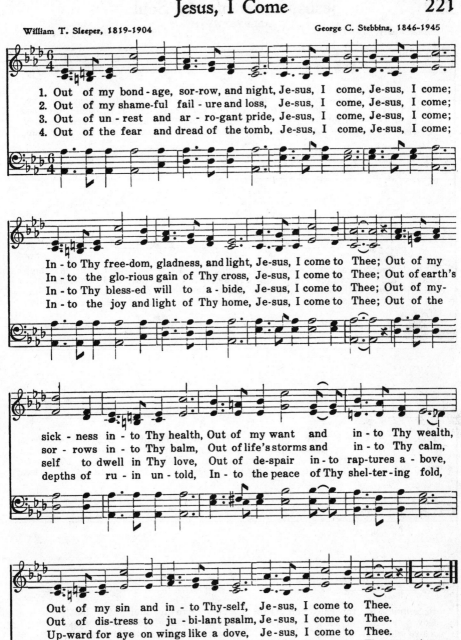

1. Out of my bond-age, sor-row, and night, Je-sus, I come, Je-sus, I come;
2. Out of my shame-ful fail-ure and loss, Je-sus, I come, Je-sus, I come;
3. Out of un-rest and ar-ro-gant pride, Je-sus, I come, Je-sus, I come;
4. Out of the fear and dread of the tomb, Je-sus, I come, Je-sus, I come;

In-to Thy free-dom, gladness, and light, Je-sus, I come to Thee; Out of my
In-to the glo-rious gain of Thy cross, Je-sus, I come to Thee; Out of earth's
In-to Thy bless-ed will to a-bide, Je-sus, I come to Thee; Out of my-
In-to the joy and light of Thy home, Je-sus, I come to Thee; Out of the

sick-ness in-to Thy health, Out of my want and in-to Thy wealth,
sor-rows in-to Thy balm, Out of life's storms and in-to Thy calm,
self to dwell in Thy love, Out of de-spair in-to rap-tures a-bove,
depths of ru-in un-told, In-to the peace of Thy shel-ter-ing fold,

Out of my sin and in-to Thy-self, Je-sus, I come to Thee.
Out of dis-tress to ju-bi-lant psalm, Je-sus, I come to Thee.
Up-ward for aye on wings like a dove, Je-sus, I come to Thee.
Ev-er Thy glo-rious face to be-hold, Je-sus, I come to Thee. A-MEN.

222 Jesus, Lover of My Soul

ABERYSTWYTH

Charles Wesley, 1707-1788

Joseph Parry, 1841-1903

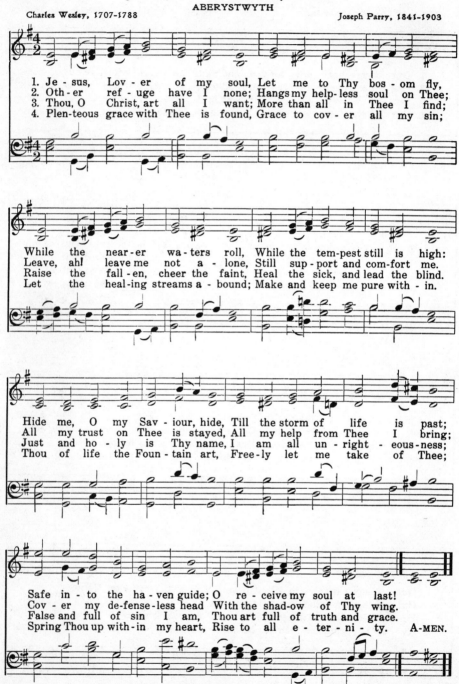

1. Je - sus, Lov - er of my soul, Let me to Thy bos - om fly,
2. Oth - er ref - uge have I none; Hangs my help - less soul on Thee;
3. Thou, O Christ, art all I want; More than all in Thee I find;
4. Plen - teous grace with Thee is found, Grace to cov - er all my sin;

While the near - er wa - ters roll, While the tem - pest still is high:
Leave, ah! leave me not a - lone, Still sup - port and com - fort me.
Raise the fall - en, cheer the faint, Heal the sick, and lead the blind.
Let the heal - ing streams a - bound; Make and keep me pure with - in.

Hide me, O my Sav - iour, hide, Till the storm of life is past;
All my trust on Thee is stayed, All my help from Thee I bring;
Just and ho - ly is Thy name, I am all un - right - eous - ness;
Thou of life the Foun - tain art, Free - ly let me take of Thee;

Safe in - to the ha - ven guide; O re - ceive my soul at last!
Cov - er my de - fense - less head With the shad - ow of Thy wing.
False and full of sin I am, Thou art full of truth and grace.
Spring Thou up with - in my heart, Rise to all e - ter - ni - ty. A-MEN.

Jesus, Lover of My Soul 222

MARTYN

(Second Tune)
Words on opposite page

Simeon B. Marsh, 1798-1875

FINE.

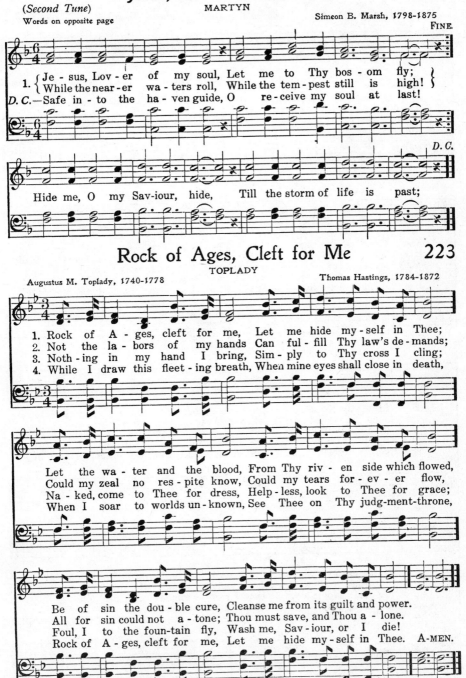

1. { Je - sus, Lov - er of my soul, Let me to Thy bos - om fly;
   { While the near - er wa - ters roll, While the tem - pest still is high!
D. C.—Safe in - to the ha - ven guide, O re - ceive my soul at last!

Hide me, O my Sav - iour, hide, Till the storm of life is past;

D. C.

Rock of Ages, Cleft for Me 223

TOPLADY

Augustus M. Toplady, 1740-1778

Thomas Hastings, 1784-1872

1. Rock of A - ges, cleft for me, Let me hide my - self in Thee;
2. Not the la - bors of my hands Can ful - fill Thy law's de - mands;
3. Noth - ing in my hand I bring, Sim - ply to Thy cross I cling;
4. While I draw this fleet - ing breath, When mine eyes shall close in death,

Let the wa - ter and the blood, From Thy riv - en side which flowed,
Could my zeal no res - pite know, Could my tears for - ev - er flow,
Na - ked, come to Thee for dress, Help - less, look to Thee for grace;
When I soar to worlds un - known, See Thee on Thy judg-ment-throne,

Be of sin the dou - ble cure, Cleanse me from its guilt and power.
All for sin could not a - tone; Thou must save, and Thou a - lone.
Foul, I to the foun-tain fly, Wash me, Sav - iour, or I die!
Rock of A - ges, cleft for me, Let me hide my - self in Thee. A-MEN.

Arise, My Soul, Arise!

Charles Wesley, 1707-1788

Source Unknown
Har. by Daniel B. Towner, 1850-1919

1. A - rise, my soul, a - rise! Shake off thy guilt - y fears;
2. He ev - er lives a - bove, For me to in - ter - cede;
3. Five bleed - ing wounds He bears, Re - ceived on Cal - va - ry;
4. The Fa - ther hears Him pray, His dear a - noint - ed One;
5. My God is rec - on - ciled, His par - doning voice I hear;

The bleed - ing Sac - ri - fice In my be - half ap-pears.
His all - re - deem - ing love, His pre - cious blood to plead;
They pour ef - fec - tual prayers, They strong-ly plead for me;
He can - not turn a - way The pres - ence of His Son:
He owns me for His child, I can no long - er fear:

Be - fore the throne my Sure - ty stands; My name is writ - ten
His blood a - toned for all our race, And sprin-kles now the
"For - give him, O for - give," they cry, "Nor let that ran - somed
His Spir - it an - swers to the blood, And tells me I am
With con - fi - dence I now draw nigh, And "Fa - ther, Ab - ba,

on His hands, My name is writ - ten on His hands.
throne of grace, And sprin - kles now the throne of grace.
sin - ner die! Nor let that ran - somed sin - ner die!"
born of God, And tells me I am born of God.
Fa - ther!" cry, And "Fa - ther, Ab - ba, Fa - ther" cry. A - MEN.

Since I Have Been Redeemed

Edwin O. Excell, 1851-1921

Edwin O. Excell, 1851-1921

1. I have a song I love to sing, Since I have been re-deemed,
2. I have a Christ who sat-is-fies, Since I have been re-deemed;
3. I have a wit-ness bright and clear, Since I have been re-deemed,
4. I have a home pre-pared for me, Since I have been re-deemed,

Of my Re-deem-er, Sav-iour, King, Since I have been re-deemed.
To do His will my high-est prize, Since I have been re-deemed.
Dis-pel-ling ev-ery doubt and fear, Since I have been re-deemed.
Where I shall dwell e-ter-nal-ly, Since I have been re-deemed.

REFRAIN

Since I have been re-deemed, Since I have been re-
Since I have been redeemed, Since I have been redeemed,

deemed, I will glo-ry in His name; Since I have been re-
Since I have been re-deemed, Since

deemed, I will glo-ry in my Sav-iour's name.
I have been re-deemed,

226 At Calvary

William R. Newell, 1868-1956

Daniel B. Towner, 1850-1919

1. Years I spent in van-i-ty and pride, Car-ing not my Lord was
2. By God's Word at last my sin I learned; Then I trem-bled at the
3. Now I've given to Je-sus ev-ery-thing; Now I glad-ly own Him
4. Oh, the love that drew sal-va-tion's plan! Oh, the grace that brought it

cru-ci-fied, Know-ing not it was for me He died On Cal-va-ry.
law I'd spurned, Till my guilt-y soul im-plor-ing turned To Cal-va-ry.
as my King; Now my rap-tured soul can on-ly sing Of Cal-va-ry.
down to man! Oh, the might-y gulf that God did span At Cal-va-ry!

REFRAIN

Mer-cy there was great, and grace was free; Par-don there was mul-ti-

plied to me; There my burdened soul found lib-er-ty, At Cal-va-ry.

227 Amazing Grace! How Sweet the Sound

McINTOSH

John Newton, 1725-1807

Early American Melody
Arr. by Edwin O. Excell, 1851-1921

1. A-maz-ing grace! how sweet the sound, That saved a wretch like me! I
2. 'Twas grace that taught my heart to fear, And grace my fears re-lieved; How
3. Through man-y dan-gers, toils and snares, I have al-read-y come; 'Tis
4. When we've been there ten thou-sand years, Bright shin-ing as the sun, We've

Alternate tune: ARLINGTON, No. 457

Amazing Grace! How Sweet the Sound

once was lost, but now am found, Was blind, but now I see.
pre - cious did that grace ap - pear The hour I first be - lieved!
grace hath brought me safe thus far, And grace will lead me home.
no less days to sing God's praise Than when we first be - gun. A - MEN.

Glory to His Name 228

Elisha A. Hoffman, 1839-1929   John H. Stockton, 1813-1877

1. Down at the cross where my Sav - iour died, Down where for cleansing from
2. I am so won-drous - ly saved from sin, Je - sus so sweet - ly a -
3. Oh, pre-cious foun-tain that saves from sin, I am so glad I have
4. Come to this foun-tain so rich and sweet; Cast thy poor soul at the

sin I cried, There to my heart was the blood ap-plied; Glo - ry to His name!
bides with-in, There at the cross where He took me in; Glo - ry to His name!
en - tered in; There Je-sus saves me and keeps me clean; Glo - ry to His name!
Saviour's feet; Plunge in to - day, and be made com-plete; Glo - ry to His name!

REFRAIN

Glo - ry to His name, Glo - ry to His name;

There to my heart was the blood ap - plied; Glo - ry to His name!

229 I Know Whom I Have Believed

Daniel W. Whittle, 1840-1901

James McGranahan, 1840-1907

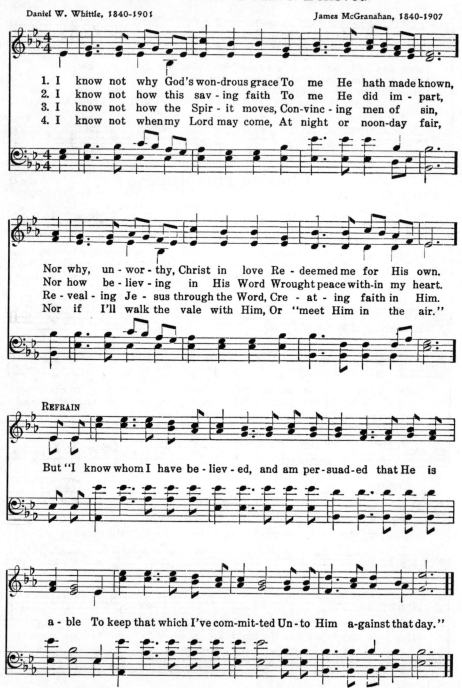

1. I know not why God's won-drous grace To me He hath made known,
2. I know not how this sav-ing faith To me He did im-part,
3. I know not how the Spir-it moves, Con-vinc-ing men of sin,
4. I know not when my Lord may come, At night or noon-day fair,

Nor why, un-wor-thy, Christ in love Re-deemed me for His own.
Nor how be-liev-ing in His Word Wrought peace with-in my heart.
Re-veal-ing Je-sus through the Word, Cre-at-ing faith in Him.
Nor if I'll walk the vale with Him, Or "meet Him in the air."

REFRAIN

But "I know whom I have be-liev-ed, and am per-suad-ed that He is

a-ble To keep that which I've com-mit-ted Un-to Him a-gainst that day."

Praise Him! Praise Him!

Fanny J. Crosby, 1820-1915

Chester G. Allen, 1838-1878

1. Praise Him! praise Him! Je-sus, our bless-ed Re-deem-er! Sing, O Earth, His
2. Praise Him! praise Him! Je-sus, our bless-ed Re-deem-er! For our sins He
3. Praise Him! praise Him! Je-sus, our bless-ed Re-deem-er! Heavenly por-tals

won-der-ful love pro-claim! Hail Him! hail Him! highest archangels in glo-ry;
suffered, and bled and died; He our Rock, our hope of e-ter-nal sal-va-tion,
loud with ho-san-nas ring! Je-sus, Sav-iour, reigneth for-ev-er and ev-er;

Strength and hon-or give to His ho-ly name! Like a shep-herd Je-sus will
Hail Him! hail Him! Je-sus the Cru-ci-fied. Sound His prais-es! Je-sus who
Crown Him! crown Him! Prophet and Priest and King! Christ is com-ing! o-ver the

REFRAIN

guard His children, In His arms He carries them all day long:
bore our sor-rows; Love unbounded, wonderful, deep and strong: Praise Him! praise Him!
world vic-to-rious, Power and glo-ry un-to the Lord be-long:

tell of His ex-cel-lent greatness; Praise Him! praise Him! ever in joy-ful song!

231 I Love to Tell the Story

A. Catherine Hankey, 1834-1911

William G. Fischer, 1835-1912

1. I love to tell the sto - ry Of un - seen things a - bove, Of Je - sus and His glo - ry, Of Je - sus and His love. I love to tell the sto - ry, Be - cause I know 'tis true; It sat - is - fies my long-ings As noth-ing else can do.

2. I love to tell the sto - ry, More won-der - ful it seems Than all the gold - en fan - cies Of all our gold - en dreams. I love to tell the sto - ry, It did so much for me; And that is just the rea - son I tell it now to thee.

3. I love to tell the sto - ry, 'Tis pleas-ant to re - peat What seems, each time I tell it, More won - der - ful - ly sweet. I love to tell the sto - ry, For some have nev - er heard The mes - sage of sal - va - tion From God's own Ho-ly Word.

4. I love to tell the sto - ry, For those who know it best Seem hun - ger - ing and thirst-ing To hear it like the rest. And when, in scenes of glo - ry, I sing the new, new song, 'Twill be the old, old sto - ry That I have loved so long.

REFRAIN

I love to tell the sto - ry, 'Twill be my theme in glo - ry To tell the old, old sto - ry Of Je - sus and His love.

I Will Sing the Wondrous Story

Francis H. Rowley, 1854-1952

Peter P. Bilhorn, 1861-1936

1. I will sing the won-drous sto - ry Of the Christ who died for me,
2. I was lost, but Je - sus found me, Found the sheep that went a - stray,
3. I was bruised, but Je - sus healed me; Faint was I from man-y a fall;
4. Days of dark - ness still come o'er me, Sor-row's paths I oft - en tread,
5. He will keep me till the riv - er Rolls its wa - ters at my feet;

How He left His home in glo - ry For the cross of Cal - va - ry.
Threw His lov - ing arms a - round me, Drew me back in - to His way.
Sight was gone, and fears pos-sessed me, But He freed me from them all.
But the Sav - iour still is with me; By His hand I'm safe - ly led.
Then He'll bear me safe - ly o - ver, Where the loved ones I shall meet.

REFRAIN

Yes, I'll sing the won-drous sto - ry Of the
Yes, I'll sing the won-drous sto-ry

Christ who died for me Sing it with the saints in
Of the Christ who died for me, Sing it with

glo - ry, Gath-ered by the crys-tal sea.
the saints in glo - ry, Gath-ered by the crys-tal sea.

233　O Could I Speak the Matchless Worth

ARIEL

Samuel Medley, 1738-1799

Wolfgang A. Mozart, 1756-1791
Arr. by Lowell Mason, 1792-1872

1. O could I speak the match-less worth,
2. I'd sing the pre-cious blood He spilt,
3. I'd sing the char-ac-ters He bears,
4. Soon the de-light-ful day will come

O could I sound the glo-ries forth Which in my Sav-iour shine,
My ran-som from the dread-ful guilt Of sin and wrath di-vine!
And all the forms of love He wears, Ex-alt-ed on His throne:
When my dear Lord will bring me home, And I shall see His face;

I'd soar and touch the heav'nly strings, And vie with Ga-briel while he sings
I'd sing His glo-rious right-eous-ness, In which all-per-fect heavenly dress
In loft-iest songs of sweet-est praise, I would to ev-er-last-ing days
Then with my Sav-iour, Brother, Friend, A blest e-ter-ni-ty I'll spend,

In notes al-most di-vine, In notes al-most di-vine.
My soul shall ev-er shine, My soul shall ev-er shine.
Make all His glo-ries known, Make all His glo-ries known.
Tri-um-phant in His grace, Tri-um-phant in His grace. A-MEN.

I Heard the Voice of Jesus Say

VOX DILECTI

Horatius Bonar, 1808-1889

John B. Dykes, 1823-1876

1. I heard the voice of Je - sus say, "Come un - to Me and rest;
2. I heard the voice of Je - sus say, "Be - hold, I free - ly give
3. I heard the voice of Je - sus say, "I am this dark world's Light;

Lay down, thou wea - ry one, lay down Thy head up - on My breast."
The liv - ing wa - ter; thirst - y one, Stoop down, and drink, and live."
Look un - to Me, thy morn shall rise, And all thy day be bright."

I came to Je - sus as I was, Wea - ry, and worn, and sad;
I came to Je - sus, and I drank Of that life - giv - ing stream;
I looked to Je - sus, and I found In Him my Star, my Sun;

I found in Him a rest - ing-place, And He has made me glad.
My thirst was quenched, my soul revived, And now I live in Him.
And in that Light of life I'll walk, Till travel-ing days are done. A-MEN.

I Need Jesus

George O. Webster, 1866-1942   Charles H. Gabriel, 1856-1932

1. I need Je-sus, my need I now con-fess; No friend like Him in times of
2. I need Je-sus, I need a friend like Him, A friend to guide when paths of
3. I need Je-sus, I need Him to the end; No one like Him, He is the

deep dis-tress; I need Je-sus, the need I glad-ly own; Though some may bear their
life are dim; I need Je-sus, when foes my soul as-sail; A - lone I know I
sin-ner's Friend; I need Je-sus, no oth-er friend will do; So con-stant, kind, so

REFRAIN

load a-lone, Yet, I need Je-sus. I need Je-sus, I need Je-sus,
can but fail, So I need Je-sus.
strong and true, Yes, I need Je-sus. I need Je-sus with me, I need Je-sus al-ways,

I need Je-sus ev-ery day; Need Him in the sun-shine hour,
ev-ery day;

Need Him when the storm-clouds lower; Every day along my way, Yes, I need Je-sus.

No, Not One!

Johnson Oatman, Jr., 1856-1926

George C. Hugg, 1848-1907

1. There's not a friend like the low-ly Je-sus, No, not one! no, not one!
2. No friend like Him is so high and ho-ly, No, not one! no, not one!
3. There's not an hour that He is not near us, No, not one! no, not one!
4. Did ev-er saint find this Friend for-sake him? No, not one! no, not one!
5. Was e'er a gift like the Sav-iour giv-en? No, not one! no, not-one!

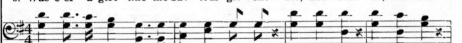

None else could heal all our soul's dis-eas-es, No, not one! no, not one!
And yet no friend is so meek and low-ly, No, not one! no, not one!
No night so dark but His love can cheer us, No, not one! no, not one!
Or sin-ner find that He would not take him? No, not one! no, not one!
Will He re-fuse us a home in heav-en? No, not one! no, not one!

REFRAIN

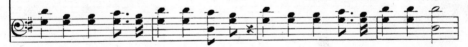

Je-sus knows all a-bout our struggles, He will guide till the day is done;

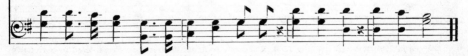

There's not a friend like the low-ly Je-sus, No, not one! no, not one!

He Keeps Me Singing

Luther B. Bridgers, 1884-1948   Luther B. Bridgers, 1884-1948

1. There's with-in my heart a mel-o-dy, Je-sus whispers sweet and low,
2. All my life was wrecked by sin and strife, Dis-cord filled my heart with pain,
3. Feast-ing on the rich-es of His grace, Resting 'neath His sheltering wing,
4. Soon He's com-ing back to wel-come me Far be-yond the star-ry sky;

Fear not, I am with thee, peace, be still, In all of life's ebb and flow.
Je-sus swept a-cross the bro-ken strings, Stirred the slumbering chords a-gain.
Al-ways look-ing on His smil-ing face, That is why I shout and sing.
I shall wing my flight to worlds unknown, I shall reign with Him on high.

REFRAIN

Je-sus, Je-sus, Je-sus— Sweet-est name I know,

Fills my ev-ery long-ing, Keep me sing-ing as I go.

Jesus, I Am Resting, Resting

TRANQUILLITY

Jean S. Pigott, 19th Century

James Mountain, 1843-1933

1. Je - sus, I am rest - ing, rest - ing In the joy of what Thou art;
2. Oh, how great Thy lov - ing kind - ness, Vast - er, broad - er than the sea!
3. Sim - ply trust - ing Thee, Lord Je - sus, I be - hold Thee as Thou art,
4. Ev - er lift Thy face up - on me, As I work and wait for Thee;

REFRAIN—*Je - sus, I am rest - ing, rest - ing, In the joy of what Thou art,*

FINE.

I am find - ing out the great - ness Of Thy lov - ing heart.
Oh, how mar - vel - lous Thy good - ness, Lav - ished all on me!
And Thy love, so pure, so change - less, Sat - is - fies my heart;
Rest - ing 'neath Thy smile, Lord Je - sus, Earth's dark shad - ows flee.

I am find - ing out the great - ness Of Thy lov - ing heart.

Thou hast bid me gaze up - on Thee, And Thy beau - ty fills my soul,
Yes, I rest in Thee, Be - lov - ed, Know what wealth of grace is Thine,
Sat - is - fies its deep - est long - ings, Meets, supplies its ev - ery need,
Brightness of my Fa - ther's glo - ry, Sun - shine of my Fa - ther's face,

D. C. Refrain

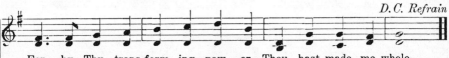

For by Thy trans - form - ing pow - er, Thou hast made me whole.
Know Thy cer - tain - ty of prom - ise, And have made it mine.
Com - pass - eth me round with bless - ings: Thine is love in - deed!
Keep me ev - er trust - ing, rest - ing, Fill me with Thy grace.

Sunshine in My Soul

Eliza E. Hewitt, 1851-1920   John R. Sweney, 1837-1899

1. There's sun-shine in my soul to - day, More glo - ri - ous and bright
2. There's mu - sic in my soul to - day, A car - ol to my King,
3. There's springtime in my soul to - day, For when the Lord is near
4. There's glad-ness in my soul to - day, And hope and praise and love,

Than glows in an - y earth-ly sky, For Je - sus is my light.
And Je - sus, lis - ten - ing can hear The songs I can - not sing.
The dove of peace sings in my heart, The flowers of grace ap - pear.
For bless - ings which He gives me now, For joys "laid up" a - bove.

REFRAIN

O there's sun - - - shine, bless - ed sun - - - shine,
O there's sun - shine in the soul, bless - ed sun - shine in the soul,

When the peace - ful, hap - py mo - ments roll;   When
                          hap - py mo-ments roll;

Je - sus shows His smil - ing face, There is sun-shine in my soul.

Love Lifted Me

James Rowe, 1865-1933

Howard E. Smith, 1863-1918

1. I was sink-ing deep in sin, Far from the peace-ful shore, Ver-y deep-ly stained with-in, Sink-ing to rise no more; But the Mas-ter of the sea Heard my de-spair-ing cry, From the wa-ters lift-ed me, Now safe am I.

2. All my heart to Him I give, Ev-er to Him I'll cling, In His bless-ed pres-ence live, Ev-er His prais-es sing. Love so might-y and so true Mer-its my soul's best songs; Faith-ful, lov-ing serv-ice, too, To Him be-longs.

3. Souls in dan-ger, look a-bove, Je-sus com-plete-ly saves; He will lift you by His love Out of the an-gry waves. He's the Mas-ter of the sea, Bil-lows His will o-bey; He your Sav-iour wants to be—Be saved to-day.

REFRAIN

Love lift-ed me! Love lift-ed me! When noth-ing
e-ven me! e-ven me!

else could help, Love lift-ed me. Love lift-ed me.

241 To God Be the Glory

Fanny J. Crosby, 1820-1915

William H. Doane, 1832-1915

1. To God be the glo-ry, great things He hath done, So loved He the world that He
2. O per - fect redemption, the pur-chase of blood, To ev - 'ry be-liev - er the
3. Great things He hath taught us, great things He hath done, And great our re - joic - ing thro'

gave us His Son, Who yield-ed His life an a-tone-ment for sin, And o-pened the
prom-ise of God; The vil - est of-fen-der who tru-ly believes, That moment from
Je - sus the Son; But pu - rer, and higher, and greater will be Our won-der, our

REFRAIN

Life-gate that all may go in.
Je - sus a par-don re-ceives. Praise the Lord, praise the Lord, Let the earth hear His
transport, when Jesus we see.

voice! Praise the Lord, praise the Lord, Let the peo-ple re-joice! O come to the

Fa-ther thro' Je-sus the Son, And give Him the glo-ry, great things He hath done.

Jesus Has Lifted Me!

Avis B. Christiansen, b. 1895

Haldor Lillenas, b. 1885

1. Out of the depths to the glo - ry a - bove, I have been
2. Out of the world in - to heav - en - ly rest, In - to the
3. Out of my - self in - to Him I a - dore, There to a -

lift - ed in won - der - ful love; From ev - ery fet - ter my
land of the ran-somed and blest; There in the glo - ry with
bide in His love ev - er - more; Thro' end - less a - ges His

spir - it is free— For Je - sus has lift - ed me!
Him I shall be— For Je - sus has lift - ed me!
glo - ry to see— My Je - sus has lift - ed me!
lift - ed me!

REFRAIN

Je - sus has lift - ed me! Je - sus has lift - ed me!
lift - ed me! lift - ed me!

Out of the night in - to glo - ri - ous light, Yes, Je - sus has lift - ed me!
lift-ed me!

243 Heavenly Sunlight

H. J. Zelley, 20th Century

George H. Cook, 20th Century

1. Walk-ing in sun - light, all of my jour-ney, O - ver the moun-tains,
2. Shad-ows a - round me, shad-ows a - bove me, Nev - er con-ceal my
3. In the bright sun - light, ev - er re - joic - ing, Press-ing my way to

through the deep vale; Je - sus has said, "I'll nev - er for - sake thee,"
Sav - iour and Guide; He is the Light, in Him is no dark - ness;
man - sions a - bove; Sing-ing His prais - es, glad - ly I'm walk - ing,

REFRAIN

Prom - ise di - vine that nev - er can fail.
Ev - er I'm walk - ing close to His side. Heav - en - ly sun - light,
Walk - ing in sun - light, sun-light of love.

heav - en - ly sun-light, Flood-ing my soul with glo - ry di - vine; Hal - le-

lu - jah! I am re - joic - ing, Sing-ing His prais - es, Je - sus is mine.

How Sweet the Name of Jesus Sounds 244

ST. PETER

John Newton, 1725-1807

Alexander R. Reinagle, 1799-1877

1. How sweet the name of Je - sus sounds In a be - liev - er's ear!
2. Dear name! the Rock on which I build, My Shield and Hid - ing - place,
3. Je - sus, my Shep-herd, Broth-er, Friend, My Proph-et, Priest, and King,
4. Weak is the ef - fort of my heart, And cold my warm-est thought;
5. Till then I would Thy love pro - claim With ev - ery fleet - ing breath;

It soothes his sor-rows, heals his wounds, And drives a - way his fear.
My nev - er - fail - ing Treas'ry, filled With bound-less stores of grace;
My Lord, my Life, my Way, my End, Ac - cept the praise I bring.
But when I see Thee as Thou art, I'll praise Thee as I ought.
And may the mu - sic of Thy name Re-fresh my soul in death. A-MEN.

Alternate tune: ORTONVILLE, No. 65

O Holy Saviour, Friend Unseen 245

FLEMMING

Charlotte Elliott, 1789-1871

Friedrich F. Flemming, 1778-1813

1. O ho - ly Sav-iour, Friend un - seen, Since on Thine arm Thou bidd'st me lean,
2. What tho' the world de - ceit - ful prove, And earth-ly friends and hopes re-move;
3. Tho' oft I seem to tread a - lone Life's dreary waste, with thorns o'er-grown,
4. Tho' faith and hope are of - ten tried, I ask not, need not aught be - side;
5. Blest is my lot, what-e'er be - fall; What can dis-turb me, who ap - pall,

Help me throughout life's changing scene, By faith to cling to Thee.
With pa-tient, un-com-plain-ing love, Still would I cling to Thee.
Thy voice of love in gen - tlest tone, Still whispers, "Cling to Me!"
So safe, so calm, so sat - is - fied, The soul that clings to Thee.
While as my Strength, my Rock, my All, Sav-iour, I cling to Thee? A-MEN.

246 We're Marching to Zion

Isaac Watts, 1674-1748
Refrain by Robert Lowry, 1826-1899

Robert Lowry, 1826-1899

1. Come, we that love the Lord, And let our joys be known,
2. Let those re-fuse to sing Who nev-er knew our God;
3. The hill of Zi-on yields A thou-sand sa-cred sweets
4. Then let our songs a-bound, And ev-ery tear be dry;

Join in a song with sweet ac-cord, Join in a song with sweet ac-cord,
But chil-dren of the heaven-ly King, But chil-dren of the heaven-ly King,
Be-fore we reach the heaven-ly fields, Be-fore we reach the heaven-ly fields,
We're marching thro' Im-manuel's ground, We're march-ing thro' Im-man-uel's ground,

And thus sur-round the throne, And thus sur-round the throne.
May speak their joys a-broad, May speak their joys a-broad.
Or walk the gold-en streets, Or walk the gold-en streets.
To fair-er worlds on high, To fair-er worlds on high.

And thus sur-round the throne, And thus sur-round the throne.

REFRAIN

We're march-ing to Zi-on, Beau-ti-ful, beau-ti-ful Zi-on;
We're march-ing on to Zi-on,

We're march-ing up-ward to Zi-on, The beau-ti-ful cit-y of God.
Zi-on, Zi-on,

Alternate tune without Refrain: ST. THOMAS, No. 247 on opposite page

Come, We That Love the Lord
ST. THOMAS
247

Isaac Watts, 1674-1748

Aaron Williams, 1731-1776

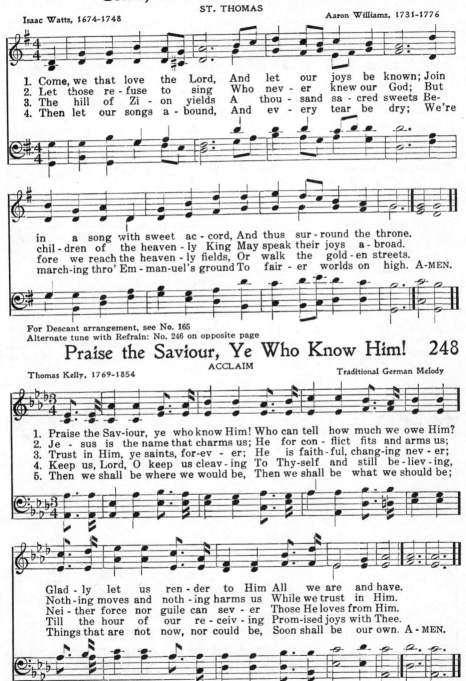

1. Come, we that love the Lord, And let our joys be known; Join
2. Let those re - fuse to sing Who nev - er knew our God; But
3. The hill of Zi - on yields A thou - sand sa - cred sweets Be-
4. Then let our songs a - bound, And ev - ery tear be dry; We're

in a song with sweet ac - cord, And thus sur - round the throne.
chil - dren of the heaven - ly King May speak their joys a - broad.
fore we reach the heaven - ly fields, Or walk the gold - en streets.
march - ing thro' Em - man - uel's ground To fair - er worlds on high. A-MEN.

For Descant arrangement, see No. 165
Alternate tune with Refrain: No. 246 on opposite page

Praise the Saviour, Ye Who Know Him!
ACCLAIM
248

Thomas Kelly, 1769-1854

Traditional German Melody

1. Praise the Sav - iour, ye who know Him! Who can tell how much we owe Him?
2. Je - sus is the name that charms us; He for con - flict fits and arms us;
3. Trust in Him, ye saints, for-ev - er; He is faith - ful, chang-ing nev - er;
4. Keep us, Lord, O keep us cleav - ing To Thy-self and still be - liev - ing,
5. Then we shall be where we would be, Then we shall be what we should be;

Glad - ly let us ren - der to Him All we are and have.
Noth - ing moves and noth - ing harms us While we trust in Him.
Nei - ther force nor guile can sev - er Those He loves from Him.
Till the hour of our re - ceiv - ing Prom-ised joys with Thee.
Things that are not now, nor could be, Soon shall be our own. A - MEN.

249 Redeemed

Fanny J. Crosby, 1820-1915

William J. Kirkpatrick, 1838-1921

1. Redeemed—how I love to pro-claim it! Re-deemed by the blood of the Lamb;
2. Redeemed and so hap-py in Je - sus, No lan-guage my rapture can tell;
3. I think of my bless-ed Re-deem-er, I think of Him all the day long;
4. I know I shall see in His beau-ty The King in whose law I de-light;

Redeemed through His in-fi-nite mer - cy, His child, and for-ev - er, I am.
I know that the light of His pres-ence With me doth con-tin-ual-ly dwell.
I sing, for I can-not be si - lent; His love is the theme of my song.
Who lov-ing-ly guard-eth my foot-steps, And giv-eth me songs in the night.

REFRAIN

Re - deemed, re - deemed, Re-deemed by the blood of the Lamb;
re-deemed, re-deemed,

Re - deemed, re - deemed, His child, and for-ev - er, I am.
re-deemed, re-deemed,

I've Heard the King

Grant C. Tullar, 1869-1950

Donald P. Hustad, b. 1918

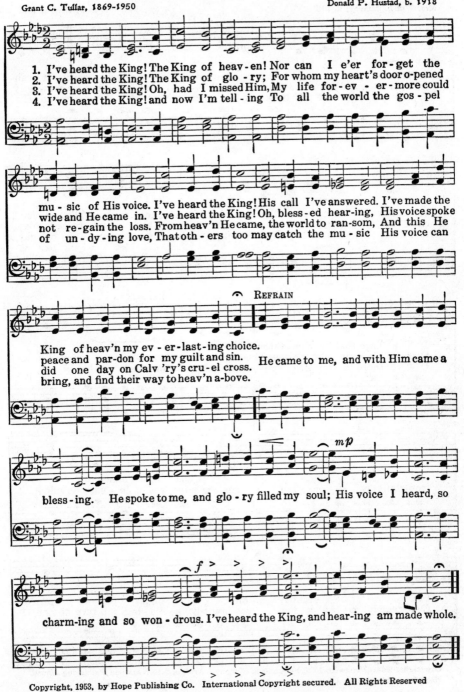

1. I've heard the King! The King of heav-en! Nor can I e'er for-get the
2. I've heard the King! The King of glo-ry; For whom my heart's door o-pened
3. I've heard the King! Oh, had I missed Him, My life for-ev-er-more could
4. I've heard the King! and now I'm tell-ing To all the world the gos-pel

mu-sic of His voice. I've heard the King! His call I've answered. I've made the
wide and He came in. I've heard the King! Oh, bless-ed hear-ing, His voice spoke
not re-gain the loss. From heav'n He came, the world to ran-som, And this He
of un-dy-ing love, That oth-ers too may catch the mu-sic His voice can

REFRAIN

King of heav'n my ev-er-last-ing choice.
peace and par-don for my guilt and sin. He came to me, and with Him came a
did one day on Calv'ry's cru-el cross.
bring, and find their way to heav'n a-bove.

bless-ing. He spoke to me, and glo-ry filled my soul; His voice I heard, so

charm-ing and so won-drous. I've heard the King, and hear-ing am made whole.

251 Constantly Abiding

Mrs. Will L. Murphy, d. 1942   Mrs. Will L. Murphy, d. 1942

1. There's a peace in my heart that the world nev-er gave, A peace it can
2. All the world seemed to sing of a Sav-iour and King, When peace sweetly
3. This treas-ure I have in a tem-ple of clay, While here on His

not take a - way; Tho' the tri - als of life may sur-round like a cloud,
came to my heart; Trou-bles all fled a - way and my night turned to day,
foot-stool I roam: But He's com-ing to take me some glo - ri - ous day,

REFRAIN

I've a peace that has come there to stay! Con - - - - stant-ly a-
Bless-ed Je - sus, how glorious Thou art! Con-stant-ly a - bid - ing,
O - ver there to my heav-en - ly home!

bid - - - - ing, Je - - - - sus is mine;
con-stant-ly a - bid - ing, Je - sus is mine, yes, Je - sus is mine;

Con - stant-ly a - bid - - - ing, rap - - ture di -
Con-stant-ly a - bid - ing, con-stant-ly a - bid - ing, rap-ture di-vine, O

Constantly Abiding

vine; He nev-er leaves me lone - - - - ly, whis-pers,
rap-ture di-vine; He nev-er leaves me, nev-er leaves me lone-ly, whis-pers,

O, so kind:— "I will nev-er leave thee," Je - sus is mine.
whis-pers, O so kind:— nev-er leave thee, Je-sus, Je-sus is mine.

My Hope Is in the Lord 252

Norman J. Clayton, b. 1903   Norman J. Clayton, b. 1903

1. My hope is in the Lord Who gave Him-self for me, And
2. No mer-it of my own His an-ger to sup-press. My
3. And now for me He stands Be - fore the Fa-ther's throne. He
4. His grace has planned it all, 'Tis mine but to be - lieve, And

REFRAIN

paid the price of all my sin at Cal-va-ry.
on - ly hope is found in Je - sus' right-eous-ness. For me He died, For
shows His wounded hands, and names me as His own. For me He died,
rec - og-nize His work of love and Christ re - ceive.

me He lives, And ev - er-last-ing life and light He free-ly gives.
For me He lives,

Copyright, 1945, by Norman J. Clayton in "Word of Life Melodies No. 2." Used by permission

253   Sweeter as the Years Go By

Lelia N. Morris, 1862-1929   Lelia N. Morris, 1862-1929

1. Of Je-sus' love that sought me, When I was lost in sin; Of won-drous
2. He trod in old Ju-de-a Life's path-way long a-go; The peo-ple
3. 'Twas wondrous love which led Him For us to suf-fer loss— To bear with-

grace that brought me Back to His fold a-gain; Of heights and depths of
thronged a-bout Him His sav-ing grace to know; He healed the bro-ken-
out a mur-mur The an-guish of the cross; With saints re-deemed in

mer-cy, Far deep-er than the sea, And high-er than the heav-ens,
heart-ed, And caused the blind to see; And still His great heart yearn-eth
glo-ry Let us our voi-ces raise, Till heaven and earth re-ech-o

REFRAIN

My theme shall ev-er be. Sweet-er as the years go by,
In love for e-ven me. Sweet-er as the years go by, 'Tis
With our Re-deem-er's praise.

Sweet-er as the years go by; Rich-er, full-er, deep-er,
sweet-er as the years go by;

Sweeter as the Years Go By

Je - sus' love is sweet - er, Sweet - er as the years go by.

No Other Plea

254

Lidie H. Edmunds, 19th Century

Arr. by William J. Kirkpatrick, 1838-1921

Norse Air

1. My faith has found a rest-ing-place, Not in de-vice nor creed;
2. E - nough for me that Je - sus saves, This ends my fear and doubt;
3. My heart is lean - ing on the Word, The writ-ten Word of God,
4. My great Phy - si - cian heals the sick, The lost He came to save;

I trust the Ev - er - liv - ing One, His wounds for me shall plead.
A sin - ful soul I come to Him, He'll nev - er cast me out.
Sal - va - tion by my Sav-iour's name, Sal - va - tion thro' His blood.
For me His pre-cious blood He shed, For me His Life He gave.

REFRAIN

I need no oth - er ar - gu - ment, I need no oth - er plea,

It is e - nough that Je - sus died, And that He died for me.

255

Saved!

Oswald J. Smith, b. 1890

In unison, ad lib

Roger M. Hickman, b. 1888

1. Saved! saved! saved! my sins are all for-giv'n; Christ is
2. Saved! saved! saved! by grace and grace a-lone; Oh, what
3. Saved! saved! saved! oh, joy be-yond com-pare! Christ my

mine! I'm on my way to heav'n; Once a guilt-y
won-drous love to me was shown, In my stead Christ
life, and I His con-stant care; Yield-ing all and

sin-ner, lost, un-done, Now a child of God, saved thro' His Son.
Je-sus bled and died, Bore my sins, for me was cru-ci-fied.
trust-ing Him a-lone, Liv-ing now each mo-ment as His own.

REFRAIN

Saved! I'm saved thro' Christ, my all in all; Saved! I'm saved, what-
my all in all;

ev-er may be-fall; He died up-on the cross for me, He bore the aw-ful

Saved!

pen - al - ty; And now I'm saved e - ter - nal - ly—I'm saved! saved! saved!

Jesus Never Fails

256

Arthur A. Luther, b. 1891

Arthur A. Luther, b. 1891

1. Earth - ly friends may prove un - true, Doubts and fears as - sail;
2. Though the sky be dark and drear, Fierce and strong the gale,
3. In life's dark and bit - ter hour Love will still pre - vail;

One still loves and cares for you: Je - sus nev - er fails.
nev-er fails.
Just re - mem - ber He is near, And He will not fail.
will not fail.
Trust His ev - er - last - ing pow'r, Je - sus will not fail.
will not fail.

REFRAIN

Je - sus nev - er fails, Je - sus nev - er fails;

Heav'n and earth may pass a - way, But Je - sus nev - er fails.

He Lives

Alfred H. Ackley, b. 1887

Alfred H. Ackley, b. 1887

1. I serve a ris - en Sav-iour, He's in the world to -day; I know that He is
2. In all the world a-round me I see His lov-ing care, And tho' my heart grows
3. Rejoice, rejoice, O Christian, lift up your voice and sing E - ter - nal hal - le-

liv - ing, what-ev - er men may say; I see His hand of mer - cy, I
wea-ry, I nev - er will de - spair; I know that He is lead - ing thro'
lu - jahs to Je - sus Christ the King! The Hope of all who seek Him, the

hear His voice of cheer, And just the time I need Him He's al - ways near.
all · the storm-y blast, The day of His ap - pear-ing will come at last.
Help of all who find, None oth-er is so lov - ing, so good and kind.

REFRAIN

He lives, He lives, Christ Je - sus lives to - day! He walks with me and
He lives, He lives,

talks with me a - long life's nar - row way. He lives, He lives, sal-
He lives, He lives,

He Lives

va - tion to im - part! You ask me how I know He lives? He lives within my heart.

Now I Belong to Jesus

258

Norman J. Clayton, b. 1903

Norman J. Clayton, b. 1903

1. Je - sus my Lord will love me for-ev - er, From Him no pow'r of e - vil can
2. Once I was lost in sin's deg-ra-da-tion, Je - sus came down to bring me sal-
3. Joy floods my soul for Jesus has saved me, Freed me from sin that long had en-

sev - er, He gave His life to ran - som my soul, Now I be-long to Him;
va - tion, Lift - ed me up from sor-row and shame, Now I be-long to Him;
slaved me, His pre-cious blood He gave to re-deem, Now I be-long to Him;

REFRAIN

Now I be - long to Je - sus, Je - sus be - longs to me,

Not for the years of time a - lone, But for e - ter - ni - ty.

Copyright, 1943, by Norman J. Clayton in "Word of Life Melodies, No. 1." Used by permission

259 And Can It Be That I Should Gain?

SAGINA

Charles Wesley, 1707-1788

Thomas Campbell, 1777-1844

1. And can it be that I should gain An in - terest in the
2. 'Tis mys-tery all! Th' Im-mor - tal dies! Who can ex - plore His
3. He left His Fa - ther's throne a - bove, So free, so in - fi-
4. Long my im-pris - oned spir - it lay Fast bound in sin and
5. No con-dem - na - tion now I dread; Je - sus, and all in

Sav - iour's blood? Died He for me, who caused His pain? For me, who
strange de - sign? In vain the first-born ser - aph tries To sound the
nite His grace; Emp-tied Him - self of all but love, And bled for
na - ture's night; Thine eye dif - fused a quick'ning ray, I woke, the
Him, is mine! A - live in Him, my liv - ing Head, And clothed in

Him to death pur-sued? A - maz - ing love! how can it be That
depths of love Di - vine! 'Tis mer - cy all! let earth a - dore, Let
A - dam's help-less race; 'Tis mer - cy all, im - mense and free; For,
dun-geon flamed with light; My chains fell off, my heart was free; I
right-eous-ness Di - vine, Bold I ap-proach th' e - ter - nal throne, And

REFRAIN

Thou, my God, shouldst die for me?
an - gel minds in - quire no more.
O my God, it found out me.   A - maz - ing love! how
rose, went forth, and fol - lowed Thee.
claim the crown, thro' Christ my own.   A - maz-ing love!

And Can It Be That I Should Gain?

can it be   That Thou, my   God, shouldst die for   me.   A-MEN.
How can it be   That Thou, my God, shouldst die for   me.

He Lifted Me   260

Charles H. Gabriel, 1856-1932   Charles H. Gabriel, 1856-1932

1. In lov - ing kind - ness Je - sus came My soul in mer - cy to re - claim,
2. He called me long be - fore I heard, Be - fore my sin - ful heart was stirred,
3. His brow was pierced with many a thorn, His hands by cru - el nails were torn,
4. Now on a high - er plane I dwell, And with my soul I know 'tis well;

And from the depths of sin and shame Thro' grace He lift - ed me.
But when I took Him at His word, For - giv'n He lift - ed me.
When from my guilt and grief, for - lorn, In love He lift - ed me.
Yet how or why, I can - not tell, He should have lift - ed me.

(He lift-ed me.)

REFRAIN

From sink-ing sand He lift - ed me, With ten - der hand He lift - ed me,

From shades of night to plains of light, Oh, praise His name, He lift - ed me!

261 ## Wonderful Grace of Jesus

Haldor Lillenas, b. 1885

Haldor Lillenas, b. 1885

1. Won-der-ful grace of Je-sus, Great-er than all my sin;
2. Won-der-ful grace of Je-sus, Reach-ing to all the lost,
3. Won-der-ful grace of Je-sus, Reach-ing the most de-filed,

How shall my tongue de-scribe it, Where shall its praise be-gin?
By it I have been par-doned, Saved to the ut-er-most;
By its trans-form-ing pow-er, Mak-ing him God's dear child,

Tak-ing a-way my bur-den, Set-ting my spir-it free;
Chains have been torn a-sun-der, Giv-ing me lib-er-ty;
Pur-chas-ing peace and heav-en, For all e-ter-ni-ty;

For the won-der-ful grace of Je-sus reach-es me.
For the won-der-ful grace of Je-sus reach-es me.
And the won-der-ful grace of Je-sus reach-es me.

REFRAIN

the match-less grace of Je-sus,

Won-der-ful the matchless grace of Je - - - sus, Deep-er than the

Wonderful Grace of Jesus

the roll - ing sea; Won - - - der - ful
might - y roll - ing sea; High - er than the moun - tain,

grace, all - suf - fi - - - cient for
spar - kling like a foun - tain, All - suf - fi - cient grace for e - ven

me, for e - ven me, Broad - er than the scope of my trans-
me, trans-

gres - sions, Great - er far than all my sin and shame;
gres - sions, sing it! my sin and shame;

O mag - ni - fy the pre - cious name of Je - sus, Praise His name!

262   I've Found a Friend

James G. Small, 1817-1888   George C. Stebbins, 1846-1945

1. I've found a Friend, oh, such a Friend! He loved me ere I knew Him;
2. I've found a Friend, oh, such a Friend! He bled, He died to save me;
3. I've found a Friend, oh, such a Friend! All power to Him is giv - en,
4. I've found a Friend, oh, such a Friend! So kind, and true, and ten - der,

He drew me with the cords of love, And thus He bound me to Him.
And not a - lone the gift of life, But His own self He gave me.
To guard me on my on-ward course, And bring me safe to heav - en.
So wise a Coun - sel - lor and Guide, So might - y a De - fend - er!

And round my heart still close - ly twine Those ties which naught can sev - er,
Naught that I have my own I call, I hold it for the Giv - er;
Th' e - ter - nal glo - ries gleam a - far, To nerve my faint en - deav - or;
From Him who loves me now so well, What power my soul can sev - er?

For I am His, and He is mine, For - ev - er and for - ev - er.
My heart, my strength, my life, my all, Are His, and His for - ev - er.
So now to watch, to work, to war, And then to rest for - ev - er.
Shall life or death, or earth or hell? No; I am His for - ev - er.

Joy in Serving Jesus

Oswald J. Smith, b. 1890

Bentley D. Ackley, b. 1872

1. There is joy in serv-ing Je-sus, As I jour-ney on my way,
2. There is joy in serv-ing Je-sus, Joy that tri-umphs o-ver pain;
3. There is joy in serv-ing Je-sus, As I walk a-lone with God;
4. There is joy in serv-ing Je-sus, Joy a-mid the dark-est night,

Joy that fills the heart with prais-es, Ev-ery hour and ev-ery day.
Fills my soul with heav-en's mu-sic, Till I join the glad re-frain.
'Tis the joy of Christ, my Sav-iour, Who the path of suf-fering trod.
For I've learned the won-drous se-cret, And I'm walk-ing in the light.

REFRAIN

There is joy, joy, Joy in serv-ing Je-sus, Joy that throbs with-

in my heart; Ev-ery mo-ment, ev-ery hour, As I draw up-

on His power, There is joy, joy, Joy that nev-er shall de-part.

My Saviour's Love

Charles H. Gabriel, 1856-1932

Charles H. Gabriel, 1856-1932

1. I stand a - mazed in the pres - ence Of Je - sus the Naz - a - rene,
2. For me it was in the gar - den He prayed: "Not My will, but Thine;"
3. He took my sins and my sor - rows, He made them His ver - y own;
4. When with the ran-somed in glo - ry His face I at last shall see,

And won - der how He could love me, A sin - ner, con-demned, un - clean.
He had no tears for His own griefs, But sweat-drops of blood for mine.
He bore the bur - den to Cal - vary, And suf-fered, and died a - lone.
'Twill be my joy through the a - ges To sing of His love for me.

REFRAIN

How mar-vel-ous! how won - der-ful! And my song shall ev - er be:
Oh, how mar-vel-ous! oh, how won - der-ful!

How mar-vel-ous! how won - der-ful Is my Sav-iour's love for me!
Oh, how mar-vel-ous! oh, how won - der-ful

Since Jesus Came Into My Heart

Rufus H. McDaniel, 1850-1940   Charles H. Gabriel, 1856-1932

1. What a won-der-ful change in my life has been wrought Since Je-sus came
2. I have ceased from my wandering and go-ing a-stray, Since Je-sus came
3. There's a light in the val-ley of death now for me, Since Je-sus came
4. I shall go there to dwell in that Cit-y, I know, Since Je-sus came

in-to my heart! I have light in my soul for which long I have sought,
in-to my heart! And my sins, which were man-y, are all washed a-way,
in-to my heart! And the gates of the Cit-y be-yond I can see,
in-to my heart! And I'm hap-py, so hap-py, as on-ward I go,

Since Je-sus came in-to my heart!

REFRAIN

Since Je-sus came in-to my
Since Je-sus came in, came

heart, Since Je-sus came in-to my heart, Floods of joy o'er my
in-to my heart, Since Je-sus came in, came in-to my heart,

soul like the sea bil-lows roll, Since Je-sus came in-to my heart.

266
My Redeemer

Philip P. Bliss, 1838-1876

James McGranahan, 1840-1907

1. I will sing of my Re-deem-er, And His won-drous love to me;
2. I will tell the won-drous sto-ry, How my lost es-tate to save,
3. I will praise my dear Re-deem-er, His tri-um-phant power I'll tell,
4. I will sing of my Re-deem-er, And His heaven-ly love to me;

On the cru-el cross He suf-fered, From the curse to set me free.
In His bound-less love and mer-cy, He the ran-som free-ly gave.
How the vic-to-ry He giv-eth O-ver sin, and death, and hell.
He from death to life hath brought me, Son of God, with Him to be.

REFRAIN

Sing, oh, sing of my Re-deem-er,
of my Re-deem-er, Sing, oh, sing of my Re-deem-er,

With His blood He pur-chased me,
He pur-chased me, With His blood He pur-chased me,

On the cross He sealed my par-don,
He sealed my par-don, On the cross He sealed my par-don,

My Redeemer

Paid the debt, and made me free.
and made me free,
and made me free.

Nothing But the Blood 267

Robert Lowry, 1826-1899

Robert Lowry, 1826-1899

1. What can wash a - way my sin? Noth-ing but the blood of Je - sus;
2. For my par - don this I see— Noth-ing but the blood of Je - sus;
3. Noth - ing can for sin a - tone— Noth-ing but the blood of Je - sus;
4. This is all my hope and peace— Noth-ing but the blood of Je - sus;

What can make me whole a - gain? Noth-ing but the blood of Je - sus.
For my cleans-ing, this my plea— Noth-ing but the blood of Je - sus.
Naught of good that I have done— Noth-ing but the blood of Je - sus.
This is all my right- eous- ness— Noth-ing but the blood of Je - sus.

REFRAIN

Oh! pre - cious is the flow That makes me white as snow;

No oth - er fount I know, Noth-ing but the blood of Je - sus.

268 I Am His, and He Is Mine

George Wade Robinson, 1838-1877   James Mountain, 1843-1933

1. Loved with ev - er - last - ing love, Led by grace that love to know;
2. Heav'n a - bove is soft - er blue, Earth a - round is sweet-er green!
3. Things that once were wild a - larms Can-not now dis-turb my rest;
4. His for - ev - er, on - ly His; Who the Lord and me shall part?

Spir - it, breath-ing from a - bove, Thou hast taught me it is so!
Some-thing lives in ev - ery hue Christ-less eyes have nev - er seen:
Closed in ev - er - last - ing arms, Pil - lowed on the lov - ing breast.
Ah, with what a rest of bliss Christ can fill the lov - ing heart!

Oh, this full and per - fect peace! Oh, this trans - port all di - vine!
Birds with glad - der songs o'er - flow, Flow'rs with deep - er beau-ties shine,
Oh, to lie for - ev - er here, Doubt, and care, and self re - sign,
Heav'n and earth may fade and flee, First-born light in gloom de - cline;

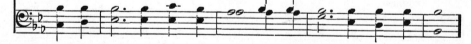

In a love which can - not cease, I am His, and He is mine.
Since I know, as now I know, I am His, and He is mine.
While He whis - pers in my ear, I am His, and He is mine.
But while God and I shall be, I am His, and He is mine.

My Sins Are Blotted Out, I Know! 269

Merrill Dunlop, b. 1905

Merrill Dunlop, b. 1905

1. What a won-drous mes-sage in God's Word! My sins are blot-ted
2. Once my heart was black but now, what joy, My sins are blot-ted
3. I shall stand some day be-fore my King, My sins all blot-ted

out, I know! If I trust in His re-deem-ing blood, My
out, I know! I have peace that noth-ing can de-stroy, My
out, I know! With the ran-somed host I then shall sing: "My

REFRAIN

sins are blot-ted out, I know!
sins are blot-ted out, I know! My sins are blot-ted out, I know!
sins are blot-ted out, I know!" I know!

My sins are blot-ted out, I know! They are bur-ied in the
I know!

depths of the deep-est sea; My sins are blot-ted out, I know!
I know!

270 Beulah Land

Edgar P. Stites, 1836-1921

John R. Sweney, 1837-1899

1. I've reached the land of corn and wine, And all its rich - es free - ly mine;
2. My Sav-iour comes and walks with me, And sweet com-mun-ion here have we;
3. A sweet per-fume up - on the breeze Is borne from ev - er - ver-nal trees,
4. The zeph-yrs seem to float to me Sweet sounds of Heaven's mel - o - dy,

Here shines un-dimmed one blissful day, For all my night has passed a-way.
He gen - tly leads me by His hand, For this is Heav-en's bor - der-land.
And flow'rs, that nev-er - fad - ing grow, Where streams of life for - ev - er flow.
As an-gels with the white-robed throng Join in the sweet Re - demp-tion song.

REFRAIN

O Beu - lah Land, sweet Beu-lah Land, As on thy high - est mount I stand,

I look a - way a - cross the sea, Where mansions are pre-pared for me,

And view the shin - ing glo - ry-shore, My Heav'n, my home for - ev - er-more!

Only a Sinner

James M. Gray, 1851-1935

Daniel B. Towner, 1850-1919

1. Naught have I got-ten but what I re-ceived; Grace hath be-stowed it since
2. Once I was fool-ish, and sin ruled my heart, Caus-ing my foot-steps from
3. Tears un-a-vail-ing, no mer-it had I; Mer-cy had saved me, or
4. Suf-fer a sin-ner whose heart o-ver-flows, Lov-ing his Sav-iour to

I have be-lieved; Boast-ing ex-clud-ed, pride I a-base; I'm
God to de-part; Je-sus hath found me, hap-py my case; I
else I must die; Sin had a-larmed me, fear-ing God's face; But
tell what he knows; Once more to tell it would I em-brace—I'm

REFRAIN

on-ly a sin-ner saved by grace!
now am a sin-ner saved by grace! On-ly a sin-ner saved by grace!
now I'm a sin-ner saved by grace!
on-ly a sin-ner saved by grace!

On-ly a sin-ner saved by grace! This is my sto-ry, to

God be the glo-ry—I'm on-ly a sin-ner saved by grace!

272 Oh, How I Love Jesus

Frederick Whitfield, 1829-1904

Traditional Melody

1. There is a name I love to hear, I love to sing its worth; It sounds like
2. It tells me of a Sav-iour's love, Who died to set me free; It tells me
3. It tells me what my Fa-ther hath In store for ev-ery day, And though I
4. It tells of One whose lov-ing heart Can feel my deep-est woe, Who in each

mu-sic in mine ear, The sweetest name on earth.
of His pre-cious blood, The sin-ner's per-fect plea. Oh, how I love Je - sus,
tread a darksome path, Yields sunshine all the way.
sor-row bears a part, That none can bear be - low.

REFRAIN

Oh, how I love Je - sus, Oh, how I love Je - sus, Be-cause He first loved me!

273 There's a Wideness in God's Mercy

WELLESLEY

Frederick W. Faber, 1814-1863

Lizzie S. Tourjée, 1858-1913

1. There's a wide-ness in God's mer-cy, Like the wide - ness of the sea;
2. There is wel-come for the sin-ner, And more grac - es for the good;
3. For the love of God is broad-er Than the meas - ure of man's mind;
4. If our love were but more sim-ple, We should take Him at His word,

There's a Wideness in God's Mercy

There's a kind - ness in His jus - tice, Which is more than lib - er - ty.
There is mer - cy with the Sav - iour; There is heal - ing in His blood.
And the heart of the E - ter - nal Is most won - der - ful - ly kind.
And our lives would be all sun-shine In the sweet-ness of our Lord. A-MEN.

Take the Name of Jesus with You — 274

Lydia Baxter, 1809-1874

William H. Doane, 1832-1915

1. Take the name of Je - sus with you, Child of sor - row and of woe;
2. Take the name of Je - sus ev - er, As a shield from ev - ery snare;
3. Oh, the pre-cious name of Je - sus! How it thrills our souls with joy,
4. At the name of Je - sus bow - ing, Fall - ing pros-trate at His feet,

It will joy and com - fort give you, Take it, then, wher-e'er you go.
If temp - ta - tions 'round you gath - er, Breathe that ho - ly name in prayer.
When His lov - ing arms re-ceive us, And His songs our tongues employ.
King of kings in heav'n we'll crown Him, When our jour - ney is com-plete.

REFRAIN

Pre-cious name, oh, how sweet! Hope of earth and joy of heaven;
Precious name, oh, how sweet!

Pre-cious name, oh, how sweet! Hope of earth and joy of heaven.
Precious name, oh, how sweet, how sweet!

275 In Tenderness He Sought Me

W. Spencer Walton, 19th Century

Adoniram J. Gordon, 1836-1895

1. In ten - der - ness He sought me, Wea - ry and sick with sin,
2. He washed the bleed-ing sin-wounds, And poured in oil and wine;
3. He point - ed to the nail - prints, For me His blood was shed,
4. I'm sit - ting in His pres - ence, The sun - shine of His face,
5. So while the hours are pass - ing, All now is per - fect rest;

And on His shoul-ders brought me Back to His fold a - gain. While
He whis-pered to as - sure me, "I've found thee, thou art Mine;" I
A mock - ing crown so thorn - y Was placed up - on His head: I
While with a - dor - ing won - der His bless - ings I re - trace. It
I'm wait - ing for the morn - ing, The bright - est and the best, When

an - gels in His pres-ence sang Un - til the courts of heav - en rang.
nev - er heard a sweet-er voice; It made my ach - ing heart re - joice!
won-dered what He saw in me, To suf - fer such deep ag - o - ny.
seems as if e - ter - nal days Are far too short to sound His praise.
He will call us to His side, To be with Him, His spot - less bride.

REFRAIN

Oh, the love that sought me! Oh, the blood that bought me! Oh, the grace that

brought me to the fold, Won-drous grace that brought me to the fold!

In My Heart There Rings a Melody

Elton M. Roth, 1891-1951

Elton M. Roth, 1891-1951

1. I have a song that Je - sus gave me, It was sent from
2. I love the Christ who died on Cal - vary, For He washed my
3. 'Twill be my end - less theme in glo - ry, With the an - gels

heaven a - bove; There nev - er was a sweet - er mel - o - dy, 'Tis a
sins a - way; He put with - in my heart a mel - o - dy, And I
I will sing; 'Twill be a song with glo - rious har - mo - ny, When the

REFRAIN

mel - o - dy of love.
know it's there to stay. In my heart there rings a mel - o - dy, There
courts of heav - en ring.

rings a mel - o - dy with heav - en's har - mo - ny; In my heart there

rings a mel - o - dy; There rings a mel - o - dy of love.

277 Jesus Is All the World to Me

Will L. Thompson, 1847-1909   Will L. Thompson, 1847-1909

1. Je - sus is all the world to me, My life, my joy, my all;
2. Je - sus is all the world to me, My Friend in tri - als sore;
3. Je - sus is all the world to me, And true to Him I'll be;
4. Je - sus is all the world to me, I want no bet - ter friend;

He is my strength from day to day, With-out Him I would fall.
I go to Him for bless-ings, and He gives them o'er and o'er.
Oh, how could I this Friend de - ny, When He's so true to me?
I trust Him now, I'll trust Him when Life's fleet-ing days shall end.

When I am sad to Him I go, No oth - er one can cheer me so;
He sends the sun-shine and the rain, He sends the har-vest's gold - en grain;
Fol - low-ing Him I know I'm right, He watch-es o'er me day and night;
Beau-ti - ful life with such a Friend; Beau-ti - ful life that has no end;

When I am sad He makes me glad, He's my Friend.
Sun - shine and rain, har - vest of grain, He's my Friend.
Fol - low-ing Him, by day and night, He's my Friend.
E - ter - nal life, e - ter - nal joy, He's my Friend.

A Shelter in the Time of Storm

Vernon J. Charlesworth, b. 1839
Arr. by Ira D. Sankey, 1840-1908

Ira D. Sankey, 1840-1908

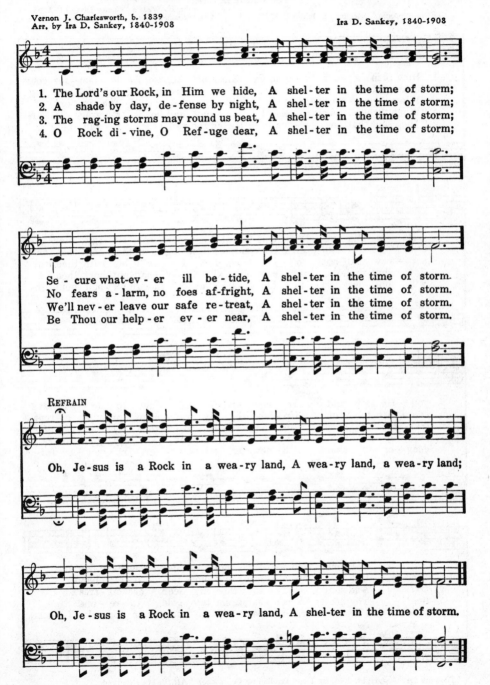

1. The Lord's our Rock, in Him we hide, A shel-ter in the time of storm;
2. A shade by day, de-fense by night, A shel-ter in the time of storm;
3. The rag-ing storms may round us beat, A shel-ter in the time of storm;
4. O Rock di-vine, O Ref-uge dear, A shel-ter in the time of storm;

Se-cure what-ev-er ill be-tide, A shel-ter in the time of storm.
No fears a-larm, no foes af-fright, A shel-ter in the time of storm.
We'll nev-er leave our safe re-treat, A shel-ter in the time of storm.
Be Thou our help-er ev-er near, A shel-ter in the time of storm.

REFRAIN

Oh, Je-sus is a Rock in a wea-ry land, A wea-ry land, a wea-ry land;

Oh, Je-sus is a Rock in a wea-ry land, A shel-ter in the time of storm.

How Firm a Foundation

PORTUGUESE HYMN

John F. Wade's "Cantus Diversi," 1751

"K" in Rippon's "Selection of Hymns," 1787

Descant (small notes), William Lester, b. 1889

1. How firm a foun - da - tion, ye saints of the Lord, Is laid for your
2. "Fear not, I am with thee, O be not dis - mayed, For I am thy
3. "When through the deep waters I call thee to go, The riv - ers of
4. "When through fi - ery tri - als thy path - way shall lie, My grace all - suf -
5. "The soul that on Je - sus hath leaned for re - pose, I will not, I

faith in His ex - cel - lent Word! What more can He say than to
God, I will still give thee aid; I'll strength - en thee, help thee, and
sor - row shall not o - ver - flow, For I will be with thee, thy
fi - cient shall be thy sup - ply; The flame shall not hurt thee; I
will not de - sert to his foes; That soul, though all hell should en -

you He hath said, To you who for ref - uge to Je - sus have
cause thee to stand, Up - held by My gra - cious, om - nip - o - tent
tri - als to bless, And sanc - ti - fy to thee thy deep - est dis -
on - ly de - sign Thy dross to con - sume, and thy gold to re -
deav - or to shake, I'll nev - er, no nev - er, no nev - er for -

fled? To you who for ref - uge to Je - sus have fled?
hand, Up - held by My gra - cious, om - nip - o - tent hand.
tress, And sanc - ti - fy to thee thy deep - est dis - tress.
fine, Thy dross to con - sume, and thy gold to re - fine.
sake! I'll nev - er, no nev - er, no nev - er for - sake!" A-MEN.

For alternate Descant to same tune, see No. 36

How Firm a Foundation

279

(*Second Tune*) FOUNDATION
Words on opposite page

Early American Melody

1. How firm a foun-da-tion, ye saints of the Lord, Is laid for your faith in His

D. S. To you who for ref-uge to

ex - cel-lent Word! What more can He say than to you He hath said,

Je - sus have fled?

Walk in the Light!

280

MANOAH

Bernard Barton, 1784-1849

From Henry W. Greatorex's "Collection," 1851

1. Walk in the light! so shalt thou know That fel - low-ship of love
2. Walk in the light! and thou shalt find Thy heart made tru - ly His,
3. Walk in the light! and thou shalt own Thy dark-ness passed a - way,
4. Walk in the light! and e'en the tomb No fear - ful shade shall wear;
5. Walk in the light! thy path shall be A path, though thorn-y, bright;

His Spir - it on - ly can be - stow Who reigns in light a - bove.
Who dwells in cloud-less light enshrined, In whom no dark-ness is.
Be - cause that light hath on thee shone In which is per - fect day.
Glo - ry shall chase a - way its gloom, For Christ hath conquered there.
For God, by grace, shall dwell in thee, And God Him-self is light. A-MEN.

281 He Leadeth Me

Joseph H. Gilmore, 1834-1918

William B. Bradbury, 1816-1868

1. He lead-eth me, O bless-ed thought! O words with heavenly com-fort fraught!
2. Sometimes 'mid scenes of deep-est gloom, Sometimes where Eden's bowers bloom,
3. Lord, I would clasp Thy hand in mine, Nor ev-er mur-mur nor re-pine;
4. And when my task on earth is done, When, by Thy grace, the vic-tory's won,

What-e'er I do, wher-e'er I be, Still 'tis God's hand that lead-eth me.
By wa-ters still, o'er troub-led sea, Still 'tis His hand that lead-eth me.
Con-tent, what-ev-er lot I see, Since 'tis my God that lead-eth me.
E'en death's cold wave I will not flee, Since God through Jor-dan lead-eth me.

REFRAIN

{ He lead-eth me, He lead-eth me! By His own hand He lead-eth me!
His faithful follower I would be, For by His hand He (*Omit*....) lead-eth me.

282 I Am Trusting Thee, Lord Jesus

BULLINGER

Frances R. Havergal, 1836-1879

Ethelbert W. Bullinger, 1837-1913

1. I am trust-ing Thee, Lord Je-sus, Trust-ing on-ly Thee;
2. I am trust-ing Thee to guide me; Thou a-lone shalt lead,
3. I am trust-ing Thee for pow-er: Thine can nev-er fail;
4. I am trust-ing Thee, Lord Je-sus; Nev-er let me fall;

I Am Trusting Thee, Lord Jesus

Trust - ing Thee for full sal - va - tion, Great and free.
Ev - ery day and hour sup - ply - ing All my need.
Words which Thou Thy - self shalt give me Must pre - vail.
I am trust - ing Thee for - ev - er, And for all. A-MEN.

It Is Well with My Soul

283

Horatio G. Spafford, 1828-1888

Philip P. Bliss, 1838-1876

1. When peace, like a riv - er, at - tend-eth my way, When sor-rows like
2. Though Sa - tan should buf - fet, tho' tri - als should come, Let this blest as-
3. My sin— oh, the bliss of this glo - ri-ous thought, My sin— not in
4. And, Lord, haste the day when the faith shall be sight, The clouds be rolled

sea - bil-lows roll; What-ev - er my lot, Thou hast taught me to say,
sur - ance con-trol, That Christ has re-gard - ed my help - less es - tate,
part, but the whole, Is nailed to the cross and I bear it no more,
back as a scroll, The trump shall re-sound and the Lord shall de-scend,

REFRAIN

"It is well, it is well with my soul." It is well with my
And hath shed His own blood for my soul.
Praise the Lord, praise the Lord, O my soul!
"E - ven so"— it is well with my soul. It is well

soul, It is well, it is well with my soul.
with my soul,

284 I Belong to the King

Ida L. Reed, b. 1865

Maurice A. Clifton, 20th Century
Arr. by Donald P. Hustad, b. 1918

1. I be-long to the King, I'm a child of His love, I shall dwell in His
2. I be-long to the King, and He loves me, I know, For His mer-cy and
3. I be-long to the King, and His prom-ise is sure, That we all shall be

pal - ace so fair; For He tells of its bliss in yon heav-en a-bove, And His
kindness, so free, Are un-ceas-ing - ly mine, where-so-ev - er I go, And my
gathered at last In His king-dom a - bove, by life's wa-ters so pure, When this

chil - dren in splen - dor shall share.
ref - uge un - fail - ing is He.
life with its tri - als is past.

REFRAIN

I be-long to the King, I'm a child of His love, And He nev - er for-sak-eth His own; He will call me some day to His pal-ace a-bove, I shall dwell by His glo-ri-fied throne.

Wonderful, Wonderful Jesus

Anna B. Russell, 1862-1954

Ernest O. Sellers, 1869-1952

1. There is nev-er a day so drear-y, There is nev-er a
2. There is nev-er a cross so heav-y, There is nev-er a
3. There is nev-er a care or bur-den, There is nev-er a
4. There is nev-er a guilt-y sin-ner, There is nev-er a

night so long (so long), But the soul that is trust-ing Je-sus Will
weight of woe (of woe), But that Je-sus will help to car-ry Be-
grief or loss (or loss), But that Je-sus in love will light-en When
wan-d'ring one (not one), But that God can in mer-cy par-don Thro'

REFRAIN

some-where find a song (a song).
cause He lov-eth so (loves so). Won-der-ful, won-der-ful Je-sus,
car-ried to the cross (the cross).
Je-sus Christ, His Son (His Son).

In the heart He im-plant-eth a song; A song of de-liv-'rance, of

He plant-eth a song,

cour-age, of strength, In the heart He im-plant-eth a song (a song).

My Anchor Holds

W. C. Martin, 19th Century, alt.

Daniel B. Towner, 1850-1919

1. Though the an - gry surg - es roll   On my tem - pest-driv - en   soul,
2. Might - y tides a - bout me sweep, Per - ils lurk with - in the deep,
3. I can feel the an - chor fast   As I meet each sud - den blast,
4. Troub - les al - most 'whelm the soul; Griefs like bil - lows o'er me roll;

I am peace - ful, for I know, Wild - ly though the winds may blow,
An - gry clouds o'er-shade the sky, And the tem - pest ris - es high;
And the ca - ble, though un - seen, Bears the heav - y strain be - tween;
Tempters seek to lure a - stray; Storms ob-scure the light of day:

I've an an - chor safe and sure, That can ev - er - more en - dure.
Still I stand the tem-pest's shock, For my an - chor grips the Rock.
Through the storm I safe - ly ride, Till the turn - ing of the tide.
But in Christ I can be bold, I've an an - chor that shall hold.

REFRAIN

And it holds, my an - chor holds;   Blow your wild - est, then, O
And it holds,   my an - chor holds; Blow your wild - - - est,

gale,   On my bark so small and frail; By His grace I shall not
then, O gale,

My Anchor Holds

fail, For my an - - chor holds, . . my an - chor holds.
For my an - chor holds, it firm - ly holds,

Hiding in Thee 287

William O. Cushing, 1823-1902

Ira D. Sankey, 1840-1908

1. O safe to the Rock that is high - er than I, My soul in its
2. In the calm of the noon-tide, in sor - row's lone hour, In times when temp-
3. How oft in the con-flict, when pressed by the foe, I have fled to my

con - flicts and sor - rows would fly; So sin - ful, so wea - ry, Thine,
ta - tion casts o'er me its power; In the tem - pests of life, on its
Ref - uge and breathed out my woe; How oft - en, when tri - als like

Thine would I be; Thou blest "Rock of A - ges," I'm hid - ing in Thee.
wide, heav-ing sea, Thou blest "Rock of A - ges," I'm hid - ing in Thee.
sea - bil - lows roll, Have I hid - den in Thee, O Thou Rock of my soul.

REFRAIN

Hid-ing in Thee, Hid-ing in Thee, Thou blest "Rock of Ages," I'm hid-ing in Thee.

We Have an Anchor

Priscilla J. Owens, 1829-1907

William J. Kirkpatrick, 1838-1921

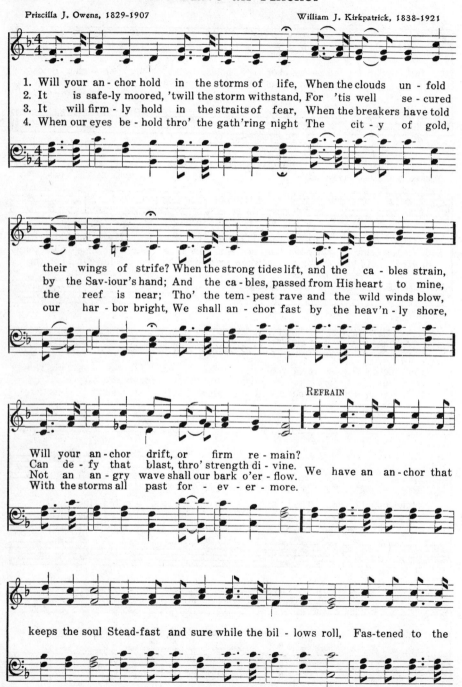

1. Will your an-chor hold in the storms of life, When the clouds un-fold
2. It is safe-ly moored, 'twill the storm withstand, For 'tis well se-cured
3. It will firm-ly hold in the straits of fear, When the breakers have told
4. When our eyes be-hold thro' the gath'ring night The cit-y of gold,

their wings of strife? When the strong tides lift, and the ca-bles strain,
by the Sav-iour's hand; And the ca-bles, passed from His heart to mine,
the reef is near; Tho' the tem-pest rave and the wild winds blow,
our har-bor bright, We shall an-chor fast by the heav'n-ly shore,

REFRAIN

Will your an-chor drift, or firm re-main?
Can de-fy that blast, thro' strength di-vine.
Not an an-gry wave shall our bark o'er-flow.
With the storms all past for-ev-er-more.

We have an an-chor that

keeps the soul Stead-fast and sure while the bil-lows roll, Fas-tened to the

We Have an Anchor

Rock which can-not move, Ground-ed firm and deep in the Sav-iour's love.

'Tis So Sweet to Trust in Jesus 289

Louisa M. R. Stead, 19th Century   William J. Kirkpatrick, 1838-1921

1. 'Tis so sweet to trust in Je-sus, Just to take Him at His word;
2. O how sweet to trust in Je-sus, Just to trust His cleans-ing blood;
3. Yes, 'tis sweet to trust in Je-sus, Just from sin and self to cease;
4. I'm so glad I learned to trust Thee, Pre-cious Je-sus, Sav-iour, Friend;

Just to rest up-on His prom-ise; Just to know, "Thus saith the Lord."
Just in sim-ple faith to plunge me 'Neath the heal-ing, cleans-ing flood!
Just from Je-sus sim-ply tak-ing Life and rest, and joy and peace.
And I know that Thou art with me, Wilt be with me to the end.

REFRAIN

Je-sus, Je-sus, how I trust Him! How I've proved Him o'er and o'er!

Je-sus, Je-sus, pre-cious Je-sus! O for grace to trust Him more!

290 All Things in Jesus

Harry Dixon Loes, b. 1892   Harry Dixon Loes, b. 1892

1. Friends all a-round us are try-ing to find What the heart yearns for, by
2. Some car-ry bur-dens whose weight has for years Crushed them with sorrow and
3. No oth-er name stirs the joy-chords with-in, And thro' none else is re-
4. Je - sus is all this sad world needs to - day; Blind-ly men strive, for sin

sin un-der-mined; I have the se - cret, I know where 'tis found:
blind - ed with tears; Yet One stands read - y to help them just now,
mis - sion of sin; He knows the pain of the heart sore - ly tried,
dark - ens the way. O to draw back the grim cur - tains of night—

REFRAIN

On - ly in Je - sus true pleas-ures a - bound.
If they with faith and in pen - i - tence bow.
All of its needs will in Him be sup - plied.   All that I want is in
One glimpse of Je - sus, and all will be bright!

Je - sus; He sat - is - fies, joy He sup - plies;
Je-sus, in Je - sus, with the free - ly;

Life would be worthless without Him, All things in Je - sus I find.
without Him, without Him,

Copyright, 1915. Renewal, 1943, by H. D. Loes. Assigned to Hope Publishing Co. All Rights Reserved

Be Still, My Soul
FINLANDIA

From Psalm 46
Katharina von Schlegel, b. 1697
Trans. by Jane L. Borthwick, 1813-1897

Jean Sibelius, b. 1865
Arr. for "The Hymnal," 1933

1. Be still, my soul: the Lord is on thy side; Bear pa-tient-ly the cross of grief or pain; Leave to thy God to or-der and pro-vide; In ev-ery change He faith-ful will re-main. Be still, my soul: thy best, thy heav'n-ly Friend Thro' thorn-y ways leads to a joy-ful end.

2. Be still, my soul: thy God doth un-der-take To guide the fu-ture as He has the past. Thy hope, thy con-fi-dence let noth-ing shake; All now mys-te-rious shall be bright at last. Be still, my soul: the waves and winds still know His voice who ruled them while He dwelt be-low.

3. Be still, my soul: the hour is has-t'ning on When we shall be for-ev-er with the Lord, When dis-ap-point-ment, grief, and fear are gone, Sor-row for-got, love's pur-est joys re-stored. Be still, my soul: when change and tears are past, All safe and bless-ed we shall meet at last. A-MEN.

Under His Wings

William O. Cushing, 1823-1902

Ira D. Sankey, 1840-1908

1. Un - der His wings I am safe - ly a - bid - ing; Though the night
2. Un - der His wings, what a ref - uge in sor - row! How the heart
3. Un - der His wings, O what pre - cious en - joy - ment! There will I

deep - ens and tem - pests are wild, Still I can trust Him; I
yearn - ing - ly turns to His rest! Oft - en when earth has no
hide till life's tri - als are o'er; Shel - tered, pro - tect - ed, no

know He will keep me; He has re - deemed me, and I am His child.
balm for my heal - ing, There I find com - fort, and there I am blest.
e - vil can harm me; Rest - ing in Je - sus I'm safe ev - er - more.

REFRAIN

Un - der His wings, un - der His wings, Who from His love can sev - er?

Un - der His wings my soul shall a - bide, Safe - ly a - bide for - ev - er.

The Solid Rock

Edward Mote, 1797-1874

William B. Bradbury, 1816-1868

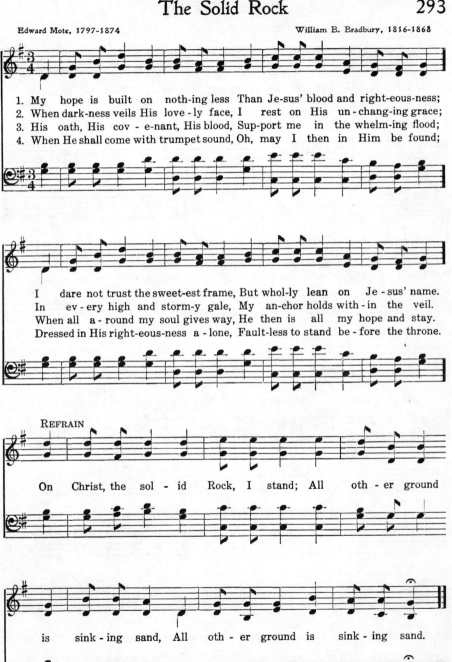

1. My hope is built on noth-ing less Than Je-sus' blood and right-eous-ness;
2. When dark-ness veils His love - ly face, I rest on His un - chang-ing grace;
3. His oath, His cov - e-nant, His blood, Sup-port me in the whelm-ing flood;
4. When He shall come with trumpet sound, Oh, may I then in Him be found;

I dare not trust the sweet-est frame, But whol-ly lean on Je - sus' name.
In ev - ery high and storm-y gale, My an-chor holds with - in the veil.
When all a - round my soul gives way, He then is all my hope and stay.
Dressed in His right-eous-ness a - lone, Fault-less to stand be - fore the throne.

REFRAIN

On Christ, the sol - id Rock, I stand; All oth - er ground

is sink - ing sand, All oth - er ground is sink - ing sand.

Never Give Up

Fanny J. Crosby, 1820-1915

I. Allan Sankey, 1874-1915

1. Nev-er be sad or de-spond-ing, If thou hast faith to be-lieve;
2. What if thy bur-dens op-press thee; What though thy life may be drear;
3. Nev-er be sad or de-spond-ing, There is a mor-row for thee;
4. Nev-er be sad or de-spond-ing, Lean on the arm of thy Lord;

Grace, for the du-ties be-fore thee, Ask of thy God and re-ceive.
Look on the side that is bright-est, Pray, and thy path will be clear.
Soon thou shalt dwell in its bright-ness, There with the Lord thou shalt be.
Dwell in the depths of His mer-cy, Thou shalt re-ceive thy re-ward.

REFRAIN

Nev - - er give up, Nev - - er give up,
Nev-er give up, nev-er give up, Nev-er give up, nev-er give up,

Nev-er give up to thy sor-rows, Je-sus will bid them de-part;

Trust in the Lord, Trust in the Lord,
Trust in the Lord, trust in the Lord, Trust in the Lord, trust in the Lord,

Never Give Up

Sing when your tri - als are great - est, Trust in the Lord and take heart.

Fade, Fade, Each Earthly Joy 295
LUNDIE

Jane C. Bonar, 1821-1884   Theodore E. Perkins, b. 1831

1. Fade, fade, each earth - ly joy; Je - sus is mine. Break ev - ery
2. Tempt not my soul a - way; Je - sus is mine. Here would I
3. Fare - well, ye dreams of night; Je - sus is mine. Lost in this
4. Fare - well, mor - tal - i - ty; Je - sus is mine. Wel - come, e-

ten - der tie; Je - sus is mine. Dark is the wil - der - ness,
ev - er stay; Je - sus is mine. Per - ish - ing things of clay,
dawn - ing bright, Je - sus is mine. All that my soul has tried
ter - ni - ty; Je - sus is mine. Wel - come, O loved and blest,

Earth has no rest-ing-place, Je - sus a - lone can bless; Je - sus is mine.
Born but for one brief day, Pass from my heart a - way; Je - sus is mine.
Left but a dis - mal void; Je - sus has sat - is - fied; Je - sus is mine.
Welcome, sweet scenes of rest, Wel - come, my Saviour's breast; Je - sus is mine.

296 In Heavenly Love Abiding

SEASONS

Anna L. Waring, 1820-1910

Felix Mendelssohn, 1809-1847
Arr. by Donald P. Hustad, b. 1918

1. In heaven-ly love a-bid-ing, No change my heart shall fear;
2. Wher-ev-er He may guide me, No want shall turn me back;
3. Green pas-tures are be-fore me, Which yet I have not seen;

And safe is such con-fid-ing, For noth-ing chang-es here.
My Shep-herd is be-side me, And noth-ing can I lack.
Bright skies will soon be o'er me, Where dark-est clouds have been.

The storm may roar with-out me, My heart may low be laid,
His wis-dom ev-er wak-eth, His sight is nev-er dim;
My hope I can-not meas-ure, My path to life is free;

But God is round a-bout me—And can I be dis-mayed?
He knows the way He tak-eth, And I will walk with Him.
My Sav-iour has my treas-ure, And He will walk with me. A-MEN.

Trust and Obey

John H. Sammis, 1846-1919

Daniel B. Towner, 1850-1919

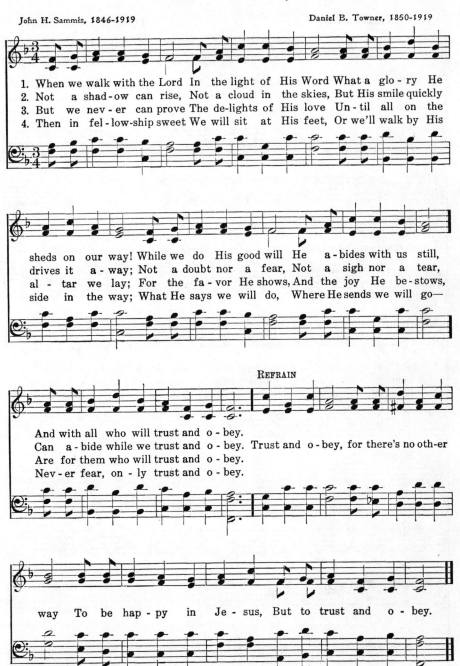

1. When we walk with the Lord In the light of His Word What a glo-ry He
2. Not a shad-ow can rise, Not a cloud in the skies, But His smile quickly
3. But we nev-er can prove The de-lights of His love Un-til all on the
4. Then in fel-low-ship sweet We will sit at His feet, Or we'll walk by His

sheds on our way! While we do His good will He a-bides with us still,
drives it a-way; Not a doubt nor a fear, Not a sigh nor a tear,
al-tar we lay; For the fa-vor He shows, And the joy He be-stows,
side in the way; What He says we will do, Where He sends we will go—

REFRAIN

And with all who will trust and o-bey.
Can a-bide while we trust and o-bey. Trust and o-bey, for there's no oth-er
Are for them who will trust and o-bey.
Nev-er fear, on-ly trust and o-bey.

way To be hap-py in Je-sus, But to trust and o-bey.

298 Anywhere with Jesus

Jessie B. Pounds, 1861-1921   Daniel B. Towner, 1850-1919

1. An - y-where with Je - sus I can safe - ly go; An - y-where He
2. An - y-where with Je - sus I am not a - lone; Oth - er friends may
3. An - y-where with Je - sus I can go to sleep, When the darkening

leads me in this world be - low; An - y-where with-out Him dear - est
fail me, He is still my own; Though His hand may lead me o - ver
shad-ows round a - bout me creep; Know-ing I shall wak - en nev - er

joys would fade; An - y-where with Je - sus I am not a - fraid.
drear - y ways, An - y-where with Je - sus is a house of praise.
more to roam, An - y-where with Je - sus will be home, sweet home.

REFRAIN

An - y - where! an - y - where! Fear I can - not know;

An - y - where with Je - sus I can safe - ly go.

He Hideth My Soul

Fanny J. Crosby, 1820-1915

William J. Kirkpatrick, 1838-1921

1. A won-der-ful Sav-iour is Je-sus my Lord, A won-der-ful
2. A won-der-ful Sav-iour is Je-sus my Lord, He tak-eth my
3. With num-ber-less bless-ings each mo-ment He crowns, And, filled with His
4. When clothed in His bright-ness, trans-port-ed I rise To meet Him in

Sav-iour to me; He hid-eth my soul in the cleft of the rock, Where
bur-den a-way; He hold-eth me up, and I shall not be moved, He
full-ness di-vine, I sing in my rap-ture, oh, glo-ry to God For
clouds of the sky, His per-fect sal-va-tion, His won-der-ful love, I'll

REFRAIN

riv-ers of pleas-ure I see.
giv-eth me strength as my day. He hid-eth my soul in the cleft of the rock
such a Re-deem-er as mine!
shout with the millions on high.

That shadows a dry, thirst-y land; He hid-eth my life in the depths of His love,

And cov-ers me there with His hand, And cov-ers me there with His hand.

300 Precious Promise

Nathaniel Niles, b. 1835   Philip P. Bliss, 1838-1876

1. Pre - cious prom-ise God hath giv - en To the wea-ry pass - er - by,
2. When temp-ta - tions al - most win thee, And thy trust-ed watch-ers fly,
3. When thy se - cret hopes have perished In the grave of years gone by,
4. When the shades of life are fall-ing, And the hour has come to die,

On the way from earth to heav-en, "I will guide thee with Mine eye."
Let this prom-ise ring with-in thee, "I will guide thee with Mine eye."
Let this prom-ise still be cher-ished, "I will guide thee with Mine eye."
Hear the trust-y Pi - lot call-ing, "I will guide thee with Mine eye."

REFRAIN

I will guide thee, I will guide thee, I will guide thee with Mine eye;

On the way from earth to heav-en, I will guide thee with Mine eye.

Trusting Jesus

Edgar P. Stites, 1836-1921

Ira D. Sankey, 1840-1908

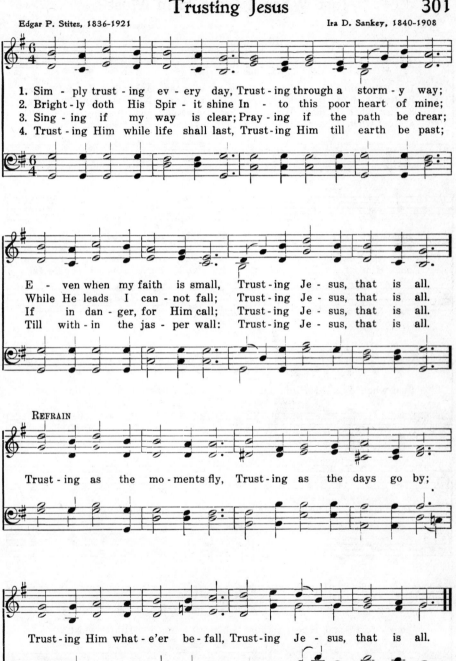

1. Sim - ply trust - ing ev - ery day, Trust - ing through a storm - y way;
2. Bright - ly doth His Spir - it shine In - to this poor heart of mine;
3. Sing - ing if my way is clear; Pray - ing if the path be drear;
4. Trust - ing Him while life shall last, Trust - ing Him till earth be past;

E - ven when my faith is small, Trust - ing Je - sus, that is all.
While He leads I can - not fall; Trust - ing Je - sus, that is all.
If in dan - ger, for Him call; Trust - ing Je - sus, that is all.
Till with - in the jas - per wall: Trust - ing Je - sus, that is all.

REFRAIN

Trust - ing as the mo - ments fly, Trust - ing as the days go by;

Trust - ing Him what - e'er be - fall, Trust - ing Je - sus, that is all.

302 Just When I Need Him Most

William C. Poole, 1875-1949

Charles H. Gabriel, 1856-1932

1. Just when I need Him, Je-sus is near, Just when I fal-ter,
2. Just when I need Him, Je-sus is true, Nev-er for-sak-ing
3. Just when I need Him, Je-sus is strong, Bear-ing my bur-dens
4. Just when I need Him, He is my all, An-swer-ing when up-

just when I fear; Read-y to help me, read-y to cheer,
all the way through; Giv-ing for bur-dens pleas-ures a-new,
all the day long; For all my sor-row giv-ing a song,
on Him I call; Ten-der-ly watch-ing lest I should fall,

REFRAIN

Just when I need Him most. Just when I need Him most,

Just when I need Him most; Je-sus is near to

com-fort and cheer, Just when I need Him most.

Blessed Assurance

Fanny J. Crosby, 1820-1915

Phoebe P. Knapp, 1839-1908

1. Bless-ed as-sur-ance, Je-sus is mine! Oh, what a fore-taste of
2. Per-fect sub-mis-sion, per-fect de-light, Vi-sions of rap-ture now
3. Per-fect sub-mis-sion, all is at rest, I in my Sav-iour am

glo-ry di-vine! Heir of sal-va-tion, pur-chase of God,
burst on my sight; An-gels de-scend-ing, bring from a-bove
hap-py and blest; Watch-ing and wait-ing, look-ing a-bove,

Born of His Spir-it, washed in His blood.
Ech-oes of mer-cy, whis-pers of love.
Filled with His goodness, lost in His love.

REFRAIN

This is my sto-ry, this is my

song, Prais-ing my Sav-iour all the day long; This is my sto-ry,

this is my song, Prais-ing my Sav-iour all the day long.

304 If Thou But Suffer God to Guide Thee

NEUMARK (Bremen)

Georg Neumark, 1621-1681
Trans. by Catherine Winkworth, 1829-1878

Chorale by Georg Neumark, 1621-1681
Arr. with Descant by William Lester, b. 1889

DESCANT

CHORALE

1. If thou but suf - fer God to guide thee, And hope in Him through all thy ways,

1. If thou but suf - fer God to guide thee, And hope in Him through all thy ways,
2. Be pa-tient and a - wait His leis-ure In cheer-ful hope, with heart con-tent,
3. He knows the time for joy, and, tru-ly, Will send it when He sees it meet;

He'll give thee strength, whate'er be-tide thee, And bear thee thro' the e-vil days;

He'll give thee strength, whate'er betide thee, And bear thee through the e - vil days;
To take what-e'er Thy Fa-ther's pleas-ure And His dis-cern-ing love hath sent;
When He has tried and purged thee du - ly And finds thee free from all de-ceit.

Who trusts in God's unchanging love Builds on the rock that naught can move. A - MEN.

Who trusts in God's un-chang-ing love Builds on the rock that naught can move.
Nor doubt our in - most wants are known To Him who chose us for His own.
He comes to thee all un - a-ware And makes thee own His loving care. A - MEN.

All the Way My Saviour Leads Me   305

Fanny J. Crosby, 1820-1915   Robert Lowry, 1826-1899

1. All the way my Sav-iour leads me; What have I to ask be-side?
2. All the way my Sav-iour leads me, Cheers each wind-ing path I tread,
3. All the way my Sav-iour leads me; Oh, the full-ness of His love!

Can I doubt His ten-der mer-cy, Who through life has been my Guide?
Gives me grace for ev-ery tri-al, Feeds me with the liv-ing bread.
Per-fect rest to me is prom-ised In my Fa-ther's house a-bove.

Heaven-ly peace, di-vin-est com-fort, Here by faith in Him to dwell!
Though my wea-ry steps may fal-ter, And my soul a-thirst may be,
When my spir-it, clothed im-mor-tal, Wings its flight to realms of day,

For I know, what-e'er be-fall me, Je-sus do-eth all things well; well.
Gush-ing from the Rock be-fore me, Lo! a spring of joy I see; see.
This my song through endless a-ges: Je-sus led me all the way; way.

306 Is My Name Written There?

Mary A. Kidder, 1820-1905   Frank M. Davis, 1839-1896

1. Lord, I care not for rich-es, Nei-ther sil-ver nor gold; I would
2. Lord, my sins they are man-y, Like the sands of the sea, But Thy
3. Oh! that beau-ti-ful cit-y, With its man-sions of light, With its

make sure of heav-en, I would en-ter the fold. In the book of Thy
blood, O my Sav-iour, Is suf-fi-cient for me; For Thy prom-ise is
glo-ri-fied be-ings, In pure gar-ments of white; Where no e-vil thing

king-dom, With its pa-ges so fair, Tell me, Je-sus, my Sav-iour, Is my
writ-ten, In bright let-ters that glow, "Tho' your sins be as scar-let, I will
com-eth To de-spoil what is fair; Where the an-gels are watch-ing, Yes, my

REFRAIN

name writ-ten there?
make them like snow." Is my name writ-ten there, On the page white and fair?
name's writ-ten there. (3) Yes, my name's, etc.

In the book of Thy king-dom, Is my name writ-ten there?
(3) Yes, my name's writ-ten there.

Jesus Is a Friend of Mine

307

John H. Sammis, 1846-1919

Daniel B. Towner, 1850-1919

1. Why should I charge my soul with care? The wealth in ev - ery mine
2. The gold - en sun, the sil - ver moon, And all the stars that shine,
3. He dai - ly spreads a boun-teous feast, And at His ta - ble dine
4. And when He comes in bright ar - ray, And leads the con-quering line,

Be - longs to Christ, God's Son and Heir, And He's a Friend of mine.
Are His a - lone, yes, ev - ery one, And He's a Friend of mine.
The whole cre - a - tion, man and beast, And He's a Friend of mine.
It will be glo - ry then to say, That He's a Friend of mine.

REFRAIN

Yes, He's a Friend of mine, And He with me doth all things share;

Since all is Christ's and Christ is mine, Why should I have a

care? For Je - sus is a Friend of mine.

308 Faith Is the Victory!

John H. Yates, 1837-1900

Ira D. Sankey, 1840-1908

1. En-camped a-long the hills of light, Ye Chris-tian sol-diers, rise, And
2. His ban-ner o-ver us is love, Our sword the Word of God; We
3. On ev-ery hand the foe we find Drawn up in dread ar-ray; Let
4. To him that o-ver-comes the foe, White rai-ment shall be giv'n; Be-

press the bat-tle ere the night Shall veil the glow-ing skies. A-gainst the foe in
tread the road the saints a-bove With shouts of tri-umph trod. By faith they, like a
tents of ease be left be-hind, And on-ward to the fray; Sal-va-tion's helmet
fore the an-gels he shall know His name confessed in heav'n. Then onward from the

vales be-low, Let all our strength be hurled; Faith is the vic-to-ry, we know,
whirlwind's breath, Swept on o'er ev-'ry field; The faith by which they conquered death
on each head, With truth all girt a-bout, The earth shall tremble 'neath our tread,
hills of light, Our hearts with love a-flame, We'll vanquish all the hosts of night,

That o-ver-comes the world.
Is still our shin-ing shield.
And ech-o with our shout.
In Je-sus' conquering name.

REFRAIN

Faith is the vic-to-ry! Faith is the

vic-to-ry! Oh, glo-ri-ous vic-to-ry, That o-ver-comes the world.

A Child of the King

Harriet E. Buell, 1834-1910

John B. Sumner, 1838-1918

1. My Fa - ther is rich in hous - es and lands, He hold - eth the
2. My Fa - ther's own Son, the Sav - iour of men, Once wan - dered on
3. I once was an out - cast stran - ger on earth, A sin - ner by
4. A tent or a cot - tage, why should I care? They're build-ing a

wealth of the world in His hands! Of ru - bies and dia-monds, of
earth as the poor - est of them; But now He is reign-ing for-
choice, and an al - ien by birth; But I've been a - dopt-ed, my
pal - ace for me o - ver there; Tho' ex - iled from home, yet

sil - ver and gold, His cof - fers are full, He has rich - es un - told.
ev - er on high, And will give me a home in heaven by and by.
name's writ-ten down, An heir to a man - sion, a robe, and a crown.
still I may sing: All glo - ry to God, I'm a child of the King.

REFRAIN

I'm a child of the King, A child of the King:

With Je - sus my Sav - iour, I'm a child of the King.

310 He Is Able to Deliver Thee

William A. Ogden, 1841-1897   William A. Ogden, 1841-1897

1. 'Tis the grand-est theme through the a-ges rung; 'Tis the grand-est theme for a
2. 'Tis the grand-est theme in the earth or main; 'Tis the grand-est theme for a
3. 'Tis the grand-est theme, let the ti-dings roll To the guilt-y heart, to the

mor-tal tongue; 'Tis the grand-est theme that the world e'er sung, "Our God is
mor-tal strain; 'Tis the grand-est theme, tell the world a-gain, "Our God is
sin-ful soul; Look to God in faith, He will make thee whole; "Our God is

REFRAIN

a-ble to de-liv-er thee." He is a - - - ble to de-liv-er thee,
a-ble, He is a-ble

He is a - - - ble to de-liv-er thee; Though by sin op-pressed,
a-ble, He is a-ble

Go to Him for rest; "Our God is a-ble to de-liv-er thee."

In the Garden

C. Austin Miles, 1868-1946   C. Austin Miles, 1868-1946

1. I come to the gar-den a-lone, While the dew is still on the
2. He speaks, and the sound of His voice Is so sweet the birds hush their
3. I'd stay in the gar-den with Him Though the night a-round me be

ros-es; And the voice I hear, fall-ing on my ear; The
sing-ing, And the mel-o-dy that He gave to me, With-
fall-ing, But He bids me go; through the voice of woe, His

REFRAIN

Son of God dis-clos-es.
in my heart is ring-ing. And He walks with me, and He
voice to me is call-ing.

talks with me, And He tells me I am His own, And the

joy we share as we tar-ry there, None oth-er has ev-er known.

312 My Jesus, as Thou Wilt

Benjamin Schmolck, 1672-1737   **JEWETT**   Carl M. von Weber, 1786-1826
Trans. by Jane L. Borthwick, 1813-1897   Arr. by Joseph P. Holbrook, 1822-1888

1. My Je - sus, as Thou wilt: O may Thy will be mine! In-to Thy hand of love
2. My Je - sus, as Thou wilt: Tho' seen thro' man-y'a tear, Let not my star of hope
3. My Je - sus, as Thou wilt: All shall be well for me; Each changing future scene

I would my all re - sign. Through sor-row or thro' joy, Con-duct me
Grow dim or dis-ap - pear. Since Thou on earth hast wept And sor-rowed
I glad-ly trust with Thee. Straight to my home a - bove I trav-el

as Thine own, And help me still to say, "My Lord, Thy will be done."
oft a - lone, If I must weep with Thee, "My Lord, Thy will be done."
calm-ly on, And sing in life or death, "My Lord, Thy will be done." A-MEN.

313 My Gracious Lord, I Own Thy Right

QUEBEC (Hesperus)

Philip Doddridge, 1702-1751   Henry Baker, 1835-1910

1. My gra-cious Lord, I own Thy right To ev - er-y ser-vice I can pay,
2. What is my be - ing but for Thee, Its sure sup-port, its no-blest end?
3. I would not breathe for world-ly joy, Or to in-crease my world-ly good;
4. 'Tis to my Sav-iour I would live, To Him who for my ran-som died;
5. His work my hoar - y age shall bless, When youthful vig-our is no more;

My Gracious Lord, I Own Thy Right

And call it my supreme de-light To hear Thy dic-tates, and o-bey.
Thy ev-er-smil-ing face to see, And serve the cause of such a Friend.
Nor future days or powers em-ploy To spread a sound-ing name a-broad.
Nor could un-taint-ed E-den give Such bliss as blos-soms at His side.
And my last hour of life con-fess His love hath an-i-mat-ing power. A-MEN.

Channels Only

314

Mary E. Maxwell, 20th Century

Ada Rose Gibbs, 20th Century

1. How I praise Thee, pre-cious Sav-iour, That Thy love laid hold of me;
2. Emp-tied that Thou should-est fill me, A clean ves-sel in Thy hand;
3. Wit-ness-ing Thy pow'r to save me, Set-ting free from self and sin;
4. Je-sus, fill now with Thy Spir-it Hearts that full sur-ren-der know;

Thou hast saved and cleansed and filled me That I might Thy chan-nel be.
With no pow'r but as Thou giv-est Gra-cious-ly with each com-mand.
Thou who bought-est to pos-sess me, In Thy full-ness, Lord, come in.
That the streams of liv-ing wa-ter From our in-ner man may flow.

REFRAIN

Chan-nels on-ly, bless-ed Mas-ter, But with all Thy won-drous pow'r

Flow-ing thro' us, Thou canst use us Ev-'ry day and ev-'ry hour.

Nothing Between

Charles A. Tindley, 1851-1933

Charles A. Tindley, 1851-1933
Arr. by F. A. Clark, 19th Century

1. Noth-ing be-tween my soul and the Sav-iour, Naught of this world's de-
2. Noth-ing be-tween, like world - ly pleas-ure, Hab-its of life though
3. Noth-ing be-tween, like pride or sta-tion, Self or friends shall
4. Noth-ing be-tween, e'en man-y hard tri-als, Tho' the whole world a-

lu - sive dream; I have re-nounced all sin - ful pleas-ure,
harm-less they seem, Must not my heart from Him e'er sev - er,
not in - ter - vene, Tho' it may cost me much trib - u - la - tion,
gainst me con - vene; Watching with prayer and much self - de - ni - al, I'll

REFRAIN

Je - sus is mine; there's noth-ing be-tween.
He is my all; there's noth-ing be-tween.
I am re - solved; there's noth-ing be-tween. Noth-ing be-tween my
tri - umph at last, with noth-ing be-tween.

soul and the Sav-iour, So that His bless - ed face may be seen; Noth-ing pre-

vent-ing the least of His fa-vor, Keep the way clear! Let noth-ing be-tween.

I Surrender All

Judson W. Van DeVenter, 1855-1939

Winfield S. Weeden, 1847-1908
Arr. by Donald P. Hustad, b. 1918

1. All to Je-sus I sur-ren-der, All to Him I free-ly give;
2. All to Je-sus I sur-ren-der, Hum-bly at His feet I bow,
3. All to Je-sus I sur-ren-der, Make me, Sav-iour, whol-ly Thine;
4. All to Je-sus I sur-ren-der, Lord, I give my-self to Thee;

I will ev-er love and trust Him, In His pres-ence dai-ly live.
World-ly pleas-ures all for-sak-en, Take me, Je-sus, take me now.
Let me feel the Ho-ly Spir-it, Tru-ly know that Thou art mine.
Fill me with Thy love and pow-er, Let Thy bless-ing fall on me.

REFRAIN

I sur-ren-der all, I sur-ren-der all.
I sur-ren-der all, I sur-ren-der all.

All to Thee, my bless-ed Sav-iour, I sur-ren-der all.

317 O for a Heart to Praise My God

AZMON

Charles Wesley, 1707-1788

Carl G. Glaser, 1784-1829
Arr. by Lowell Mason, 1792-1872

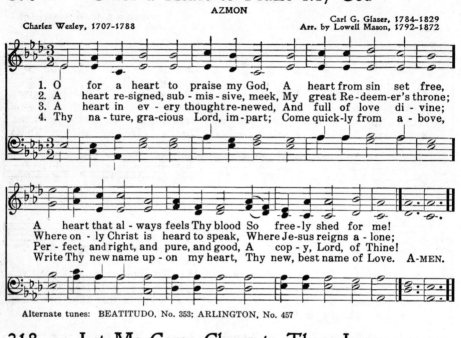

1. O for a heart to praise my God, A heart from sin set free,
2. A heart re-signed, sub-mis-sive, meek, My great Re-deem-er's throne;
3. A heart in ev-ery thought re-newed, And full of love di-vine;
4. Thy na-ture, gra-cious Lord, im-part; Come quick-ly from a-bove,

A heart that al-ways feels Thy blood So free-ly shed for me!
Where on-ly Christ is heard to speak, Where Je-sus reigns a-lone;
Per-fect, and right, and pure, and good, A cop-y, Lord, of Thine!
Write Thy new name up-on my heart, Thy new, best name of Love. A-MEN.

Alternate tunes: BEATITUDO, No. 353; ARLINGTON, No. 457

318 Let Me Come Closer to Thee, Jesus

LLANTHONY ABBEY

J. L. Lyne, 19th Century

John H. Lester, 19th Century

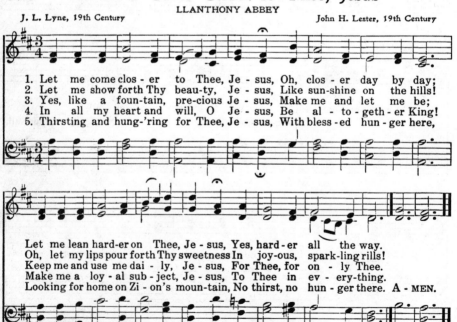

1. Let me come clos-er to Thee, Je-sus, Oh, clos-er day by day;
2. Let me show forth Thy beau-ty, Je-sus, Like sun-shine on the hills!
3. Yes, like a foun-tain, pre-cious Je-sus, Make me and let me be;
4. In all my heart and will, O Je-sus, Be al-to-geth-er King!
5. Thirsting and hung-'ring for Thee, Je-sus, With bless-ed hun-ger here,

Let me lean hard-er on Thee, Je-sus, Yes, hard-er all the way.
Oh, let my lips pour forth Thy sweetness In joy-ous, spark-ling rills!
Keep me and use me dai-ly, Je-sus, For Thee, for on-ly Thee.
Make me a loy-al sub-ject, Je-sus, To Thee in ev-ery-thing.
Looking for home on Zi-on's moun-tain, No thirst, no hun-ger there. A-MEN.

Draw Me Nearer

Fanny J. Crosby, 1820-1915

William H. Doane, 1832-1915

1. I am Thine, O Lord, I have heard Thy voice, And it
2. Con - se - crate me now to Thy serv - ice, Lord, By the
3. Oh, the pure de - light of a sin - gle hour That be -
4. There are depths of love that I can - not know Till I

told Thy love to me; But I long to rise in the arms of faith,
power of grace di - vine; Let my soul look up with a stead-fast hope,
fore Thy throne I spend, When I kneel in prayer, and with Thee, my God,
cross the nar - row sea; There are heights of joy that I may not reach

REFRAIN

And be clos - er drawn to Thee.
And my will be lost in Thine. Draw me near - er,
I com - mune as friend with friend!
Till I rest in peace with Thee. near - er, near - er,

near - er, bless - ed Lord, To the cross where Thou hast died; Draw me

near - er, near - er, near - er, bless - ed Lord, To Thy pre - cious, bleed-ing side.

320 A Charge to Keep I Have

BOYLSTON

Charles Wesley, 1707-1788

Lowell Mason, 1792-1872

1. A charge to keep I have, A God to glo - ri - fy, A
2. To serve the pres - ent age, My call - ing to ful - fill; O
3. Arm me with jeal - ous care, As in Thy sight to live, And
4. Help me to watch and pray And on Thy - self re - ly, And

nev - er - dy - ing soul to save, And fit it for the sky.
may it all my powers en - gage, To do my Mas - ter's will!
O Thy serv - ant, Lord, pre - pare, A strict ac - count to give!
let me ne'er my trust be - tray, But press to realms on high. A - MEN.

321 Nearer, My God, to Thee

BETHANY

Sarah F. Adams, 1805-1848

Lowell Mason, 1792-1872

1. Near - er, my God, to Thee, Near - er to Thee! E'en though it
2. Though like the wan - der - er, The sun gone down, Dark - ness be
3. There let the way ap - pear Steps un - to heaven; All that Thou
4. Then, with my wak - ing thoughts Bright with Thy praise, Out of my
5. Or if on joy - ful wing, Cleav - ing the sky, Sun, moon, and

be a cross That rais - eth me; Still all my song shall be, Near - er, my
o - ver me, My rest a stone; Yet in my dreams I'd be Near - er, my
send - est me In mer - cy given; An - gels to beck - on me Near - er, my
ston - y griefs, Beth - el I'll raise; So by my woes to be Near - er, my
stars for - got, Up - ward I fly, Still all my song shall be, Near - er, my

Nearer, My God, to Thee

God, to Thee, Near-er, my God, to Thee, Near-er to Thee. A-MEN.

Beneath the Cross of Jesus 322

ST. CHRISTOPHER

Elizabeth C. Clephane, 1830-1869

Frederick C. Maker, 1844-1927

1. Be - neath the cross of Je - sus I fain would take my stand—
2. Up - on that cross of Je - sus Mine eye at times can see
3. I take, O cross, thy shad - ow For my a - bid - ing - place;

The shad - ow of a might - y Rock With - in a wea - ry land;
The ver - y dy - ing form of One Who suf - fered there for me;
I ask no oth - er sun - shine than The sun - shine of His face;

A home with - in the wil - der - ness, A rest up - on the way,
And from my smit - ten heart with tears Two won - ders I con - fess—
Con - tent to let the world go by, To know no gain nor loss,

From the burn-ing of the noon-tide heat, And the bur-den of the day.
The won - ders of re-deem-ing love And my un - wor - thi-ness.
My sin - ful self my on - ly shame, My glo - ry all the cross. A-MEN.

323 O Love That Wilt Not Let Me Go

ST. MARGARET

George Matheson, 1842-1906

Albert L. Peace, 1844-1912

1. O Love that wilt not let me go,
2. O Light that fol-lowest all my way,
3. O Joy that seek-est me through pain,
4. O Cross that lift-est up my head,

I rest my wea-ry
I yield my flick-ering
I can-not close my
I dare not ask to

soul in Thee; I give Thee back the life I owe, That
torch to Thee; My heart re-stores its bor-rowed ray, That
heart to Thee; I trace the rain-bow through the rain, And
fly from Thee; I lay in dust life's glo-ry dead, And

in Thine o-cean depths its flow May rich-er, full-er be.
in Thy sun-shine's blaze its day May bright-er, fair-er be.
feel the prom-ise is not vain That morn shall tear-less be.
from the ground there blossoms red Life that shall end-less be. A-MEN.

By permission of Novello & Co., Ltd.

324 Lord Jesus, Think on Me

SOUTHWELL

Synesius of Cyrene, c.375-430
Trans. by Allen W. Chatfield, 1808-1896

From "Damon's Psalms," 1579

1. Lord Je-sus, think on me, And purge a-way my sin;
2. Lord Je-sus, think on me, With care and woe op-pressed;
3. Lord Je-sus, think on me, Nor let me go a-stray;
4. Lord Je-sus, think on me, That, when the flood is past,

Lord Jesus, Think on Me

From earth-born pas-sions set me free, And make me pure with - in.
Let me Thy lov - ing serv-ant be, And taste Thy prom-ised rest.
Through darkness and per-plex - i - ty Point Thou the heav'n-ly way.
I may th'e - ter - nal bright-ness see, And share Thy joy at last. A-MEN.

Take Time to Be Holy 325

LONGSTAFF

William D. Longstaff, 1822-1894   George C. Stebbins, 1846-1945

1. Take time to be ho - ly, Speak oft with thy Lord; A - bide in Him
2. Take time to be ho - ly, The world rush-es on; Much time spend in
3. Take time to be ho - ly, Let Him be thy Guide, And run not be-
4. Take time to be ho - ly, Be calm in thy soul; Each thought and each

al - ways, And feed on His Word. Make friends of God's children; Help those who are
se - cret With Je - sus a - lone; By look-ing to Je - sus, Like Him thou shalt
fore Him, What-ev-er be - tide; In joy or in sor - row, Still fol - low thy
mo - tive Be-neath His con-trol; Thus led by His Spir - it To foun-tains of

weak; For - get-ting in noth - ing His bless-ing to seek.
be; Thy friends in thy con - duct His like-ness shall see.
Lord, And, look - ing to Je - sus, Still trust in His Word.
love, Thou soon shalt be fit - ted For serv-ice a - bove. A-MEN.

326 Make Me a Captive, Lord

PARADOXY

George Matheson, 1842-1906

Donald P. Hustad, b. 1918

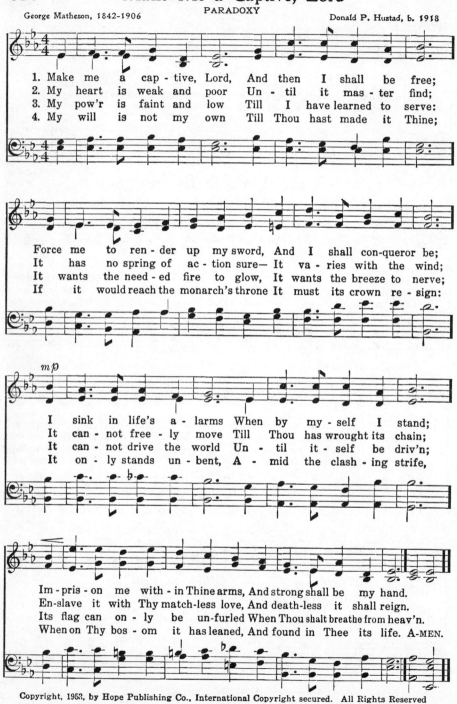

1. Make me a cap-tive, Lord, And then I shall be free;
2. My heart is weak and poor Un-til it mas-ter find;
3. My pow'r is faint and low Till I have learned to serve:
4. My will is not my own Till Thou hast made it Thine;

Force me to ren-der up my sword, And I shall con-quer-or be;
It has no spring of ac-tion sure— It va-ries with the wind;
It wants the need-ed fire to glow, It wants the breeze to nerve;
If it would reach the monarch's throne It must its crown re-sign:

mp

I sink in life's a-larms When by my-self I stand;
It can-not free-ly move Till Thou has wrought its chain;
It can-not drive the world Un-til it-self be driv'n;
It on-ly stands un-bent, A-mid the clash-ing strife,

Im-pris-on me with-in Thine arms, And strong shall be my hand.
En-slave it with Thy match-less love, And death-less it shall reign.
Its flag can on-ly be un-furled When Thou shalt breathe from heav'n.
When on Thy bos-om it has leaned, And found in Thee its life. A-MEN.

Fill All My Vision

Avis B. Christiansen, b. 1895

Homer Hammontree, b. 1884

1. Fill all my vi - sion, Sav - iour, I pray, Let me see on - ly
2. Fill all my vi - sion, ev - ery de - sire Keep for Thy glo - ry;
3. Fill all my vi - sion, let naught of sin Shad - ow the bright - ness

Je - sus to - day; Though thro' the val - ley Thou lead - est me,
my soul in - spire With Thy per - fec - tion, Thy ho - ly love
shin - ing with - in. Let me see on - ly Thy bless - ed face,

REFRAIN

Thy fade - less glo - ry en - com - pass - eth me. Fill all my vi - sion,
Flood - ing my path - way with light from a - bove.
Feast - ing my soul on Thy in - fi - nite grace.

Sav - iour di - vine, Till with Thy glo - ry my spir - it shall shine. Fill all my

vi - sion, that all may see Thy ho - ly Im - age re - flect - ed in me.

Copyright, 1940, by Homer Hammontree. Used by permission

328 Jesus, Thy Boundless Love to Me

Paul Gerhardt, 1607-1676
Trans. by John Wesley, 1703-1791

ST. CATHERINE

Henri F. Hemy, 1818-1888
Alt. by James G. Walton, 1821-1905

1. Je - sus, thy boundless love to me No thought can reach, no tongue de-clare;
2. O, grant that noth-ing in my soul May dwell, but Thy pure love a - lone;
3. O Love, how cheer-ing is Thy ray! All pain be-fore Thy pres-ence flies;
4. Still let Thy love point out my way; What wondrous things Thy love hath wrought!
5. In suf-f'ring, be Thy love my peace; In weak-ness, be Thy love my power;

O, knit my thank-ful heart to Thee, And reign with-out a ri - val there:
O, may Thy love pos - sess me whole, My joy, my treas-ure, and my crown.
Care, an-guish, sor - row, melt a-way, Wher-e'er Thy heal-ing beams a - rise.
Still lead me, lest I go a-stray; Di - rect my work, in - spire my thought;
And when the storms of life shall cease, Je - sus, in that e - vent-ful hour,

Thine whol-ly, Thine a-lone, I am; Be Thou a-lone my con-stant Flame.
Strange fires far from my soul re-move; May ev - ery act, word, thought be love.
O Je-sus, noth-ing may I see, Noth-ing de-sire, or seek, but Thee!
And if I fall, soon may I hear Thy voice, and know that love is near.
In death, as life, be Guide and Friend, That I may love Thee with-out end. A - MEN.

329 O for a Faith That Will Not Shrink

EVAN

William H. Bathurst, 1796-1877

William H. Havergal, 1793-1870

1. O for a faith that will not shrink Though pressed by man - y a foe,
2. That will not mur - mur nor com-plain Be - neath the chast'ning rod,
3. A faith that shines more bright and clear When tem-pests rage with - out,
4. Lord, give me such a faith as this, And then, what-e'er may come,

Alternate tune: ARLINGTON, No. 457

O for a Faith That Will Not Shrink

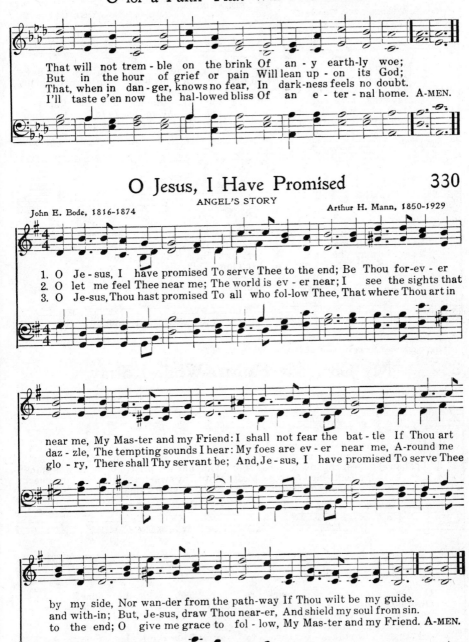

That will not trem - ble on the brink Of an - y earth-ly woe;
But in the hour of grief or pain Will lean up - on its God;
That, when in dan - ger, knows no fear, In dark-ness feels no doubt.
I'll taste e'en now the hal-lowed bliss Of an e - ter - nal home. A-MEN.

O Jesus, I Have Promised 330

ANGEL'S STORY

John E. Bode, 1816-1874

Arthur H. Mann, 1850-1929

1. O Je - sus, I have promised To serve Thee to the end; Be Thou for-ev - er
2. O let me feel Thee near me; The world is ev - er near; I see the sights that
3. O Je-sus, Thou hast promised To all who fol-low Thee, That where Thou art in

near me, My Mas - ter and my Friend: I shall not fear the bat - tle If Thou art
daz - zle, The tempting sounds I hear: My foes are ev - er near me, A-round me
glo - ry, There shall Thy servant be; And, Je - sus, I have promised To serve Thee

by my side, Nor wan-der from the path-way If Thou wilt be my guide.
and with-in; But, Je-sus, draw Thou near-er, And shield my soul from sin.
to the end; O give me grace to fol - low, My Mas-ter and my Friend. A-MEN.

Music used by permission of E. R. Goodliffe

331 May the Mind of Christ, My Saviour
ST. LEONARDS

Kate B. Wilkinson, 20th Century   A. Cyril Barham-Gould, 1891-1953

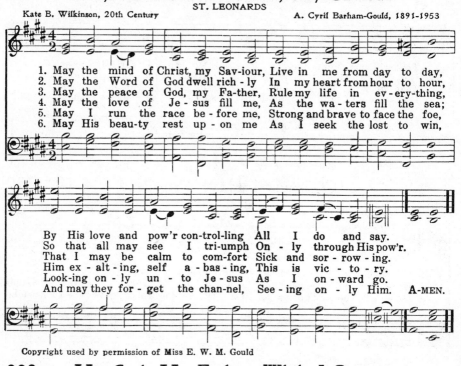

1. May the mind of Christ, my Sav-iour, Live in me from day to day,
2. May the Word of God dwell rich-ly In my heart from hour to hour,
3. May the peace of God, my Fa-ther, Rule my life in ev-ery-thing,
4. May the love of Je-sus fill me, As the wa-ters fill the sea;
5. May I run the race be-fore me, Strong and brave to face the foe,
6. May His beau-ty rest up-on me As I seek the lost to win,

By His love and pow'r con-trol-ling All I do and say.
So that all may see I tri-umph On-ly through His pow'r.
That I may be calm to com-fort Sick and sor-row-ing.
Him ex-alt-ing, self a-bas-ing, This is vic-to-ry.
Look-ing on-ly un-to Je-sus As I on-ward go.
And may they for-get the chan-nel, See-ing on-ly Him. A-MEN.

Copyright used by permission of Miss E. W. M. Gould

332 My God, My Father, While I Stray
HANFORD

Charlotte Elliott, 1789-1871, alt.   Arthur S. Sullivan, 1842-1900

1. My God, my Fa-ther, while I stray Far from my home in life's rough way,
2. Though dark my path, and sad my lot, Let me be still and mur-mur not,
3. If Thou should'st call me to re-sign What most I prize, it ne'er was mine;
4. Let but my faint-ing heart be blest With Thy sweet Spir-it for its guest,
5. Re-new my will from day to day, Blend it with Thine, and take a-way

O teach me from my heart to say, "Thy will be done!"
Or breathe the prayer di-vine-ly taught, "Thy will be done!"
I on-ly yield Thee what is Thine; "Thy will be done!"
My God, to Thee I leave the rest; "Thy will be done!"
All that now makes it hard to say, "Thy will be done!" A-MEN.

More About Jesus

Eliza E. Hewitt, 1851–1920   John R. Sweney, 1837–1899

1. More a-bout Je - sus would I know, More of His grace to oth - ers show;
2. More a-bout Je - sus let me learn, More of His ho - ly will dis-cern;
3. More a-bout Je - sus; in His Word, Holding com-mun - ion with my Lord;
4. More a-bout Je - sus on His throne, Rich-es in glo - ry all His own;

More of His sav - ing full-ness see, More of His love who died for me.
Spir - it of God, my teach - er be, Show-ing the things of Christ to me.
Hear - ing His voice in ev - ery line, Mak - ing each faith - ful say - ing mine.
More of His kingdom's sure in-crease; More of His com-ing, Prince of Peace.

REFRAIN

More, more a - bout Je - sus, More, more a - bout Je - sus;

More of His sav - ing full - ness see, More of His love who died for me.

334 Saviour, Thy Dying Love

SOMETHING FOR THEE

Sylvanus D. Phelps, 1816-1895

Robert Lowry, 1826-1899
Descant (small notes), William Lester, b. 1889

1. Sav - iour, Thy dy - ing love Thou gav - est me, Nor should I
2. At the blest mer - cy - seat, Plead-ing for me, My fee - ble
3. Give me a faith - ful heart, Like - ness to Thee, That each de -
4. All that I am and have— Thy gifts so free— In joy, in

aught with-hold, Dear Lord, from Thee: In love my soul would bow, My heart ful-
faith looks up, Je - sus, to Thee: Help me the cross to bear, Thy won-drous
part - ing day Henceforth may see Some work of love be - gun, Some deed of
grief, through life, Dear Lord, for Thee! And when Thy face I see, My ran-somed

fill its vow, Some of-fering bring Thee now, Some-thing for Thee.
love de-clare, Some song to raise, or prayer, Some-thing for Thee.
kind-ness done, Some wanderer sought and won, Some-thing for Thee.
soul shall be, Through all e - ter - ni - ty, Some-thing for Thee. A - MEN.

Descant arr. Copyright, 1935, by Hope Publishing Co., owner. All Rights Reserved

335 Take My Life, and Let It Be

HENDON

Frances R. Havergal, 1836-1879

H. A. César Malan, 1787-1864

1. Take my life, and let it be Con - se - crat-ed, Lord, to Thee; Take my hands, and
2. Take my feet, and let them be Swift and beau-ti - ful for Thee; Take my voice, and
3. Take my lips, and let them be Filled with mes-sa-ges for Thee; Take my sil - ver
4. Take my love, my God, I pour At Thy feet its treasure store; Take my-self and

Take My Life, and Let It Be

let them move At the im-pulse of Thy love, At the im-pulse of Thy love.
let me sing Al-ways, on-ly, for my King, Al-ways, on-ly, for my King.
and my gold, Not a mite would I with-hold, Not a mite would I with-hold.
I will be Ev-er, on-ly, all for Thee, Ev-er, on-ly, all for Thee. A-MEN.

My Jesus, I Love Thee   336

GORDON

William R. Featherstone, 1842-1878   Adoniram J. Gordon, 1836-1895

1. My Je - sus, I love Thee, I know Thou art mine; For Thee all the
2. I love Thee, be - cause Thou hast first lov - ed me, And pur-chased my
3. I'll love Thee in life, I will love Thee in death, And praise Thee as
4. In man-sions of glo - ry and end - less de - light, I'll ev - er a-

fol - lies of sin I re-sign; My gra-cious Re - deem - er, my Sav - iour art
par - don on Cal - va - ry's tree; I love Thee for wear-ing the thorns on Thy
long as Thou lend-est me breath; And say when the death-dew lies cold on my
dore Thee in heav-en so bright; I'll sing with the glit - ter-ing crown on my

Thou; If ev - er I loved Thee, my Je - sus, 'tis now.
brow; If ev - er I loved Thee, my Je - sus, 'tis now.
brow, If ev - er I loved Thee, my Je - sus, 'tis now.
brow, If ev - er I loved Thee, my Je - sus, 'tis now. A - MEN.

337 Saviour, More than Life

Fanny J. Crosby, 1820-1915

William H. Doane, 1832-1915

1. Sav-iour, more than life to me, I am cling-ing, cling-ing close to Thee.
2. Thro' this changing world be-low Lead me gen-tly, gen-tly as I go.
3. Let me love Thee more and more Till this fleet-ing, fleet-ing life is o'er;

Let Thy pre-cious blood ap-plied Keep me ev-er, ev-er near Thy side.
Trust-ing Thee, I can-not stray; I can nev-er, nev-er lose my way.
Till my soul is lost in love In a bright-er, bright-er world a-bove.

REFRAIN

Ev-ery day, ev-ery hour, Let me feel Thy cleansing pow'r.
Ev-ery day and hour, ev-ery day and hour,

May Thy ten-der love to me Bind me clos-er, clos-er, Lord, to Thee.

338 Lord, Speak to Me
CANONBURY

Frances R. Havergal, 1836-1879

Robert Schumann, 1810-1856

1. Lord, speak to me, that I may speak In liv-ing ech-oes of Thy tone;
2. O teach me; Lord, that I may teach The pre-cious things Thou dost impart;
3. O fill me with Thy full-ness, Lord, Un-til my ver-y heart o'er-flow
4. O use me, Lord, use e-ven me, Just as Thou wilt, and when, and where;

Alternate tune: HOLLEY, No. 96

Lord, Speak to Me

As Thou hast sought, so let me seek Thy err-ing chil-dren lost and lone.
And wing my words, that they may reach The hid-den depths of many a heart.
In kindling thought and glow-ing word, Thy love to tell, Thy praise to show.
Un - til Thy bless-ed face I see, Thy rest, Thy joy, Thy glo - ry share. AMEN.

Nearer, Still Nearer   339

MORRIS

Lelia N. Morris, 1862-1929   Lelia N. Morris, 1862-1929

1. Near-er, still near-er, close to Thy heart, Draw me, my Sav-iour, so pre-cious Thou
2. Near-er, still near-er, noth-ing I bring, Naught as an of-fering to Je - sus my
3. Near-er, still near-er, Lord, to be Thine, Sin, with its fol - lies, I glad - ly re-
4. Near-er, still near-er, while life shall last, Till safe in glo - ry my an - chor is

art; Fold me, O fold me close to Thy breast, Shel - ter me safe in that
King; On - ly my sin - ful, now con-trite heart, Grant me the cleansing Thy
sign; All of its pleas-ures, pomp and its pride, Give me but Je - sus, my
cast; Through endless a - ges, ev - er to be, Near - er, my Sav-iour, still

"Ha - ven of Rest," Shel-ter me safe in that "Ha - ven of Rest."
blood doth im-part, Grant me the cleansing Thy blood doth im-part.
Lord cru - ci - fied, Give me but Je - sus, my Lord cru - ci - fied.
near - er to Thee, Near-er, my Sav-iour, still near - er to Thee. A-MEN.

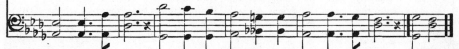

340 I Want a Principle Within

GERALD

Charles Wesley, 1707-1788

Louis Spohr, 1784-1859

1. I want a prin - ci - ple with - in Of watch - ful, god - ly fear,
2. From Thee that I no more may stray, No more Thy good - ness grieve,
3. Al - might - y God of truth and love, To me Thy power im - part;

A sen - si - bil - i - ty of sin, A pain to feel it near.
Grant me the fil - ial awe, I pray, The ten - der con-science give.
The bur - den from my soul re - move, The hard-ness from my heart.

Help me the first ap-proach to feel Of pride or wrong de - sire;
Quick as the ap - ple of an eye, O God, my con-science make!
O may the least o - mis - sion pain My re - a - wak-ened soul,

To catch the wan-dering of my will, And quench the kind-ling fire.
A - wake my soul when sin is nigh, And keep it still a - wake.
And drive me to that grace a - gain, Which makes the wound-ed whole. A-MEN.

Whiter than Snow

James Nicholson, c.1828-1896

William G. Fischer, 1835-1912

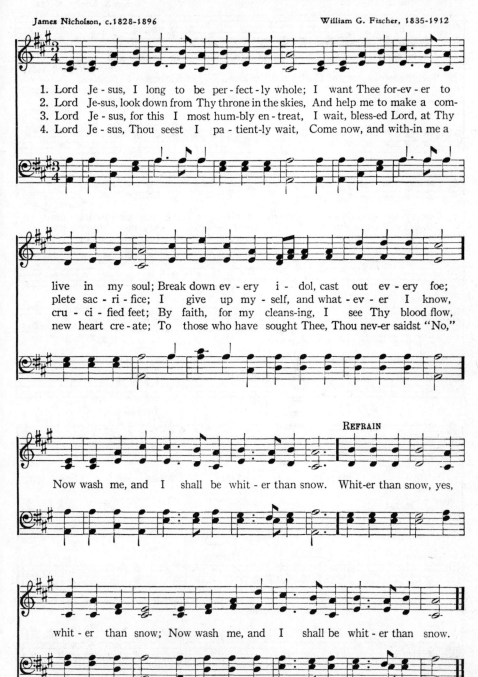

1. Lord Je - sus, I long to be per - fect - ly whole; I want Thee for-ev - er to
2. Lord Je-sus, look down from Thy throne in the skies, And help me to make a com-
3. Lord Je - sus, for this I most hum-bly en - treat, I wait, bless-ed Lord, at Thy
4. Lord Je - sus, Thou seest I pa - tient-ly wait, Come now, and with-in me a

live in my soul; Break down ev - ery i - dol, cast out ev - ery foe;
plete sac - ri - fice; I give up my - self, and what - ev - er I know,
cru - ci - fied feet; By faith, for my cleans-ing, I see Thy blood flow,
new heart cre - ate; To those who have sought Thee, Thou nev-er saidst "No,"

REFRAIN

Now wash me, and I shall be whit - er than snow. Whit-er than snow, yes,

whit - er than snow; Now wash me, and I shall be whit - er than snow.

342 Make Me a Blessing

Ira B. Wilson, 1880-1950

George S. Schuler, b. 1882

1. Out in the highways and byways of life, Man-y are weary and sad;
   are wea-ry and sad;
2. Tell the sweet story of Christ and His love, Tell of His power to forgive;
   His power to for-give;
3. Give as 'twas giv-en to you in your need, Love as the Master loved you;
   the Mas-ter loved you;

Car - ry the sunshine where darkness is rife, Mak - ing the sor-row-ing glad.
Oth-ers will trust Him if on - ly you prove True, ev - ery mo-ment you live.
Be to the help-less a help - er in-deed, Un - to your mis-sion be true.

REFRAIN *Men or Unison*   *Women*

Make me a bless - ing, Make me a bless - ing, Out of my

life may Je - sus shine; Make me a bless - ing,
Out of my life
Men

Women   *Parts*

O Sav - iour, I pray, Make me a bless-ing to some-one to - day.
I pray Thee, my Saviour,
Tenors

All for Jesus

Mary D. James, 19th Century

Source Unknown

1. All for Je-sus, all for Je-sus! All my be-ing's ransomed pow'rs:
2. Let my hands per-form His bid-ding, Let my feet run in His ways;
3. Since my eyes were fixed on Je-sus, I've lost sight of all be-side;
4. Oh, what won-der! how a-maz-ing! Je-sus, glo-rious King of kings,

All my tho'ts and words and do-ings, All my days and all my hours.
Let my eyes see Je-sus on-ly, Let my lips speak forth His praise.
So en-chained my spir-it's vi-sion, Look-ing at the Cru-ci-fied.
Deigns to call me His be-lov-ed, Lets me rest be-neath His wings.

REFRAIN *(omit with second tune)*

All for Je-sus! all for Je-sus! All my days and all my hours; hours.
All for Je-sus! all for Je-sus! Let my lips speak forth His praise; praise.
All for Je-sus! all for Je-sus! Look-ing at the Cru-ci-fied; fied.
All for Je-sus! all for Je-sus! Rest-ing now be-neath His wings; wings.

All for Jesus

(Second Tune)
Without Refrain

WYCLIFF

John Stainer, 1840-1901

1. All for Je-sus! All for Je-sus! All my be-ing's ransomed pow'rs;

All my thoughts and words and do-ings, All my days and all my hours. A-MEN.

344 Jesus Only, Let Me See

Oswald J. Smith, b. 1890

Daniel B. Towner, 1850-1919

1. For sal-va-tion full and free, Purchased once on Cal-va-ry, Christ a-lone shall
2. He's my Guide from day to day, As I jour-ney on life's way; Close be-side Him
3. May my Mod-el ev-er be Christ the Lord, and none save He, That the world may
4. He shall reign from shore to shore; His the glo-ry ev-er-more. Heav'n and earth shall

REFRAIN

be my plea—Je-sus! Je-sus on-ly!
let me stay—Je-sus! Je-sus on-ly!
see in me—Je-sus! Je-sus on-ly!
bow be-fore—Je-sus! Je-sus on-ly!

Je-sus on-ly, let me see, Je-sus

on-ly, none save He, Then my song shall ev-er be— Je-sus! Je-sus on-ly!

345 Take Up Thy Cross

QUEBEC (Hesperus)

Charles W. Everest, 1814-1877

Henry Baker, 1835-1910

1. "Take up thy cross," the Sav-iour said, "If thou wouldst My dis-ci-ple be;
2. Take up thy cross; let not its weight Fill thy weak soul with vain a-larm;
3. Take up thy cross, nor heed the shame, And let thy fool-ish pride be still:
4. Take up thy cross, then, in His strength, And calm-ly ev-ery dan-ger brave;
5. Take up thy cross, and fol-low Christ, Nor think till death to lay it down;

Music copyright by W. Garrett Horder. Used by permission
Alternate tune: GERMANY, No. 465

Take Up Thy Cross

Take up thy cross with willing heart, And humbly fol-low af - ter Me."
His strength shall bear thy spirit up, And brace thy heart and nerve thine arm.
Thy Lord re-fused not e'en to die Up-on a cross on Cal - v'ry's hill.
'Twill guide thee to a bet-ter home, And lead to vic - t'ry o'er the grave.
For on - ly he who bears the cross May hope to wear the glo-rious crown. A-MEN.

Revive Us Again   346

William P. Mackay, 1839-1885

John J. Husband, 1760-1825

1. We praise Thee, O God, for the Son of Thy love, For Je - sus who
2. We praise Thee, O God, for Thy Spir - it of light, Who has shown us our
3. All glo - ry and praise to the Lamb that was slain, Who has borne all our
4. Re - vive us a - gain, fill each heart with Thy love; May each soul be re-

REFRAIN

died and is now gone a - bove.
Sav-iour and scat-tered our night.
sins, and has cleansed ev-ery stain.
kin - dled with fire from a - bove.

Hal - le - lu - jah! Thine the glo - ry, Hal - le-

lu - jah! A - men; Hal - le - lu - jah! Thine the glo - ry; Re - vive us a - gain.

347 Revive Thy Work

Albert Midlane, 1825-1909

James McGranahan, 1840-1907

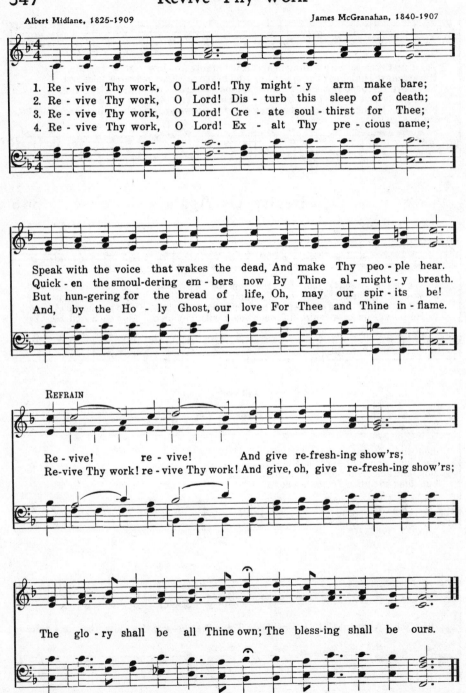

1. Re - vive Thy work, O Lord! Thy might - y arm make bare;
2. Re - vive Thy work, O Lord! Dis - turb this sleep of death;
3. Re - vive Thy work, O Lord! Cre - ate soul - thirst for Thee;
4. Re - vive Thy work, O Lord! Ex - alt Thy pre - cious name;

Speak with the voice that wakes the dead, And make Thy peo - ple hear.
Quick - en the smoul-dering em - bers now By Thine al - might - y breath.
But hun-gering for the bread of life, Oh, may our spir - its be!
And, by the Ho - ly Ghost, our love For Thee and Thine in - flame.

REFRAIN

Re - vive! re - vive! And give re-fresh-ing show'rs;
Re-vive Thy work! re - vive Thy work! And give, oh, give re-fresh-ing show'rs;

The glo - ry shall be all Thine own; The bless-ing shall be ours.

Not I, But Christ

EXALTATION

Mrs. A. A. Whiddington, 19th Century   C. H. Forrest, 19th Century

1. Not I, but Christ, be hon-ored, loved, ex-alt-ed; Not I, but Christ,
2. Not I, but Christ, to gen-tly soothe in sor-row; Not I, but Christ,
3. Not I, but Christ, in low-ly, si-lent la-bor; Not I, but Christ,
4. Christ, on-ly Christ, ere long will fill my vi-sion; Glo-ry ex-cel-

be seen, be known, be heard; Not I, but Christ, in ev-ery look and
to wipe the fall-ing tear; Not I, but Christ, to lift the wea-ry
in hum-ble, ear-nest toil; Christ, on-ly Christ! no show, no os-ten-
ling, soon, full soon, I'll see— Christ, on-ly Christ, my ev-ery wish ful-

ac-tion; Not I, but Christ, in ev-ery thought and word.
bur-den! Not I, but Christ, to hush a-way all fear.
ta-tion! Christ, none but Christ, the gath-erer of the spoil.
fil-ling— Christ, on-ly Christ, my All in all to be.

REFRAIN

Oh, to be saved from my-self, dear Lord, Oh, to be lost in Thee;

Oh, that it may be no more I, But Christ that lives in me. A-MEN.

Refrain may be omitted. In this case, the Amen will follow the fourth verse.

349 Must Jesus Bear the Cross Alone?

MAITLAND

Thomas Shepherd, 1665-1739

George N. Allen, 1812-1877

1. Must Je - sus bear the cross a - lone, And all the world go free?
2. The con - se - crat - ed cross I'll bear, Till death shall set me free,
3. Up - on the crys - tal pave-ment, down At Je - sus' pierc - ed feet,
4. O pre - cious cross! O glo - rious crown! O res - ur - rec - tion day!

No; there's a cross for ev - ery one, And there's a cross for me.
And then go home my crown to wear, For there's a crown for me.
Joy - ful, I'll cast my gold - en crown, And His dear name re - peat.
Ye an - gels, from the stars come down, And bear my soul a - way. A-MEN.

350 I'll Live for Him

Ralph E. Hudson, 1843-1901

C. R. Dunbar, 19th Century

1. My life, my love I give to Thee, Thou Lamb of God who died for me;
2. I now be - lieve Thou dost re - ceive, For Thou hast died that I might live;
3. O Thou who died on Cal - va - ry, To save my soul and make me free,

REF. I'll live for Him who died for me, How hap - py then my life shall be!

D. C. Refrain

Oh, may I ev - er faith - ful be, My Sav - iour and my God!
And now hence-forth I'll trust in Thee, My Sav - iour and my God!
I'll con - se - crate my life to Thee, My Sav - iour and my God!
I'll live for Him who died for me, My Sav - iour and my God!

Love Divine

BEECHER

Charles Wesley, 1707-1788

John Zundel, 1815-1882
Descant (small notes), William Lester, b. 1889

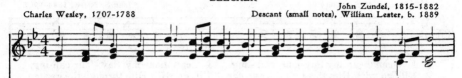

1. Love di - vine, all loves ex - cel - ling, Joy of heaven, to earth come down;
2. Breathe, O breathe Thy lov - ing Spir - it In - to ev - ery troub-led breast!
3. Come, al - might-y to de - liv - er, Let us all Thy life re - ceive;
4. Fin - ish then Thy new cre - a - tion, Pure and spot-less let us be;

Fix in us Thy hum - ble dwell-ing; All Thy faith-ful mer - cies crown.
Let us all in Thee in - her - it, Let us find that sec - ond rest.
Sud - den - ly re - turn, and nev - er, Nev - er - more Thy tem - ples leave:
Let us see Thy great sal - va - tion Per-fect - ly re - stored in Thee:

Je - sus, Thou art all com - pas-sion, Pure, un-bound-ed love Thou art;
Take a - way our bent to sin-ning, Al - pha and O - me - ga be;
Thee we would be al - ways bless-ing, Serve Thee as Thy hosts a - bove,
Changed from glory in - to glo-ry, Till in heaven we take our place,

Vis - it us with Thy sal - va - tion; En - ter ev - ery trem-bling heart.
End of faith, as its be - gin - ning, Set our hearts at lib - er - ty.
Pray, and praise Thee without ceas-ing, Glo-ry in Thy per-fect love.
Till we cast our crowns be - fore Thee, Lost in won-der, love, and praise. A-MEN.

Alternate tune: HYFRYDOL, No. 469

352 Where He Leads Me

E. W. Blandy, 19th Century

John S. Norris, 1844-1907

1. I can hear my Sav-iour call-ing, I can hear my Sav-iour call-ing,
2. I'll go with Him through the gar-den, I'll go with Him through the garden,
3. I'll go with Him through the judgment, I'll go with Him through the judgment,
4. He will give me grace and glo-ry, He will give me grace and glo-ry,

REF.—*Where He leads me I will fol-low, Where He leads me I will fol-low,*

D.C. for Refrain

I can hear my Sav-iour call-ing, "Take thy cross and fol-low, fol-low Me."
I'll go with Him through the garden, I'll go with Him, with Him all the way.
I'll go with Him through the judgment, I'll go with Him, with Him all the way.
He will give me grace and glo-ry, And go with me, with me all the way.

Where He leads me I will fol-low, I'll go with Him, with Him all the way.

353 O for a Closer Walk with God

BEATITUDO

William Cowper, 1731-1800

John B. Dykes, 1823-1876

1. O for a clos-er walk with God, A calm and heaven-ly frame,
2. Re-turn, O ho-ly Dove, re-turn, Sweet mes-sen-ger of rest;
3. The dear-est i-dol I have known, What-e'er that i-dol be,
4. So shall my walk be close with God, Calm and se-rene my frame;

A light to shine up-on the road That leads me to the Lamb.
I hate the sins that made Thee mourn, And drove Thee from my breast.
Help me to tear it from Thy throne, And wor-ship on-ly Thee.
So pur-er light shall mark the road That leads me to the Lamb. A-MEN.

"Are Ye Able," Said the Master 354

BEACON HILL

Earl Marlatt, b. 1892   Harry S. Mason, b. 1881

1. "Are ye a - ble," said the Mas -ter, "To be cru - ci - fied with me?"
2. "Are ye a - ble " to re - mem - ber, When a thief lifts up his eyes,
3. "Are ye a - ble " when the shad-ows Close a - round you with the sod,
4. "Are ye a - ble?" Still the Mas - ter Whis-pers down e - ter - ni - ty,

"Yea," the sturd -y dream-ers an-swered, "To the death we fol - low Thee."
That his par-doned soul is wor - thy Of a place in par - a - dise?
To be - lieve that spir - it tri - umphs, To com-mend your soul to God?
And he - ro - ic spir -its an - swer Now, as then, in Gal - i - lee.

REFRAIN

"Lord, we are a - ble." Our spir - its are Thine. Re - mold them,

make us, Like Thee, di - vine. Thy guid-ing ra-diance A - bove us shall

be A bea - con to God, To love and loy - al - ty. A-MEN.

355 More Like the Master

Charles H. Gabriel, 1856-1932   Charles H. Gabriel, 1856-1932

1. More like the Mas-ter I would ev-er be, More of His meek-ness,
2. More like the Mas-ter is my dai-ly prayer; More strength to car-ry
3. More like the Mas-ter I would live and grow; More of His love to

more hu-mil-i-ty; More zeal to la-bor, more cour-age to be true,
cross-es I must bear; More ear-nest ef-fort to bring His king-dom in;
oth-ers I would show; More self-de-ni-al, like His in Gal-i-lee,

More con-se-cra-tion for work He bids me do. Take Thou my
More of His Spir-it, the wan-der-er to win.
More like the Mas-ter I long to ev-er be.

Refrain

heart, I would be Thine a-lone; Take Thou my heart and
take my heart, I would be Thine a-lone; Take my heart, O take my heart and

make it all Thine own; Purge me from sin, O Lord, I now im-
make it all Thine own; Purge Thou me from ev-'ry sin, O Lord, I

More Like the Master

plore, Wash me and keep me Thine for - ev - er - more.
now im-plore, Wash and keep, O wash and keep me Thine for - ev - er - more.

I Am Resolved 356

Palmer Hartsough, 1844-1932

James H. Fillmore, 1849-1936

1. I am re-solved no long - er to lin - ger, Charmed by the world's de-light;
2. I am re-solved to go to the Sav-iour, Leav - ing my sin and strife;
3. I am re-solved to fol - low the Sav-iour, Faith - ful and true each day;
4. I am re-solved to en - ter the Kingdom, Leav - ing the paths of sin;

Things that are high - er, things that are no - bler, These have al-lured my sight.
He is the true One, He is the just One, He hath the words of life.
Heed what He say - eth, do what He will - eth, He is the liv - ing way.
Friends may op-pose me, foes may be - set me, Still will I en - ter in.

REFRAIN

I will has-ten to Him, Has - ten so glad and free;
I will has-ten,

Has-ten glad and free;

Je - - sus, Great - est, High - est, I will come to Thee.
Je - sus, Je - sus,

Higher Ground

Johnson Oatman, Jr., 1856-1926

Charles H. Gabriel, 1856-1932

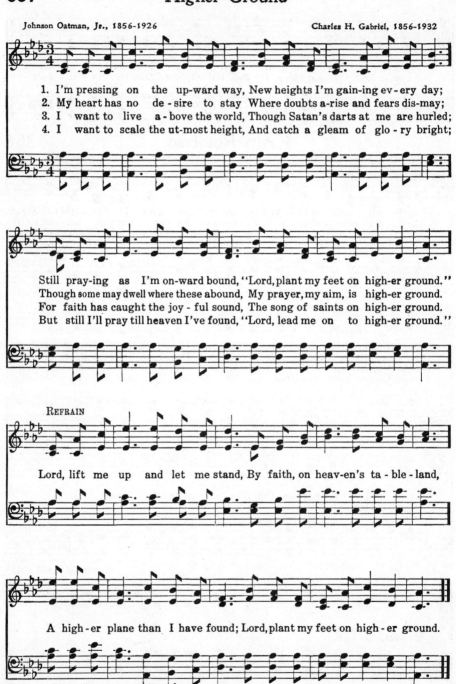

1. I'm pressing on the up-ward way, New heights I'm gain-ing ev-ery day;
2. My heart has no de-sire to stay Where doubts a-rise and fears dis-may;
3. I want to live a-bove the world, Though Satan's darts at me are hurled;
4. I want to scale the ut-most height, And catch a gleam of glo-ry bright;

Still pray-ing as I'm on-ward bound, "Lord, plant my feet on high-er ground."
Though some may dwell where these abound, My prayer, my aim, is high-er ground.
For faith has caught the joy-ful sound, The song of saints on high-er ground.
But still I'll pray till heaven I've found, "Lord, lead me on to high-er ground."

REFRAIN

Lord, lift me up and let me stand, By faith, on heav-en's ta-ble-land,

A high-er plane than I have found; Lord, plant my feet on high-er ground.

I Would Be Like Jesus

James Rowe, 1865-1933

Bentley D. Ackley, b. 1872

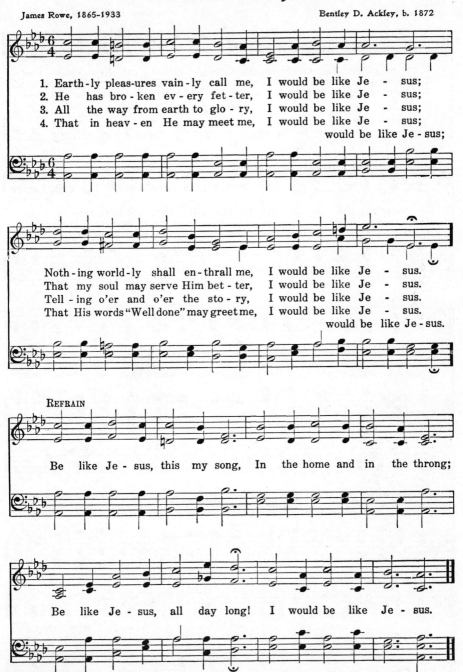

1. Earth-ly pleas-ures vain-ly call me, I would be like Je - sus;
2. He has bro - ken ev - ery fet - ter, I would be like Je - sus;
3. All the way from earth to glo - ry, I would be like Je - sus;
4. That in heav - en He may meet me, I would be like Je - sus;
would be like Je - sus;

Noth - ing world-ly shall en-thrall me, I would be like Je - sus.
That my soul may serve Him bet - ter, I would be like Je - sus.
Tell - ing o'er and o'er the sto - ry, I would be like Je - sus.
That His words "Well done" may greet me, I would be like Je - sus.
would be like Je - sus.

REFRAIN

Be like Je - sus, this my song, In the home and in the throng;

Be like Je - sus, all day long! I would be like Je - sus.

359 I'll Go Where You Want Me to Go

Charles H. Gabriel, 1856-1932   Carrie E. Rounsefell, 1861-1930

1. It may not be on the mountain's height, Or o-ver the storm-y sea;
2. Per-haps to-day there are lov-ing words Which Je-sus would have me speak,
3. There's surely somewhere a low-ly place In earth's harvest fields so wide,

It may not be at the bat-tle's front My Lord will have need of me;
There may be now, in the paths of sin, Some wand'rer whom I should seek.
Where I may la-bor thro' life's short day For Je-sus, the Cru-ci-fied.

But if by a still, small voice He calls To paths I do not know,
O Sav-iour, if Thou wilt be my Guide, Tho' dark and rug-ged the way,
So, trust-ing my all un-to Thy care, I know Thou lov-est me!

I'll an-swer, dear Lord, with my hand in Thine, I'll go where you want me to go.
My voice shall ech-o the mes-sage sweet, I'll say what you want me to say.
I'll do Thy will with a heart sin-cere, I'll be what you want me to be.

REFRAIN

I'll go where you want me to go, dear Lord, O'er mountain, or plain, or sea;

I'll Go Where You Want Me to Go

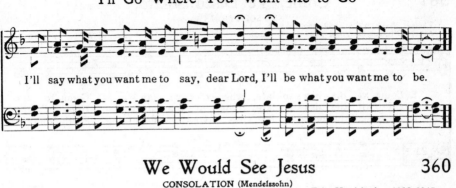

I'll say what you want me to say, dear Lord, I'll be what you want me to be.

We Would See Jesus 360

CONSOLATION (Mendelssohn)

Anna B. Warner, 1820-1915   Felix Mendelssohn, 1809-1847

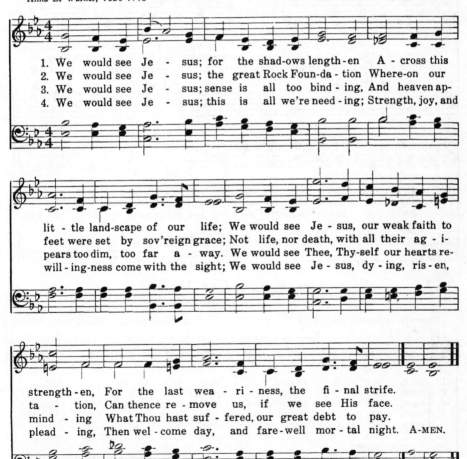

1. We would see Je - sus; for the shad-ows length-en A - cross this
2. We would see Je - sus; the great Rock Foun-da - tion Where-on our
3. We would see Je - sus; sense is all too bind - ing, And heaven ap-
4. We would see Je - sus; this is all we're need - ing; Strength, joy, and

lit - tle land-scape of our life; We would see Je - sus, our weak faith to
feet were set by sov'reign grace; Not life, nor death, with all their ag - i-
pears too dim, too far a - way. We would see Thee, Thy-self our hearts re-
will - ing-ness come with the sight; We would see Je - sus, dy - ing, ris - en,

strength - en, For the last wea - ri - ness, the fi - nal strife.
ta - tion, Can thence re - move us, if we see His face.
mind - ing What Thou hast suf - fered, our great debt to pay.
plead - ing, Then wel - come day, and fare - well mor - tal night. A-MEN.

Alternate tune: O PERFECT LOVE, No. 524

361 Come, Ye Disconsolate

CONSOLATION (Webbe)

Thomas Moore, 1779-1852; stanzas 1, 2
Alt. by Thomas Hastings, 1784-1872; stanza 3

Samuel Webbe, 1740-1816

1. Come, ye dis - con - so - late, wher - e'er ye lan - guish; Come to the
2. Joy of the des - o - late, light of the stray - ing, Hope of the
3. Here see the bread of life; see wa - ters flow - ing Forth from the

mer - cy-seat, fer - vent-ly kneel; Here bring your wounded hearts, here tell your
pen - i - tent, fade-less and pure, Here speaks the Com-fort-er, ten - der - ly
throne of God, pure from a - bove; Come to the feast of love; come, ev - er

an - guish; Earth has no sor - row that heaven can-not heal.
say - ing, "Earth has no sor - row that heaven can-not cure."
know-ing Earth has no sor - row but heaven can re - move. A - MEN.

362 Peace, Perfect Peace

PAX TECUM

Edward H. Bickersteth, 1825-1906

George T. Caldbeck, 1852-c.1912
Arr. by Charles J. Vincent, 1852-1934

1. Peace, per - fect peace, in this dark world of sin?
2. Peace, per - fect peace, by throng - ing du - ties pressed?
3. Peace, per - fect peace, with sor - rows surg - ing round?
4. Peace, per - fect peace, our fu - ture all un - known?
5. Peace, per - fect peace, death shad - ow - ing us and ours?
6. It is e - nough: earth's strug - gles soon shall cease,

Peace, Perfect Peace

The blood of Je - sus whis - pers peace with - in.
To do the will of Je - sus, this is rest.
On Je - sus' bos - om naught but calm is found.
Je - sus we know, and He is on the throne.
Je - sus has van-quished death and all its powers.
And Je - sus, call us to heaven's per - fect peace. A - MEN.

Near to the Heart of God 363

Cleland B. McAfee, 1866-1944

Cleland B. McAfee, 1866-1944

1. There is a place of qui - et rest, Near to the heart of God,
2. There is a place of com - fort sweet, Near to the heart of God,
3. There is a place of full re - lease, Near to the heart of God,

A place where sin can - not mo - lest, Near to the heart of God.
A place where we our Sav - iour meet, Near to the heart of God.
A place where all is joy and peace, Near to the heart of God.

REFRAIN

O Je - sus, blest Re - deem - er, Sent from the heart of God,

Hold us, who wait be - fore Thee, Near to the heart of God.

364 Like a River Glorious

Frances R. Havergal, 1836-1879

James Mountain, 1843-1933

1. Like a riv-er glo-rious Is God's per-fect peace, O-ver all vic-to-rious
2. Hid-den in the hol-low Of His bless-ed hand, Nev-er foe can fol-low,
3. Ev-ery joy or tri-al Fall-eth from a-bove, Traced up-on our di-al

In its bright in-crease; Per-fect, yet it flow-eth Full-er ev-ery day,
Nev-er trai-tor stand; Not a surge of wor-ry, Not a shade of care,
By the Sun of Love. We may trust Him ful-ly All for us to do;

REFRAIN

Per-fect, yet it grow-eth Deep-er all the way.
Not a blast of hur-ry Touch the spir-it there. Stayed up-on Je-ho-vah,
They who trust Him whol-ly Find Him whol-ly true.

Hearts are ful-ly blest; Find-ing, as He prom-ised, Per-fect peace and rest.

365 Name of Jesus, Softly Stealing

BEATRICE

Source Unknown

William Wallace Coe, b. 1862

1. Name of Je-sus, soft-ly steal-ing O'er a world of strife and shame,
2. Name of Je-sus, Heav'n of gladness, Cause our doubts and fears to cease;

Name of Jesus, Softly Stealing

Thou canst bring us heav'n-ly heal-ing, O Thou all - re - stor-ing Name.
Soothe a-way the ach-ing sad-ness; Name of Je - sus, give us peace. A-MEN.

Leaning on the Everlasting Arms   366

Elisha A. Hoffman, 1839-1929

Anthony J. Showalter, 1858-1924

1. What a fel-low-ship, what a joy di-vine, Lean-ing on the ev-er-last-ing arms;
2. Oh, how sweet to walk in this pilgrim way, Lean-ing on the ev-er-last-ing arms;
3. What have I to dread, what have I to fear, Lean-ing on the ev-er-last-ing arms?

What a bless-ed-ness, what a peace is mine, Lean-ing on the ev - er-last-ing arms.
Oh, how bright the path grows from day to day, Lean-ing on the ev - er-last-ing arms.
I have bless-ed peace with my Lord so near, Lean-ing on the ev - er-last-ing arms.

REFRAIN

Lean - ing, lean - ing, Safe and se-cure from all a-larms;
Lean-ing on Je-sus, lean-ing on Je - sus,

Lean - ing, lean - ing, Lean-ing on the ev - er-last-ing arms.
Lean-ing on Je-sus, lean-ing on Je-sus,

367 Sweet Peace, the Gift of God's Love

Peter P. Bilhorn, 1861-1936   Peter P. Bilhorn, 1861-1936

1. There comes to my heart one sweet strain, (sweet strain,) A
2. Thro' Christ on the cross peace was made, (was made,) My
3. When Jesus as Lord I had crowned, (had crowned,) My
4. In Jesus for peace I abide, (abide,) And

glad and a joyous refrain; (refrain;) I sing it a-
debt by His death was all paid; (all paid;) No other foun-
heart with this peace did abound; (abound;) In Him the rich
as I keep close to His side, (His side,) There's nothing but

gain and again, Sweet peace, the gift of God's love.
dation is laid For peace, the gift of God's love.
blessing I found, Sweet peace, the gift of God's love.
peace doth betide, Sweet peace, the gift of God's love.

REFRAIN

Peace, peace, sweet peace! Wonderful gift from above! (above!)

Oh, wonderful, wonderful peace! Sweet peace, the gift of God's love!

Give to the Winds Thy Fears

DIADEMATA

368

Paul Gerhardt, 1607-1676
Trans. by John Wesley, 1703-1791

George J. Elvey, 1816-1893

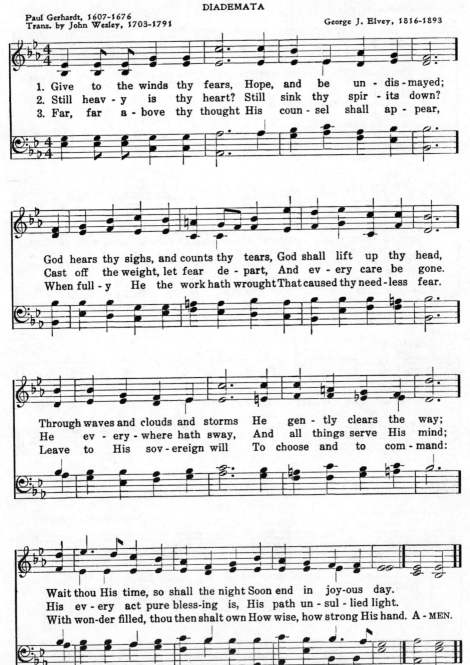

1. Give to the winds thy fears, Hope, and be un-dis-mayed;
2. Still heav-y is thy heart? Still sink thy spir-its down?
3. Far, far a-bove thy thought His coun-sel shall ap-pear,

God hears thy sighs, and counts thy tears, God shall lift up thy head,
Cast off the weight, let fear de-part, And ev-ery care be gone.
When full-y He the work hath wrought That caused thy need-less fear.

Through waves and clouds and storms He gen-tly clears the way;
He ev-ery-where hath sway, And all things serve His mind;
Leave to His sov-ereign will To choose and to com-mand:

Wait thou His time, so shall the night Soon end in joy-ous day.
His ev-ery act pure bless-ing is, His path un-sul-lied light.
With won-der filled, thou then shalt own How wise, how strong His hand. A-MEN.

For Descant arrangement, see No. 417

369 The Great Physician

William Hunter, 1811-1877

John H. Stockton, 1813-1877

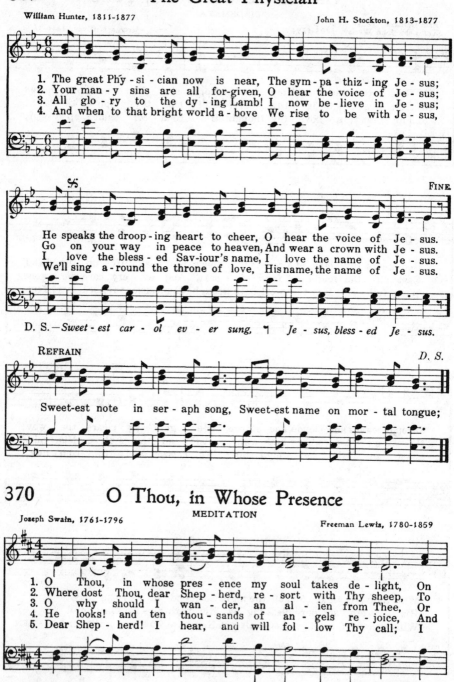

1. The great Phy-si-cian now is near, The sym-pa-thiz-ing Je-sus;
2. Your man-y sins are all for-given, O hear the voice of Je-sus;
3. All glo-ry to the dy-ing Lamb! I now be-lieve in Je-sus;
4. And when to that bright world a-bove We rise to be with Je-sus,

He speaks the droop-ing heart to cheer, O hear the voice of Je-sus.
Go on your way in peace to heaven, And wear a crown with Je-sus.
I love the bless-ed Sav-iour's name, I love the name of Je-sus.
We'll sing a-round the throne of love, His name, the name of Je-sus.

FINE

D. S.—Sweet-est car-ol ev-er sung, Je-sus, bless-ed Je-sus.

REFRAIN

D. S.

Sweet-est note in ser-aph song, Sweet-est name on mor-tal tongue;

370 O Thou, in Whose Presence

MEDITATION

Joseph Swain, 1761-1796

Freeman Lewis, 1780-1859

1. O Thou, in whose pres-ence my soul takes de-light, On
2. Where dost Thou, dear Shep-herd, re-sort with Thy sheep, To
3. O why should I wan-der, an al-ien from Thee, Or
4. He looks! and ten thou-sands of an-gels re-joice, And
5. Dear Shep-herd! I hear, and will fol-low Thy call; I

O Thou, in Whose Presence

whom in af - flic - tion I call, My com - fort by day and my
feed them in pas - tures of love? Say, why in the val - ley of
cry in the des - ert for bread? Thy foes will re - joice when my
myr - i - ads wait for His word; He speaks! and e - ter - ni - ty,
know the sweet sound of Thy voice; Re - store and de - fend me, for

song in the night, My hope, my sal - va - tion, my all!
death should I weep, Or a - lone in this wil - der - ness rove?
sor - rows they see, And smile at the tears I have shed.
filled with His voice, Re - ech - oes the praise of the Lord.
Thou art my all, And in Thee I will ev - er re - joice. A - MEN.

I Know Not What the Future Hath   371

COOLING

John G. Whittier, 1807-1892   Alonzo J. Abbey, 1825-1887

1. I know not what the fu - ture hath   Of mar - vel or sur - prise,
2. And if my heart and flesh are weak   To bear an un - tried pain,
3. And Thou, O Lord, by whom are seen   Thy crea - tures as they be,
4. And so be - side the si - lent sea   I wait the muf - fled oar:
5. I know not where His is - lands lift   Their frond - ed palms in air;

As - sured a - lone that life and death God's mer - cy un - der - lies.
The bruis - ed reed He will not break, But strength-en and sus - tain.
For - give me if too close I lean My hu - man heart on Thee.
No harm from Him can come to me On o - cean or on shore.
I on - ly know I can - not drift Be - yond His love and care. A - MEN.

372   It's Just Like His Great Love

Edna R. Worrell, 19th Century   Clarence B. Strouse, 19th Century

1. A Friend I have, called Jesus, Whose love is strong and true, And nev-er
2. Sometimes the clouds of troub-le Be-dim the sky a-bove, I can-not
3. When sor-row's clouds o'ertake me, And break up-on my head, When life seems
4. Oh, I could sing for-ev-er Of Je-sus' love di-vine, Of all His

fails how-e'er 'tis tried, No mat-ter what I do; I've sinned a-gainst this
see my Sav-iour's face, I doubt His won-drous love; But He, from Heav-en's
worse than use-less, And I were bet-ter dead; I take my grief to
care and ten-der-ness For this poor life of mine; His love is in and

love of His, But when I knelt to pray, Con-fess-ing all my
mer-cy-seat, Be-hold-ing my de-spair, In pit-y bursts the
Je-sus then, Nor do I go in vain, For heav'n-ly hope He
o-ver all, And wind and waves o-bey When Je-sus whis-pers

REFRAIN

guilt to Him, The sin-clouds rolled a-way.
clouds be-tween, And shows me He is there.   It's just like Je-sus to
gives that cheers Like sun-shine aft-er rain.
"Peace, be still!" And rolls the clouds a-way.

It's Just Like His Great Love

roll the clouds a - way, It's just like Je - sus to keep me day by day,

It's just like Je - sus all a - long the way, It's just like His great love.

Jesus, My Saviour, Look on Me   373
HANFORD

Charlotte Elliott, 1789-1871

Arthur S. Sullivan, 1842-1900

1. Je - sus, my Sav - iour, look on me, For I am wea - ry and op-prest;
2. Look down on me, for I am weak; I feel the toil-some journey's length:
3. I am be - wil - dered on my way, Dark and tem-pest-uous is the night;
4. When Sa - tan flings his fi - ery darts, I look to Thee, my ter-rors cease;
5. Stand-ing a - lone on Jordan's brink, In that tre - men-dous, lat - est strife,
6. Thou wilt my ev - ery want sup - ply, E'en to the end, what-e'er be - fall;

I come to cast my - self on Thee: Thou art my Rest.
Thine aid om - nip - o - tent I seek: Thou art my Strength.
O send Thou forth some cheer-ing ray! Thou art my Light.
Thy Cross a hid - ing - place im - parts: Thou art my Peace.
Thou wilt not suf - fer me to sink: Thou art my Life.
Through life, in death, e - ter - nal - ly, Thou art my All.   A-MEN.

374 Wonderful Peace

W. D. Cornell, 19th Century, alt.

W. G. Cooper, 19th Century

1. Far a-way in the depths of my spir-it to-night Rolls a
2. What a treas-ure I have in this won-der-ful peace, Bur-ied
3. I am rest-ing to-night in this won-der-ful peace, Rest-ing
4. And me-thinks when I rise to that Cit-y of peace, Where the
5. Ah! soul, are you here with-out com-fort or rest, March-ing

mel-o-dy sweet-er than psalm; In ce-les-tial-like strains it un-
deep in the heart of my soul; So se-cure that no pow-er can
sweet-ly in Je-sus' con-trol; For I'm kept from all dan-ger by
Au-thor of peace I shall see, That one strain of the song which the
down the rough path-way of time? Make Je-sus your friend ere the

ceas-ing-ly falls O'er my soul like an in-fi-nite calm.
mine it a-way, While the years of e-ter-ni-ty roll.
night and by day, And His glo-ry is flood-ing my soul.
ran-somed will sing, In that heav-en-ly king-dom shall be:
shad-ows grow dark; Oh, ac-cept this sweet peace so sub-lime.

REFRAIN

Peace! Peace! won-der-ful peace, Coming down from the Fa-ther a-bove; Sweep

o-ver my spir-it for-ev-er, I pray, In fath-om-less bil-lows of love.

The Rock That Is Higher than I

Erastus Johnson, 1826-1909   William G. Fischer, 1835-1912

1. O some-times the shad-ows are deep, And rough seems the path to the goal,
2. O some-times how long seems the day, And some-times how wea-ry my feet;
3. O near to the Rock let me keep, If bless-ings or sor-rows pre-vail;

And sor-rows, sometimes how they sweep Like tempests down o-ver the soul!
But toil-ing in life's dust-y way, The Rock's blessed shad-ow, how sweet!
Or climb-ing the mountain way steep, Or walk-ing the shad-ow-y vale.

REFRAIN

O then to the Rock let me fly, let me fly, To the

Rock that is high-er than I; is high-er than I; O then to the

Rock let me fly, let me fly, To the Rock that is high-er than I!

Moment by Moment

Daniel W. Whittle, 1840-1901

May Whittle Moody, b. 1870

1. Dy - ing with Je - sus, by death reck-oned mine; Liv - ing with Je - sus, a
2. Nev - er a tri - al that He is not there, Nev - er a bur - den that
3. Nev - er a heart-ache and nev - er a groan, Nev - er a tear-drop and
4. Nev - er a weak-ness that He doth not feel, Nev - er a sick-ness that

new life di - vine; Look-ing to Je - sus till glo - ry doth shine, Mo-ment by
He doth not bear, Nev - er a sor - row that He doth not share, Mo-ment by
nev - er a moan; Nev - er a dan - ger, but there on the throne, Mo-ment by
He can - not heal; Mo - ment by mo-ment, in woe or in weal, Je - sus, my

mo - ment, O Lord, I am Thine.
mo - ment I'm un - der His care;   Mo-ment by mo-ment I'm kept in His love;
mo - ment, He thinks of His own.
Sav-iour, a - bides with me still.

REFRAIN

Mo - ment by mo-ment I've life from a - bove; Look - ing to Je - sus till

glo - ry doth shine; Mo - ment by mo - ment, O Lord, I am Thine.

Does Jesus Care?

Frank E. Graeff, 1860-1919

J. Lincoln Hall, 1866-1930

1. Does Je- sus care when my heart is pained Too deep - ly for mirth and song;
2. Does Je- sus care when my way is dark With a name - less dread and fear?
3. Does Je- sus care when I've tried and failed To re-sist some temp-ta-tion strong;
4. Does Je- sus care when I've said "good-by" To the dear-est on earth to me,

As the burdens press, and the cares distress, And the way grows weary and long?
As the day-light fades into deep night shades, Does He care e-nough to be near?
When for my deep grief I find no re-lief, Though my tears flow all the night long?
And my sad heart aches till it near-ly breaks Is it aught to Him? Does He see?

REFRAIN

O yes, He cares; I know He cares, His heart is touched with my grief;

When the days are weary, the long nights dreary, I know my Saviour cares. (He cares).

378

In the Hour of Trial

PENITENCE

James Montgomery, 1771-1854

Spencer Lane, 1843-1903

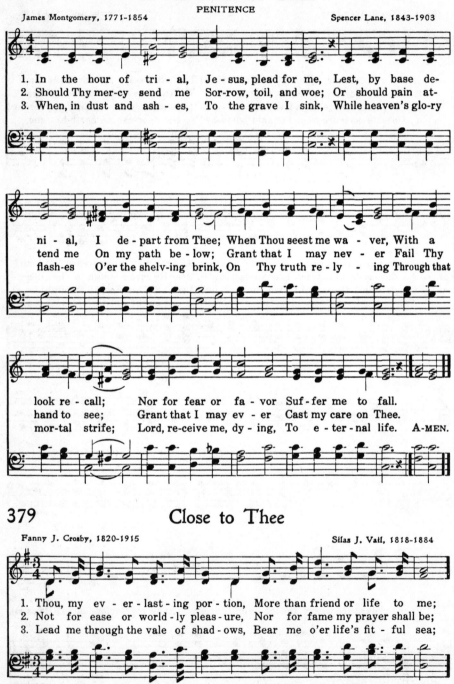

1. In the hour of tri - al, Je - sus, plead for me, Lest, by base de-
2. Should Thy mer-cy send me Sor-row, toil, and woe; Or should pain at-
3. When, in dust and ash - es, To the grave I sink, While heaven's glo-ry

ni - al, I de-part from Thee; When Thou seest me wa - ver, With a
tend me On my path be - low; Grant that I may nev - er Fail Thy
flash-es O'er the shelv-ing brink, On Thy truth re - ly - ing Through that

look re - call; Nor for fear or fa - vor Suf-fer me to fall.
hand to see; Grant that I may ev - er Cast my care on Thee.
mor-tal strife; Lord, re-ceive me, dy - ing, To e - ter - nal life. A-MEN.

379

Close to Thee

Fanny J. Crosby, 1820-1915

Silas J. Vail, 1818-1884

1. Thou, my ev - er - last - ing por - tion, More than friend or life to me;
2. Not for ease or world - ly pleas - ure, Nor for fame my prayer shall be;
3. Lead me through the vale of shad - ows, Bear me o'er life's fit - ful sea;

Close to Thee

FINE

D.S.—All a-long my pil-grim jour-ney, Sav-iour, let me walk with Thee.
D.S.—Glad-ly will I toil and suf-fer, On-ly let me walk with Thee.
D.S.—Then the gate of life e-ter-nal May I en-ter, Lord, with Thee.

REFRAIN

D.S.

Close to Thee, close to Thee, Close to Thee, close to Thee;

More Love to Thee

380

Elizabeth P. Prentiss, 1818-1878

William H. Doane, 1832-1915

1. More love to Thee, O Christ, More love to Thee! Hear Thou the
2. Once earth-ly joy I craved, Sought peace and rest; Now Thee a-
3. Let sor-row do its work, Send grief and pain; Sweet are Thy
4. Then shall my lat-est breath Whis-per Thy praise; This be the

prayer I make On bend-ed knee; This is my ear-nest plea:
lone I seek, Give what is best; This all my prayer shall be:
mes-sen-gers, Sweet their re-frain, When they can sing with me:
part-ing cry My heart shall raise; This still its prayer shall be:

More love, O Christ, to Thee, More love to Thee, More love to Thee! A-MEN.

381 My Faith Looks Up to Thee
OLIVET

Ray Palmer, 1808-1887

Lowell Mason, 1792-1872

1. My faith looks up to Thee, Thou Lamb of Cal - va - ry,
2. May Thy rich grace im - part Strength to my faint - ing heart,
3. While life's dark maze I tread, And griefs a - round me spread,
4. When ends life's tran - sient dream, When death's cold, sul - len stream

Sav - iour di - vine! Now hear me while I pray, Take all my
My zeal in - spire; As Thou hast died for me, O may my
Be Thou my Guide; Bid dark - ness turn to day, Wipe sor - row's
Shall o'er me roll; Blest Sav - iour, then, in love, Fear and dis-

guilt a - way, O let me from this day Be whol - ly Thine!
love to Thee Pure, warm, and changeless be, A liv - ing fire!
tears a - way, Nor let me ev - er stray From Thee a - side.
trust re - move; O bear me safe a - bove, A ran-somed soul! A-MEN.

382 Speak, Lord, in the Stillness
QUIETUDE

E. May Grimes, 1868-1927

Harold Green, 1871-1931

1. Speak, Lord, in the still - ness, While I wait on Thee;
2. Speak, O bless - ed Mas - ter, In this qui - et hour;
3. For the words Thou speak - est, They are life in - deed;
4. All to Thee is yield - ed, I am not my own;
5. Speak, Thy ser - vant hear - eth, Be not si - lent, Lord;
6. Fill me with the know - ledge Of Thy glo - rious will;

By permission of the South Africa General Mission, London

Speak, Lord, in the Stillness

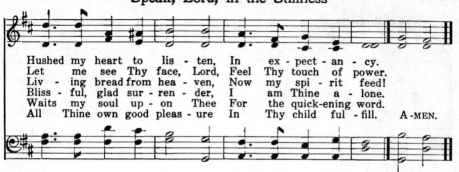

Hushed my heart to lis - ten, In ex - pect - an - cy.
Let me see Thy face, Lord, Feel Thy touch of power.
Liv - ing bread from hea - ven, Now my spi - rit feed!
Bliss - ful, glad sur - ren - der, I am Thine a - lone.
Waits my soul up - on Thee For the quick-ening word.
All Thine own good pleas - ure In Thy child ful - fill. A-MEN.

Sweet Hour of Prayer 383

William W. Walford, 1772-1850

William B. Bradbury, 1816-1868

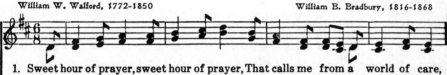

1. Sweet hour of prayer, sweet hour of prayer, That calls me from a world of care,
2. Sweet hour of prayer, sweet hour of prayer, Thy wings shall my pe - ti - tion bear,
3. Sweet hour of prayer, sweet hour of prayer, May I thy con - so - la - tion share,

FINE

And bids me at my Fa-ther's throne Make all my wants and wish-es known;
To Him whose truth and faith-ful-ness En - gage the wait-ing soul to bless;
Till, from Mount Pisgah's loft - y height, I view my home, and take my flight:

D.S.—*And oft es - caped the tempt-er's snare, By thy re - turn, sweet hour of prayer.*
D.S.—*I'll cast on Him my ev - ery care, And wait for thee, sweet hour of prayer.*
D.S.—*And shout, while pass-ing through the air, Fare-well, fare - well, sweet hour of prayer!*

D. S.

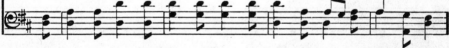

In sea-sons of dis - tress and grief, My soul has oft - en found re - lief,
And since He bids me seek His face, Be - lieve His word and trust His grace,
This robe of flesh I'll drop, and rise To seize the ev - er - last-ing prize;

384 Tell It to Jesus

Jeremiah E. Rankin, 1828-1904

Edmund S. Lorenz, 1854-1942

1. Are you wea - ry, are you heav - y - heart - ed? Tell it to Je - sus,
2. Do the tears flow down your cheeks un - bid - den? Tell it to Je - sus,
3. Do you fear the gath-'ring clouds of sor - row? Tell it to Je - sus,
4. Are you troub - led at the thought of dy - ing? Tell it to Je - sus,

Tell it to Je - sus; Are you griev - ing o - ver joys de - part - ed?
Tell it to Je - sus; Have you sins that to men's eyes are hid - den?
Tell it to Je - sus; Are you anx - ious what shall be to - mor - row?
Tell it to Je - sus; For Christ's com - ing King-dom are you sigh - ing?

REFRAIN

Tell it to Je - sus a - lone. Tell it to Je - sus, tell it to Je - sus,

He is a friend that's well known; You've no oth - er

such a friend or broth - er, Tell it to Je - sus a - lone.

Teach Me to Pray

Albert S. Reitz, b. 1879

Albert S. Reitz, b. 1879

1. Teach me to pray, Lord, teach me to pray; This is my heart-cry,
   day un-to day; I long to know Thy will and Thy way; Teach me to
   pray, Lord, teach me to pray.

2. Pow-er in prayer, Lord, pow-er in prayer, Here 'mid earth's sin and
   sor-row and care; Men lost and dy-ing, souls in des-pair; O give me
   pow-er, pow-er in prayer!

3. My weak-ened will, Lord, Thou canst re-new; My sin-ful na-ture
   Thou canst sub-due; Fill me just now with pow-er a-new, Pow-er to
   pray and pow-er to do!

4. Teach me to pray, Lord, teach me to pray; Thou art my Pat-tern,
   day un-to day; Thou art my Sure-ty, now and for aye; Teach me to
   pray, Lord, teach me to pray.

REFRAIN

Liv-ing in Thee, Lord, and Thou in me; Con-stant a-bid-ing, this is my plea; Grant me Thy pow-er, boundless and free: Pow-er with men and pow-er with Thee.

386 Have Thine Own Way, Lord!

ADELAIDE

Adelaide A. Pollard, 1862-1934

George C. Stebbins, 1846-1945

1. Have Thine own way, Lord! Have Thine own way! Thou art the Pot-ter; I am the clay. Mould me and make me Aft-er Thy will, While I am wait-ing, Yield-ed and still.

2. Have Thine own way, Lord! Have Thine own way! Search me and try me, Mas-ter, to-day! Whit-er than snow, Lord, Wash me just now, As in Thy pres-ence Hum-bly I bow.

3. Have Thine own way, Lord! Have Thine own way! Wound-ed and wea-ry, Help me, I pray! Pow-er—all pow-er— Sure-ly is Thine! Touch me and heal me, Sav-iour di-vine!

4. Have Thine own way, Lord! Have Thine own way! Hold o'er my be-ing Ab-so-lute sway! Fill with Thy Spir-it Till all shall see Christ on-ly, al-ways, Liv-ing in me! A-MEN.

Copyright, 1907. Renewal, 1935, by G. C. Stebbins. Assigned to Hope Publishing Co. All Rights Reserved

387 Prayer Is the Soul's Sincere Desire

NAOMI

James Montgomery, 1771-1854

Hans G. Nägeli, 1773-1836
Arr. by Lowell Mason, 1792-1872

1. Prayer is the soul's sin-cere de-sire, Un-ut-tered or ex-pressed,
2. Prayer is the bur-den of a sigh, The fall-ing of a tear,
3. Prayer is the sim-plest form of speech That in-fant lips can try;
4. Prayer is the Chris-tian's vi-tal breath, The Chris-tian's na-tive air,
5. O Thou, by whom we come to God, The Life, the Truth, the Way,

Alternate tune: ST. AGNES, No. 472

Prayer Is the Soul's Sincere Desire

The mo-tion of a hid-den fire That trem-bles in the breast.
The up-ward glanc-ing of an eye When none but God is near.
Prayer the sub-lim-est strains that reach The Ma - jes - ty on high.
His watch-word at the gates of death; He en-ters heaven with prayer.
The path of prayer Thy-self hast trod; Lord, teach us how to pray. A-MEN.

Dear Lord and Father of Mankind   388

REST (Whittier)

John G. Whittier, 1807-1892, alt.   Frederick C. Maker, 1844-1927

1. Dear Lord and Fa - ther of man - kind, For - give our fool - ish
2. In sim - ple trust like theirs who heard, Be - side the Syr - ian
3. Drop Thy still dews of qui - et - ness, Till all our striv - ings
4. Breathe through the heats of our de - sire Thy cool - ness and Thy

ways! Re - clothe us in our right - ful mind; In pur - er
sea, The gra - cious call - ing of the Lord, Let us, like
cease; Take from our souls the strain and stress, And let our
balm; Let sense be dumb, let flesh re - tire; Speak through the

lives Thy serv - ice find, In deep - er rev - erence, praise.
them, with - out a word, Rise up and fol - low Thee.
or - dered lives con - fess The beau - ty of Thy peace.
earth-quake, wind, and fire, O still small voice of calm! A - MEN.

389 Jesus, Saviour, Pilot Me

PILOT

Edward Hopper, 1816-1888

John E. Gould, 1822-1875

1. Je - sus, Sav - iour, pi - lot me O - ver life's tem - pes - tuous sea;
2. As a moth - er stills her child, Thou canst hush the o - cean wild;
3. When at last I near the shore, And the fear - ful break - ers roar

Un-known waves be - fore me roll, Hid - ing rock and treacherous shoal;
Bois-terous waves o - bey Thy will When Thou say'st to them, "Be still!"
'Twixt me and the peace-ful rest, Then, while lean - ing on Thy breast,

Chart and com-pass came from Thee: Je - sus, Sav - iour, pi - lot me.
Won-drous Sovereign of the sea, Je - sus, Sav - iour, pi - lot me.
May I hear Thee say to me, "Fear not, I will pi - lot thee." A - MEN.

390 Pass Me Not

Fanny J. Crosby, 1820-1915

William H. Doane, 1832-1915

1. Pass me not, O gen - tle Sav - iour, Hear my hum - ble cry; While on oth - ers
2. Let me at a throne of mer - cy Find a sweet re - lief; Kneel-ing there in
3. Trust-ing on - ly in Thy mer - it, Would I seek Thy face; Heal my wounded,
4. Thou the spring of all my com - fort, More than life to me, Whom have I on

Pass Me Not

REFRAIN

Thou art call - ing, Do not pass me by.
deep con - tri - tion, Help my un - be - lief.
bro - ken spir - it, Save me by Thy grace.
earth be - side Thee? Whom in heaven but Thee?

Sav - iour, Sav - iour, hear my

hum - ble cry; While on oth-ers Thou art call - ing, Do not pass me by.

I Need Thee Every Hour   391

Annie S. Hawks, 1835-1918

Robert Lowry, 1826-1899

1. I need Thee ev - ery hour, Most gra - cious Lord; No ten - der voice like
2. I need Thee ev - ery hour, Stay Thou near by; Temp-ta-tions lose their
3. I need Thee ev - ery hour, In joy or pain; Come quick-ly and a-
4. I need Thee ev - ery hour, Most Ho - ly One; O make me Thine in-

REFRAIN

Thine Can peace af - ford.
power When Thou art nigh.
bide, Or life is vain.
deed, Thou bless - ed Son!

I need Thee, O I need Thee; Ev - ery hour I

need Thee; O bless me now, my Sav - iour, I come to Thee!

392 Lord, I Have Shut the Door
SANCTUARY

William M. Runyan, b. 1870 · William M. Runyan, b. 1870

1. Lord, I have shut the door, Speak now the word Which in the
2. Lord, I have shut the door, Here do I bow; Speak, for my
3. In this blest qui - et - ness Clam - or - ings cease; Here in Thy
4. Lord, I have shut the door, Strength-en my heart; Yon - der a-

din and throng Could not be heard; Hushed now my in - ner heart,
soul at - tent Turns to Thee now. Re - buke Thou what is vain,
pres - ence dwells In - fi - nite peace; Yon - der, the strife and cry,
waits the task— I share a part. On - ly through grace be-stowed

Whis-per Thy will, While I have come a-part, While all is still.
Coun-sel my soul, Thy ho - ly will re-veal, My will con - trol.
Yon - der, the sin: Lord, I have shut the door, Thou art with - in!
May I be true; Here, while alone with Thee, My strength re - new. A - MEN.

Copyright, 1923. Renewal, 1951, by W. M. Runyan. Assigned to Hope Publishing Co. All Rights Reserved

393 Come, Thou My Light, That I May See
OMBERSLEY

Hugh T. Kerr, 1871-1950 · William H. Gladstone, 1840-1891

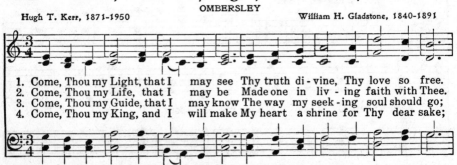

1. Come, Thou my Light, that I may see Thy truth di - vine, Thy love so free.
2. Come, Thou my Life, that I may be Made one in liv - ing faith with Thee.
3. Come, Thou my Guide, that I may know The way my seek - ing soul should go;
4. Come, Thou my King, and I will make My heart a shrine for Thy dear sake;

Words copyright, 1942, by the Hymn Society of America. Used by permission

Come, Thou My Light, That I May See

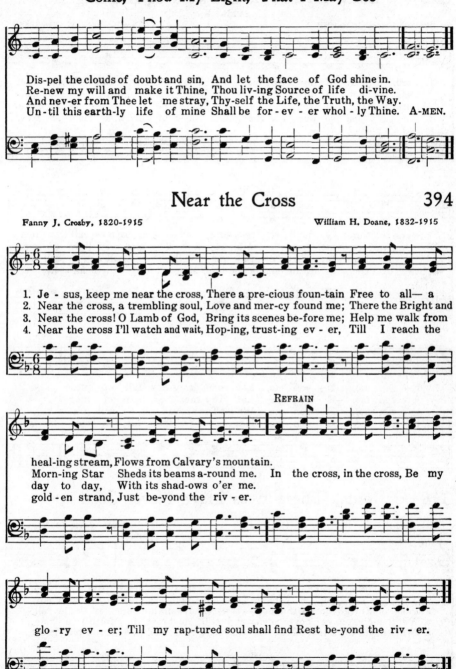

Dis-pel the clouds of doubt and sin, And let the face of God shine in.
Re-new my will and make it Thine, Thou liv-ing Source of life di-vine.
And nev-er from Thee let me stray, Thy-self the Life, the Truth, the Way.
Un-til this earth-ly life of mine Shall be for-ev-er whol-ly Thine. A-MEN.

Near the Cross 394

Fanny J. Crosby, 1820-1915   William H. Doane, 1832-1915

1. Je - sus, keep me near the cross, There a pre-cious foun-tain Free to all— a
2. Near the cross, a trembling soul, Love and mer-cy found me; There the Bright and
3. Near the cross! O Lamb of God, Bring its scenes be-fore me; Help me walk from
4. Near the cross I'll watch and wait, Hop-ing, trust-ing ev - er, Till I reach the

REFRAIN

heal-ing stream, Flows from Calvary's mountain.
Morn-ing Star Sheds its beams a-round me. In the cross, in the cross, Be my
day to day, With its shad-ows o'er me.
gold-en strand, Just be-yond the riv - er.

glo - ry ev - er; Till my rap-tured soul shall find Rest be-yond the riv - er.

395 Lord, I Hear of Showers of Blessing

EVEN ME

Elizabeth Codner, 1824-1919

William B. Bradbury, 1816-1868

1. Lord, I hear of showers of bless-ing Thou art scat-tering full and free;
2. Pass me not, O gra-cious Fa-ther, Sin-ful though my heart may be;
3. Pass me not, O ten-der Sav-iour, Let me love and cling to Thee;
4. Love of God, so pure and changeless, Blood of Christ, so rich, so free,

Showers, the thirst-y land re-fresh-ing; Let some drops now fall on me,
Thou mightst leave me, but the rath-er Let Thy mer-cy light on me,
I am long-ing for Thy fa-vor; Whilst Thou'rt call-ing, O call me,
Grace of God, so strong and bound-less, Mag-ni-fy them all in me,

E-ven me, E-ven me, Let some drops now fall on me.
E-ven me, E-ven me, Let Thy mer-cy light on me.
E-ven me, E-ven me, Whilst Thou'rt call-ing, O call me.
E-ven me, E-ven me, Mag-ni-fy them all in me. A-MEN.

396 Jesus, These Eyes Have Never Seen

SAWLEY

Ray Palmer, 1808-1887

James Walch, 1837-1901

1. Je-sus, these eyes have nev-er seen That ra-diant form of Thine;
2. I see Thee not, I hear Thee not, Yet art Thou oft with me;
3. Like some bright dream that comes un-sought When slumbers o'er me roll,
4. Yet though I have not seen, and still Must rest in faith a-lone;
5. When death these mortal eyes shall seal, And still this throb-bing heart,

Jesus, These Eyes Have Never Seen

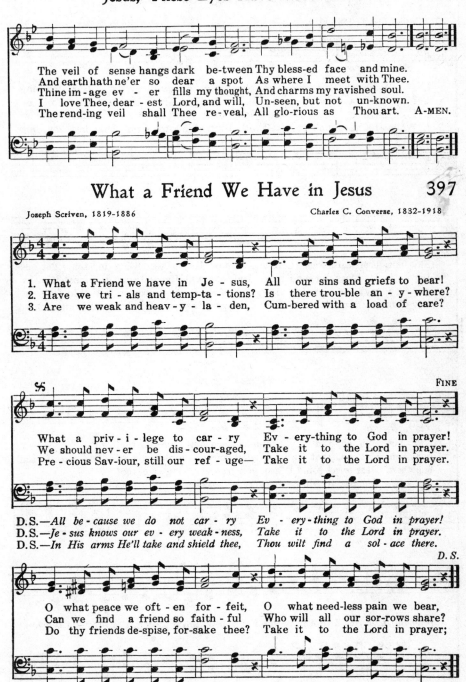

The veil of sense hangs dark be-tween Thy bless-ed face and mine.
And earth hath ne'er so dear a spot As where I meet with Thee.
Thine im-age ev - er fills my thought, And charms my ravished soul.
I love Thee, dear - est Lord, and will, Un-seen, but not un-known.
The rend-ing veil shall Thee re-veal, All glo-rious as Thou art. A-MEN.

What a Friend We Have in Jesus 397

Joseph Scriven, 1819-1886

Charles C. Converse, 1832-1918

1. What a Friend we have in Je - sus, All our sins and griefs to bear!
2. Have we tri - als and temp-ta - tions? Is there trou-ble an - y - where?
3. Are we weak and heav - y - la - den, Cum-bered with a load of care?

FINE

What a priv - i - lege to car - ry Ev - ery-thing to God in prayer!
We should nev - er be dis-cour-aged, Take it to the Lord in prayer.
Pre - cious Sav-iour, still our ref - uge— Take it to the Lord in prayer.

D.S.—All be - cause we do not car - ry Ev - ery-thing to God in prayer!
D.S.—Je - sus knows our ev - ery weak-ness, Take it to the Lord in prayer.
D.S.—In His arms He'll take and shield thee, Thou wilt find a sol - ace there.

D. S.

O what peace we oft - en for - feit, O what need-less pain we bear,
Can we find a friend so faith - ful Who will all our sor-rows share?
Do thy friends de-spise, for-sake thee? Take it to the Lord in prayer;

398 I Am Praying for You

S. O'Malley Clough, 1837-1910

Ira D. Sankey, 1840-1908

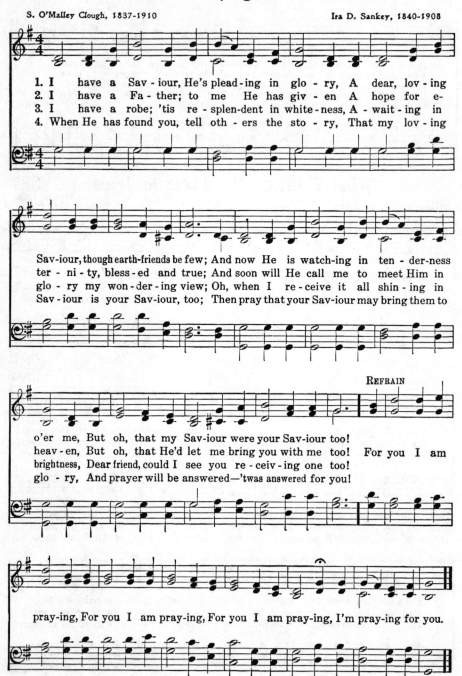

1. I have a Sav-iour, He's plead-ing in glo-ry, A dear, lov-ing
2. I have a Fa-ther; to me He has giv-en A hope for e-
3. I have a robe; 'tis re-splen-dent in white-ness, A-wait-ing in
4. When He has found you, tell oth-ers the sto-ry, That my lov-ing

Sav-iour, though earth-friends be few; And now He is watch-ing in ten-der-ness
ter-ni-ty, bless-ed and true; And soon will He call me to meet Him in
glo-ry my won-der-ing view; Oh, when I re-ceive it all shin-ing in
Sav-iour is your Sav-iour, too; Then pray that your Sav-iour may bring them to

REFRAIN

o'er me, But oh, that my Sav-iour were your Sav-iour too!
heav-en, But oh, that He'd let me bring you with me too! For you I am
brightness, Dear friend, could I see you re-ceiv-ing one too!
glo-ry, And prayer will be answered—'twas answered for you!

pray-ing, For you I am pray-ing, For you I am pray-ing, I'm pray-ing for you.

'Tis the Blessed Hour of Prayer

Fanny J. Crosby, 1820-1915

William H. Doane, 1832-1915

1. 'Tis the bless - ed hour of prayer, when our hearts low - ly bend,
2. 'Tis the bless - ed hour of prayer, when the Sav - iour draws near,
3. 'Tis the bless - ed hour of prayer, when the tempt - ed and tried
4. At the bless - ed hour of prayer, trust-ing Him we be - lieve

And we gath - er to Je - sus, our Sav - iour and Friend; If we
With a ten - der com - pas - sion His chil - dren to hear; When He
To the Sav - iour who loves them their sor - row con - fide; With a
That the bless - ings we're need - ing we'll sure - ly re - ceive; In the

come to Him in faith, His pro - tec - tion to share, What a balm for the
tells us we may cast at His feet ev - ery care, What a balm for the
sym - pa-thiz-ing heart He re-moves ev - ery care, What a balm for the
full - ness of this trust we shall lose ev - ery care; What a balm for the

REFRAIN

wea - ry! O how sweet to be there! Bless-ed hour of prayer, Bless-ed

hour of prayer; What a balm for the wea - ry! O how sweet to be there!

Pentecostal Power

Charles H. Gabriel, 1856-1932   Charles H. Gabriel, 1856-1932

1. Lord, as of old at Pen - te - cost Thou didst Thy power dis - play,
2. For might - y works for Thee, pre - pare And strength-en ev - ery heart;
3. All self con - sume, all sin de-stroy! With ear - nest zeal en - due
4. Speak, Lord! be - fore Thy throne we wait, Thy prom - ise we be - lieve,

With cleans-ing, pu - ri - fy - ing flame De - scend on us to - day.
Come, take pos - ses - sion of Thine own, And nev - er - more de - part.
Each wait - ing heart to work for Thee; O Lord, our faith re - new!
And will not let Thee go un - til The bless - ing we re - ceive.

REFRAIN

Lord, send the old - time power, The Pen-te-cos - tal power! Thy flood-gates of

bless-ing on us throw o - pen wide! Lord, send the old - time power, the

Pen - te - cos - tal power, That sinners be con-vert-ed and Thy name glo - ri-fied!

Guide Me, O Thou Great Jehovah 401

CWM RHONDDA

William Williams, 1717-1791

John Hughes, 1873-1932

1. Guide me, O Thou great Je - ho - vah, Pil - grim through this bar - ren land;
2. O - pen now the crys-tal foun-tain, Whence the heal - ing stream doth flow;
3. When I tread the verge of Jor - dan, Bid my anx - ious fears sub-side;

I am weak, but Thou art might-y; Hold me with Thy pow-er-ful hand;
Let the fire and cloud-y pil - lar Lead me all my jour-ney through;
Death of death, and hell's de-struc-tion, Land me safe on Ca-naan's side;

Bread of heav - en, Bread of heav - en, Feed me till I want no
Strong De - liv - erer, strong De - liv - er-er, Be Thou still my strength and
Songs of prais - es, songs of prais - es I will ev - er give to

more, (want no more,) Feed me till I want no more.
shield, (strength and shield,) Be Thou still my strength and shield.
Thee. (give to Thee,) I will ev - er give to Thee. A - MEN.

Music used by permission of Mrs. John Hughes, owner of copyright

402 From Every Stormy Wind That Blows

RETREAT

Hugh Stowell, 1799-1865

Thomas Hastings, 1784-1872

1. From ev-ery storm-y wind that blows, From ev-ery swell-ing tide of woes,
2. There is a place where Je-sus sheds The oil of glad-ness on our heads;
3. There is a scene where spirits blend, Where friend holds fel-low-ship with friend;
4. Ah! whith-er could we flee for aid, When tempted, des-o-late, dis-mayed;
5. Ah! there on ea-gle wings we soar, And sin and sense mo-lest no more:

There is a calm, a sure re-treat:'Tis found be-neath the mer-cy seat.
A place than all besides more sweet:It is the blood-bought mer-cy seat.
Though sundered far, by faith they meet A-round one com-mon mer-cy seat.
Or how the hosts of hell de-feat, Had suffering saints no mer-cy seat?
And heav'n comes down our souls to greet, While glo-ry crowns the mer-cy seat. A-MEN.

403 Come, My Soul, Thy Suit Prepare

HENDON

John Newton, 1725-1807

Henri A. César Malan, 1787-1864

1. Come, my soul, thy suit pre-pare, Je-sus loves to an-swer prayer; He Him-self has
2. Thou art com-ing to a King; Large pe-ti-tions with thee bring; For His grace and
3. Lord, I come to Thee for rest; Take pos-ses-sion of my breast; There Thy blood-bought
4. While I am a pil-grim here, Let Thy love my spir-it cheer: As my guide, my
5. Show me what I have to do; Ev-ery hour my strength renew; Let me live a

bid thee pray, Therefore will not say thee nay, Therefore will not say thee nay.
power are such, None can ev-er ask too much, None can ev-er ask too much.
right maintain, And with-out a ri-val reign, And with-out a ri-val reign.
guard, my friend, Lead me to my journey's end, Lead me to my journey's end.
life of faith, Let me die Thy peo-ple's death, Let me die Thy people's death. A-MEN.

I Must Tell Jesus

Elisha A. Hoffman, 1839-1929   Elisha A. Hoffman, 1839-1929

1. I must tell Je - sus all of my tri - als; I can - not bear these
2. I must tell Je - sus all of my troub - les; He is a kind, com -
3. Tempted and tried I need a great Sav - iour, One who can help my
4. O how the world to e - vil al - lures me! O how my heart is

bur - dens a - lone; In my dis - tress He kind - ly will help me;
pas - sion - ate Friend; If I but ask Him, He will de - liv - er,
bur - dens to bear; I must tell Je - sus, I must tell Je - sus;
tempt - ed to sin! I must tell Je - sus, and He will help me

He ev - er loves and cares for His own.
Make of my troub - les quick - ly an end.
He all my cares and sor - rows will share.
O - ver the world the vic - tory to win.

REFRAIN

I must tell Je - sus!

I must tell Je - sus! I can - not bear my bur - dens a - lone; I must tell

Je - sus! I must tell Je - sus! Je - sus can help me, Je - sus a - lone.

405 Jesus, I My Cross Have Taken

ELLESDIE

Henry F. Lyte, 1793-1847

Ascribed to Wolfgang A. Mozart, 1756-1791
Arr. by Hubert P. Main, 1839-1925

1. Je - sus, I my cross have tak - en, All to leave and fol - low Thee;
2. Let the world de-spise and leave me, They have left my Sav-iour, too;
3. Man may troub-le and dis - tress me, 'Twill but drive me to Thy breast;
4. Haste thee on from grace to glo - ry, Armed by faith and winged by prayer;

Des - ti - tute, de-spised, for - sak - en, Thou, from hence, my all shalt be:
Hu - man hearts and looks de - ceive me; Thou art not, like man, un - true;
Life with tri - als hard may press me, Heaven will bring me sweet - er rest.
Heaven's e - ter - nal day's be - fore thee, God's own hand shall guide thee there.

Per - ish ev - ery fond am - bi - tion, All I've sought, and hoped, and known;
And, while Thou shalt smile up - on me, God of wis - dom, love, and might,
O 'tis not in grief to harm me, While Thy love is left to me;
Soon shall close thy earth - ly mis - sion, Swift shall pass thy pil - grim days,

Yet how rich is my con-di - tion, God and heaven are still my own!
Foes may hate, and friends may shun me; Show Thy face, and all is bright.
O 'twere not in joy to charm me, Were that joy un-mixed with Thee.
Hope shall change to glad fru-i - tion, Faith to sight, and prayer to praise. AMEN.

Christian, Dost Thou See Them?

ST. ANDREW OF CRETE

Andrew of Crete, 660-732
Trans. by John M. Neale, 1818-1866

John B. Dykes, 1823-1876

1. Chris - tian, dost thou see them On the ho - ly ground,
2. Chris - tian, dost thou feel them, How they work with - in,
3. Chris - tian, dost thou hear them, How they speak thee fair,
4. "Well I know thy trou - ble, O my serv - ant true.

How the powers of dark - ness Com - pass thee a - round?
Striv - ing, tempt-ing, lur - ing, Goad - ing in - to sin?
"Al - ways fast and vig - il, Al - ways watch and prayer."
Thou art ver - y wea - ry; I was wea - ry too.

Chris - tian, up and smite them, Count - ing gain but loss,
Chris - tian, nev - er trem - ble, Nev - er be down-cast;
Chris - tian, an - swer bold - ly, "While I breathe I pray."
But that toil shall make thee Some day all mine own,

In the strength that com - eth, By the ho - ly cross.
Gird thee for the bat - tle, Watch and pray and fast.
Peace shall fol - low bat - tle, Night shall end in day.
And the end of sor - row Shall be near my throne." A-MEN.

407 Jesus Calls Us
GALILEE (Jude)

Cecil F. Alexander, 1818-1895

William H. Jude, 1852-1922

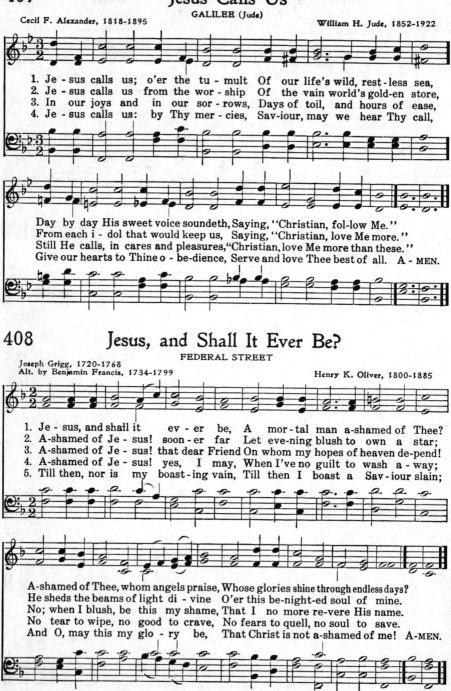

1. Je - sus calls us; o'er the tu - mult Of our life's wild, rest - less sea,
2. Je - sus calls us from the wor - ship Of the vain world's gold-en store,
3. In our joys and in our sor - rows, Days of toil, and hours of ease,
4. Je - sus calls us: by Thy mer - cies, Sav-iour, may we hear Thy call,

Day by day His sweet voice soundeth, Saying, "Christian, fol-low Me."
From each i - dol that would keep us, Saying, "Christian, love Me more."
Still He calls, in cares and pleasures, "Christian, love Me more than these."
Give our hearts to Thine o - be-dience, Serve and love Thee best of all. A - MEN.

408 Jesus, and Shall It Ever Be?
FEDERAL STREET

Joseph Grigg, 1720-1768
Alt. by Benjamin Francis, 1734-1799

Henry K. Oliver, 1800-1885

1. Je - sus, and shall it ev - er be, A mor-tal man a-shamed of Thee?
2. A-shamed of Je - sus! soon-er far Let eve-ning blush to own a star;
3. A-shamed of Je - sus! that dear Friend On whom my hopes of heaven de-pend!
4. A-shamed of Je - sus! yes, I may, When I've no guilt to wash a - way;
5. Till then, nor is my boast-ing vain, Till then I boast a Sav-iour slain;

A-shamed of Thee, whom angels praise, Whose glories shine through endless days?
He sheds the beams of light di - vine O'er this be-night-ed soul of mine.
No; when I blush, be this my shame, That I no more re-vere His name.
No tear to wipe, no good to crave, No fears to quell, no soul to save.
And O, may this my glo - ry be, That Christ is not a-shamed of me! A-MEN.

My Soul, Be on Thy Guard

409

LABAN

George Heath, 1750-1822

Lowell Mason, 1792-1872

1. My soul, be on thy guard, Ten thou-sand foes a - rise; The
2. O watch, and fight, and pray, The bat - tle ne'er give o'er; Re-
3. Ne'er think the vic - tory won, Nor lay thine ar - mor down; The
4. Fight on, my soul, till death Shall bring thee to thy God; He'll

hosts of sin are press - ing hard To draw thee from the skies.
new it bold - ly ev - ery day, And help di - vine im - plore.
work of faith will not be done, Till thou ob - tain the crown.
take thee, at thy part - ing breath, To His di - vine a - bode. A - MEN.

Children of the Heavenly King

410

PLEYEL'S HYMN

John Cennick, 1718-1755

Ignaz J. Pleyel, 1757-1831

1. Chil - dren of the heaven-ly King, As we jour - ney let us sing;
2. We are trav-eling home to God, In the way our fa - thers trod;
3. O ye ban - ished seed, be glad; Christ our Ad - vo - cate is made:
4. Fear not, breth-ren, joy - ful stand On the bor - ders of our land;
5. Lord, o - be - dient-ly we'll go, Glad - ly leav - ing all be - low:

Sing our Sav-iour's wor-thy praise, Glo - rious in His works and ways.
They are hap - py now, and we Soon their hap - pi - ness shall see.
Us to save our flesh as - sumes, Broth - er to our souls be - comes.
Je - sus Christ, our Fa-ther's Son, Bids us un - dis-mayed go on.
On - ly Thou our Lead - er be, And we still will fol - low Thee. A - MEN.

Stepping in the Light

Eliza E. Hewitt, 1851-1920

William J. Kirkpatrick, 1838-1921

1. Try - ing to walk in the steps of the Sav-iour, Try - ing to fol - low our
2. Press-ing more close - ly to Him who is lead-ing, When we are tempt-ed to
3. Walk-ing in foot - steps of gen - tle for-bear-ance, Foot-steps of faith-ful-ness,
4. Try - ing to walk in the steps of the Sav-iour, Up-ward, still up-ward we'll

Sav - iour and King; Shap - ing our lives by His bless - ed ex - am - ple,
turn from the way; Trust - ing the arm that is strong to de - fend us,
mer - cy and love; Look - ing to Him for the grace free - ly prom - ised,
fol - low our Guide; When we shall see Him, "the King in His beau - ty,"

REFRAIN

Hap - py, how hap - py, the songs that we bring.
Hap - py, how hap - py, our prais - es each day. How beau - ti - ful to walk in the
Hap - py, how hap - py, our jour - ney a - bove!
Hap - py, how hap - py, our place at His side!

steps of the Sav - iour, Step-ping in the light, Step-ping in the light; How

beau - ti - ful to walk in the steps of the Sav-iour, Led in paths of light!

He Who Would Valiant Be

ST. DUNSTAN'S

John Bunyan, 1628-1688, alt.

Charles W. Douglas, 1867-1944

1. He who would val - iant be 'Gainst all dis - as - ter,
2. Who - so be - set him round With dis - mal sto - ries,
3. Since, Lord, thou dost de - fend Us with Thy Spir - it,

Let him in con - stan - cy Fol - low the Mas - ter.
Do but them - selves con - found, His strength the more is.
We know we at the end Shall life in - her - it.

There's no dis - cour - age - ment Shall make him once re - lent His
No foes shall stay his might; Though he with gi - ants fight, He
Then fan - cies, flee a - way! I'll fear not what men say, I'll

first a - vowed in - tent To be a pil - grim.
will make good his right To be a pil - grim.
la - bor night and day To be a pil - grim. A - MEN.

Words from "Songs of Praise," Enlarged. Used by permission of the Oxford University Press
Music copyright, 1918, by Winfred Douglas. Used by permission of the Church Pension Fund

413 Loyalty to Christ

E. Taylor Cassel, 1849-1930

Flora H. Cassel, 1852-1911

1. From o - ver hill and plain There comes the signal strain, 'Tis loy-al-ty, loy-al-ty,
2. O hear, ye brave, the sound That moves the earth around, 'Tis loy-al-ty, loy-al-ty,
3. Come, join our loyal throng, We'll rout the gi-ant wrong, 'Tis loy-al-ty, loy-al-ty,
4. The strength of youth we lay At Je-sus' feet to - day, 'Tis loy-al-ty, loy-al-ty,

loy - al - ty to Christ; Its mu - sic rolls a - long, The hills take up the song,
loy - al - ty to Christ; A - rise to dare and do, Ring out the watch-word true,
loy - al - ty to Christ; Where Sa-tan's banners float We'll send the bu - gle note,
loy - al - ty to Christ; His gos - pel we'll pro-claim Throughout the world's domain,

REFRAIN

Of loy - al - ty, loy - al-ty, Yes, loy-al-ty to Christ. "On to vic-to-ry! On to

vic-to-ry!" Cries our great Commander; "On!" We'll move at His com-mand,
great Commander; "On!"

We'll soon possess the land, Thro' loy-al-ty, loy - al - ty, Yes, loy-al-ty to Christ.

Lead On, O King Eternal

LANCASHIRE

Ernest W. Shurtleff, 1862-1917

Henry Smart, 1813-1879

1. Lead on, O King E - ter - nal, The day of march has come;
2. Lead on, O King E - ter - nal, Till sin's fierce war shall cease,
3. Lead on, O King E - ter - nal, We fol - low, not with fears;

Hence-forth in fields of con - quest Thy tents shall be our home.
And ho - li - ness shall whis - per The sweet A - men of peace;
For glad - ness breaks like morn - ing Wher-e'er Thy face ap - pears;

Through days of prep - a - ra - tion Thy grace has made us strong,
For not with swords loud clash - ing, Nor roll of stir - ring drums,
Thy cross is lift - ed o'er us; We jour - ney in its light:

And now, O King E - ter - nal, We lift our bat - tle song.
With deeds of love and mer - cy The heaven-ly king - dom comes.
The crown a - waits the con - quest; Lead on, O God of might. A-MEN.

415 Who Is on the Lord's Side?

ARMAGEDDON

Francis R. Havergal, 1836-1879

German Melody Arr. by John Goss, 1800-1880
Descant (small notes), William Lester, b. 1889

1. Who is on the Lord's side? Who will serve the King? Who will be His
2. Not for weight of glo - ry, Not for crown and palm, En - ter we the
3. Je - sus, Thou hast bought us, Not with gold or gem, But with Thine own
4. Fierce may be the con - flict, Strong may be the foe, But the King's own

help - ers, Oth - er lives to bring? Who will leave the world's side?
ar - my, Raise the war - rior psalm; But for love that claim - eth
life - blood, For Thy di - a - dem. With Thy bless - ing fill - ing
ar - my None can o - ver - throw. Round His stand - ard rang - ing

Who will face the foe? Who is on the Lord's side? Who for
Lives for whom He died; He whom Je - sus nam - eth Must be
Each who comes to Thee, Thou hast made us will - ing, Thou hast
Vic - tory is se - cure; For His truth un-chang - ing Makes the

Him will go? By Thy call of mer - cy, By Thy grace di - vine,
on His side. By Thy love con-strain - ing, By Thy grace di - vine,
made us free. By Thy grand re - demp - tion, By Thy grace di - vine,
tri - umph sure. Joy - ful - ly en - list - ing By Thy grace di - vine,

We are on the Lord's side, Sav - iour, we are Thine. A - MEN.

The Banner of the Cross

Daniel W. Whittle, 1840-1901

James McGranahan, 1840-1907

1. There's a roy-al ban-ner giv-en for dis-play To the sol-diers
2. Though the foe may rage and gath-er as the flood, Let the stand-ard
3. O - ver land and sea, wher-ev - er man may dwell, Make the glo - rious
4. When the glo - ry dawns—'tis draw-ing ver - y near— It is has-tening

of the King; As an en-sign fair we lift it up to-day,
be dis-played; And be-neath its folds, as sol-diers of the Lord,
ti-dings known; Of the crim-son ban-ner now the sto-ry tell,
day by day— Then be-fore our King the foe shall dis-ap-pear,

REFRAIN

While as ran-somed ones we sing. March-ing on, march-ing
For the truth be not dis-mayed! on, on,
While the Lord shall claim His own!
And the cross the world shall sway!

on, For Christ count ev - ery-thing but loss! And to
on, on, ev - ery-thing, ev - ery-thing but loss!

crown Him King, toil and sing 'Neath the ban-ner of the cross!
we'll Be-neath

417 Soldiers of Christ, Arise
DIADEMATA

Charles Wesley, 1707-1788

George J. Elvey, 1816-1893
Descant, (small notes), William Lester, b. 1889

1. Sol - diers of Christ, a - rise, And put your ar - mor on,
2. Stand then in His great might, With all His strength en - dued,
3. Leave no un - guard - ed place, No weak - ness of the soul;

Strong in the strength which God sup - plies Through His e - ter - nal Son;
And take, to arm you for the fight, The pan - o - ply of God;
Take ev - ery vir - tue, ev - ery grace, And for - ti - fy the whole.

Strong in the Lord of hosts, And in His might - y power, Who
That hav - ing all things done, And all your con - flicts past, Ye
From strength to strength go on, Wres - tle and fight and pray; Tread

in the strength of Je - sus trusts Is more than con - quer - or.
may o'er-come through Christ a-lone, And stand en - tire at last.
all the powers of dark - ness down, And win the well-fought day. A-MEN.

Fight the Good Fight with All Thy Might 418

PENTECOST

John S. B. Monsell, 1811-1875

William Boyd, 1847-1928

1. Fight the good fight with all thy might! Christ is thy strength, and Christ thy right;
2. Run the straight race through God's good grace, Lift up thine eyes, and seek His face;
3. Cast care a-side, lean on thy Guide, His bound-less mer-cy will pro-vide;
4. Faint not nor fear, His arms are near, He chang-eth not, and thou art dear;

Lay hold on life, and it shall be Thy joy and crown e-ter-nal-ly.
Life with its way be-fore us lies, Christ is the path, and Christ the prize.
Trust, and thy trusting soul shall prove Christ is its life, and Christ its love.
On-ly be-lieve, and thou shalt see That Christ is all in all to thee. A-MEN.

Music used by permission of Novello & Co., Ltd. This tune in higher key, No. 428

Awake, My Soul, Stretch Every Nerve 419

CHRISTMAS

Philip Doddridge, 1702-1751

Arr. from George F. Handel, 1685-1759

1. A-wake, my soul, stretch every nerve, And press with vig-or on! A heaven-ly
2. A cloud of wit-ness-es a-round Hold thee in full sur-vey; For-get the
3. 'Tis God's all-an-i-mat-ing voice That calls thee from on high; 'Tis His own
4. Blest Saviour, in-tro-duced by Thee, Have I my race be-gun; And, crowned with

race demands thy zeal, And an im-mor-tal crown, And an im-mor-tal crown.
steps al-read-y trod, And onward urge thy way, And on-ward urge thy way.
hand presents the prize To thine as-pir-ing eye, To thine as-pir-ing eye.
vic-tory, at Thy feet I'll lay my hon-ors down, I'll lay my hon-ors down. A-MEN.

420 Sound the Battle Cry

William F. Sherwin, 1826-1888   William F. Sherwin, 1826-1888

1. Sound the bat-tle cry! See, the foe is nigh; Raise the stand-ard high
2. Strong to meet the foe, March-ing on we go, While our cause we know,
3. O Thou God of all, Hear us when we call, Help us one and all

For the Lord; Gird your ar-mor on, Stand firm, ev-ery one; Rest your
Must pre-vail; Shield and ban-ner bright, Gleam-ing in the light; Bat-tling
By Thy grace; When the bat-tle's done, And the vic-tory's won, May we

REFRAIN

cause up-on His ho-ly Word.
for the right We ne'er can fail. Rouse, then, sol-diers, ral-ly round the
wear the crown Be-fore Thy face.

ban-ner, Read-y, stead-y, pass the word a-long; On-ward, for-ward,

shout a-loud Ho-san-na! Christ is Cap-tain of the might-y throng.

The Son of God Goes Forth to War 421

ALL SAINTS, NEW

Reginald Heber, 1783-1826   Henry S. Cutler, 1824-1902

1. The Son of God goes forth to war, A king-ly crown to gain;
2. The mar-tyr first, whose ea-gle eye Could pierce be-yond the grave,
3. A glo-rious band, the cho-sen few On whom the Spir-it came,
4. A no-ble ar-my, men and boys, The ma-tron and the maid,

His blood-red ban-ner streams a-far: Who fol-lows in His train?
Who saw his Mas-ter in the sky, And called on Him to save:
Twelve va-liant saints, their hope they knew, And mocked the cross and flame:
A-round the Sav-iour's throne re-joice, In robes of light ar-rayed:

Who best can drink his cup of woe, Tri-um-phant o-ver pain,
Like Him, with par-don on his tongue In midst of mor-tal pain,
They met the ty-rant's brandished steel, The li-on's go-ry mane;
They climbed the steep as-cent of heaven Through per-il, toil, and pain;

Who pa-tient bears his cross be-low, He fol-lows in His train.
He prayed for them that did the wrong: Who fol-lows in his train?
They bowed their necks the death to feel: Who fol-lows in their train?
O God, to us may grace be given To fol-low in their train. A-MEN.

422 A Passion for Souls

Herbert G. Tovey, b. 1888   Foss L. Fellers, 1887-1924

1. Give me a pas-sion for souls, dear Lord, A pas-sion to save the lost;
2. Though there are dan-gers un-told and stern Con-front-ing me in the way,
3. How shall this pas-sion for souls be mine? Lord, make Thou the an-swer clear;

O that Thy love were by all a-dored, And wel-comed at an-y cost.
Will-ing-ly still would I go, nor turn, But trust Thee for grace each day.
Help me to throw out the old Life-Line To those who are strug-gling near.

REFRAIN

Je-sus, I long, I long to be win-ning Men who are

lost, and con-stant-ly sin-ning; O may this hour be

one of be-gin-ning The sto-ry of par-don to tell.

Throw Out the Life-Line

Edward S. Ufford, 1851-1929

Edward S. Ufford, 1851-1929
Arr. by George C. Stebbins, 1846-1945

1. Throw out the Life-Line a - cross the dark wave, There is a broth-er whom
2. Throw out the Life-Line with hand quick and strong: Why do you tar - ry, why
3. Throw out the Life-Line to dan - ger fraught men, Sink - ing in an-guish where
4. Soon will the sea - son of res - cue be o'er, Soon will they drift to e-

some one should save; Some-bod - y's broth - er! oh, who then will dare To
lin - ger so long? See! he is sink - ing; oh, has - ten to - day— And
you've nev - er been: Winds of temp - ta - tion and bil - lows of woe Will
ter - ni - ty's shore; Haste then, my broth - er, no time for de - lay, But

REFRAIN

throw out the Life-Line, his per - il to share?
out with the Life - Boat! a - way, then, a - way!   Throw out the Life - Line!
soon hurl them out where the dark wa - ters flow.
throw out the Life - Line and save them to - day.

Throw out the Life-Line! Some-one is drift - ing a - way; Throw out the

Life - Line! Throw out the Life-Line! Some one is sink - ing to - day.

424 Will There Be Any Stars?

Eliza E. Hewitt, 1851-1920

John R. Sweney, 1837-1899

1. I am think-ing to-day of that beau-ti-ful land I shall reach when the sun go-eth down; When through won-der-ful grace by my Sav-iour I stand, Will there be an-y stars in my crown?

2. In the strength of the Lord let me la-bor and pray, Let me watch as a win-ner of souls; That bright stars may be mine in the glo-ri-ous day, When His praise like the sea-bil-low rolls.

3. Oh, what joy it will be when His face I be-hold, Liv-ing gems at His feet to lay down; It would sweet-en my bliss in the cit-y of gold, Should there be an-y stars in my crown.

REFRAIN

Will there be an-y stars, an-y stars in my crown When at eve-ning the sun go-eth down? When I wake with the blest In the go-eth down?

Will There Be Any Stars?

man-sions of rest, Will there be an-y stars in my crown?

an-y stars in my crown?

Bring Them In

425

Alexcenah Thomas, 19th Century

William A. Ogden, 1841-1897

1. Hark! 'tis the Shep-herd's voice I hear, Out in the des-ert dark and drear,
2. Who'll go and help this Shep-herd kind, Help Him the wand-ering ones to find?
3. Out in the des-ert hear their cry, Out on the moun-tains wild and high;

Call-ing the sheep who've gone a-stray Far from the Shep-herd's fold a-way.
Who'll bring the lost ones to the fold, Where they'll be shel-tered from the cold?
Hark! 'tis the Mas-ter speaks to thee, "Go find my sheep wher-e'er they be."

REFRAIN

Bring them in, bring them in, Bring them in from the fields of sin;

Bring them in, bring them in, Bring the wand-ering ones to Je-sus.

426

Rescue the Perishing

Fanny J. Crosby, 1820-1915   William H. Doane, 1832-1915

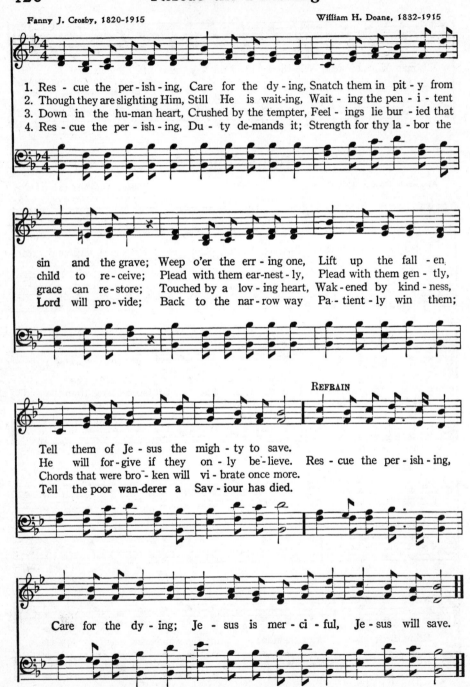

1. Res - cue the per - ish - ing, Care for the dy - ing, Snatch them in pit - y from
2. Though they are slighting Him, Still He is wait-ing, Wait - ing the pen - i - tent
3. Down in the hu - man heart, Crushed by the tempter, Feel - ings lie bur - ied that
4. Res - cue the per - ish - ing, Du - ty de-mands it; Strength for thy la - bor the

sin and the grave; Weep o'er the err - ing one, Lift up the fall - en
child to re - ceive; Plead with them ear-nest - ly, Plead with them gen - tly,
grace can re - store; Touched by a lov - ing heart, Wak - ened by kind - ness,
Lord will pro - vide; Back to the nar - row way Pa - tient - ly win them;

REFRAIN

Tell them of Je - sus the migh - ty to save.
He will for - give if they on - ly be - lieve. Res - cue the per - ish - ing,
Chords that were bro - ken will vi - brate once more.
Tell the poor wan-derer a Sav - iour has died.

Care for the dy - ing; Je - sus is mer - ci - ful, Je - sus will save.

Hasten, Lord, the Glorious Time
ST. BEES

427

Harriet Auber, 1773-1862   John B. Dykes, 1823-1876

1. Has - ten, Lord, the glo - rious time, When be-neath Mes - si - ah's sway,
2. Mightiest kings His power shall own; Heath-en tribes His name a - dore.
3. Then shall wars and tu-mults cease, Then be ban-ished grief and pain;
4. Bless we, then, our gra-cious Lord; Ev - er praise His glo - rious name;

Ev - ery na - tion, ev - ery clime, Shall the gos - pel call o - bey.
Sa - tan and his host o'erthrown, Bound in chains, shall hurt no more.
Righteousness and joy and peace, Un - disturbed, shall ev - er reign.
All His might-y acts re - cord, All His won-drous love pro-claim. A-MEN.

Go, Labor On; Spend, and Be Spent
PENTECOST

428

Horatius Bonar, 1808-1889   William Boyd, 1847-1928

1. Go, la - bor on; spend, and be spent, Thy joy to do the Fa-ther's will:
2. Go, la - bor on; 'tis not for naught; Thy earthly loss is heaven-ly gain:
3. Go, la - bor on while it is day: The world's dark night is hastening on;
4. Toil on, faint not, keep watch and pray, Be wise the err - ing soul to win;

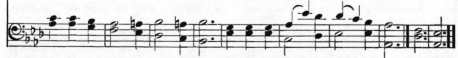

It is the way the Mas-ter went; Should not the servant tread it still?
Men heed thee, love thee, praise thee not; The Master prais-es: what are men?
Speed, speed thy work, cast sloth away; It is not thus that souls are won.
Go forth in - to the world's highway, Compel the wanderer to come in. A-MEN.

Music used by permission of Novello & Co. Ltd. This tune in lower key, No. 418
Alternate tunes: MISSIONARY CHANT, No. 434; DUKE STREET, No. 444

429 Hark, the Voice of Jesus Calling

ELLESDIE

Daniel March, 1816-1909

Ascribed to Wolfgang A. Mozart, 1756-1791
Arr. by Hubert P. Main, 1839-1925

1. Hark, the voice of Je-sus call-ing, "Who will go and work to-day?
2. If you can-not cross the o-cean And the heath-en lands ex-plore,
3. Let none hear you i-dly say-ing, "There is noth-ing I can do,"

Fields are white, and har-vests wait-ing, Who will bear the sheaves a-way?"
You can find the heath-en near-er, You can help them at your door:
While the souls of men are dy-ing, And the Mas-ter calls for you:

Loud and long the Mas-ter call-eth, Rich re-ward He of-fers thee;
If you can-not give your thousands, You can give the wid-ow's mite;
Glad-ly take the task He gives you; Let His work your pleas-ure be;

Who will an-swer, glad-ly say-ing, "Here am I; send me, send me"?
And the least you give for Je-sus Will be pre-cious in His sight.
An-swer quickly when He call-eth, "Here am I; send me, send me." A-MEN.

Alternate tune: HYFRYDOL, No. 469

O Zion, Haste

TIDINGS

Mary A. Thomson, 1834-1923

James Walch, 1837-1901

1. O   Zi - on, haste, thy mis - sion high ful - fill - ing,   To   tell   to   all   the
2. Be-hold how man - y thous- ands still are   ly - ing,   Bound in the dark - some
3. Pro-claim to ev - ery peo - ple, tongue and na - tion   That God in whom they
4. Give of thy sons to   bear the mes-sage glo - rious;   Give of thy wealth to

world that God is Light; That He who made   all   na - tions is not will - ing
pris - on-house of   sin,   With none to tell them of   the Sav-iour's dy - ing,
live and move is love: Tell how He stooped to save His lost cre - a - tion,
speed them on their way; Pour out thy soul for them in prayer vic - to- rious;

REFRAIN

One soul should per - ish,   lost   in shades of   night .
Or   of   the life He   died for them to   win. Pub - lish glad ti - dings,
And died   on earth that   man might live   a - bove.
And   all thou spend - est   Je - sus will re - pay.

Ti - dings of peace; Ti - dings of Je - sus, Re - demp-tion, and re - lease.

431 From Greenland's Icy Mountains

MISSIONARY HYMN

Reginald Heber, 1783-1826   Lowell Mason, 1792-1872

1. From Green-land's i - cy moun-tains, From In - dia's cor - al strand,
2. What though the spi - cy breez - es Blow soft o'er Cey-lon's isle;
3. Shall we, whose souls are light - ed With wis-dom from on high,
4. Waft, waft, ye winds, His sto - ry, And you, ye wa - ters, roll,

Where Af - ric's sun - ny foun - tains Roll down their gold - en sand,
Though ev - ery pros - pect pleas - es, And on - ly man is vile?
Shall we to men be - night - ed The lamp of life de - ny?
Till, like a sea of glo - ry, It spreads from pole to pole:

From man - y an an - cient riv - er, From man - y a palm - y plain,
In vain with lav - ish kind - ness The gifts of God are strown;
Sal - va -tion! O sal - va - tion! The joy - ful sound pro - claim,
Till o'er our ran-somed na - ture The Lamb for sin - ners slain,

They call us to de - liv - er Their land from er - ror's chain.
The hea - then in his blind - ness Bows down to wood and stone.
Till earth's re - mot - est na - tion Has learned Mes - si - ah's name.
Re - deem - er, King, Cre - a - tor, In bliss re - turns to reign. A-MEN.

The Morning Light Is Breaking

WEBB

Samuel F. Smith, 1808-1895 George J. Webb, 1803-1887

1. The morn - ing light is break - ing, The dark - ness dis - ap - pears;
2. See hea - then na - tions bend - ing Be - fore the God we love,
3. Blest riv - er of sal - va - tion, Pur - sue thine on - ward way;

The sons of earth are wak - ing To pen - i - ten - tial tears;
And thou - sand hearts as - cend - ing In grat - i - tude a - bove;
Flow thou to ev - ery na - tion, Nor in thy rich - ness stay;

Each breeze that sweeps the o - cean Brings ti - dings from a - far,
While sin - ners, now con - fess - ing, The gos - pel call o - bey,
Stay not till all the low - ly Tri - um - phant reach their home;

Of na - tions in com - mo - tion, Pre - pared for Zi - on's war.
And seek the Sav - iour's bless - ing, A na - tion in a day.
Stay not till all the ho - ly Pro - claim, "The Lord is come!" A-MEN.

433 Go Ye into All the World

James McGranahan, 1840-1907

James McGranahan, 1840-1907

1. Far, far a-way, in hea-then dark-ness dwell-ing, Mil-lions of souls for-
2. See o'er the world wide-o-pen doors in-vit-ing, Sol-diers of Christ, a-
3. "Why will ye die?" the voice of God is call-ing, "Why will ye die?" re-
4. God speed the day, when those of ev-ery na-tion "Glo-ry to God!" tri-

ev-er may be lost; Who, who will go, sal-va-tion's sto-ry tell-ing,
rise and en-ter in! Chris-tians, a-wake! your forc-es all u-nit-ing,
ech-o in His name; Je-sus hath died to save from death ap-pall-ing,
um-phant-ly shall sing; Ran-somed, redeemed, re-joic-ing in sal-va-tion,

REFRAIN

Look-ing to Je-sus, minding not the cost?
Send forth the gos-pel, break the chains of sin.
Life and sal-va-tion therefore go pro-claim. "All pow'r is giv-en un-to Me,
Shout Hal-le-lu-jah; for the Lord is King.

All pow'r is giv-en un-to Me, Go ye in-to all the world and

preach the gos-pel, And lo, I am with you al-way."

Ye Christian Heralds!
MISSIONARY CHANT

Bourne H. Draper. 1775-1843

Charles H. C. Zeuner, 1795-1857

1. Ye Chris-tian her- alds, go pro-claim Sal - va - tion through Em-man-uel's name;
2. God shield you with a wall of fire, With flam-ing zeal your hearts in - spire,
3. And when our la - bors all are o'er, Then we shall meet to part no more;

To dis-tant climes the ti-dings bear, And plant the Rose of Shar-on there.
Bid rag'- ing winds their fu - ry cease, And hush the tem-pests in- to peace.
Meet with the blood-bought throng to fall, And crown our Je-sus Lord of all. A-MEN.

Alternate tune: DUKE STREET, No. 444

The Call for Reapers
435

John O. Thompson, 1782-1818

J. B. O. Clemm, 19th Century

1. Far and near the fields are teem-ing With the waves of ri - pened grain;
2. Send them forth with morn's first beaming, Send them in the noon-tide's glare;
3. O thou, whom thy Lord is send-ing, Gath - er now the sheaves of gold;

FINE

Far and near their gold is gleam-ing O'er the sun - ny slope and plain.
When the sun's last rays are gleam-ing, Bid them gath - er ev - ery-where.
Heavenward then at eve-ning wend- ing, Thou shalt come with joy un - told.

D.S.—*Send them now the sheaves to gath - er, Ere the har - vest - time pass by.*

REFRAIN

D.S.

Lord of har - vest, send forth reap-ers! Hear us, Lord, to Thee we cry;

436 We've a Story to Tell to the Nations

H. Ernest Nichol, 1862-1928

H. Ernest Nichol, 1862-1928

1. We've a sto - ry to tell to the na - tions That shall
2. We've a song to be sung to the na - tions That shall
3. We've a mes - sage to give to the na - tions That the
4. We've a Sav - iour to show to the na - tions Who the

turn their hearts to the right, A sto - ry of truth and mer - cy,
lift their hearts to the Lord, A song that shall con - quer e - vil
Lord who reign-eth a - bove Hath sent us His Son to save us,
path of sor - row hath trod, That all of the world's great peo - ples

A sto - ry of peace and light, A sto - ry of peace and light.
And shat - ter the spear and sword, And shat - ter the spear and sword.
And show us that God is love, And show us that God is love.
Might come to the truth of God, Might come to the truth of God.

REFRAIN

For the dark-ness shall turn to dawn - ing, And the dawn-ing to noon-day bright,

And Christ's great king-dom shall come to earth, The king-dom of love and light.

Words and music copyright. Used by permission of H. E. Nichol and Son.

Send the Light

Charles H. Gabriel, 1856-1932

Charles H. Gabriel, 1856-1932

1. There's a call comes ring - ing o'er the rest-less wave, "Send the light!
2. We have heard the Mac - e - do - nian call to - day, "Send the light!
3. Let us pray that grace may ev - ery-where a-bound; Send the light!
4. Let us not grow wea - ry in the work of love, Send the light!

Send the light!

Send the light!" There are souls to res - cue, there are souls to save,
Send the light!" And a gold - en of - fering at the cross we lay,
Send the light! And a Christ-like spir - it ev - ery-where be found,
Send the light! Let us gath - er jew - els for a crown a-bove,

Send the light!

REFRAIN

Send the light! Send the light! Send the light! the
Send the light! Send the light! Send the light!

1

bless - ed gos - pel light; Let it shine from shore to
the bless - ed gos - pel light; Let it shine

2

shore! shine for - ev - er - more.
from shore to shore! Let it shine for - ev - er - more.

438   Let the Lower Lights Be Burning

Philip P. Bliss, 1838-1876   Philip P. Bliss, 1838-1876

1. Bright-ly beams our Fa-ther's mer - cy From His light-house ev - er - more,
2. Dark the night of sin has set - tled, Loud the an - gry bil - lows roar;
3. Trim your fee - ble lamp, my broth - er; Some poor sail - or tem-pest tossed,

But to us He gives the keep - ing Of the lights a - long the shore.
Ea - ger eyes are watch-ing, long - ing, For the lights a - long the shore.
Try - ing now to make the har - bor, In the dark-ness may be lost.

REFRAIN

Let the low - er lights be burn-ing! Send a gleam a - cross the wave!

Some poor faint - ing, strug-gling sea-man You may res - cue, you may save.

439   In Christ There Is No East or West

ST. PETER

John Oxenham, 1852-1941   Alexander R. Reinagle, 1799-1877

1. In Christ there is no East or West, In Him no South or North;
2. In Him shall true hearts ev - ery-where Their high com - mun - ion find;
3. Join hands then, broth-ers of the faith, Whate'er your race may be;
4. In Christ now meet both East and West, In Him meet South and North;

Words from "Bees in Amber," by John Oxenham. Used by permission of Miss Erica Oxenham

In Christ There Is No East or West

But one great fel-low-ship of love Throughout the whole wide earth.
His serv-ice is the gold-en cord Close-bind-ing all man-kind.
Who serves my Fa-ther as a son Is sure-ly kin to me.
All Christ-ly souls are one in Him Throughout the whole wide earth. A-MEN.

Hail to the Brightness   440
WESLEY

Thomas Hastings, 1784-1872

Lowell Mason, 1792-1872
Descant (small notes), William Lester, b. 1889

1. Hail to the bright-ness of Zi-on's glad morn-ing! Joy to the
2. Hail to the bright-ness of Zi-on's glad morn-ing, Long by the
3. Lo, in the des-ert rich flow-ers are spring-ing, Streams ev-er
4. See, from all lands, from the isles of the o-cean, Praise to Je-

lands that in dark-ness have lain! Hushed be the ac-cents of sor-row and
proph-ets of Is-rael fore-told! Hail to the mil-lions from bond-age re-
co-pious are glid-ing a-long; Loud from the moun-tain-tops ech-oes are
ho-vah as-cend-ing on high; Fall-en the en-gines of war and com-

mourn-ing; Zi-on in tri-umph be-gins her mild reign.
turn-ing! Gen-tiles and Jews the blest vi-sion be-hold.
ring-ing, Wastes rise in ver-dure and min-gle in song.
mo-tion, Shouts of sal-va-tion are rend-ing the sky. A-MEN.

441   Let the Song Go Round the Earth

MOEL LLYS

Sarah G. Stock, 19th Century   Sarah G. Stock, 19th Century

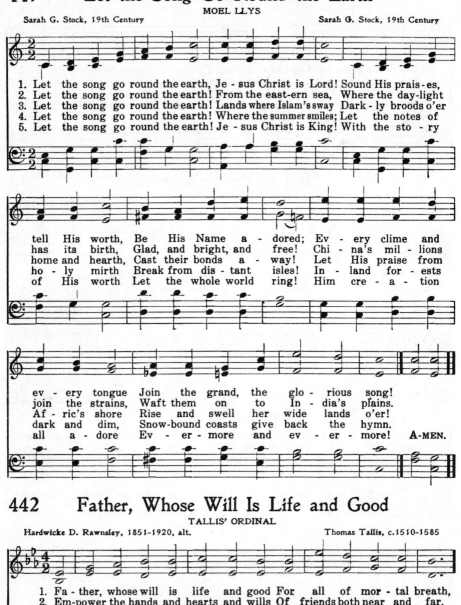

1. Let the song go round the earth, Je - sus Christ is Lord! Sound His prais - es,
2. Let the song go round the earth! From the east-ern sea, Where the day-light
3. Let the song go round the earth! Lands where Islam's sway Dark - ly broods o'er
4. Let the song go round the earth! Where the summer smiles; Let the notes of
5. Let the song go round the earth! Je - sus Christ is King! With the sto - ry

tell His worth, Be His Name a - dored; Ev - ery clime and
has its birth, Glad, and bright, and free! Chi - na's mil - lions
home and hearth, Cast their bonds a - way! Let His praise from
ho - ly mirth Break from dis - tant isles! In - land for - ests
of His worth Let the whole world ring! Him cre - a - tion

ev - ery tongue Join the grand, the glo - rious song!
join the strains, Waft them on to In - dia's plains.
Af - ric's shore Rise and swell her wide lands o'er!
dark and dim, Snow-bound coasts give back the hymn.
all a - dore Ev - er - more and ev - er - more! A-MEN.

442   Father, Whose Will Is Life and Good

TALLIS' ORDINAL

Hardwicke D. Rawnsley, 1851-1920, alt.   Thomas Tallis, c.1510-1585

1. Fa - ther, whose will is life and good For all of mor - tal breath;
2. Em-power the hands and hearts and wills Of friends both near and far,
3. Wher-e'er they heal the maimed and blind, Let love of Christ at - tend:
4. O Fa - ther, look from heaven and bless, Wher-e'er Thy ser - vants be,

Words by permission of Mrs. Hardwicke D. Rawnsley.
Alternate tune: ST. PETER, No. 439

Father, Whose Will Is Life and Good

Bind strong the bond of broth-er-hood Of those who fight with death.
Who bat-tle with the bod-y's ills, And wage Thy ho-ly war.
Pro-claim the good Phy-si-cian's mind, And prove the Sav-iour friend.
Their works of pure un-self-ish-ness, Made con-se-crate to Thee! A-MEN.

Christ for the World! We Sing 443

ITALIAN HYMN

Samuel Wolcott, 1813-1886   Felice de Giardini, 1716-1796

1. Christ for the world! we sing; The world to Christ we bring,
2. Christ for the world! we sing; The world to Christ we bring,
3. Christ for the world! we sing; The world to Christ we bring,
4. Christ for the world! we sing; The world to Christ we bring,

With lov-ing zeal; The poor and them that mourn, The faint and
With fer-vent prayer; The way-ward and the lost, By rest-less
With one ac-cord; With us the work to share, With us re-
With joy-ful song; The new-born souls whose days, Re-claimed from

o-ver-borne, Sin-sick and sor-row-worn, Whom Christ doth heal.
pas-sions tossed, Re-deemed at count-less cost, From dark de-spair.
proach to dare, With us the cross to bear, For Christ our Lord.
er-ror's ways, In-spired with hope and praise, To Christ be-long. A-MEN.

Alternate tune: KIRBY BEDON, No. 509

444 Jesus Shall Reign

DUKE STREET

From Psalm 72
Isaac Watts, 1674-1748

John Hatton, c.1710-1793

1. Je - sus shall reign wher-e'er the sun Does his suc - ces - sive jour-neys run;
2. From north to south the prin - ces meet To pay their hom-age at His feet;
3. To Him shall end - less prayer be made, And end- less prais-es crown His head;
4. Peo - ple and realms of ev - ery tongue Dwell on His love with sweet-est song,

His kingdom spread from shore to shore, Till moons shall wax and wane no more.
While west-ern em-pires own their Lord, And sav-age tribes at-tend His word.
His name like sweet per-fume shall rise With ev-ery morn-ing sac - ri - fice.
And in - fant voic - es shall pro-claim Their ear-ly bless-ings on His name. A-MEN.

445 Fling Out the Banner! Let It Float

WALTHAM (Doane)

George W. Doane, 1799-1859

John B. Calkin, 1827-1905

1. Fling out the ban - ner! let it float Sky-ward and sea-ward, high and wide;
2. Fling out the ban - ner! heath - en lands Shall see from far the glo - rious sight,
3. Fling out the ban - ner! sin - sick souls That sink and per - ish in the strife,
4. Fling out the ban - ner! let it float Sky-ward and sea-ward, high and wide,

The sun that lights its shin-ing folds, The cross on which the Sav-iour died.
And na - tions, crowd-ing to be born, Bap-tize their spir-its in its light.
Shall touch in faith its ra-diant hem, And spring im-mor-tal in - to life.
Our glo - ry, on - ly in the cross; Our on - ly hope, the Cru - ci - fied. A-MEN.

Jesus Saves

Priscilla J. Owens, 1829-1907

William J. Kirkpatrick, 1838-1921

1. We have heard the joy - ful sound: Je - sus saves! Je - sus saves!
2. Waft it on the roll - ing tide; Je - sus saves! Je - sus saves!
3. Sing a - bove the bat - tle strife, Je - sus saves! Je - sus saves!
4. Give the winds a might - y voice, Je - sus saves! Je - sus saves!

Spread the ti - dings all a - round: Je - sus saves! Je - sus saves!
Tell to sin - ners far and wide: Je - sus saves! Je - sus saves!
By His death and end - less life, Je - sus saves! Je - sus saves!
Let the na - tions now re - joice— Je - sus saves! Je - sus saves!

Bear the news to ev - ery land, Climb the steeps and cross the waves;
Sing, ye is - lands of the sea; Ech - o back, ye o - cean caves;
Sing it soft - ly through the gloom, When the heart for mer - cy craves;
Shout sal - va - tion full and free, High - est hills and deep - est caves;

On - ward!—'tis our Lord's com - mand; Je - sus saves! Je - sus saves!
Earth shall keep her ju - bi - lee; Je - sus saves! Je - sus saves!
Sing in tri - umph o'er the tomb— Je - sus saves! Je - sus saves!
This our song of vic - to - ry— Je - sus saves! Je - sus saves!

447   O Lord of Heaven and Earth and Sea

RADIANT MORN

Christopher Wordsworth, 1807-1885   Charles F. Gounod, 1818-1893

1. O Lord of heav'n and earth and sea, To Thee all praise and glo - ry be;
2. Thou didst not spare Thine on - ly Son, But gav'st Him for a world un - done,
3. For souls re-deemed, for sins for-giv'n, For means of grace and hopes of heav'n,
4. We lose what on our-selves we spend, We have as trea - sure with-out end
5. To Thee, from whom we all de - rive Our life, our gifts, our power to give:

How shall we show our love to Thee, Who giv - est all?
And free - ly, with that Bless - ed One, Thou giv - est all.
Fa - ther, what can to Thee be giv'n, Who giv - est all?
What - ev - er, Lord, to Thee we lend, Who giv - est all;
O may we ev - er with Thee live, Who giv - est all! A-MEN.

Alternate tune: ALMSGIVING, below

448   All Labor Gained New Dignity

ALMSGIVING

John Oxenham, 1852-1941   John B. Dykes, 1823-1876

1. All la - bor gained new dig - ni - ty Since He who all cre - a - tion made
2. No work is com-mon-place, if all Be done as un - to Him a - lone;
3. Each smallest com-mon thing He makes Serves Him with its mi - nut - est part;
4. His serv-ice is life's high - est joy, It yields fair fruit a hun-dred-fold,

Toiled with His hands for dai - ly bread Right man-ful - ly.
Life's sim-plest toil to Him is known, Who know-eth all.
Man on - ly, with his wan-d'ring heart, His way for - sakes.
Be this our prayer—"Not fame, nor gold, But Thine em-ploy!" A-MEN.

Master, No Offering

LOVE'S OFFERING

Edwin P. Parker, 1836-1925

Edwin P. Parker, 1836-1925

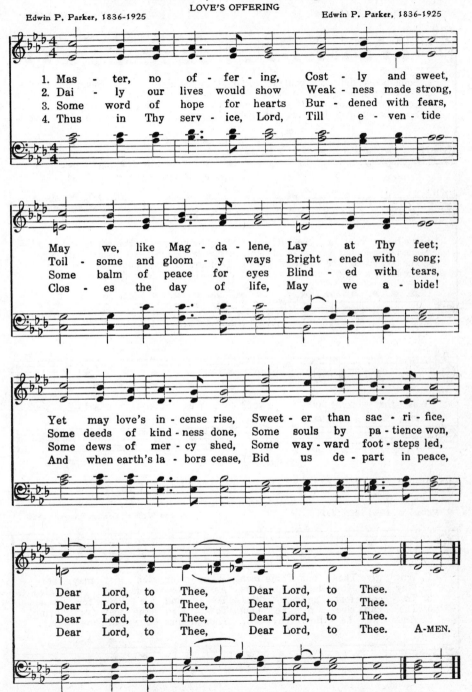

1. Mas - ter, no of - fer - ing, Cost - ly and sweet,
2. Dai - ly our lives would show Weak - ness made strong,
3. Some word of hope for hearts Bur - dened with fears,
4. Thus in Thy serv - ice, Lord, Till e - ven - tide

May we, like Mag - da - lene, Lay at Thy feet;
Toil - some and gloom - y ways Bright - ened with song;
Some balm of peace for eyes Blind - ed with tears,
Clos - es the day of life, May we a - bide!

Yet may love's in - cense rise, Sweet - er than sac - ri - fice,
Some deeds of kind - ness done, Some souls by pa - tience won,
Some dews of mer - cy shed, Some way - ward foot - steps led,
And when earth's la - bors cease, Bid us de - part in peace,

Dear Lord, to Thee, Dear Lord, to Thee.
Dear Lord, to Thee, Dear Lord, to Thee.
Dear Lord, to Thee, Dear Lord, to Thee.
Dear Lord, to Thee, Dear Lord, to Thee. A-MEN.

450 Somebody Did a Golden Deed

John R. Clements, 1868-1946

Winfield S. Weeden, 1847-1908

1. Some-bod-y did a gold-en deed, Prov-ing him-self a friend in need;
2. Some-bod-y thought 'tis sweet to live, Will-ing-ly said, "I'm glad to give;"
3. Some-bod-y made a lov-ing gift, Cheer-ful-ly tried a load to lift;
4. Some-bod-y filled the days with light, Con-stant-ly chased a-way the night;

Some-bod-y sang a cheer-ful song, Brightening the sky the whole day long,—
Some-bod-y fought a val-iant fight, Brave-ly he lived to shield the right,—
Some-bod-y told the love of Christ, Told how His will was sac-ri-ficed,—
Some-bod-y's work bore joy and peace, Sure-ly his life shall nev-er cease,—

rit.

Was that some-bod-y you? Was that some-bod-y you?

451 We Give Thee But Thine Own

SCHUMANN

William W. How, 1823-1897

Mason and Webb's "Cantica Laudis," 1850

1. We give Thee but Thine own, What-e'er the gift may be:
2. May we Thy boun-ties thus As stew-ards true re-ceive,
3. To com-fort and to bless, To find a balm for woe,
4. The cap-tive to re-lieve, To God the lost to bring,
5. And we be-lieve Thy word, Though dim our faith may be:

We Give Thee But Thine Own

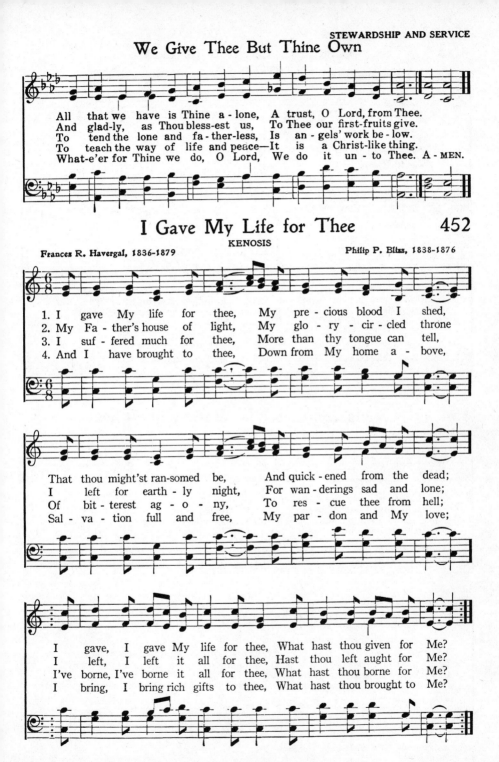

All that we have is Thine a-lone, A trust, O Lord, from Thee.
And glad-ly, as Thou bless-est us, To Thee our first-fruits give.
To tend the lone and fa-ther-less, Is an - gels' work be - low.
To teach the way of life and peace—It is a Christ-like thing.
What-e'er for Thine we do, O Lord, We do it un - to Thee. A - MEN.

I Gave My Life for Thee   452
KENOSIS

Frances R. Havergal, 1836-1879   Philip P. Bliss, 1838-1876

1. I gave My life for thee, My pre - cious blood I shed,
2. My Fa - ther's house of light, My glo - ry - cir - cled throne
3. I suf - fered much for thee, More than thy tongue can tell,
4. And I have brought to thee, Down from My home a - bove,

That thou might'st ran-somed be, And quick - ened from the dead;
I left for earth - ly night, For wan - derings sad and lone;
Of bit - terest ag - o - ny, To res - cue thee from hell;
Sal - va - tion full and free, My par - don and My love;

I gave, I gave My life for thee, What hast thou given for Me?
I left, I left it all for thee, Hast thou left aught for Me?
I've borne, I've borne it all for thee, What hast thou borne for Me?
I bring, I bring rich gifts to thee, What hast thou brought to Me?

453 Rise Up, O Men of God!

FESTAL SONG

William P. Merrill, 1867-1954

William H. Walter, 1825-1893

1. Rise up, O men of God! Have done with less-er things;
2. Rise up, O men of God! His King-dom tar-ries long;
3. Rise up, O men of God! The Church for you doth wait,
4. Lift high the cross of Christ! Tread where His feet have trod;

Give heart and soul and mind and strength To serve the King of kings.
Bring in the day of broth-er-hood And end the night of wrong.
Her strength un-e-qual to her task; Rise up, and make her great!
As broth-ers of the Son of Man, Rise up, O men of God! A-MEN.

Words used by permission of "The Presbyterian Outlook."
Alternate tune: ST. THOMAS, No. 247

454 O Master, Let Me Walk with Thee

MARYTON

Washington Gladden, 1836-1918

H. Percy Smith, 1825-1898

1. O Mas-ter, let me walk with Thee In low-ly paths of serv-ice free;
2. Help me the slow of heart to move By some clear, winning word of love;
3. Teach me Thy patience! still with Thee In clos-er, dear-er com-pa-ny,
4. In hope that sends a shin-ing ray Far down the fu-ture's broad'ning way,

Tell me Thy se-cret; help me bear The strain of toil, the fret of care.
Teach me the wayward feet to stay, And guide them in the homeward way.
In work that keeps faith sweet and strong, In trust that tri-umphs o-ver wrong;
In peace that on-ly Thou canst give, With Thee, O Mas-ter, let me live. A-MEN.

Alternate tune: CANONBURY, No. 338

Our Best

S. C. Kirk, 20th Century

Grant C. Tullar, 1869-1950

1. Hear ye the Mas-ter's call, "Give Me thy best!" For, be it great or small,
2. Wait not for men to laud, Heed not their slight; Win-ning the smile of God
3. Night soon comes on a-pace, Day has-tens by; Workman and work must face

That is His test. Do then the best you can, Not for re-ward, Not for the
Brings its de-light! Aid-ing the good and true Ne'er goes un-blest, All that we
Test-ing on high. Oh, may we in that day Find rest, sweet rest, Which God has

REFRAIN

praise of man, But for the Lord.
think or do, Be it the best. Ev-ery work for Je-sus will be blest,
prom-ised those Who do their best.

But He asks from ev-ery-one His best. Our tal-ents may be few,

These may be small, But un-to Him is due Our best, our all.

456 Must I Go, and Empty-Handed?

Charles C. Luther, 1847-1924

George C. Stebbins, 1846-1945

1. "Must I go, and emp - ty hand - ed," Thus my dear Re-deem-er meet?
2. Not at death I shrink nor fal - ter, For my Sav-iour saves me now;
3. O the years in sin - ning wast - ed, Could I but re - call them now,
4. O ye saints, a-rouse, be ear - nest, Up and work while yet 'tis day;

Not one day of serv - ice give Him, Lay no tro - phy at His feet?
But to meet Him emp - ty - hand - ed, Tho't of that now clouds my brow.
I would give them to my Sav - iour, To His will I'd glad - ly bow.
Ere the night of death o'er-take thee, Strive for souls while still you may.

REFRAIN

"Must I go, and emp - ty - hand - ed?" Must I meet my Sav - iour so?

Not one soul with which to greet Him: Must I emp - ty - hand - ed go?

457 Am I a Soldier of the Cross?

ARLINGTON

Isaac Watts, 1674-1748

Thomas A. Arne, 1710-1778

1. Am I a sol - dier of the cross, A fol - lower of the Lamb,
2. Must I be car - ried to the skies On flow - ery beds of ease,
3. Are there no foes for me to face? Must I not stem the flood?
4. Sure I must fight, if I would reign; In - crease my cour - age, Lord;

Am I a Soldier of the Cross?

And shall I fear to own His cause, Or blush to speak His name?
While oth-ers fought to win the prize, And sailed thro' blood-y seas?
Is this vile world a friend to grace, To help me on to God?
I'll bear the toil, en - dure the pain, Sup-port-ed by Thy word. A-MEN.

Work, for the Night Is Coming   458

WORK SONG

Annie L. Coghill, 1836-1907
Alt. by Lowell Mason, 1792-1872

Lowell Mason, 1792-1872

1. Work, for the night is com - ing, Work thro' the morn - ing hours;
2. Work, for the night is com - ing, Work thro' the sun - ny noon;
3. Work, for the night is com - ing, Un - der the sun - set skies;

Work while the dew is spark - ling; Work 'mid spring - ing flowers.
Fill bright-est hours with la - bor, Rest comes sure and soon.
While their bright tints are glow - ing, Work, for day - light flies.

Work when the day grows bright-er, Work in the glow - ing sun;
Give ev - er-y fly - ing min - ute Some-thing to keep in store;
Work till the last beam fad - eth, Fad - eth to shine no more;

Work, for the night is com - ing, When man's work is done.
Work, for the night is com - ing, When man works no more.
Work, while the night is dark - 'ning, When man's work is o'er. A-MEN.

Stand Up, Stand Up for Jesus

GEIBEL

George Duffield. 1818-1888

Adam Geibel, 1855-1933

Unison

1. Stand up, stand up for Je - sus, Ye sol - diers of the cross;
2. Stand up, stand up for Je - sus, The trump-et call o - bey;
3. Stand up, stand up for Je - sus, The strife will not be long;

Lift high His roy - al ban - ner, It must not suf - fer loss:
Forth to the might - y con - flict, In this His glo - rious day:
This day the noise of bat - tle, The next, the vic - tor's song:

From vic - tory un - to vic - tory His ar - my shall He lead,
"Ye that are men, now serve Him" A - gainst un - num-bered foes;
To Him that o - ver - com - eth, A crown of life shall be:

rit.

Till ev - ery foe is van - quished, And Christ is Lord in - deed.
Let cour - age rise with dan - ger, And strength to strength op - pose.
He with the King of glo - ry Shall reign e - ter - nal - ly.

Alternate tune without Refrain: WEBB, No. 460 on opposite page

Stand Up, Stand Up for Jesus

REFRAIN

Stand up for Je - sus, Ye sol - diers of the cross;...
Stand up, stand up for Je - sus,

Lift high His roy-al ban - ner, It must not, it must not suf - fer loss.

Stand Up, Stand Up for Jesus   460

WEBB

George Duffield, 1818-1888   George J. Webb, 1803-1887

1. Stand up, stand up for Je - sus, Ye sol - diers of the cross, Lift high His
2. Stand up, stand up for Je - sus, The trump-et call o - bey; Forth to the
3. Stand up, stand up for Je - sus, Stand in His strength a - lone; The arm of
4. Stand up, stand up for Je - sus, The strife will not be long; This day the

roy - al ban - ner, It must not suf - fer loss; From vic-tory un - to vic - tory, His
might-y con-flict, In this His glorious day. "Ye that are men, now serve Him," A-
flesh will fail you—Ye dare not trust your own; Put on the gos - pel ar - mor, Each
noise of bat - tle, The next, the vic-tor's song; To him that o - ver - com - eth, A

ar - my shall He lead, Till ev - ery foe is vanquished And Christ is Lord in-deed.
gainst unnumbered foes; Let courage rise with dan-ger, And strength to strength oppose.
piece put on with prayer; Where du-ty calls, or dan-ger, Be nev-er want-ing there.
crown of life shall be; He with the King of glo - ry Shall reign e - ter-nal-ly. A-MEN.

Alternate tune with Refrain: GEIBEL, No. 459 on opposite page

461 God the Omnipotent!

RUSSIAN HYMN

Henry F. Chorley, 1808-1872; 1, 3
John Ellerton, 1826-1893; 2, 4

Alexis F. Lwoff, c.1798-1870

1. God the Om - nip - o - tent! King, who or - dain - est
2. God the All - mer - ci - ful! earth hath for - sak - en
3. God the All - right-eous One! man hath de - fied Thee;
4. So shall Thy peo - ple, with thank - ful de - vo - tion,

Thun - der Thy clar - ion, the light - ning Thy sword;
Meek - ness and mer - cy, and slight - ed Thy Word;
Yet to e - ter - ni - ty stand - eth Thy Word;
Praise Him who saved them from per - il and sword,

Show forth Thy pit - y on high where Thou reign - est;
Let not Thy wrath in its ter - rors a - wak - en;
False - hood and wrong shall not tar - ry be - side Thee;
Sing - ing in cho - rus from o - cean to o - cean,

Give to us peace in our time, O Lord.
Give to us peace in our time, O Lord.
Give to us peace in our time, O Lord.
Peace to the na - tions, and praise to the Lord. A - MEN.

Great God of Nations

462

MENDON

Alfred A. Woodhull, 1810-1836

German Traditional Melody
Arr. by Samuel Dyer, 1785-1835

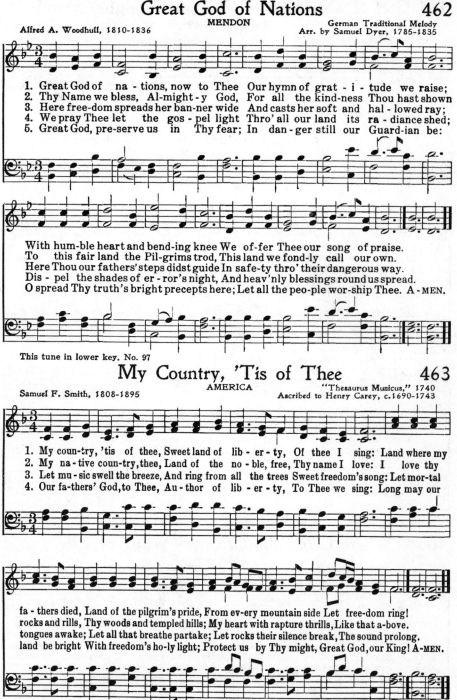

1. Great God of na - tions, now to Thee Our hymn of grat - i - tude we raise;
2. Thy Name we bless, Al - might - y God, For all the kind - ness Thou hast shown
3. Here free - dom spreads her ban - ner wide And casts her soft and hal - lowed ray;
4. We pray Thee let the gos - pel light Thro' all our land its ra - diance shed;
5. Great God, pre - serve us in Thy fear; In dan - ger still our Guard - ian be:

With hum - ble heart and bend - ing knee We of - fer Thee our song of praise.
To this fair land the Pil - grims trod, This land we fond - ly call our own.
Here Thou our fathers' steps didst guide In safe - ty thro' their dangerous way.
Dis - pel the shades of er - ror's night, And heav'nly blessings round us spread.
O spread Thy truth's bright precepts here; Let all the peo - ple wor - ship Thee. A - MEN.

This tune in lower key, No. 97

My Country, 'Tis of Thee

463

AMERICA

Samuel F. Smith, 1808-1895

"Thesaurus Musicus," 1740
Ascribed to Henry Carey, c.1690-1743

1. My coun - try, 'tis of thee, Sweet land of lib - er - ty, Of thee I sing: Land where my
2. My na - tive coun - try, thee, Land of the no - ble, free, Thy name I love: I love thy
3. Let mu - sic swell the breeze, And ring from all the trees Sweet freedom's song: Let mor - tal
4. Our fa - thers' God, to Thee, Au - thor of lib - er - ty, To Thee we sing: Long may our

fa - thers died, Land of the pilgrim's pride, From ev - ery mountain side Let free - dom ring!
rocks and rills, Thy woods and templed hills; My heart with rapture thrills, Like that a - bove.
tongues awake; Let all that breathe partake; Let rocks their silence break, The sound prolong.
land be bright With freedom's ho - ly light; Protect us by Thy might, Great God, our King! A - MEN.

464 God of Our Fathers, Whose Almighty Hand

NATIONAL HYMN

Daniel C. Roberts, 1841-1907

George W. Warren, 1828-1902
Descant (small notes), William Lester, b. 1889

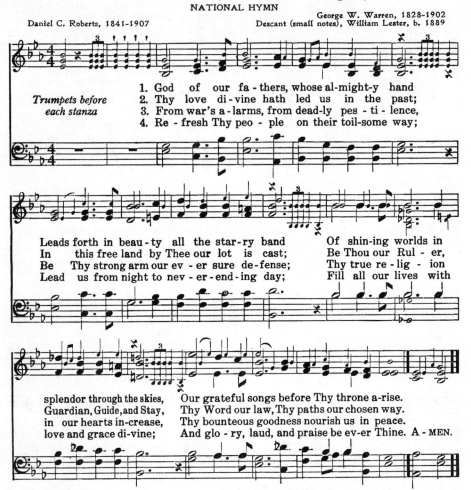

Trumpets before
each stanza

1. God of our fa - thers, whose al-might-y hand
2. Thy love di - vine hath led us in the past;
3. From war's a - larms, from dead-ly pes - ti - lence,
4. Re - fresh Thy peo - ple on their toil-some way;

Leads forth in beau - ty all the star-ry band   Of shin-ing worlds in
In this free land by Thee our lot is cast;   Be Thou our Rul - er,
Be Thy strong arm our ev - er sure de-fense;   Thy true re - lig - ion
Lead us from night to nev - er-end-ing day;   Fill all our lives with

splendor through the skies,   Our grateful songs before Thy throne a-rise.
Guardian, Guide, and Stay,   Thy Word our law, Thy paths our chosen way.
in our hearts in-crease,   Thy bounteous goodness nourish us in peace.
love and grace di-vine;   And glo - ry, laud, and praise be ev-er Thine. A - MEN.

465 Where Cross the Crowded Ways of Life

GERMANY

Frank M. North, 1850-1935

William Gardiner's "Sacred Melodies," 1815

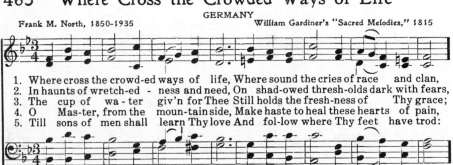

1. Where cross the crowd-ed ways of life, Where sound the cries of race   and clan,
2. In haunts of wretch-ed - ness and need, On shad-owed thresh-olds dark with fears,
3. The cup of wa - ter giv'n for Thee Still holds the fresh-ness of   Thy grace,
4. O Mas-ter, from the moun-tain side, Make haste to heal these hearts of pain,
5. Till sons of men shall learn Thy love And fol-low where Thy feet   have trod:

Where Cross the Crowded Ways of Life

A - bove the noise of self - ish strife, We hear Thy voice, O Son of man!
From paths where hide the lures of greed, We catch the vi-sion of Thy tears.
Yet long these mul-ti-tudes to see The sweet com-pas-sion of Thy face.
A-mong these rest-less throngs a-bide, O tread the cit - y's streets a - gain;
Till glo-rious from Thy heaven a-bove Shall come the cit-y of our God. A-MEN.

Hope of the World

ANCIENT OF DAYS

466

Georgia Harkness, b. 1891

J. Albert Jeffery, 1854-1929

1. Hope of the world, Thou Christ of great com-pas-sion, Speak to our fear - ful
2. Hope of the world, God's gift from high-est heav-en, Bring-ing to hun-gry
3. Hope of the world, a - foot on dust - y high-ways, Show-ing to wan - dering
4. Hope of the world, who by Thy cross didst save us From death and dark de-
5. Hope of the world, O Christ, o'er death vic-tor - ious, Who by this sign didst

hearts, by con - flict rent. Save us, Thy peo - ple, from con-sum-ing pas - sion,
souls the bread of life, Still let Thy Spir - it un - to us be giv - en
souls the path of light; Walk Thou be - side us, lest the tempt-ing by - ways
spair, from sin and guilt; We ren-der back the love Thy mer - cy gave us;
con - quer grief and pain, We would be faith - ful to Thy gos - pel glo - rious:

Who by our own false hopes and aims are spent.
To heal earth's wounds and end her bit - ter strife.
Lure us a - way from Thee to end - less night.
Take Thou our lives and use them as Thou wilt.
Thou art our Lord! Thou dost for - ev - er reign! A-MEN.

467 O Beautiful for Spacious Skies

MATERNA

Katharine Lee Bates, 1859-1929　　　　　　　　Samuel A. Ward, 1847-1903

1. O beau-ti-ful for spa-cious skies, For am-ber waves of grain,
2. O beau-ti-ful for pil-grim feet, Whose stern, im-pas-sioned stress
3. O beau-ti-ful for he-roes proved In lib-er-at-ing strife,
4. O beau-ti-ful for pa-triot dream That sees be-yond the years

For pur-ple moun-tain maj-es-ties A-bove the fruit-ed plain!
A thor-ough-fare for free-dom beat A-cross the wil-der-ness!
Who more than self their coun-try loved, And mer-cy more than life!
Thine al-a-bas-ter cit-ies gleam, Un-dimmed by hu-man tears!

A-mer-i-ca! A-mer-i-ca! God shed His grace on thee,
A-mer-i-ca! A-mer-i-ca! God mend thine ev-ery flaw,
A-mer-i-ca! A-mer-i-ca! May God thy gold re-fine
A-mer-i-ca! A-mer-i-ca! God shed His grace on thee,

And crown thy good with broth-er-hood From sea to shin-ing sea!
Con-firm thy soul in self-con-trol, Thy lib-er-ty in law!
Till all suc-cess be no-ble-ness And ev-ery gain di-vine!
And crown thy good with broth-er-hood From sea to shin-ing sea! A-MEN.

Once to Every Man and Nation

EBENEZER (Ton-Y-Botel)

James Russell Lowell, 1819-1891, alt.

Thomas John Williams, 1869-1944

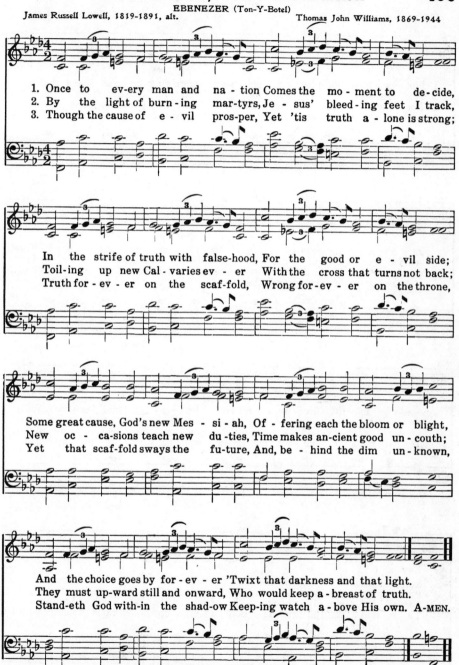

1. Once to ev-ery man and na-tion Comes the mo-ment to de-cide,
2. By the light of burn-ing mar-tyrs, Je - sus' bleed-ing feet I track,
3. Though the cause of e - vil pros-per, Yet 'tis truth a - lone is strong;

In the strife of truth with false-hood, For the good or e - vil side;
Toil-ing up new Cal - varies ev - er With the cross that turns not back;
Truth for - ev - er on the scaf-fold, Wrong for-ev - er on the throne,

Some great cause, God's new Mes - si - ah, Of - fering each the bloom or blight,
New oc - ca-sions teach new du - ties, Time makes an-cient good un - couth;
Yet that scaf-fold sways the fu - ture, And, be - hind the dim un - known,

And the choice goes by for - ev - er 'Twixt that darkness and that light.
They must up-ward still and onward, Who would keep a - breast of truth.
Stand-eth God with-in the shad-ow Keep-ing watch a - bove His own. A-MEN.

Music by permission of Gwenlyn Evans, Ltd., Caernarvon
Alternate tune: AUSTRIAN HYMN, No. 171

469 Not Alone for Mighty Empire
HYFRYDOL

William P. Merrill, 1867-1954   Rowland H. Prichard, 1811-1887

1. Not a - lone for might - y em - pire, Stretch-ing far o'er land and sea;
2. Not for bat - tle - ship and for - tress, Not for con - quests of the sword;
3. For the ar - mies of the faith - ful, Souls that passed and left no name;
4. God of jus - tice, save the peo - ple From the clash of race and creed,

Not a - lone for boun - teous har - vests, Lift we up our hearts to Thee.
But for con - quests of the spir - it Give we thanks to Thee, O Lord;
For the glo - ry that il - lu - mines Pa - triot lives of death-less fame;
From the strife of class and fac - tion: Make our na - tion free in - deed.

Stand-ing in the liv - ing pres - ent, Mem - o - ry and hope be - tween,
For the her - it - age of free - dom, For the home, the church, the school;
For our proph - ets and a - pos - tles, Loy - al to the liv - ing Word;
Keep her faith in sim - ple man-hood Strong as when her life be - gan,

Lord, we would with deep thanks-giv-ing Praise Thee most for things unseen.
For the o - pen door to man - hood In a land the peo-ple rule.
For all he - roes of the Spir - it, Give we thanks to Thee, O Lord.
Till it find its full fru - i - tion In the broth - er - hood of man. A-MEN.

Alternate tune: AUSTRIAN HYMN, No. 171

Lord of Life and King of Glory

470

SICILIAN MARINERS' HYMN

Christian Burke, 1859-c.1915　　　　　　　　　　　　Arr. from a Sicilian Melody, 1794

1. Lord of life and King of glo - ry, Who didst deign a
2. Since the day the bless - ed moth-er Thee, the world's Re-
3. Grant us then pure hearts and pa - tient, That in all we
4. When our grow-ing sons and daughters Look on life with
5. May we keep our ho - ly call - ing Stain - less in its

child to be, Cra - dled on a moth - er's bo - som,
deem - er, bore, Thou hast crowned us with an hon - or
do or say Lit - tle ones our deeds may cop - y,
ea - ger eyes, Grant us then a deep - er in - sight
fair re - nown, That, when all the work is o - ver

Throned up - on a moth - er's knee: For the chil - dren
Wom - en nev - er knew be - fore; And that we may
And be nev - er led a - stray; Lit - tle feet our
And new powers of sac - ri - fice: Hope to trust them,
And we lay the bur - den down, Then the chil - dren

Thou hast giv - en We must an - swer un - to Thee.
bear it meet - ly, We must seek Thine aid the more.
steps may fol - low In a safe and nar - row way.
faith to guide them, Love that noth - ing good de - nies.
Thou hast giv - en Still may be our joy and crown. A - MEN.

Words used by permission of The Mothers' Union

471 O Happy Home, Where Thou Art Loved

ALVERSTOKE

Carl J. P. Spitta, 1801-1859
Trans. by Sarah B. Findlater, 1823-1907, alt.

Joseph Barnby, 1838-1896

1. O hap-py home, where Thou art loved the dear-est, Thou lov-ing
2. O hap-py home, where each one serves Thee, low-ly, What-ev-er
3. O hap-py home, where Thou art not for-got-ten When joy is
4. Un-til at last, when earth's day's work is end-ed, All meet Thee

Friend, and Sav-iour of our race, And where a-mong the guests there nev-er
his ap-point-ed work may be, Till ev-ery com-mon task seems great and
o-ver-flow-ing, full, and free; O hap-py home, where ev-ery wound-ed
in the bless-ed home a-bove, From whence Thou cam-est, where Thou hast as-

com-eth One who can hold such high and hon-ored place!
ho-ly, When it is done, O Lord, as un-to Thee!
spir-it Is brought, Phy-si-cian, Com-fort-er, to Thee—
cend-ed, Thy ev-er-last-ing home of peace and love! A-MEN.

Alternate tune: CONSOLATION, No. 142

472 Happy the Home When God Is There

ST. AGNES

Henry Ware, the younger, 1794-1843

John B. Dykes, 1823-1876

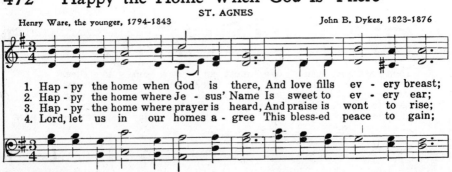

1. Hap-py the home when God is there, And love fills ev-ery breast;
2. Hap-py the home where Je-sus' Name Is sweet to ev-ery ear;
3. Hap-py the home where prayer is heard, And praise is wont to rise;
4. Lord, let us in our homes a-gree This bless-ed peace to gain;

This tune in higher key, No. 50

Happy the Home When God Is There

When one their wish, and one their prayer, And one their heav'n-ly rest.
Where chil-dren ear - ly lisp His fame, And par-ents hold Him dear.
Where par-ents love the sa - cred Word, And all its wis - dom prize.
U - nite our hearts in love to Thee, And love to all will reign. A - MEN.

Gracious Saviour, Who Didst Honor 473

MOTHERHOOD

Emily L. Shirreff, 1814-1897

L. Meadows White, 19th Century

1. Gra-cious Sav-iour, who didst hon - or Wom - an - kind as wom-an's son;
2. Je - sus, Son of hu - man moth-er, Bless our moth - er - hood, we pray;
3. Thou who didst with Jo - seph la - bor, Nor didst hum - ble work dis - dain,
4. Thou who didst go forth in sor -row, Toil - ing for the souls of men,

Ver - y Man, though God - be - got-ten, And with God the Fa - ther one—
Give us grace to lead our chil-dren, Draw them to Thee day by day;
Grant we may Thy foot-steps fol - low Pa - tient - ly through toil or pain;
Thou who shalt draw all men to Thee, Though de-spised, re - ject - ed then;

Grant that wom - an - hood may be Con - se - crat-ed, Lord, to Thee.
May our sons and daugh-ters be Ded - i - cat-ed, Lord, to Thee.
May our qui - et home - life be Lived, O Lord, in Thee, to Thee.
Hum - ble though our in-fluence be, Use it in the world for Thee. A-MEN.

Saved by Grace

George C. Stebbins, 1846-1945
Arr. by Donald P. Hustad, b. 1918

Fanny J. Crosby, 1820-1915

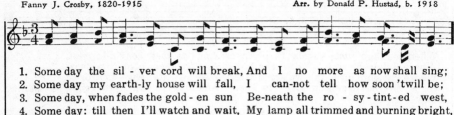

1. Some day the sil - ver cord will break, And I no more as now shall sing;
2. Some day my earth-ly house will fall, I can-not tell how soon 'twill be;
3. Some day, when fades the gold - en sun Be-neath the ro - sy - tint - ed west,
4. Some day: till then I'll watch and wait, My lamp all trimmed and burning bright,

But oh, the joy when I shall wake With-in the pal - ace of the King!
But this I know—my All in All Has now a place in heav'n for me.
My bless-ed Lord will say, "Well done!" And I shall en - ter in - to rest.
That when my Sav-iour opes the gate, My soul to Him may take its flight.

REFRAIN

And I shall see Him face to face, And tell the sto - ry—Saved by grace;
shall see to face,

And I shall see Him face to face, And tell the sto-ry— Saved by grace.
shall see to face,

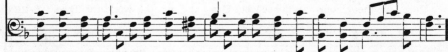

Hark, Hark, My Soul!

PILGRIMS

Frederick W. Faber, 1814-1863

Henry Smart, 1813-1879
Descant, (small notes), William Lester, b. 1889

1. Hark, hark, my soul! an - gel - ic songs are swell-ing O'er earth's green fields and
2. Far, far a - way, like bells at eve-ning peal-ing, The voice of Je - sus
3. On - ward we go, for still we hear them sing-ing, "Come, wea - ry souls, for
4. An - gels, sing on! your faith-ful watch-es keep-ing; Sing us sweet frag - ments

ocean's wave-beat shore; How sweet the truth those bless-ed strains are tell - ing
sounds o'er land and sea; And la - den souls by thou-sands meek-ly steal-ing,
Je - sus bids you come;" And through the dark, its ech - oes sweet-ly ring - ing,
of the songs a - bove; Till morn-ing's joy shall end the night of weep - ing,

REFRAIN

Of that new life when sin shall be no more! An - gels of Je - sus,
Kind Shep-herd, turn their wea - ry steps to Thee. The mu - sic of the gos - pel leads us home.
And life's long shad-ows break in cloud-less love.

an - gels of light, Sing - ing to wel - come the pil-grims of the night! A - MEN.

For All the Saints

William W. How, 1823-1897   SINE NOMINE   R. Vaughan Williams, b. 1872

UNISON, *stanzas 1, 2, and 6, 7*

1. For all the saints who from their la-bors rest, Who Thee by faith be-
2. Thou wast their rock, their fortress and their might; Thou, Lord, their cap - tain
6. But lo! there breaks a yet more glo-rious day; The saints tri - um - phant
7. From earth's wide bounds, from o - cean's far-thest coast, Thro' gates of pearl stream

fore the world con-fessed, Thy name, O Je - sus, be for - ev - er blest.
in the well-fought fight; Thou, in the dark - ness drear, their one true light.
rise in bright ar - ray; The King of Glo - ry pass - es on His way.
in the count-less host, Sing-ing to Fa - ther, Son, and Ho-ly Ghost.

(after stanza 7)

Al - le - lu - ia! Al - le - lu - ia! A - MEN.

HARMONY, *stanzas 3, 4, 5*

3. O blest com-mun - ion, fel - low-ship di - vine! We fee-bly strug - gle;
4. And when the strife is fierce, the war-fare long, Steals on the ear the
5. The gold-en eve-ning bright-ens in the west; Soon, soon to faith - ful

they in glo - ry shine. Yet all are one in Thee, for all are Thine.
dis - tant tri-umph song, And hearts are brave a - gain and arms are strong.
war-riors com - eth rest; And sweet the calm of Par - a - dise, the blest.

For All the Saints

(Sop.) Al - le - lu - ia! D. C. *stanzas 6 and 7*

Al - le - lu - ia! Al - le - lu - ia!

Face to Face 477

Carrie E. Breck, 1855-1934

Grant Colfax Tullar, 1869-1950

1. Face to face with Christ my Sav - iour, Face to face—what will it be—
2. On - ly faint-ly now I see Him, With the dark - ling veil be-tween,
3. What re - joic-ing in His pres - ence, When are ban-ished grief and pain;
4. Face to face! O bliss - ful mo - ment! Face to face—to see and know;

When with rap-ture I be - hold Him, Je - sus Christ Who died for me?
But a bless-ed day is com - ing, When His glo - ry shall be seen.
When the crook-ed ways are straightened, And the dark things shall be plain.
Face to face with my Re-deem - er, Je - sus Christ Who loves me so.

REFRAIN

Face to face I shall be-hold Him, Far be-yond the star-ry sky;

Face to face in all His glo-ry, I shall see Him by and by!

478 My Saviour First of All

Fanny J. Crosby, 1820-1915

John R. Sweney, 1837-1899

1. When my life-work is end-ed, and I cross the swell-ing tide, When the
bright and glo-rious morn-ing I shall see; I shall know my Re-deem-er when I
reach the oth-er side, And His smile will be the first to wel-come me.

2. Oh, the soul-thrill-ing rap-ture when I view His bless-ed face, And the
lus-ter of His kind-ly beam-ing eye; How my full heart will praise Him for the
mer-cy, love, and grace, That pre-pare for me a man-sion in the sky.

3. Oh, the dear ones in glo-ry, how they beck-on me to come, And our
part-ing at the riv-er I re-call; To the sweet vales of E-den they will
sing my wel-come home; But I long to meet my Sav-iour first of all.

4. Thro' the gates to the cit-y in a robe of spot-less white, He will
lead me where no tears will ev-er fall; In the glad song of a-ges I shall
min-gle with de-light; But I long to meet my Sav-iour first of all.

REFRAIN

I shall know Him, I shall know Him, And redeemed by His side I shall stand,
I shall know Him,

I shall know Him, I shall know Him By the print of the nails in His hand.
I shall know Him,

O That Will Be Glory

Charles H. Gabriel, 1856-1932   Charles H. Gabriel, 1856-1932

1. When all my la-bors and tri-als are o'er, And I am safe on that
2. When, by the gift of His in-fi-nite grace, I am ac-cord-ed in
3. Friends will be there I have loved long a-go; Joy like a riv-er a-

beau-ti-ful shore, Just to be near the dear Lord I a-dore,
heav-en a place, Just to be there and to look on His face,
round me will flow; Yet, just a smile from my Sav-iour, I know,

REFRAIN

Will through the a-ges be glo-ry for me. O that will be
O that will

glo-ry for me, Glo-ry for me, glo-ry for me; When by His grace
be glo-ry for me, Glo-ry for me, glo-ry for me;

I shall look on His face, That will be glo-ry, be glo-ry for me.

480 O What Their Joy and Their Glory Must Be

O QUANTA QUALIA

Peter Abélard, 1079-1142
Trans. by John M. Neale, 1818-1866, alt.

La Feillée's "Méthode du Plain Chant," 1808

1. O what their joy and their glo - ry must be,
2. Tru - ly Je - ru - sa - lem name we that shore,
3. There, where no trou - bles dis - trac - tion can bring,
4. Low be - fore Him with our prais - es we fall,

Those end - less Sab - baths the bless - ed ones see;
"Vi - sion of Peace," that brings joy ev - er - more;
We the sweet an - thems of Zi - on shall sing;
Of whom, and in whom, and through whom are all;

Crowns for the val - iant, to wea - ry ones rest;
Wish and ful - fill - ment can sev - ered be ne'er,
While for Thy grace, Lord, their voi - ces of praise
Of whom, the Fa - ther; and through whom, the Son;

God shall be All, and in all ev - er blest.
Nor the thing prayed for come short of the prayer.
Thy bless - ed peo - ple shall ev - er - more raise.
In whom, the Spir - it, with these ev - er One. A-MEN.

Jerusalem the Golden

EWING

Bernard of Cluny, 12th Century
Trans. by John M. Neale, 1818-1866

Alexander Ewing, 1830-1895

1. Je - ru - sa - lem the gold - en, With milk and hon - ey blest!
2. They stand, those halls of Zi - on, All ju - bi - lant with song,
3. There is the throne of Da - vid; And there, from care re - leased,
4. O sweet and bless - ed coun - try, The home of God's e - lect!

Be - neath thy con - tem - pla - tion Sink heart and voice op-pressed;
And bright with many an an - gel, And all the mar - tyr throng;
The song of them that tri - umph, The shout of them that feast;
O sweet and bless - ed coun - try That ea - ger hearts ex - pect!

I know not, oh, I know not What joys a - wait me there;
The Prince is ev - er in them, The day - light is se - rene;
And they, who with their Lead - er Have con-quered in the fight,
Je - sus, in mer - cy bring us To that dear land of rest;

What ra - dian - cy of glo - ry, What bliss be - yond com-pare.
The pas-tures of the bless - ed Are decked in glo-rious sheen.
For - ev - er and for - ev - er Are clad in robes of white.
Who art, with God the Fa - ther, And Spir - it, ev - er blest. A-MEN.

482 When the Roll Is Called Up Yonder

James M. Black, 1856-1938   James M. Black, 1856-1938

1. When the trum-pet of the Lord shall sound, and time shall be no more, And the
2. On that bright and cloud-less morn-ing when the dead in Christ shall rise, And the
3. Let us la-bor for the Mas-ter from the dawn till set-ting sun, Let us

morn-ing breaks, e-ter-nal, bright and fair; When the saved of earth shall gath-er
glo-ry of His res-ur-rec-tion share; When His cho-sen ones shall gath-er
talk of all His won-drous love and care; Then when all of life is o-ver,

o-ver on the oth-er shore, And the roll is called up yon-der, I'll be there.
to their home be-yond the skies, And the roll is called up yon-der, I'll be there.
and our work on earth is done, And the roll is called up yon-der, I'll be there.

REFRAIN

When the roll is called up yon - - - der, When the
When the roll is called up yon-der, I'll be there,

roll is called up yon - - der, When the roll is called up
When the roll is called up yon-der, I'll be there, When the roll is called up

When the Roll Is Called Up Yonder

yon - der, When the roll is called up yon - der, I'll be there.

When We All Get to Heaven   483

Eliza E. Hewitt, 1851-1920   Mrs. John G. Wilson, 1865-1942

1. Sing the won-drous love of Je - sus, Sing His mer - cy and His grace;
2. While we walk the pil - grim pathway, Clouds will o - ver-spread the sky;
3. Let us then be true and faith-ful, Trust-ing, serv - ing ev - ery day;
4. On-ward to the prize be - fore us! Soon His beau - ty we'll be - hold;

In the man - sions bright and bless - ed, He'll pre - pare for us a place.
But when trav-'ling days are o - ver, Not a shad-ow, not a sigh.
Just one glimpse of Him in glo - ry Will the toils of life re-pay.
Soon the pearl - y gates will o - pen, We shall tread the streets of gold.

REFRAIN

When we all get to heaven, What a day of re-joicing that will be!
When we all   What a day of rejoicing that will be!

When we all see Je-sus, We'll sing and shout the victory.
When we all   and shout the vic-to-ry.

484 Ten Thousand Times Ten Thousand

ALFORD

Henry Alford, 1810-1871

John B. Dykes, 1823-1876

1. Ten thou-sand times ten thou-sand In spar-kling rai-ment bright,
2. What rush of al-le-lu-ias Fills all the earth and sky!
3. O then what rap-tured greet-ings On Ca-naan's hap-py shore!
4. Bring near Thy great sal-va-tion, Thou Lamb for sin-ners slain;

The ar-mies of the ran-somed saints Throng up the steeps of light:
What ring-ing of a thou-sand harps Be-speaks the tri-umph nigh!
What knit-ting sev-ered friend-ships up, Where part-ings are no more!
Fill up the roll of Thine e-lect, Then take Thy power and reign:

'Tis fin-ished, all is fin-ished, Their fight with death and sin:
O day, for which cre-a-tion And all its tribes were made;
Then eyes with joy shall spar-kle, That brimmed with tears of late,
Ap-pear, De-sire of na-tions, Thine ex-iles long for home;

Fling o-pen wide the gold-en gates, And let the vic-tors in.
O joy, for all its for-mer woes A thou-sand-fold re-paid!
Or-phans no lon-ger fa-ther-less, Nor wid-ows des-o-late.
Show in the heavens Thy prom-ised sign; Thou Prince and Sav-iour, come. A-MEN.

Can a Little Child Like Me?

THANKSGIVING

485

Ascribed to Mary M. Dodge, 1831-1905　　　　　　W. K. Basswood, 1839-1902

1. Can a lit-tle child like me Thank the Fa-ther fit-ting-ly?
2. For the fruit up-on the tree, For the birds that sing of Thee,
3. For the sun-shine warm and bright, For the day and for the night,
4. For our com-rades and our plays, And our hap-py hol-i-days,

Yes, O yes! be good and true, Pa-tient, kind in all you do;
For the earth in beau-ty dressed, Fa-ther, mo-ther, and the rest,
For the les-sons of our youth—Hon-or, gra-ti-tude and truth,
For the joy-ful work and true That a lit-tle child may do,

Love the Lord, and do your part; Learn to say with all your heart,
For Thy pre-cious, lov-ing care, For Thy boun-ty ev-ery where,
For the love that met us here, For the home and for the cheer,
For our lives but just be-gun, For the great gift of Thy Son,

REFRAIN

Fa-ther, we thank Thee! Fa-ther, we thank Thee!

Fa-ther in heav-en, we thank Thee. A-MEN.

486 Dare to Be a Daniel

Philip P. Bliss, 1838-1876

Philip P. Bliss, 1838-1876

1. Stand-ing by a pur-pose true, Heed-ing God's command, Hon - or them, the
2. Man - y might-y men are lost, Dar-ing not to stand, Who for God had
3. Man - y gi - ants, great and tall, Stalk-ing thro' the land, Headlong to the
4. Hold the gos-pel ban-ner high! On to vic - t'ry grand! Sa - tan and his

faith - ful few! All hail to Dan-iel's Band!
been a host, By join - ing Dan-iel's Band!
earth would fall, If met by Dan-iel's Band!
host de - fy, And shout for Dan-iel's Band!

REFRAIN

Dare to be a Dan - iel,

Dare to stand a - lone! Dare to have a pur-pose firm! Dare to make it known!

487 Gentle Jesus, Meek and Mild

GENTLE JESUS

Charles Wesley, 1707-1788

Martin Shaw, b. 1875

1. Gen - tle Je - sus, meek and mild, Look up - on a lit - tle child;
2. Lamb of God, I look to Thee; Thou shalt my ex - am - ple be:
3. Fain I would be as Thou art; Give me Thine o - be-dient heart:
4. Lov - ing Je - sus, gen - tle Lamb, In Thy gra-cious hands I am;

Music copyright by J. Curwen & Sons, Ltd. Used by permission

Gentle Jesus, Meek and Mild

Pit - y my sim - plic - i - ty, Suf - fer me to come to Thee.
Thou art gen - tle, meek and mild; Thou wast once a lit - tle child.
Thou art pit - i - ful and kind; Let me have Thy lov - ing mind.
Make me, Sav - iour, what Thou art, Live Thy - self with - in my heart. A-MEN.

When He Cometh 488

JEWELS

William O. Cushing, 1823-1902

George F. Root, 1820-1895

1. When He com - eth, when He com - eth To make up His jew - els,
2. He will gath - er, He will gath - er The gems for His king - dom;
3. Lit - tle chil - dren, lit - tle chil - dren, Who love their Re - deem - er,

All His jew - els, pre - cious jew - els, His loved and His own:
All the pure ones, all the bright ones, His loved and His own.
Are the jew - els, pre - cious jew - els, His loved and His own.

REFRAIN

Like the stars of the morn - ing, His bright crown a - dorn - ing,

They shall shine in their beau - ty, Bright gems for His crown.

489 Jesus Bids Us Shine

Susan Warner, 1819-1885

Edwin O. Excell, 1851-1921

1. Je-sus bids us shine, with a clear, pure light, Like a lit-tle can-dle burn-ing in the night; In this world of dark-ness we must shine, You in your small cor-ner, and I in mine.

2. Je-sus bids us shine, first of all for Him; Well He sees and knows it if our light is dim; He looks down from heav-en, sees us shine, You in your small cor-ner, and I in mine.

3. Je-sus bids us shine, then, for all a-round Man-y kinds of dark-ness in this world a-bound— Sin, and want, and sor-row: we must shine, You in your small cor-ner, and I in mine.

4. Je-sus bids us shine, as we work for Him, Bring-ing those that wan-der from the paths of sin; He will ev-er help us, if we shine, You in your small cor-ner, and I in mine.

490 Jesus Loves Me

Anna B. Warner, 1820-1915

William B. Bradbury, 1816-1868

1. Je-sus loves me! this I know, For the Bi-ble tells me so;
2. Je-sus loves me! He who died, Heav-en's gate to o-pen wide;
3. Je-sus loves me! loves me still, Though I'm ver-y weak and ill;
4. Je-sus loves me! He will stay Close be-side me all the way;

Jesus Loves Me

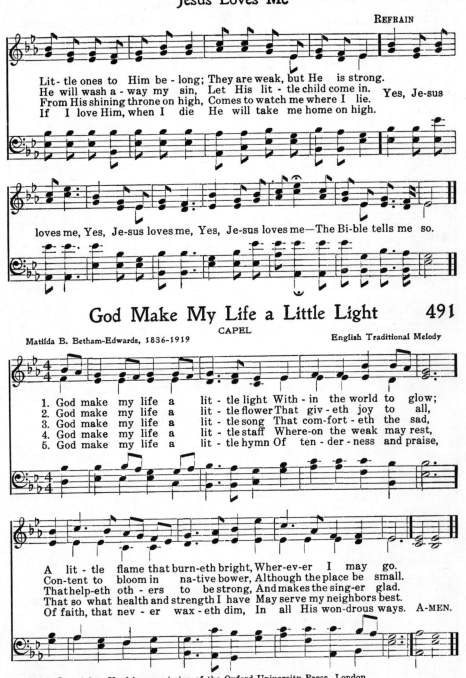

REFRAIN

Lit- tle ones to Him be - long; They are weak, but He is strong.
He will wash a - way my sin, Let His lit - tle child come in. Yes, Je-sus
From His shining throne on high, Comes to watch me where I lie.
If I love Him, when I die He will take me home on high.

loves me, Yes, Je-sus loves me, Yes, Je-sus loves me—The Bi-ble tells me so.

God Make My Life a Little Light   491

CAPEL

Matilda B. Betham-Edwards, 1836-1919   English Traditional Melody

1. God make my life a lit - tle light With - in the world to glow;
2. God make my life a lit - tle flower That giv - eth joy to all,
3. God make my life a lit - tle song That com-fort - eth the sad,
4. God make my life a lit - tle staff Where-on the weak may rest,
5. God make my life a lit - tle hymn Of ten - der - ness and praise,

A lit - tle flame that burn-eth bright, Wher-ev-er I may go.
Con-tent to bloom in na-tive bower, Although the place be small.
That help-eth oth - ers to be strong, And makes the sing-er glad.
That so what health and strength I have May serve my neighbors best.
Of faith, that nev - er wax-eth dim, In all His won-drous ways. A-MEN.

492 Hushed Was the Evening Hymn

SAMUEL

James D. Burns, 1823-1864

Arthur S. Sullivan, 1842-1900

1. Hushed was the eve - ning hymn, The tem - ple courts were dark,
2. The old man, meek and mild, The priest of Is - rael, slept;
3. O give me Sam - uel's ear! The o - pen ear, O Lord,
4. O give me Sam - uel's heart: A low - ly heart, that waits
5. O give me Sam - uel's mind: A sweet, un - mur-muring faith,

The lamp was burn-ing dim Be - fore the sa - cred ark; When sud-den-ly a
His watch the tem-ple-child, The lit - tle Le-vite, kept; And what from E - li's
A - live and quick to hear Each whis-per of Thy word! Like him to an-swer
Where in Thy house Thou art, Or watch-es at Thy gates! By day and night, a
O - be-dient and re-signed To Thee in life and death! That I may read with

Voice di - vine Rang through the si - lence of the shrine.
sense was sealed, The Lord to Han-nah's son re - vealed.
at Thy call, And to o - bey Thee first of all.
heart that still Moves at the breath-ing of Thy will.
child - like eyes Truths that are hid - den from the wise. A - MEN.

493 I Think When I Read That Sweet Story

SWEET STORY

Greek Folk Song

Jemima T. Luke, 1813-1906

Arr. by William B. Bradbury, 1816-1868

1. I think when I read that sweet sto - ry of old, When
2. I wish that His hands had been placed on my head, That His
3. Yet still to His foot - stool in prayer I may go, And

I Think When I Read That Sweet Story

Je - sus was here a - mong men, How He called lit - tle chil - dren as
arms had been thrown a-round me, And that I might have seen His kind
ask for a share in His love; And if I thus ear - nest - ly

lambs to His fold, I should like to have been with Him then.
look when He said, "Let the lit - tle ones come un - to Me."
seek Him be - low, I shall see Him and hear Him a - bove. A-MEN.

Tell Me the Stories of Jesus 494

William H. Parker, 1845-1929   Frederic A. Challinor, 1866-1952

1. Tell me the sto - ries of Je - sus I love to hear; Things I would
2. First let me hear how the chil - dren Stood round His knee; And I shall
3. In - to the cit - y I'd fol - low The chil - dren's band, Wav - ing a

ask Him to tell me If He were here; Scenes by the way - side,
fan - cy His bless - ing Rest - ing on me: Words full of kind - ness,
branch of the palm-tree High in my hand; One of His her - alds,

Tales of the sea, Sto - ries of Je - sus, Tell them to me.
Deeds full of grace, All in the love - light Of Je - sus' face.
Yes, I would sing Loud-est ho - san - nas! Je - sus is King. A-MEN.

Copyright by the National Sunday School Union. Used by permission

495

I'll Be a Sunbeam

Nellie Talbot, 19th Century

Edwin O. Excell, 1851-1921
Arr. by Donald P. Hustad, b. 1918

1. Je - sus wants me for a sun-beam, To shine for Him each day;
2. Je - sus wants me to be lov - ing, And kind to all I see;
3. I will ask Je - sus to help me To keep my heart from sin,
4. I'll be a sun-beam for Je - sus; I can if I but try;

In ev - ery way try to please Him, At home, at school, at play.
Showing how pleas-ant and hap - py His lit - tle one can be.
Ev - er re - flect - ing His good-ness, And al - ways shine for Him.
Serv-ing Him mo-ment by mo-ment, Then live with Him on high.

REFRAIN

A sun - beam, a sun - beam, Je - sus wants me for a sun - beam; A

sun - beam, a sun - beam, I'll be a sun - beam for Him.

All Things Bright and Beautiful

GREYSTONE

Cecil F. Alexander, 1818-1895

W. R. Waghorne, 1881-1942

(To be sung before stanza 1 and after stanza 5)

All things bright and beau - ti - ful, All crea - tures great and small,

Amen after last refrain

All things wise and won - der - ful, The Lord God made them all. A-MEN.

1. Each lit - tle flower that o - pens, Each lit - tle bird that sings,
2. The pur - ple - head - ed moun - tain, The riv - er run - ning by,
3. The cold wind in the win - ter, The pleas - ant sum - mer sun,
4. The tall trees in the green - wood, The mead - ows where we play,
5. He gave us eyes to see them, And lips that we might tell

D. S.

He made their glow - ing col - ors, He made their ti - ny wings.
The sun - set, and the morn - ing That bright - ens up the sky,
The ripe fruits in the gar - den, He made them ev - ery one.
The rush - es by the wa - ter, We gath - er ev - ery day,
How great is God Al - might - y, Who has made all things well. D.C.

497 Jesus, Gentlest Saviour

EUDOXIA

Frederick W. Faber, 1814-1863, alt.

Sabine Baring-Gould, 1834-1924

1. Je - sus, gen - tlest Sav - iour, God of might and power,
2. Na - ture can - not hold thee, Heav'n is all too strait
3. Out be - yond the shin - ing Of the far - thest star,
4. Yet the hearts of child - ren Hold what worlds can - not,
5. Je - sus, gent - lest Sav - iour, Thou art with us now;
6. Mul - ti - ply our gra - ces, Give us love and fear,

Thou thy - self art dwell - ing With us at this hour.
For Thine end - less glo - ry And thy roy - al state.
Thou art ev - er stretch - ing In - fi - nite - ly far.
And the God of won - ders Loves the low - ly spot.
Fill us with thy good - ness Till our hearts o'er - flow.
And, dear Lord, the chief - est, Grace to per - se - vere. A - MEN.

Music copyright by J. Curwen & Sons, Ltd. Used by permission

498 God, My Father, Loving Me

VIENNA

George W. Briggs, b. 1875

Justin H. Knecht, 1752-1817

1. God, my Fa - ther, lov - ing me, Gave His Son, my friend to be;
2. Je - sus still re - mains the same As in days of old He came;
3. How can I re - pay Thy love, Lord of all the hosts a - bove?
4. I have but my - self to give: Let me to Thy glo - ry live;

Gave His Son, my form to take, Bear - ing all things for my sake.
As my broth - er by my side, Still He seeks my steps to guide.
What have I, a child, to bring Un - to Thee, Thou heav'n - ly King?
Let me fol - low, day by day, Where Thou show - est me the way. A - MEN.

Words used by permission of Oxford University Press

Jesus Loves Even Me

Philip P. Bliss, 1838-1876

Philip P. Bliss, 1838-1876

1. I am so glad that our Fa-ther in heaven Tells of His love in the Book He has given; Won-der-ful things in the Bi-ble I see— This is the dear-est, that Je-sus loves me.

2. Though I for-get Him and wan-der a-way, Still He doth love me wher-ev-er I stray; Back to His dear lov-ing arms would I flee, When I re-mem-ber that Je-sus loves me.

3. Oh, if there's on-ly one song I can sing, When in His beau-ty I see the great King, This shall my song in e-ter-ni-ty be: "Oh, what a won-der that Je-sus loves me!"

REFRAIN

I am so glad that Je-sus loves me, Je-sus loves me, Je-sus loves me;
I am so glad that Je-sus loves me, Je-sus loves e-ven me.

500   Saviour, Like a Shepherd Lead Us

BRADBURY

From "Hymns for the Young," 1836
Ascribed to Dorothy A. Thrupp, 1779-1847

William B. Bradbury, 1816-1868

1. Sav - iour, like a shep-herd lead us, Much we need Thy ten-der care;
2. We are Thine; do Thou be - friend us, Be the Guard-ian of our way;
3. Thou hast prom-ised to re - ceive us, Poor and sin - ful though we be;
4. Ear - ly let us seek Thy fa - vor; Ear - ly let us do Thy will;

In Thy pleas-ant pas-tures feed us, For our use Thy folds pre - pare:
Keep Thy flock, from sin de - fend us, Seek us when we go a - stray:
Thou hast mer - cy to re - lieve us, Grace to cleanse, and power to free:
Bless - ed Lord and on - ly Sav - iour, With Thy love our bos-oms fill:

Bless - ed Je - sus, Bless - ed Je - sus, Thou hast bought us, Thine we are;
Bless - ed Je - sus, Bless - ed Je - sus, Hear, O hear us when we pray;
Bless - ed Je - sus, Bless - ed Je - sus, Ear - ly let us turn to Thee;
Bless - ed Je - sus, Bless - ed Je - sus, Thou hast loved us, love us still;

Bless - ed Je - sus, Bless - ed Je - sus, Thou hast bought us, Thine we are.
Bless - ed Je - sus, Bless - ed Je - sus, Hear, O hear us when we pray.
Bless - ed Je - sus, Bless - ed Je - sus, Ear - ly let us turn to Thee.
Bless - ed Je - sus, Bless - ed Je - sus, Thou hast loved us, love us still.

Alternate tune: SICILIAN MARINERS' HYMN, No. 470

Give of Your Best to the Master

Howard B. Grose, 1851-1939   Charlotte A. Barnard, 1830-1869

1. Give of your best to the Mas - ter; Give of the strength of your youth;
2. Give of your best to the Mas - ter; Give Him first place in your heart;
3. Give of your best to the Mas - ter; Naught else is wor - thy His love;

REF.—*Give of your best to the Mas - ter; Give of the strength of your youth;*

FINE

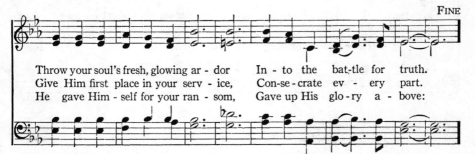

Throw your soul's fresh, glowing ar - dor   In - to the bat-tle for truth.
Give Him first place in your serv - ice,   Con-se - crate ev - ery part.
He gave Him - self for your ran - som,   Gave up His glo - ry a - bove:

Clad in sal - va - tion's full ar - mor, Join in the bat - tle for truth.

Je - sus has set the ex - am - ple; Daunt-less was He, young and brave;
Give, and to you shall be giv - en; God His be - lov - ed Son gave;
Laid down His life with-out mur - mur, You from sin's ru - in to save;

D. C.

Give Him your loy - al de - vo - tion, Give Him the best that you have.
Grate - ful - ly seek-ing to serve Him, Give Him the best that you have.
Give Him your heart's ad-o - ra - tion, Give Him the best that you have.

502 Living for Jesus

Thomas O. Chisholm, b. 1866

C. Harold Lowden, b. 1883

1. Liv-ing for Je-sus a life that is true, Striv-ing to please Him in
2. Liv-ing for Je-sus who died in my place, Bear-ing on Cal-vary my
3. Liv-ing for Je-sus wher-ev-er I am, Do-ing each du-ty in
4. Liv-ing for Je-sus through earth's little while, My dear-est treas-ure, the

all that I do; Yield-ing al-le-giance, glad-heart-ed and free,
sin and dis-grace; Such love con-strains me to an-swer His call,
His ho-ly name; Will-ing to suf-fer af-flic-tion and loss,
light of His smile; Seek-ing the lost ones He died to re-deem,

REFRAIN

This is the path-way of bless-ing for me.
Fol-low His lead-ing and give Him my all.
Deem-ing each tri-al a part of my cross.
Bring-ing the wea-ry to find rest in Him.

O Je-sus, Lord and

Sav-iour, I give my-self to Thee, For Thou, in Thy a-tone-ment, Didst

give Thy-self for me; I own no oth-er Mas-ter, My heart shall be Thy

Living for Jesus

throne; My life I give, hence-forth to live, O Christ, for Thee a - lone.

I Would Be True

503

PEEK

Howard A. Walter, 1883-1918

Joseph Yates Peek, 1843-1911

1. I would be true, for there are those who trust me; I would be
2. I would be friend of all—the foe, the friend-less; I would be
3. I would be prayer-ful through each bus - y mo - ment; I would be

pure, for there are those who care; I would be strong, for there is
giv - ing, and for - get the gift; I would be hum - ble, for I
con - stant-ly in touch with God; I would be tuned to hear His

much to suf - fer; I would be brave, for there is much to
know my weak - ness; I would look up, and laugh, and love, and
slight-est whis - per; I would have faith to keep the path Christ

dare; I would be brave, for there is much to dare.
lift; I would look up, and laugh, and love, and lift.
trod; I would have faith to keep the path Christ trod. A - MEN.

Alternate tunes: O PERFECT LOVE, No. 524; ALVERSTOKE, No. 471

504 Teach Me Thy Will, O Lord
TEACH ME

Katherine A. Grimes, b. 1877   William M. Runyan, b. 1870

1. Teach me Thy will, O Lord, Teach me Thy way; Teach me to
2. Teach me Thy won-drous grace, Bound-less and free; Lord, let Thy
3. Teach me by pain Thy power, Teach me by love; Teach me to
4. Teach Thou my lips to sing, My heart to praise; Be Thou my

know Thy word, Teach me to pray. What-e'er seems best to Thee, That be my
bless-ed face Shine up-on me. Heal Thou sin's ev-ery smart, Dwell Thou with-
know, each hour, Thou art a-bove. Teach me as seem-eth best In Thee to
Lord and King Through all my days. Teach Thou my soul to cry, "Be Thou, dear

ear-nest plea, So that Thou draw-est me Clos-er each day.
in my heart; Grant that I nev-er part, Sav-iour, from Thee.
find sweet rest; Lean-ing up-on Thy breast, All doubt re-move.
Sav-iour, nigh, Teach me to live, to die, Saved by Thy grace." A-MEN.

505 Just As I Am, Thine Own to Be
JUST AS I AM

Marianne Hearn, 1834-1909   Joseph Barnby, 1838-1896

1. Just as I am, Thine own to be, Friend of the young, who lov-est me,
2. In the glad morn-ing of my day, My life to give, my vows to pay,
3. I would live ev-er in the light, I would work ev-er for the right,
4. Just as I am, young, strong, and free, To be the best that I can be

Just As I Am, Thine Own to Be

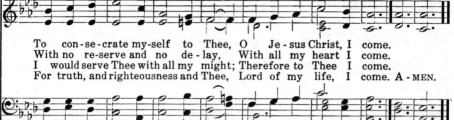

To con-se-crate my-self to Thee, O Je-sus Christ, I come.
With no re-serve and no de-lay, With all my heart I come.
I would serve Thee with all my might; Therefore to Thee I come.
For truth, and righteousness and Thee, Lord of my life, I come. A-MEN.

Open My Eyes, That I May See   506

Clara H. Scott, 1841-1897   Clara H. Scott, 1841-1897

1. O-pen my eyes, that I   may see Glimps-es of truth Thou hast for me;
2. O-pen my ears, that I   may hear Voic-es of truth Thou send-est clear;
3. O-pen my mouth, and let   me bear Glad-ly the warm truth ev-ery-where;

Place in my hands the won-der-ful key That shall un-clasp, and set me free.
And while the wave-notes fall on my ear, Ev-ery-thing false will dis-ap-pear.
O-pen my heart, and let me pre-pare Love with Thy chil-dren thus to share.

Si-lent-ly now I wait for Thee, Read-y, my God, Thy will to see;

O-pen my eyes, il-lu-mine me, Spir-it di-vine!
O-pen my ears, il-lu-mine me, Spir-it di-vine!
O-pen my heart, il-lu-mine me, Spir-it di-vine! A-MEN.

507 Lord, for Tomorrow and Its Needs

VINCENT

Sybil F. Partridge, b. 1876

Horatio R. Palmer, 1834-1907

1. Lord, for to-mor-row and its needs I do not pray; Keep me, my God, from
2. Let me be slow to do my will, Prompt to o-bey; Help me to sac-ri-
3. Let me in sea-son, Lord, be grave, In sea-son gay; Let me be faith-ful

stain of sin Just for to-day. Help me to la-bor earn-est-ly,
fice my-self, Fa-ther, to-day. Let me no wrong or i-dle word
to Thy grace, Fa-ther, to-day. Lord, for to-mor-row and its needs

And du-ly pray; Let me be kind in word and deed, Fa-ther to-day.
Un-think-ing say; Set Thou a seal up-on my lips Thro' all to-day.
I do not pray; Still keep me, guide me, love me, Lord, Thro' each to-day. A-MEN.

508 God, Who Touchest Earth with Beauty

GENEVA

Mary S. Edgar, b. 1889

C. Harold Lowden, b. 1883

1. God, who touch-est earth with beau-ty, Make me love-ly too,
2. Like Thy springs and run-ning wa-ters, Make me crys-tal pure,
3. Like Thy danc-ing waves in sun-light, Make me glad and free,
4. Like the arch-ing of the heav-ens, Lift my thoughts a-bove,
5. God, who touch-est earth with beau-ty, Make me love-ly too,

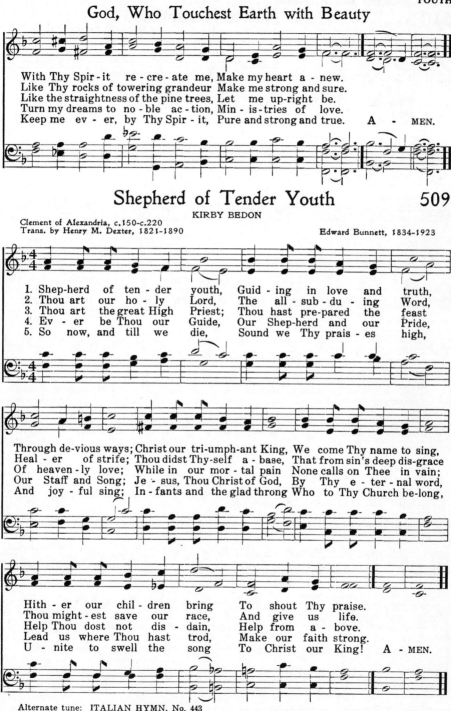

God, Who Touchest Earth with Beauty

With Thy Spir-it re-cre-ate me, Make my heart a - new.
Like Thy rocks of towering grandeur Make me strong and sure.
Like the straightness of the pine trees, Let me up-right be.
Turn my dreams to no-ble ac-tion, Min-is-tries of love.
Keep me ev-er, by Thy Spir-it, Pure and strong and true. A - MEN.

Shepherd of Tender Youth   509
KIRBY BEDON

Clement of Alexandria, c.150-c.220
Trans. by Henry M. Dexter, 1821-1890

Edward Bunnett, 1834-1923

1. Shep-herd of ten - der youth, Guid-ing in love and truth,
2. Thou art our ho-ly Lord, The all-sub-du-ing Word,
3. Thou art the great High Priest; Thou hast pre-pared the feast
4. Ev-er be Thou our Guide, Our Shep-herd and our Pride,
5. So now, and till we die, Sound we Thy prais-es high,

Through de-vious ways; Christ our tri-umph-ant King, We come Thy name to sing,
Heal-er of strife; Thou didst Thy-self a-base, That from sin's deep dis-grace
Of heaven-ly love; While in our mor-tal pain None calls on Thee in vain;
Our Staff and Song; Je-sus, Thou Christ of God, By Thy e-ter-nal word,
And joy-ful sing; In-fants and the glad throng Who to Thy Church be-long,

Hith-er our chil-dren bring To shout Thy praise.
Thou might-est save our race, And give us life.
Help Thou dost not dis-dain, Help from a-bove.
Lead us where Thou hast trod, Make our faith strong.
U-nite to swell the song To Christ our King! A - MEN.

Alternate tune: ITALIAN HYMN, No. 443

510

Yield Not to Temptation

Horatio R. Palmer, 1834-1907
Arr. by Donald P. Hustad, b. 1918

Horatio R. Palmer, 1834-1907

1. Yield not to temp-ta-tion, For yield-ing is sin, Each vic-t'ry will
2. Shun e-vil com-pan-ions, Bad lan-guage dis-dain, God's name hold in
3. To him that o'er-com-eth God giv-eth a crown, Thro' faith we shall

help you Some oth-er to win; Fight man-ful-ly on-ward,
rev-'rence, Nor take it in vain; Be thought-ful and ear-nest,
con-quer, Though of-ten cast down; He, who is our Sav-iour,

Dark pas-sions sub-due, Look ev-er to Je-sus, He will car-ry you through.
Kind-heart-ed and true, Look ev-er to Je-sus, He will car-ry you through.
Our strength will re-new, Look ev-er to Je-sus, He will car-ry you through.

REFRAIN

Ask the Sav-iour to help you, Com-fort, strengthen, and keep you,

He is will-ing to aid you, He will car-ry you through.

True-Hearted, Whole-Hearted

Frances R. Havergal, 1836-1879

George C. Stebbins, 1846-1945

1. True-heart-ed, whole-heart-ed, faith-ful and loy - al, King of our lives, by Thy
2. True-heart-ed, whole-heart-ed, full-est al - le-giance Yielding henceforth to our
3. True-heart-ed, whole-heart-ed, Sav-iour all - glo-rious! Take Thy great power and

grace we will be; Un-der the stand-ard ex - alt - ed and roy - al, Strong in Thy
glo - ri-ous King; Val-iant en-deav-or and lov - ing o-be-dience, Free-ly and
reign there a-lone, O - ver our wills and af - fec - tions vic-to-rious, Free-ly sur-

REFRAIN

strength we will battle for Thee. Peal out the watchword! si - lence it nev-er!
joy - ous-ly now would we bring. Peal out the watchword! si-lence it nev-er!
ren-dered and whol-ly Thine own. Peal out the watchword! si-lence it nev-er!

Song of our spir-its, re - joic - ing and free; Peal out the watchword!
Song of our spir-its, re-joic - ing and free; Peal out the watchword!

loy - al for - ev - er, King of our lives, by Thy grace we will be.
loy - al for - ev - er, King of our lives, by Thy grace we will be.

512 Lord and Saviour, True and Kind

BOYCE (Sharon)

Handley C. G. Moule, 1841-1920

William Boyce, 1710-1779

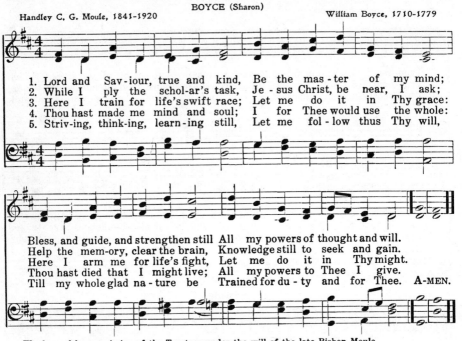

1. Lord and Sav-iour, true and kind, Be the mas-ter of my mind;
2. While I ply the schol-ar's task, Je-sus Christ, be near, I ask;
3. Here I train for life's swift race; Let me do it in Thy grace:
4. Thou hast made me mind and soul; I for Thee would use the whole:
5. Striv-ing, think-ing, learn-ing still, Let me fol-low thus Thy will,

Bless, and guide, and strengthen still All my powers of thought and will.
Help the mem-ory, clear the brain, Knowledge still to seek and gain.
Here I arm me for life's fight, Let me do it in Thy might.
Thou hast died that I might live; All my powers to Thee I give.
Till my whole glad na-ture be Trained for du-ty and for Thee. A-MEN.

513 The Lord Our God Alone Is Strong

TRURO

Caleb T. Winchester, 1847-1920

From T. Williams "Psalmodia Evangelica", 1789

1. The Lord our God a-lone is strong; His hands built not for one brief day;
2. His mountains lift their solemn forms, To watch in si-lence o'er the land;
3. Thou sov-'reign God, re-ceive this gift Thy will-ing ser-vants of-fer Thee;
4. And let those learn, who here shall meet, True wisdom is with reverence crowned,

His wondrous works, thro' a-ges long, His wis-dom and His power dis-play.
The roll-ing o-cean rocked with storms, Sleeps in the hol-low of His hand.
Ac-cept the prayers that thousands lift, And let these halls Thy tem-ple be.
And sci-ence walks with hum-ble feet To seek the God that faith hath found. A-MEN.

We Plow the Fields, and Scatter

WIR PFLÜGEN (Dresden)

514

Matthias Claudius, 1740-1815
Trans. by Jane M. Campbell, 1817-1878

Johann A. P. Schulz, 1747-1800

1. We plow the fields, and scat-ter The good seed on the land, But it is
2. He on-ly is the Mak-er Of all things near and far, He paints the
3. We thank Thee, then, O Fa-ther, For all things bright and good, The seed-time

fed and wa-tered By God's al-might-y hand; He sends the snow in
way-side flow-er, He lights the eve-ning star; The winds and waves o-
and the har-vest, Our life, our health, our food; Ac-cept the gifts we

win-ter, The warmth to swell the grain, The breez-es and the sun-shine, And
bey Him, By Him the birds are fed; Much more to us, His chil-dren, He
of-fer, For all Thy love im-parts, And what Thou most de-sir-est, Our

soft re-fresh-ing rain.
gives our dai-ly bread.
hum-ble, thank-ful hearts.

REFRAIN

All good gifts a-round us Are sent from heaven a-

bove; Then thank the Lord, O thank the Lord For all His love. A-MEN.

515   Count Your Blessings

Johnson Oatman, Jr., 1856-1926   Edwin O. Excell, 1851-1921

1. When up-on life's bil-lows you are tem - pest - tossed, When you are dis-
2. Are you ev - er bur-dened with a load of care? Does the cross seem
3. When you look at oth-ers with their lands and gold, Think that Christ has
4. So, a - mid the con-flict, wheth-er great or small, Do not be dis-

1. you are tem-pest

cour-aged, think-ing all is lost, Count your man-y bless-ings, name them
heav - y you are called to bear? Count your man-y bless-ings, ev - ery
prom-ised you His wealth un - told; Count your man-y bless-ings, mon - ey
cour-aged, God is o - ver all; Count your man-y bless-ings, an - gels

think-ing all is

one by one, And it will sur-prise you what the Lord hath done.
doubt will fly, And you will be sing-ing as the days go by.
can - not buy Your re-ward in heav-en, nor your home on high.
will at - tend, Help and com-fort give you to your jour - ney's end.

name them one by   what the Lord hath

REFRAIN

Count   your bless-ings, Name them one by one; Count your
Count your man-y bless-ings,   Name them one by one; Count your man-y

Count Your Blessings

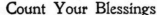

With Thankful Hearts, O Lord, We Come 516

MOHLER

J. S. Mohler, 19th Century

J. Henry Showalter, 1864-1947

517 We Gather Together

KREMSER

Source Unknown
Trans. by Theodore Baker, 1851-1934

Netherlands Folk Song, 1625
Arr. by Edward Kremser, 1838-1914

1. We gath-er to-geth-er to ask the Lord's bless-ing;
2. Be-side us to guide us, our God with us join-ing;
3. We all do ex-tol Thee, Thou Lead-er tri-um-phant,

He chas-tens and has-tens His will to make known;
Or-dain-ing, main-tain-ing His king-dom di-vine;
And pray that Thou still our De-fend-er wilt be.

The wick-ed op-press-ing now cease from dis-tress-ing,
So from the be-gin-ning the fight we were win-ning:
Let Thy con-gre-ga-tion es-cape trib-u-la-tion:

Sing prais-es to His Name: He for-gets not His own.
Thou, Lord, wast at our side, all glo-ry be Thine!
Thy Name be ev-er praised! O Lord, make us free! A-MEN.

ALTERNATE ENDING (after third stanza)

Lord, make us free.

Come, Ye Thankful People, Come

ST. GEORGE'S, WINDSOR

Henry Alford, 1810-1871

George J. Elvey, 1816-1893
Descant (small notes), William Lester, b. 1889

1. Come, ye thank-ful peo-ple, come, Raise the song of har-vest-home:
2. All the world is God's own field, Fruit un-to His praise to yield;
3. For the Lord our God shall come, And shall take His har-vest home;
4. E-ven so, Lord, quick-ly come To Thy fi-nal har-vest-home;

All is safe-ly gath-ered in, Ere the win-ter storms be-gin;
Wheat and tares to-geth-er sown, Un-to joy or sor-row grown;
From His field shall in that day All of-fens-es purge a-way;
Gath-er Thou Thy peo-ple in, Free from sor-row, free from sin;

God, our Ma-ker, doth pro-vide For our wants to be sup-plied:
First the blade, and then the ear, Then the full corn shall ap-pear:
Give His an-gels charge at last In the fire the tares to cast;
There, for-ev-er pu-ri-fied, In Thy pres-ence to a-bide:

Come to God's own tem-ple, come, Raise the song of har-vest-home.
Lord of har-vest, grant that we Whole-some grain and pure may be.
But the fruit-ful ears to store In His gar-ner ev-er-more.
Come, with all Thine an-gels, come, Raise the glo-rious har-vest-home. A-MEN.

519 Now Thank We All Our God

NUN DANKET

Martin Rinkart, 1586-1649
Trans. by Catherine Winkworth, 1829-1878

Johann Crüger, 1598-1662
Har. by Felix Mendelssohn, 1809-1847

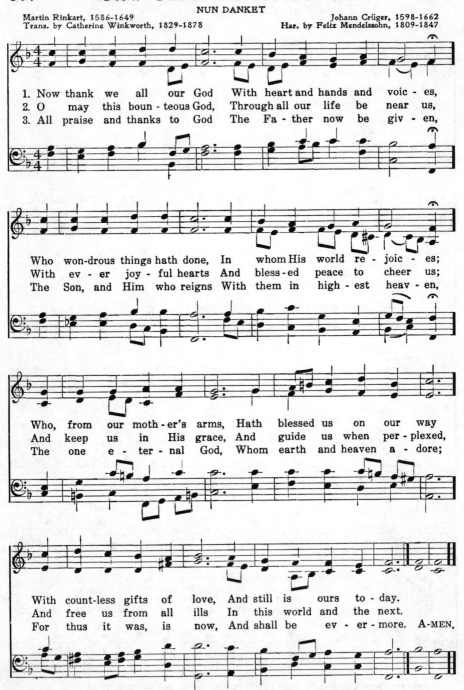

1. Now thank we all our God With heart and hands and voic - es,
2. O may this boun - teous God, Through all our life be near us,
3. All praise and thanks to God The Fa - ther now be giv - en,

Who won-drous things hath done, In whom His world re - joic - es;
With ev - er joy - ful hearts And bless - ed peace to cheer us;
The Son, and Him who reigns With them in high - est heav - en,

Who, from our moth - er's arms, Hath blessed us on our way
And keep us in His grace, And guide us when per - plexed,
The one e - ter - nal God, Whom earth and heaven a - dore;

With count-less gifts of love, And still is ours to - day.
And free us from all ills In this world and the next.
For thus it was, is now, And shall be ev - er - more. A-MEN.

Great God, We Sing That Mighty Hand 520

FEDERAL STREET

Philip Doddridge, 1702-1751

Henry K. Oliver, 1800-1885

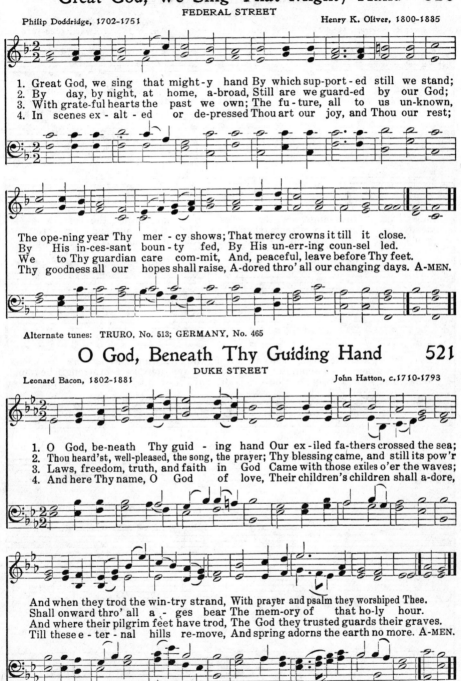

1. Great God, we sing that might-y hand By which sup-port-ed still we stand;
2. By day, by night, at home, a-broad, Still are we guard-ed by our God;
3. With grate-ful hearts the past we own; The fu-ture, all to us un-known,
4. In scenes ex-alt-ed or de-pressed Thou art our joy, and Thou our rest;

The ope-ning year Thy mer-cy shows; That mercy crowns it till it close.
By His in-ces-sant boun-ty fed, By His un-err-ing coun-sel led.
We to Thy guardian care com-mit, And, peaceful, leave before Thy feet.
Thy goodness all our hopes shall raise, A-dored thro' all our changing days. A-MEN.

Alternate tunes: TRURO, No. 513; GERMANY, No. 465

O God, Beneath Thy Guiding Hand 521

DUKE STREET

Leonard Bacon, 1802-1881

John Hatton, c.1710-1793

1. O God, be-neath Thy guid-ing hand Our ex-iled fa-thers crossed the sea;
2. Thou heard'st, well-pleased, the song, the prayer; Thy blessing came, and still its pow'r
3. Laws, freedom, truth, and faith in God Came with those exiles o'er the waves;
4. And here Thy name, O God of love, Their children's children shall a-dore,

And when they trod the win-try strand, With prayer and psalm they worshiped Thee.
Shall onward thro' all a-ges bear The mem-ory of that ho-ly hour.
And where their pilgrim feet have trod, The God they trusted guards their graves.
Till these e-ter-nal hills re-move, And spring adorns the earth no more. A-MEN.

522 Standing at the Portal

ST. ALBAN

Frances R. Havergal, 1836-1879

Franz Joseph Haydn, 1732-1809
Arr. by John B. Dykes, 1823-1876

1. Stand-ing at the por - tal Of the o-pening year, Words of com-fort
2. For the year be-fore us, O what rich sup-plies! For the poor and
3. He will nev-er fail us, He will not for-sake; His e-ter-nal

meet us, Hush-ing ev-ery fear; Spo-ken through the si-lence
need-y Liv-ing streams shall rise; For the sad and sin-ful
cov-'nant He will nev-er break. Rest-ing on His prom-ise,

By our Fa-ther's voice, Ten-der, strong and faith-ful, Mak-ing us re-joice.
Shall His grace a-bound; For the faint and fee-ble Perfect strength be found.
What have we to fear? God is all-suf-fi-cient For the com-ing year.

REFRAIN

On-ward then, and fear not, Chil-dren of the day;

For His Word shall nev-er, Nev-er pass a-way. A-MEN.

Alternate tunes: HERMAS, No. 82; ST. GERTRUDE, No. 170

Another Year Is Dawning

SALVATORI

Frances R. Havergal, 1836-1879

Arr. from J. Michael Haydn, 1737-1806

1. An - oth - er year is dawn - ing! Dear Fa - ther, let it be,
2. An - oth - er year of mer - cies, Of faith - ful - ness and grace;
3. An - oth - er year of serv - ice, Of wit - ness for Thy love;

In work - ing or in wait - ing, An - oth - er year with Thee;
An - oth - er year of glad - ness In the shin - ing of Thy face;
An - oth - er year of train - ing For ho - lier work a - bove.

An - oth - er year of lean - ing Up - on Thy lov - ing breast,
An - oth - er year of prog - ress, An - oth - er year of praise,
An - oth - er year is dawn - ing! Dear Fa - ther, let it be

An - oth - er year of trust - ing, Of qui - et, hap - py rest.
An - oth - er year of prov - ing Thy pres-ence all the days.
On earth, or else in heav - en, An - oth - er year for Thee. A-MEN.

Alternate tunes: ELLACOMBE, No. 19; AURELIA, No. 164

524 O Perfect Love, All Human Thought Transcending

O PERFECT LOVE

Dorothy F. Gurney, 1858-1932   Joseph Barnby, 1838-1896

1. O per - fect Love, all hu - man thought tran - scend - ing,
2. O per - fect Life, be Thou their full as - sur - ance
3. Grant them the joy which bright - ens earth - ly sor - row;
4. Hear us, O Fa - ther, gra - cious and for - giv - ing,

Low - ly we kneel in prayer be - fore Thy throne,
Of ten - der char - i - ty and stead - fast faith,
Grant them the peace which calms all earth - ly strife,
Through Je - sus Christ, Thy co - e - ter - nal Word,

That theirs may be the love that has no end - ing,
Of pa - tient hope, and qui - et, brave en - dur - ance,
And to life's day the glo - rious, un - known mor - row
Who, with the Ho - ly Ghost, by all things liv - ing

Whom Thou for - ev - er - more dost join in one.
With child - like trust that fears nor pain nor death.
That dawns up - on e - ter - nal love and life.
Now and to end - less a - ges art a - dored. A-MEN.

A Wedding Prayer

THOMPSON

Alfred P. Gibbs, b. 1890

Alfred P. Gibbs, b. 1890

1. Thou glo - rious Bride - groom Who, from heav - en's splen - dor,
2. We seek for them, O Lord, Thy ben - e - dic - tion,
3. O, may they prove Thy grace is all - suf - fi - cient,
4. In - to Thy gra - cious hands we now com - mend them,

Came to the cross, Thy cho - sen Bride to gain;
Each good and per - fect gift from heav'n a - bove;
Those needs to meet they can - not now fore - see;
For that rich bless - ing Thou a - lone canst give;

Draw near, we pray, and grace this hap - py un - ion,
The strength of faith, of cour - age, and for - bear - ance,
And have the con - scious sense of Thine own pres - ence,
And pray that they may grow in grace and know - ledge,

And, o'er their lives, do Thou su - preme - ly reign!
The light of wis - dom, and the warmth of love.
As they, in all their ways, ac - know - ledge Thee.
And, for Thy glo - ry, hence - forth seek to live. A-MEN.

526 O Worship the Lord

PORTER

Psalm 96: 9

Robert G. McCutchan, b. 1877

O wor-ship the Lord in the beau-ty of ho-li-ness;

Serve Him with glad-ness, all the earth. A-MEN.

527 We Praise Thee, O God

TE DEUM LAUDAMUS

Source Unknown, 4th Century

From Joseph Barnby, 1838-1896

We praise Thee, O God: We ac-knowl-edge Thee to be the Lord.

All the earth doth wor-ship Thee, the Fa-ther ev-er-last-ing. A-MEN.

528 Holy, Holy, Holy Lord of Hosts

SANCTUS

Isaiah 6:3

Arr. from "The Holy City"
Alfred R. Gaul, 1837-1913

Ho-ly, Ho-ly, Ho-ly Lord of Hosts: Ho-ly, Ho-ly, Ho-ly is the Lord of Hosts. A-MEN.

For additional "Opening Sentences" - see front inside cover

Christ, We Do All Adore Thee

From "The Seven Last Words of Christ"
Theodore Dubois, 1837-1924

Christ, we do all a - dore Thee, and we do praise Thee for - ev - er;

Christ, we do all a - dore Thee, and we do praise Thee for - ev - er,

For on the ho - ly cross hast Thou the world from sin re - deem - ed.

Christ, we do all a - dore Thee, and we do praise Thee for - ev - er.

(instrument)

Christ, we do all a - dore Thee.

530 Sanctus

Arr. from Isaiah 6:3

Alexander S. Cooper, 1835-1900

Ho - ly, Ho - ly, Ho - ly, Lord God of hosts, Heav'n and earth are

full of Thy glo - ry; Glo - ry be to Thee, O Lord Most High. A - MEN.

531 Lead Me, Lord

Psalm 5:8

Samuel S. Wesley, 1810-1876

Lead me, Lord, lead me in Thy right - eous - ness;

Make Thy way plain be - fore my face. A - MEN.

RESPONSE TO SCRIPTURE

532 Write These Words in Our Hearts

Ancient "Psalm Tone"

Write these words in our hearts, we be - seech Thee, O Lord.

Hear Our Prayer, O Lord 533

George Whelpton, 1847-1930

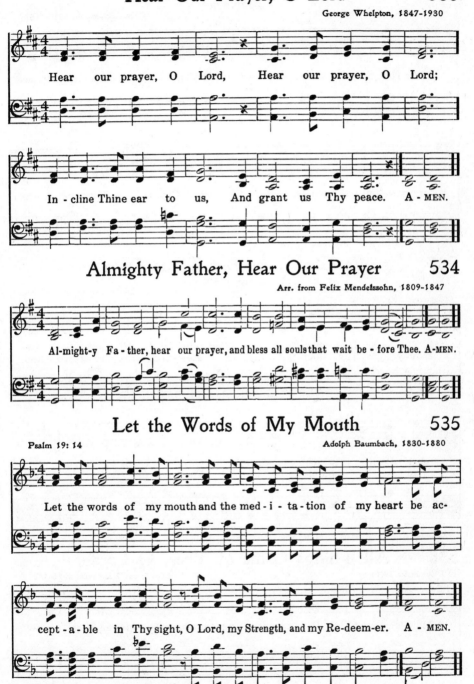

Hear our prayer, O Lord, Hear our prayer, O Lord;

In - cline Thine ear to us, And grant us Thy peace. A - MEN.

Almighty Father, Hear Our Prayer 534

Arr. from Felix Mendelssohn, 1809-1847

Al-might-y Fa - ther, hear our prayer, and bless all souls that wait be - fore Thee. A-MEN.

Let the Words of My Mouth 535

Psalm 19: 14

Adolph Baumbach, 1830-1880

Let the words of my mouth and the med - i - ta - tion of my heart be ac-

cept - a - ble in Thy sight, O Lord, my Strength, and my Re-deem-er. A - MEN.

For "Amens" - see back inside cover

536 Bless Thou the Gifts
CANONBURY

Samuel Longfellow, 1819-1892   Robert Schumann, 1810-1856

Bless Thou the gifts our hands have brought; Bless Thou the work our hearts have planned;

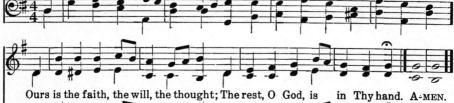

Ours is the faith, the will, the thought; The rest, O God, is   in Thy hand. A-MEN.

537 We Give Thee But Thine Own
ST. ANDREW

William W. How, 1823-1897   Joseph Barnby, 1838-1896

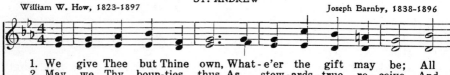

1. We give Thee but Thine own, What-e'er the gift may be; All
2. May we Thy boun-ties thus As stew-ards true re-ceive, And

that we have is Thine a-lone, A   trust, O Lord, from Thee.
glad-ly, as Thou bless-est us, To   Thee our first-fruits give. A-MEN.

Alternate tune: SCHUMANN, No. 451

538 All Things Come of Thee, O Lord

I Chronicles 29:14   Ludwig van Beethoven, 1770-1827

All things come of Thee, O Lord; and of Thine own have we giv-en Thee. A-MEN.

For "Glorias" and "Doxology"—see inside front cover

Father, Give Thy Benediction 539

ALLA TRINITA BEATA

Samuel Longfellow, 1819-1892   Arr. from "Laudi Spirituali," 1336

Fa - ther, give Thy ben - e - dic - tion, Give Thy peace be - fore we part;

Still our minds with truth's con-vic-tion, Calm with trust each anx-ious heart. A-MEN.

Lord, Let Us Now Depart in Peace 540

DISMISSAL

George Whelpton, 1847-1930

Lord, let us now de - part in peace, Who in Thy name are gath-ered here;

Dis-close the bright-ness of Thy face, and be for - ev - er near. A - MEN.

Peace, Peace; God's Wonderful Peace 541

William M. Runyan, b. 1870

Peace, peace; God's wonderful peace Be with you now and evermore. A - men,   A - men.

542 God Be in My Head

"Book of Hours," 1514

H. Walford Davies, 1869-1941

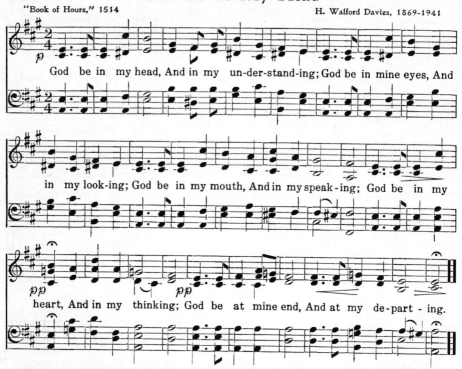

God be in my head, And in my un-der-stand-ing; God be in mine eyes, And

in my look-ing; God be in my mouth, And in my speak-ing; God be in my

heart, And in my thinking; God be at mine end, And at my de-part-ing.

543 May the Grace of Christ Our Saviour

DORRNANCE

John Newton, 1725-1807

Isaac B. Woodbury, 1819-1858

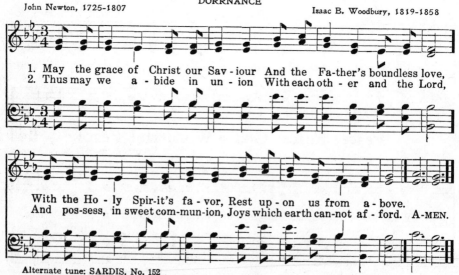

1. May the grace of Christ our Sav-iour And the Fa-ther's boundless love,
2. Thus may we a-bide in un-ion With each oth-er and the Lord,

With the Ho-ly Spir-it's fa-vor, Rest up-on us from a-bove.
And pos-sess, in sweet com-mun-ion, Joys which earth can-not af-ford. A-MEN.

Alternate tune: SARDIS, No. 152

SCRIPTURE READINGS

The readings are in consecutive scriptural order with relation to the beginning passage of each reading. The text used is the King James Version, 1611, with a few exceptions, when the American Standard Version, 1901, is used for easier congregational participation. Alphabetical, Subject and Scriptural Indexes are provided at the end of the Readings on pages 487 and 488.

544 GOD THE CREATOR

In the beginning God created the heaven and the earth.

And the earth was without form, and void; and darkness was upon the face of the deep.

And the Spirit of God moved upon the face of the waters. And God said, Let there be light: and there was light.

And God saw the light, that it was good: and God divided the light from the darkness.

And God called the light Day, and the darkness he called Night.

And the evening and the morning were the first day. —Genesis 1: 1-5.

By the word of the Lord were the heavens made; and all the host of them by the breath of his mouth.

He gathereth the waters of the sea together as an heap: he layeth up the depth in storehouses.

Let all the earth fear the Lord: let all the inhabitants of the world stand in awe of him.

For he spake, and it was done; he commanded, and it stood fast. —Psalm 33: 6-9.

Let us come before his presence with thanksgiving, and make a joyful noise unto him with psalms.

For the Lord is a great God, and a great King above all gods.

In his hand are the deep places of the earth: the strength of the hills is his also.

The sea is his, and he made it: and his hands formed the dry land.

O come, let us worship and bow down: let us kneel before the Lord our maker.

For he is our God; and we are the people of his pasture, and the sheep of his hand. —Psalm 95: 2-7.

545 GOD'S COMMANDMENTS

And God spake all these words, saying,

I am the Lord thy God, which have brought thee out of the land of Egypt, out of the house of bondage.

Thou shalt have no other gods before me.

Thou shalt not make unto thee any graven image, or any likeness of any thing that is in heaven above, or that is in the earth beneath, or that is in the water under the earth:

Thou shalt not bow down thyself to them, nor serve them: for I the Lord thy God am a jealous God, visiting the iniquity of the fathers upon the children unto the third and fourth generation of them that hate me;

And showing mercy unto thousands of them that love me, and keep my commandments.

Thou shalt not take the name of the Lord thy God in vain;

For the Lord will not hold him guiltless that taketh his name in vain.

Remember the sabbath day, to keep it holy. Six days shalt thou labour, and do all thy work:

But the seventh day is the sabbath of the Lord thy God: in it thou shalt not do any work, thou, nor thy son, nor thy daughter, thy manservant, nor thy maidservant, nor thy cattle, nor thy stranger that is within thy gates:

For in six days the Lord made heaven and earth, the sea, and all that in them is, and rested the seventh day:

Wherefore the Lord blessed the sabbath day, and hallowed it. (over)

Honour thy father and thy mother: that thy days may be long upon the land which the Lord thy God giveth thee.

Thou shalt not kill.

Thou shalt not commit adultery.

Thou shalt not steal.

Thou shalt not bear false witness against thy neighbour.

Thou shalt not covet thy neighbour's house, thou shalt not covet thy neighbour's wife, nor his manservant, nor his maidservant, nor his ox, nor his ass, nor any thing that is thy neighbour's. —Exodus 20: 1-17.

Then one of them, which was a lawyer, asked him a question, tempting him, and saying, Master, which is the great commandment in the law?

Jesus said unto him, Thou shalt love the Lord thy God with all thy heart, and with all thy soul, and with all thy mind. This is the first and great commandment.

And the second is like unto it, Thou shalt love thy neighbour as thyself.

On these two commandments hang all the law and the prophets. —Matthew 22: 35-40.

546 GOD AND THE FAMILY

Now these are the commandments, the statutes, and the judgments, which the Lord your God commanded to teach you, that ye might do them in the land whither ye go to possess it:

That thou mightest fear the Lord thy God, to keep all his statutes and his commandments, which I command thee, thou, and thy son, and thy son's son, all the days of thy life; and that thy days may be prolonged.

And thou shalt love the Lord thy God with all thine heart, and with all thy soul, and with all thy might.

And these words, which I command thee this day, shall be in thine heart:

And thou shalt teach them diligently unto thy children, and shalt talk of them when thou sittest in thine house, and when thou walkest by the way, and when thou liest down, and when thou risest up.

And thou shalt bind them for a sign upon thine hand, and they shall be as frontlets between thine eyes. And thou shalt write them upon the posts of thy house, and on thy gates. —Deuteronomy 6: 1, 2, 5–9.

The fear of the Lord is the beginning of knowledge: but fools despise wisdom and instruction.

My son, hear the instruction of thy father, and forsake not the law of thy mother:

For they shall be an ornament of grace unto thy head, and chains about thy neck.

Train up a child in the way he should go: and when he is old, he will not depart from it. —Proverbs 1: 7-9; 22:6.

Children, obey your parents in Lord: for this is right.

Honour thy father and mother; which is the first commandment with promise;

That it may be well with thee, and thou mayest live long on the earth.

And, ye fathers, provoke not your children to wrath: but bring them up in the nurture and admonition of the Lord. —Ephesians 6: 1-4.

547 GOD AND THE NATION

All the commandments which I command thee this day shall ye observe to do, that ye may live,

And thou shalt remember all the way which the Lord thy God led thee.

For the Lord thy God bringeth thee into a good land, a land of brooks of water, of fountains and depths that spring out of valleys and hills;

A land of wheat, and barley, and vines, and fig trees, and pomegranates; a land of olive trees and honey;

A land wherein thou shalt eat bread without scarceness, thou shalt not lack any thing in it; a land whose stones are iron, and out of whose hills thou mayest dig brass.

When thou hast eaten and art full, then thou shalt bless the Lord thy God for the good land which he hath given thee.

Beware that thou forget not the Lord thy God, in not keeping his commandments, and his judgments, and his statutes, which I command thee this day:

Lest when thou hast eaten and art full, and hast built goodly houses, and dwelt therein;

And when thy herds and thy flocks multiply, and thy silver and thy gold is multiplied, and all that thou hast is multiplied;

Then thine heart be lifted up, and thou forget the Lord thy God,

And thou say in thine heart, My power and the might of mine hand hath gotten me this wealth.

But thou shalt remember the Lord thy God: for it is he that giveth thee power to get wealth that he may establish his covenant which he sware unto thy fathers, as it is this day.

And it shall be, if thou do at all forget the Lord thy God, and walk after other gods, and serve them, and worship them, I testify against you this day that ye shall surely perish.

As the nations which the Lord destroyeth before your face, so shall ye perish; because ye would not be obedient unto the voice of the Lord your God. —Deuteronomy 8: 1, 2, 7-14, 17-20.

548   THE WAY OF LIFE

Blessed is the man that walketh not in the counsel of the ungodly, nor standeth in the way of sinners, nor sitteth in the seat of the scornful.

But his delight is in the law of the Lord; and in his law doth he meditate day and night.

And he shall be like a tree planted by the rivers of water, that bringeth forth his fruit in his season; his leaf also shall not wither; and whatsoever he doeth shall prosper.

The ungodly are not so: but are like the chaff which the wind driveth away.

Therefore the ungodly shall not stand in the judgment, nor sinners in the congregation of the righteous.

For the Lord knoweth the way of the righteous: but the way of the ungodly shall perish. —Psalm 1.

There is a way which seemeth right unto a man, but the end thereof are the ways of death. —Proverbs 14:12.

Enter ye in at the strait gate: for wide is the gate, and broad is the way, that leadeth to destruction, and many there be which go in thereat:

Because strait is the gate, and narrow is the way, which leadeth unto life, and few there be that find it. —Matthew 7:13, 14.

Jesus saith unto him, I am the way, the truth, and the life: no man cometh unto the Father, but by me. —John 14:6.

549   GOD'S ATTRIBUTES

The heavens declare the glory of God; and the firmament showeth his handywork.

Day unto day uttereth speech, and night unto night showeth knowledge.

There is no speech nor language, where their voice is not heard.

Their line is gone out through all the earth, and their words to the end of the world.

In them hath he set a tabernacle for the sun, which is as a bridegroom coming out of his chamber, and rejoiceth as a strong man to run a race.

His going forth is from the end of the heaven, and his circuit unto the ends of it: and there is nothing hid from the heat thereof.   (over)

The law of the Lord is perfect, converting the soul:

The testimony of the Lord is sure, making wise the simple.

The statutes of the Lord are right, rejoicing the heart:

The commandment of the Lord is pure, enlightening the eyes.

The fear of the Lord is clean, enduring for ever:

The judgments of the Lord are true and righteous altogether.

More to be desired are they than gold, yea, than much fine gold; sweeter also than honey and the honeycomb.

Moreover, by them is thy servant warned: and in keeping of them there is great reward.

Who can understand his errors? cleanse thou me from secret faults.

Keep back thy servant also from presumptuous sins; let them not have dominion over me:

Then shall I be upright, and I shall be innocent from the great transgression.

Let the words of my mouth, and the meditation of my heart, be acceptable in thy sight, O Lord, my strength, and my redeemer.　—Psalm 19.

550　THE SHEPHERD PSALM

The Lord is my shepherd; I shall not want.

He maketh me to lie down in green pastures: he leadeth me beside the still waters.

He restoreth my soul: he leadeth me in the paths of righteousness for his name's sake.

Yea, though I walk through the valley of the shadow of death, I will fear no evil:

For thou art with me; thy rod and thy staff they comfort me.

Thou preparest a table before me in the presence of mine enemies:

Thou anointest my head with oil; my cup runneth over.

Surely goodness and mercy shall follow me all the days of my life; and I will dwell in the house of the Lord for ever.　—Psalm 23.

551　THE MAJESTY OF GOD

The earth is the Lord's, and the fulness thereof; the world, and they that dwell therein.

For he hath founded it upon the seas, and established it upon the floods.

Who shall ascend into the hill of the Lord? or who shall stand in his holy place?

He that hath clean hands, and a pure heart; who hath not lifted up his soul unto vanity, nor sworn deceitfully.

He shall receive the blessing from the Lord, and righteousness from the God of his salvation.

This is the generation of them that seek him, that seek thy face, O Jacob.

Lift up your heads, O ye gates; and be ye lifted up, ye everlasting doors; and the King of glory shall come in.

Who is this King of glory?

The Lord strong and mighty, the Lord mighty in battle.

Lift up your heads, O ye gates; even lift them up, ye everlasting doors; and the King of glory shall come in.

Who is this King of glory?

The Lord of hosts, he is the King of glory.　—Psalm 24.

552　CHRISTIAN STEWARDSHIP

The earth is the Lord's, and the fulness thereof; the world, and they that dwell therein.　—Psalm 24:1.

In all thy ways acknowledge him, and he shall direct thy paths.
　—Proverbs 3:6.

And all the tithe of the land, whether of the seed of the land, or of the fruit of the tree, is the Lord's: it is holy unto the Lord.—Leviticus 27:30.

Render therefore unto Caesar the things which are Caesar's; and unto God the things that are God's.
—Matthew 22:21.

Honour the Lord with thy substance, and with the firstfruits of all thine increase. —Proverbs 3:9.

Bring ye all the tithes into the storehouse, that there may be meat in mine house, and prove me now herewith, saith the Lord of hosts, if I will not open you the windows of heaven, and pour you out a blessing, that there shall not be room enough to receive it. —Malachi 3:10.

But this I say, He which soweth sparingly shall reap also sparingly; and he which soweth bountifully shall reap also bountifully.

Every man according as he purposeth in his heart, so let him give; not grudgingly, or of necessity: for God loveth a cheerful giver.

And God is able to make all grace abound toward you; that ye, always having all sufficiency in all things, may abound to every good work.
—II Corinthians 9: 6-8.

As every man hath received the gift, even so minister the same one to another, as good stewards of the manifold grace of God. —I Peter 4:10.

553 FAITH AND CONFIDENCE

The Lord is my light and my salvation; whom shall I fear? the Lord is the strength of my life; of whom shall I be afraid?

When the wicked, even mine enemies and my foes, came upon me to eat up my flesh, they stumbled and fell.

Though an host should encamp against me, my heart shall not fear: though war should rise against me, in this will I be confident.

One thing have I desired of the Lord, that will I seek after; that I may dwell in the house of the Lord all the days of my life, to behold the beauty of the Lord, and to inquire in his temple.

For in the time of trouble he shall hide me in his pavilion: in the secret of his tabernacle shall he hide me; he shall set me up upon a rock.

And now shall mine head be lifted up above mine enemies round about me; therefore will I offer in his tabernacle sacrifices of joy; I will sing, yea, I will sing praises unto the Lord.

Hear, O Lord, when I cry with my voice: have mercy also upon me, and answer me.

When thou saidst, Seek ye my face; my heart said unto thee, Thy face, Lord, will I seek.

Hide not thy face far from me; put not thy servant away in anger: thou hast been my help; leave me not, neither forsake me, O God of my salvation.

Deliver me not over unto the will of mine enemies: for false witnesses are risen up against me, and such as breathe out cruelty.

I had fainted, unless I had believed to see the goodness of the Lord in the land of the living.

Wait on the Lord: be of good courage, and he shall strengthen thine heart: wait, I say, on the Lord.
From Psalm 27.

554 DIVINE DELIVERANCE

Rejoice in the Lord, O ye righteous: for praise is comely for the upright.

For the word of the Lord is right; and all his works are done in truth.

He loveth righteousness and judgment: the earth is full of the goodness of the Lord.

Let all the earth fear the Lord: let all the inhabitants of the world stand in awe of him.

The Lord bringeth the counsel of the heathen to nought: he maketh the devices of the people of none effect.

(over)

The counsel of the Lord standeth forever, the thoughts of his heart to all generations.

Blessed is the nation whose God is the Lord; and the people whom he hath chosen for his own inheritance.

The Lord looketh from heaven; he beholdeth all the sons of men.

From the place of his habitation he looketh upon all the inhabitants of the earth.

He fashioneth their hearts alike; he considereth all their works.

There is no king saved by the multitude of an host: a mighty man is not delivered by much strength.

An horse is a vain thing for safety: neither shall he deliver any by his great strength.

Behold, the eye of the Lord is upon them that fear him, upon them that hope in his mercy;

To deliver their soul from death, and to keep them alive in famine.

Our soul waiteth for the Lord: he is our help and our shield.

For our heart shall rejoice in him, because we have trusted in his holy name.

Let thy mercy, O Lord, be upon us, according as we hope in thee.
—Psalm 33:1, 4, 5, 8, 10-22.

Some trust in chariots, and some in horses: but we will remember the name of the Lord our God.
—Psalm 20:7.

555   DIVINE PROVIDENCE

I will bless the Lord at all times: his praise shall continually be in my mouth.

My soul shall make her boast in the Lord: the humble shall hear thereof, and be glad.

O magnify the Lord with me, and let us exalt his name together.

I sought the Lord, and he heard me, and delivered me from all my fears.

They looked unto him, and were lightened; and their faces were not ashamed.

This poor man cried, and the Lord heard him, and saved him out of all his troubles.

The angel of the Lord encampeth round about them that fear him, and delivereth them.

O taste and see that the Lord is good: blessed is the man that trusteth in him.

O fear the Lord, ye his saints; for there is no want to them that fear him.

The young lions do lack, and suffer hunger; but they that seek the Lord shall not want any good thing.

The righteous cry, and the Lord heareth, and delivereth them out of all their troubles.

The Lord is nigh unto them that are of a broken heart; and saveth such as be of a contrite spirit.

Many are the afflictions of the righteous: but the Lord delivereth him out of them all.

The Lord redeemeth the soul of his servants; and none of them that trust in him shall be desolate.
—Psalm 34: 1-10, 17-19, 22.

556   PATIENCE AND TRUST

Fret not thyself because of evildoers, neither be thou envious against the workers of iniquity.

For they shall soon be cut down like the grass, and wither as the green herb.

Trust in the Lord, and do good; so shalt thou dwell in the land, and verily thou shalt be fed.

Delight thyself also in the Lord; and he shall give thee the desires of thine heart.

Commit thy way unto the Lord; trust also in him; and he shall bring it to pass.

And he shall bring forth thy righteousness as the light, and thy judgment as the noonday.

Rest in the Lord, and wait patiently for him: fret not thyself because of him who prospereth in his way, because of the man who bringeth wicked devices to pass.

Cease from anger, and forsake wrath: fret not thyself in any wise to do evil.

For evildoers shall be cut off: but those that wait upon the Lord, they shall inherit the earth.

For yet a little while, and the wicked shall not be: yea, thou shalt diligently consider his place, and it shall not be.

But the meek shall inherit the earth; and shall delight themselves in the abundance of peace.

The Lord knoweth the days of the upright: and their inheritance shall be for ever.

The steps of a good man are ordered by the Lord: and he delighteth in his way.

Though he fall, he shall not be utterly cast down: for the Lord upholdeth him with his hand.

I have been young, and now am old; yet have I not seen the righteous forsaken, nor his seed begging bread.

He is ever merciful and lendeth; and his seed is blessed.

Mark the perfect man, and behold the upright: for the end of that man is peace.

But the salvation of the righteous is of the Lord: he is their strength in the time of trouble. —From Psalm 37.

557 SONG OF DELIVERANCE

I waited patiently for the Lord; and he inclined unto me, and heard my cry.

He brought me up also out of an horrible pit, out of the miry clay, and set my feet upon a rock, and established my goings.

And he hath put a new song in my mouth, even praise unto our God: many shall see it, and fear, and shall trust in the Lord.

Blessed is that man that maketh the Lord his trust, and respecteth not the proud, nor such as turn aside to lies.

Many, O Lord my God, are thy wonderful works which thou hast done, and thy thoughts which are to us-ward:

They cannot be reckoned up in order unto thee: if I would declare and speak of them, they are more than can be numbered.

I delight to do thy will, O my God: yea, thy law is within my heart.

I have preached righteousness in the great congregation: lo, I have not refrained my lips, O Lord, thou knowest.

I have not hid thy righteousness within my heart; I have declared thy faithfulness and thy salvation:

I have not concealed thy lovingkindness and thy truth from the great congregation.

Withhold not thou thy tender mercies from me, O Lord: let thy lovingkindness and thy truth continually preserve me.

For innumerable evils have compassed me about: mine iniquities have taken hold upon me, so that I am not able to look up; they are more than the hairs of mine head; therefore my heart faileth me.

Be pleased, O Lord, to deliver me: O Lord, make haste to help me.

Let all those that seek thee rejoice and be glad in thee: let such as love thy salvation say continually, The Lord be magnified. —Psalm 40: 1-5, 8-13, 16.

558 PRAYER OF PENITENCE

Have mercy upon me, O God, according to thy lovingkindness:

According unto the multitude of thy tender mercies blot out my transgressions.

Wash me thoroughly from mine iniquity, and cleanse me from my sin.

For I acknowledge my transgressions; and my sin is ever before me.

Against thee, thee only, have I sinned, and done this evil in thy sight; that thou mightest be justified when thou speakest, and be clear when thou judgest.

Behold, I was shapen in iniquity; and in sin did my mother conceive me.

Behold, thou desirest truth in the inward parts; and in the hidden part thou shalt make me to know wisdom.

Purge me with hyssop, and I shall be clean: wash me, and I shall be whiter than snow.

Make me to hear joy and gladness; that the bones which thou hast broken may rejoice.

Hide thy face from my sins, and blot out all mine iniquities.

Create in me a clean heart, O God; and renew a right spirit within me.

Cast me not away from thy presence; and take not thy holy spirit from me.

Restore unto me the joy of thy salvation; and uphold me with thy free spirit.

Then will I teach transgressors thy ways; and sinners shall be converted unto thee.

Deliver me from bloodguiltiness, O God, thou God of my salvation; and my tongue shall sing aloud of thy righteousness.

O Lord, open thou my lips; and my mouth shall show forth thy praise.

For thou desirest not sacrifice; else would I give it: thou delightest not in burnt offering.

The sacrifices of God are a broken spirit: a broken and a contrite heart, O God, thou wilt not despise.
—Psalm 51: 1-17.

559　THE ETERNAL GOD

Lord, thou hast been our dwelling place in all generations.

Before the mountains were brought forth, or ever thou hadst formed the earth and the world, even from everlasting to everlasting, thou art God.

Thou turnest man to destruction; and sayest, Return, ye children of men.

For a thousand years in thy sight are but as yesterday when it is past, and as a watch in the night.

For all our days are passed away in thy wrath: we spend our years as a tale that is told.

The days of our years are threescore years and ten; and if by reason of strength they be fourscore years, yet is their strength labour and sorrow; for it is soon cut off, and we fly away.

So teach us to number our days, that we may apply our hearts unto wisdom.

O satisfy us early with thy mercy; that we may rejoice and be glad all our days.

But thou, O Lord, shalt endure for ever; and thy remembrance unto all generations.

O my God, take me not away in the midst of my days: thy years are throughout all generations.

Of old hast thou laid the foundation of the earth; and the heavens are the work of thy hands.

They shall perish, but thou shalt endure: yea, all of them shall wax old like a garment;

As a vesture shalt thou change them, and they shall be changed:

But thou art the same, and thy years shall have no end.
—Psalm 90: 1-4, 9, 10, 12, 14; 102: 12, 24-27.

560 A PSALM OF TRUST

He that dwelleth in the secret place of the Most High shall abide under the shadow of the Almighty.

I will say of the Lord, He is my refuge and my fortress: my God; in him will I trust.

Surely he shall deliver thee from the snare of the fowler, and from the noisome pestilence.

He shall cover thee with his feathers, and under his wings shalt thou trust: his truth shall be thy shield and buckler.

Thou shalt not be afraid for the terror by night, nor for the arrow that flieth by day;

Nor for the pestilence that walketh in darkness, nor for the destruction that wasteth at noonday.

A thousand shall fall at thy side, and ten thousand at thy right hand; but it shall not come nigh thee.

Only with thine eyes shalt thou behold, and see the reward of the wicked.

Because thou hast made the Lord, which is my refuge, even the Most High, thy habitation;

There shall no evil befall thee, neither shall any plague come nigh thy dwelling.

For he shall give his angels charge over thee, to keep thee in all thy ways.

They shall bear thee up in their hands, lest thou dash thy foot against a stone.

Thou shalt tread upon the lion and adder: the young lion and the dragon shalt thou trample under feet.

Because he hath set his love upon me, therefore will I deliver him: I will set him on high, because he hath known my name.

He shall call upon me, and I will answer him: I will be with him in trouble; I will deliver him, and honour him.

With long life will I satisfy him, and show him my salvation. —Psalm 91.

561 BLESSINGS FROM GOD

Bless the Lord, O my soul; and all that is within me, bless his holy name.

Bless the Lord, O my soul, and forget not all his benefits:

Who forgiveth all thine iniquities; who healeth all thy diseases;

Who redeemeth thy life from destruction; who crowneth thee with lovingkindness and tender mercies;

Who satisfieth thy mouth with good things; so that thy youth is renewed like the eagle's.

The Lord executeth righteousness and judgment for all that are oppressed.

He made known his ways unto Moses, his acts unto the children of Israel.

The Lord is merciful and gracious, slow to anger, and plenteous in mercy.

He will not always chide; neither will he keep his anger for ever.

He hath not dealt with us after our sins, nor rewarded us according to our iniquities.

For as the heaven is high above the earth, so great is his mercy toward them that fear him.

As far as the east is from the west, so far hath he removed our transgressions from us.

Like as a father pitieth his children, so the Lord pitieth them that fear him.

For he knoweth our frame; he remembereth that we are dust.

As for man, his days are as grass; as a flower of the field, so he flourisheth.

For the wind passeth over it, and it is gone; and the place thereof shall know it no more.

But the mercy of the Lord is from everlasting to everlasting upon them that fear him, and his righteousness unto children's children;

To such as keep his covenant, and to those that remember his commandments to do them. (over)

The Lord hath prepared his throne in the heavens; and his kingdom ruleth over all.

Bless the Lord, ye his angels, that excel in strength, that do his commandments, hearkening unto the voice of his word.

Bless ye the Lord, all ye his hosts; ye ministers of his, that do his pleasure.

Bless the Lord, all his works, in all places of his dominion: bless the Lord, O my soul. —Psalm 103.

562 GOD'S OMNIPOTENCE

Bless the Lord, O my soul. O Lord my God, thou art very great; thou art clothed with honour and majesty:

Who coverest thyself with light as with a garment; who stretchest out the heavens like a curtain:

Who layeth the beams of his chambers in the waters: who maketh the clouds his chariot: who walketh upon the wings of the wind:

Who maketh his angels spirits; his ministers a flaming fire:

Who laid the foundations of the earth, that it should not be removed for ever.

Thou coveredst it with the deep as with a garment: the water stood above the mountains.

At thy rebuke they fled; at the voice of thy thunder they hasted away.

They go up by the mountains; they go down by the valleys unto the place which thou hast founded for them.

Thou hast set a bound that they may not pass over; that they turn not again to cover the earth.

He sendeth the springs into the valleys, which run among the hills.

He watereth the hills from his chambers: the earth is satisfied with the fruit of thy works.

He causeth the grass to grow for the cattle, and herb for the service of man: that he may bring forth food out of the earth;

O Lord, how manifold are thy works! in wisdom hast thou made them all: the earth is full of thy riches.

So is this great and wide sea, wherein are things creeping innumerable, both small and great beasts.

These wait all upon thee, that thou mayest give them their meat in due season.

That thou givest them they gather: thou openest thine hand, they are filled with good.

Thou hidest thy face, they are troubled; thou takest away their breath, they die, and return to their dust.

Thou sendest forth thy spirit, they are created; and thou renewest the face of the earth.

The glory of the Lord shall endure for ever: the Lord shall rejoice in his works.

He looketh on the earth, and it trembleth: he toucheth the hills, and they smoke.

I will sing unto the Lord as long as I live: I will sing praise to my God while I have my being.

My meditation of him shall be sweet: I will be glad in the Lord.
—Psalm 104: 1-10, 13-14, 24, 25, 27-34.

563 SONG OF THANKSGIVING

O give thanks unto the Lord, for he is good; for his mercy endureth for ever.

Let the redeemed of the Lord say so, whom he hath redeemed from the hand of the enemy;

And gathered them out of the lands, from the east, and from the west, from the north, and from the south.

They wandered in the wilderness in a solitary way; they found no city to dwell in.

Hungry and thirsty, their soul fainted in them.

Then they cried unto the Lord in their trouble, and he delivered them out of their distresses.

And he led them forth by the right way, that they might go to a city of habitation.

Oh that men would praise the Lord for his goodness, and for his wonderful works to the children of men!

For he satisfieth the longing soul, and filleth the hungry soul with goodness.

Such as sit in darkness and in the shadow of death, being bound in affliction and iron;

Because they rebelled against the words of God, and contemned the counsel of the Most High:

Therefore he brought down their heart with labour; they fell down, and there was none to help.

Then they cried unto the Lord in their trouble, and he saved them out of their distresses.

He brought them out of darkness and the shadow of death, and brake their bands in sunder.

Oh that men would praise the Lord for his goodness, and for his wonderful works to the children of men!

For he hath broken the gates of brass, and cut the bars of iron in sunder.

Fools because of their transgression, and because of their iniquities, are afflicted.

Their soul abhorreth all manner of meat; and they draw near unto the gates of death.

Then they cry unto the Lord in their trouble, and he saveth them out of their distresses.

He sent his word, and healed them, and delivered them from their destructions.

Oh that men would praise the Lord for his goodness, and for his wonderful works to the children of men!

And let them sacrifice the sacrifices of thanksgiving, and declare his works with rejoicing. —Psalm 107: 1-22.

564   GRATITUDE TO GOD

I love the Lord, because he hath heard my voice and my supplications.

Because he hath inclined his ear unto me, therefore will I call upon him as long as I live.

The sorrows of death compassed me, and the pains of sheol gat hold upon me: I found trouble and sorrow.

Then called I upon the name of the Lord; O Lord, I beseech thee, deliver my soul.

Gracious is the Lord, and righteous; yea, our God is merciful.

The Lord preserveth the simple: I was brought low, and he helped me.

Return unto thy rest, O my soul; for the Lord hath dealt bountifully with thee.

For thou hast delivered my soul from death, mine eyes from tears, and my feet from falling.

What shall I render unto the Lord for all his benefits toward me?

I will take the cup of salvation, and call upon the name of the Lord.

I will pay my vows unto the Lord now in the presence of all his people.

I will walk before the Lord in the land of the living.

O Lord, truly I am thy servant; I am thy servant, and the son of thine handmaid: thou hast loosed my bonds.

I will offer to thee the sacrifice of thanksgiving, and will call upon the name of the Lord. I will pay my vows unto the Lord now in the presence of all his people. —From Psalm 116

565 OBEDIENCE TO GOD

Blessed are the undefiled in the way, who walk in the law of the Lord.

Blessed are they that keep his testimonies, and that seek him with the whole heart.

They also do no iniquity: they walk in his ways.

Thou hast commanded us to keep thy precepts diligently.

O that my ways were directed to keep thy statutes!

Then shall I not be ashamed, when I have respect unto all thy commandments.

I will praise thee with uprightness of heart, when I shall have learned thy righteous judgments.

I will keep thy statutes: O forsake me not utterly.

Wherewithal shall a young man cleanse his way? By taking heed thereto according to thy word.

With my whole heart have I sought thee: O let me not wander from thy commandments.

Thy word have I hid in mine heart, that I might not sin against thee.

Blessed art thou, O Lord: teach me thy statutes.

With my lips have I declared all the judgments of thy mouth.

I have rejoiced in the way of thy testimonies, as much as in all riches.

I will meditate in thy precepts, and have respect unto thy ways.

I will delight myself in thy statutes: I will not forget thy word.

Deal bountifully with thy servant, that I may live, and keep thy word.

Open thou mine eyes, that I may behold wondrous things out of thy law. —Psalm 119: 1-18.

566 PRAISE AND WORSHIP

I was glad when they said unto me, Let us go into the house of the Lord.

I will praise thee with my whole heart: before the gods will I sing praise unto thee.

I will worship toward thy holy temple, and praise thy name for thy lovingkindness and for thy truth: for thou hast magnified thy word above all thy name.

In the day when I cried thou answeredst me, and strengthenedst me with strength in my soul.

All the kings of the earth shall praise thee, O Lord, when they hear the words of thy mouth.

Yea, they shall sing in the ways of the Lord: for great is the glory of the Lord.

Though the Lord be high, yet hath he respect unto the lowly: but the proud he knoweth afar off.

Though I walk in the midst of trouble, thou wilt revive me; thou shalt stretch forth thine hand against the wrath of mine enemies, and thy right hand shall save me.

The Lord will perfect that which concerneth me: thy mercy, O Lord, endureth for ever: forsake not the works of thine own hands.

I was glad when they said unto me, Let us go into the house of the Lord. —Psalms 122:1; 138.

567 CHRISTIAN UNITY

Behold, how good and how pleasant it is for brethren to dwell together in unity!

It is like the precious ointment upon the head, that ran down upon the beard, even Aaron's beard: that went down to the skirts of his garments;

As the dew of Hermon, and as the dew that descended upon the mountains of Zion:

For there the Lord commanded the blessing, even life for evermore.
—Psalm 133.

These words spake Jesus, and lifted up his eyes to heaven, and said, Father, the hour is come; glorify thy Son, that thy Son also may glorify thee:

I have manifested thy name unto the men which thou gavest me out of the world: thine they were, and thou gavest them me; and they have kept thy word.

I pray for them: I pray not for the world, but for them which thou hast given me; for they are thine.

And all mine are thine, and thine are mine; and I am glorified in them.

Neither pray I for these alone, but for them also which shall believe on me through their word; that they all may be one; as thou, Father, art in me, and I in thee,

That they also may be one in us: that the world may believe that thou hast sent me. —John 17: 1, 6, 9, 10, 20, 21.

I therefore, the prisoner of the Lord, beseech you that ye walk worthy of the vocation wherewith ye are called,

With all lowliness and meekness, with longsuffering, forbearing one another in love;

Endeavouring to keep the unity of the Spirit in the bond of peace.

There is one body, and one Spirit, even as ye are called in one hope of your calling;

One Lord, one faith, one baptism,

One God and Father of all, who is above all, and through all, and in you all. —Ephesians 4: 1-6.

568   GOD'S OMNISCIENCE

O Lord, thou hast searched me, and known me.

Thou knowest my downsitting and mine uprising; thou understandest my thought afar off.

Thou compassest my path and my lying down, and art acquainted with all my ways.

For there is not a word in my tongue, but, lo, O Lord, thou knowest it altogether.

Thou hast beset me behind and before, and laid thine hand upon me.

Such knowledge is too wonderful for me; it is high, I cannot attain unto it.

Whither shall I go from thy spirit? or whither shall I flee from thy presence?

If I ascend up into heaven, thou art there: if I make my bed in sheol, behold, thou art there.

If I take the wings of the morning, and dwell in the uttermost parts of the sea;

Even there shall thy hand lead me, and thy right hand shall hold me.

If I say, Surely the darkness shall cover me; even the night shall be light about me.

Yea, the darkness hideth not from thee; but the night shineth as the day: the darkness and the light are both alike to thee.

Search me, O God, and know my heart: try me, and know my thoughts;

And see if there be any wicked way in me, and lead me in the way everlasting.   —Psalm 139: 1-12, 17, 18, 23, 24.

569   GOD'S COMPASSION

I will extol thee, my God, O King; and I will bless thy name for ever and ever.

Every day will I bless thee; and I will praise thy name for ever and ever.

Great is the Lord, and greatly to be praised; and his greatness is unsearchable.

One generation shall praise thy works to another, and shall declare thy mighty acts.   (over)

I will speak of the glorious honour of thy majesty, and of thy wondrous works.

And men shall speak of the might of thy terrible acts: and I will declare thy greatness.

They shall abundantly utter the memory of thy great goodness, and shall sing of thy righteousness.

The Lord is gracious, and full of compassion; slow to anger, and of great mercy.

The Lord is good to all; and his tender mercies are over all his works.

All thy works shall praise thee, O Lord; and thy saints shall bless thee.

They shall speak of the glory of thy kingdom, and talk of thy power;

To make known to the sons of men his mighty acts, and the glorious majesty of his kingdom.

Thy kingdom is an everlasting kingdom, and thy dominion endureth throughout all generations.

The Lord upholdeth all that fall, and raiseth up all those that be bowed down.

The eyes of all wait upon thee; and thou givest them their meat in due season.

Thou openest thine hand, and satisfiest the desire of every living thing.

The Lord is righteous in all his ways, and holy in all his works.

The Lord is nigh unto all them that call upon him, to all that call upon him in truth.

He will fulfil the desire of them that fear him: he also will hear their cry, and will save them.

The Lord preserveth all them that love him: but all the wicked will he destroy. My mouth shall speak the praise of the Lord; and let all flesh bless his holy name for ever and ever.
—Psalm 145.

570   TRUE WISDOM

Happy is the man that findeth wisdom, and the man that getteth understanding.

For the merchandise of it is better than the merchandise of silver, and the gain thereof than fine gold.

She is more precious than rubies: and all the things thou canst desire are not to be compared unto her.

Length of days is in her right hand; and in her left hand riches and honour.

Her ways are ways of pleasantness, and all her paths are peace.

She is a tree of life to them that lay hold upon her: and happy is every one that retaineth her.

The Lord by wisdom hath founded the earth; by understanding hath he established the heavens.

By his knowledge the depths are broken up, and the clouds drop down the dew.

My son, let not them depart from thine eyes; keep sound wisdom and discretion:

So shall they be life unto thy soul, and grace to thy neck.

Then shalt thou walk in thy way safely, and thy foot shall not stumble.

When thou liest down thou shalt not be afraid: yea, thou shalt lie down, and thy sleep shall be sweet.

Be not afraid of sudden fear, neither of the desolation of the wicked, when it cometh.

For the Lord shall be thy confidence, and shall keep thy foot from being taken.

Trust in the Lord with all thine heart; and lean not unto thine own understanding.

In all thy ways acknowledge him, and he shall direct thy paths.
—Proverbs 3: 13-26, 5, 6.

571 CALL TO RIGHTEOUSNESS

Wine is a mocker, strong drink is raging: and whosoever is deceived thereby is not wise.

Who hath woe? who hath sorrow? who hath contentions? who hath babbling? who hath wounds without cause? who hath redness of eyes?

They that tarry long at the wine; they that go to seek mixed wine. At the last it biteth like a serpent, and stingeth like an adder.
—Proverbs 20:1; 23:29, 30, 32.

Woe unto them that rise up early in the morning, that they may follow strong drink; that continue until night, till wine inflame them!

Woe unto them that are mighty to drink wine, and men of strength to mingle strong drink:

Which justify the wicked for reward, and take away the righteousness of the righteous from him!
—Isaiah 5: 11, 22, 23.

Woe unto him that giveth his neighbour drink, that puttest thy bottle to him, and makest him drunken also, that thou mayest look on their nakedness! —Habakkuk 2:15.

Know ye not that ye are the temple of God, and that the Spirit of God dwelleth in you?

If any man defile the temple of God, him shall God destroy; for the temple of God is holy, which temple ye are. —I Corinthians 3: 16, 17.

This I say then, Walk in the Spirit, and ye shall not fulfil the lust of the flesh.

For the flesh lusteth against the Spirit, and the Spirit against the flesh: and these are contrary the one to the other: so that ye cannot do the things that ye would.

But if ye be led of the Spirit, ye are not under the law.

Now the works of the flesh are manifest, which are these; Adultery, fornication, uncleanness, lasciviousness,

Idolatry, witchcraft, hatred, variance, emulations, wrath, strife, seditions, heresies,

Envyings, murders, drunkenness, revellings, and such like:

Of the which I tell you before, as I have also told you in time past, that they which do such things shall not inherit the kingdom of God.
—Galatians 5: 16-21.

572 GODLY WOMANHOOD

Who can find a virtuous woman? for her price is far above rubies.

The heart of her husband doth safely trust in her, so that he shall have no need of spoil.

She will do him good and not evil all the days of her life.

She seeketh wool and flax, and worketh willingly with her hands.

She is like the merchants' ships; she bringeth her food from afar.

She riseth also while it is yet night, and giveth meat to her household, and a portion to her maidens.

She considereth a field, and buyeth it; with the fruit of her hands she planteth a vineyard.

She girdeth her loins with strength, and strengtheneth her arms.

She perceiveth that her merchandise is good: her candle goeth not out by night.

She layeth her hands to the spindle, and her hands hold the distaff.

She stretcheth out her hand to the poor; yea, she reacheth forth her hands to the needy.

She is not afraid of the snow for her household; for all her household are clothed with scarlet.

She maketh herself coverings of tapestry; her clothing is silk and purple.

Her husband is known in the gates, when he sitteth among the elders of the land. (over)

She maketh fine linen, and selleth it; and delivereth girdles unto the merchant.

Strength and honour are her clothing; and she shall rejoice in time to come.

She openeth her mouth with wisdom; and in her tongue is the law of kindness.

She looketh well to the ways of her household, and eateth not the bread of idleness.

Her children arise up, and call her blessed; her husband also, and he praiseth her.

Many daughters have done virtuously, but thou excellest them all.

Favour is deceitful, and beauty is vain; but a woman that feareth the Lord, she shall be praised.

Give her of the fruit of her hands; and let her own works praise her in the gates. —Proverbs 31: 10-31.

573 CHALLENGE TO YOUTH

Remember now thy Creator in the days of thy youth, while the evil days come not, nor the years draw nigh, when thou shalt say, I have no pleasure in them;

While the sun, or the light, or the moon, or the stars, be not darkened, nor the clouds return after the rain:

In the day when the keepers of the house shall tremble, and the strong men shall bow themselves, and the grinders cease because they are few, and those that look out of the windows be darkened,

And the doors shall be shut in the streets, when the sound of the grinding is low, and he shall rise up at the voice of the bird, and all the daughters of music shall be brought low;

Also when they shall be afraid of that which is high, and fears shall be in the way, and the almond tree shall flourish, and the grasshopper shall be a burden, and desire shall fail:

Because man goeth to his long home, and the mourners go about the streets:

Or ever the silver cord be loosed, or the golden bowl be broken, or the pitcher be broken at the fountain, or the wheel broken at the cistern.

Then shall the dust return to the earth as it was: and the spirit shall return unto God who gave it.

Let us hear the conclusion of the whole matter: Fear God, and keep his commandments: for this is the whole duty of man.

For God shall bring every work into judgment, with every secret thing, whether it be good, or whether it be evil. —Ecclesiastes 12: 1-7, 13, 14.

574 CHRIST IN PROPHECY

And there shall come forth a rod out of the stem of Jesse, and a Branch shall grow out of his roots:

And the spirit of the Lord shall rest upon him, the spirit of wisdom and understanding, the spirit of counsel and might, the spirit of knowledge and of the fear of the Lord;

And shall make him of quick understanding in the fear of the Lord: and he shall not judge after the sight of his eyes, neither reprove after the hearing of his ears:

But with righteousness shall he judge the poor, and reprove with equity for the meek of the earth: and he shall smite the earth with the rod of his mouth, and with the breath of his lips shall he slay the wicked.

And righteousness shall be the girdle of his loins, and faithfulness the girdle of his reins.

Behold my servant, whom I uphold; mine elect, in whom my soul delighteth; I have put my spirit upon him: he shall bring forth judgment to the Gentiles.

He shall not cry, nor lift up, nor cause his voice to be heard in the street.

A bruised reed shall he not break, and the smoking flax shall he not quench: he shall bring forth judgment unto truth.

He shall not fail nor be discouraged, till he have set judgment in the earth: and the isles shall wait for his law.

Go through, go through the gates; prepare ye the way of the people; cast up, cast up the highway; gather out the stones; lift up a standard for the people.

Behold, the Lord hath proclaimed unto the end of the world, Say ye to the daughter of Zion, Behold, thy salvation cometh; behold, his reward is with him, and his work before him.
—Isaiah 11: 1-5; 42: 1-4; 62: 10, 11.

Behold, the days come, saith the Lord, that I will raise unto David a righteous Branch, and a King shall reign and prosper, and shall execute judgment and justice in the earth.

In his days Judah shall be saved, and Israel shall dwell safely; and this is his name whereby he shall be called, The Lord Our Righteousness.
—Jeremiah 23: 5, 6.

Unto you that fear my name shall the Sun of righteousness arise with healing in his wings. —Malachi 4:2.

575 COMFORT FROM GOD

Comfort ye, comfort ye my people, saith your God.

Speak ye comfortably to Jerusalem, and cry unto her, that her warfare is accomplished, that her iniquity is pardoned: for she hath received of the Lord's hand double for all her sins.

The voice of him that crieth in the wilderness, Prepare ye the way of the Lord, make straight in the desert a highway for our God.

Every valley shall be exalted, and every mountain and hill shall be made low: and the crooked shall be made straight, and the rough places plain:

And the glory of the Lord shall be revealed, and all flesh shall see it together: for the mouth of the Lord hath spoken it.

The voice said, Cry. And he said, What shall I cry? All flesh is grass, and all the goodliness thereof is as the flower of the field:

The grass withereth, the flower fadeth: because the spirit of the Lord bloweth upon it: surely the people is grass.

The grass withereth, the flower fadeth: but the word of our God shall stand for ever.

'O Zion, that bringest good tidings, get thee up into the high mountain; O Jerusalem, that bringest good tidings, lift up thy voice with strength; lift it up, be not afraid; say unto the cities of Judah, Behold your God!

Behold, the Lord God will come with strong hand, and his arm shall rule for him: behold, his reward is with him, and his work before him.

He shall feed his flock like a shepherd, he shall gather the lambs with his arm, and carry them in his bosom, and shall gently lead those that are with young.

He giveth power to the faint; and to them that have no might he increaseth strength.

Even the youths shall faint and be weary, and the young men shall utterly fall:

But they that wait upon the Lord shall renew their strength; they shall mount up with wings as eagles; they shall run, and not be weary; and they shall walk, and not faint.
—Isaiah 40: 1-11, 29-31.

576 THE LAMB OF GOD

Who hath believed our report? and to whom is the arm of the Lord revealed?

For he shall grow up before him as a tender plant, and as a root out of a dry ground: he hath no form nor comeliness; and when we shall see him, there is no beauty that we should desire him.

He is despised and rejected of men; a man of sorrows, and acquainted with grief: and we hid as it were our faces from him; he was despised, and we esteemed him not.

Surely he hath borne our griefs, and carried our sorrows: yet we did esteem him stricken, smitten of God, and afflicted.

But he was wounded for our transgressions, he was bruised for our iniquities: the chastisement of our peace was upon him; and with his stripes we are healed.

All we like sheep have gone astray; we have turned every one to his own way; and the Lord hath laid on him the iniquity of us all.

He was oppressed, and he was afflicted, yet he opened not his mouth: he is brought as a lamb to the slaughter, and as a sheep before her shearers is dumb, so he openeth not his mouth.

He was taken from prison and from judgment: and who shall declare his generation? For he was cut off out of the land of the living: for the transgression of my people was he stricken.

And he made his grave with the wicked, and with the rich in his death; because he had done no violence, neither was any deceit in his mouth.

Yet it pleased the Lord to bruise him; he hath put him to grief: when thou shalt make his soul an offering for sin, he shall see his seed, he shall prolong his days, and the pleasure of the Lord shall prosper in his hand.

He shall see of the travail of his soul, and shall be satisfied: by his knowledge shall my righteous servant justify many; for he shall bear their iniquities.

Therefore will I divide him a portion with the great, and he shall divide the spoil with the strong; because he hath poured out his soul unto death: and he was numbered with the transgressors; and he bare the sin of many, and made intercession for the transgressors. —Isaiah 53.

577 GOD'S INVITATION

Ho, every one that thirsteth, come ye to the waters, and he that hath no money; come ye, buy, and eat; yea, come, buy wine and milk without money and without price.

Wherefore do ye spend money for that which is not bread? and your labour for that which satisfieth not? hearken diligently unto me, and eat ye that which is good, and let your soul delight itself in fatness.

Incline your ear, and come unto me: hear, and your soul shall live; and I will make an everlasting covenant with you, even the sure mercies of David.

Behold, I have given him for a witness to the people, a leader and commander to the people.

Behold, thou shalt call a nation that thou knowest not, and nations that knew not thee shall run unto thee because of the Lord thy God, and for the Holy One of Israel; for he hath glorified thee.

Seek ye the Lord while he may be found, call ye upon him while he is near:

Let the wicked forsake his way, and the unrighteous man his thoughts: and let him return unto the Lord, and he will have mercy upon him; and to our God, for he will abundantly pardon.

For my thoughts are not your thoughts, neither are your ways my ways, saith the Lord.

For as the heavens are higher than the earth, so are my ways higher than your ways, and my thoughts than your thoughts.

For as the rain cometh down, and the snow from heaven, and returneth not thither, but watereth the earth, and maketh it bring forth and bud, that it may give seed to the sower, and bread to the eater:

So shall my word be that goeth forth out of my mouth: it shall not return unto me void, but it shall accomplish that which I please, and it shall prosper in the thing whereto I sent it.

For ye shall go out with joy, and be led forth with peace: the mountains and the hills shall break forth before you into singing, and all the trees of the field shall clap their hands.

Instead of the thorn shall come up the fir tree, and instead of the brier shall come up the myrtle tree:

And it shall be to the Lord for a name, for an everlasting sign that shall not be cut off. —Isaiah 55.

578 ADORATION OF THE MAGI

Now when Jesus was born in Bethlehem of Judea in the days of Herod the king, behold, there came wise men from the east to Jerusalem, saying,

Where is he that is born King of the Jews? for we have seen his star in the east, and are come to worship him.

When Herod the king had heard these things, he was troubled, and all Jerusalem with him.

And when he had gathered all the chief priests and scribes of the people together, he demanded of them where Christ should be born.

And they said unto him, In Bethlehem of Judea: for thus it is written by the prophet,

And thou Bethlehem, in the land of Judah, art not the least among the princes of Judah: for out of thee shall come a governor, that shall rule my people Israel.

Then Herod, when he had privily called the wise men, enquired of them diligently what time the star appeared. And he sent them to Bethlehem, and said,

Go and search diligently for the young child; and when ye have found him, bring me word again, that I may come and worship him also.

When they had heard the king, they departed; and, lo, the star, which they saw in the east, went before them, till it came and stood over where the young child was.

When they saw the star, they rejoiced with exceeding great joy. And when they were come into the house, they saw the young child with Mary his mother, and fell down, and worshipped him:

And when they had opened their treasures, they presented unto him gifts; gold, and frankincense, and myrrh.

And being warned of God in a dream that they should not return to Herod, they departed into their own country another way.
—Matthew 2: 1-12.

579   CHRISTIAN BAPTISM

Then cometh Jesus from Galilee to Jordan unto John, to be baptized of him. But John forbad him, saying, I have need to be baptized of thee, and comest thou to me?

And Jesus answering said unto him, Suffer it to be so now: for thus it becometh us to fulfil all righteousness. Then he suffered him.

And Jesus, when he was baptized, went up straightway out of the water: and, lo, the heavens were opened unto him, and he saw the Spirit of God descending like a dove, and lighting upon him:

And lo a voice from heaven, saying, This is my beloved Son, in whom I am well pleased.   —Matthew 3: 13-17.

And Jesus came and spake unto them, saying, All power is given unto me in heaven and in earth. Go ye therefore, and make disciples of all nations,

Baptizing them in the name of the Father, and of the Son, and of the Holy Ghost: teaching them to observe all things whatsoever I have commanded you: and, lo, I am with you alway, even unto the end of the world.   —Matthew 28: 18-20.

Therefore we are buried with him by baptism into death: that like as Christ was raised up from the dead by the glory of the Father, even so we also should walk in newness of life.

For if we have been planted together in the likeness of his death, we shall be also in the likeness of his resurrection:

Knowing this, that our old man is crucified with him, that the body of sin might be destroyed, that henceforth we should not serve sin.

For he that is dead is freed from sin. Now if we be dead with Christ, we believe that we shall also live with him:

Knowing that Christ being raised from the dead dieth no more; death hath no more dominion over him. For in that he died, he died unto sin once: but in that he liveth, he liveth unto God.

Likewise reckon ye also yourselves to be dead indeed unto sin, but alive unto God through Jesus Christ our Lord.   —Romans 6: 4-11.

580   THE BEATITUDES

And seeing the multitudes, he went up into the mountain: and when he was set, his disciples came unto him:

And he opened his mouth, and taught them, saying,

Blessed are the poor in spirit: for theirs is the kingdom of heaven.

Blessed are they that mourn: for they shall be comforted.

Blessed are the meek: for they shall inherit the earth.

Blessed are they which do hunger and thirst after righteousness: for they shall be filled.

Blessed are the merciful: for they shall obtain mercy.

Blessed are the pure in heart: for they shall see God.

Blessed are the peacemakers: for they shall be called the children of God.

Blessed are they which are persecuted for righteousness' sake: for theirs is the kingdom of heaven.

Blessed are ye, when men shall revile you, and persecute you, and shall say all manner of evil against you falsely, for my sake.

Rejoice, and be exceeding glad: for great is your reward in heaven:

For so persecuted they the prophets which were before you.

Ye are the salt of the earth: but if the salt have lost his savour, wherewith shall it be salted?

It is thenceforth good for nothing, but to be cast out, and to be trodden under foot of men.

Ye are the light of the world. A city that is set on an hill cannot be hid.

Neither do men light a candle, and put it under a bushel, but on a candlestick; and it giveth light unto all that are in the house.

Let your light so shine before men, that they may see your good works, and glorify your Father which is in heaven. —Matthew 5: 1-16.

581 HEAVENLY TREASURE

Lay not up for yourselves treasures upon earth, where moth and rust doth corrupt, and where thieves break through and steal:

But lay up for yourselves treasures in heaven, where neither moth nor rust doth corrupt, and where thieves do not break through nor steal:

For where your treasure is, there will your heart be also.

No man can serve two masters: for either he will hate the one, and love the other; or else he will hold to the one, and despise the other. Ye cannot serve God and mammon.

Therefore I say unto you, Take no thought for your life, what ye shall eat, or what ye shall drink; nor yet for your body, what ye shall put on.

Is not the life more than meat, and the body than raiment?

Behold the fowls of the air: for they sow not, neither do they reap, nor gather into barns; yet your heavenly Father feedeth them. Are ye not much better than they?

Which of you by taking thought can add one cubit unto his stature?

And why take ye thought for raiment? Consider the lilies of the field, how they grow; they toil not, neither do they spin:

And yet I say unto you, That even Solomon in all his glory was not arrayed like one of these.

Wherefore, if God so clothe the grass of the field, which today is, and tomorrow is cast into the oven, shall he not much more clothe you, O ye of little faith?

Therefore take no thought, saying, What shall we eat? or, What shall we drink? or, Wherewithal shall we be clothed?

For after all these things do the Gentiles seek: for your heavenly Father knoweth that ye have need of all these things.

But seek ye first the kingdom of God, and his righteousness; and all these things shall be added unto you. —Matthew 6:19–21, 24–33.

582 THE WHITENED HARVEST

And Jesus went about all the cities and villages, teaching in their synagogues, and preaching the gospel of the kingdom, and healing every sickness and every disease among the people.

But when he saw the multitudes, he was moved with compassion on them, because they fainted, and were scattered abroad, as sheep having no shepherd.

Then saith he unto his disciples, The harvest truly is plenteous, but the labourers are few;

Pray ye therefore the Lord of the harvest, that he will send forth labourers into his harvest. —Matthew 9: 35–38.

For there is no difference between the Jew and the Greek: for the same Lord over all is rich unto all that call upon him.

For whosoever shall call upon the name of the Lord shall be saved.

(over)

How then shall they call on him in whom they have not believed? and how shall they believe in him of whom they have not heard? and how shall they hear without a preacher?

And how shall they preach, except they be sent? as it is written, How beautiful are the feet of them that preach the gospel of peace, and bring glad tidings of good things!
—Romans 10: 12–15.

Say not ye, There are yet four months, and then cometh harvest? behold, I say unto you, Lift up your eyes, and look on the fields; for they are white already to harvest.
—John 4: 35.

He that goeth forth and weepeth, bearing precious seed, shall doubtless come again with rejoicing, bringing his sheaves with him.—Psalm 126: 6.

583　THE CHURCH

When Jesus came into the coasts of Caesarea Philippi, he asked his disciples, saying, Whom do men say that I the Son of man am?

And they said, Some say that thou art John the Baptist: some, Elijah; and others, Jeremiah, or one of the prophets.

He saith unto them, But whom say ye that I am?

And Simon Peter answered and said, Thou art the Christ, the Son of the living God.

And Jesus answered and said unto him, Blessed art thou, Simon Bar-jona: for flesh and blood hath not revealed it unto thee, but my Father which is in heaven.

And I say also unto thee, That thou art Peter, and upon this rock I will build my Church; and the gates of hell shall not prevail against it.
—Matthew 16: 13–18.

Then Peter said unto them, Repent, and be baptized every one of you in the name of Jesus Christ for the remission of sins, and ye shall receive the gift of the Holy Spirit.

Then they that gladly received his word were baptized: and the same day there were added unto them about three thousand souls.

And they continued stedfastly in the apostle's doctrine and fellowship, and in breaking of bread, and in prayers.

And the Lord added to the church daily such as should be saved.
—Acts 2: 38, 41, 42, 47.

Husbands, love your wives, even as Christ also loved the church, and gave himself for it; that he might sanctify and cleanse it with the washing of water by the word,

That he might present it to himself a glorious church, not having spot, or wrinkle, or any such thing; but that it should be holy and without blemish.
—Ephesians 5: 25–27.

Now ye are the body of Christ, and members in particular.
—I Corinthians 12: 27.

And he is the head of the body, the church: who is the beginning, the firstborn from the dead; that in all things he might have the preeminence.
—Colossians 1: 18.

584　CHRIST AND CHILDREN

At the same time came the disciples unto Jesus, saying, Who is the greatest in the kingdom of heaven?

And Jesus called a little child unto him, and set him in the midst of them, and said,

Verily I say unto you, Except ye be converted, and become as little children, ye shall not enter into the kingdom of heaven.

Whosoever therefore shall humble himself as this little child, the same is greatest in the kingdom of heaven.

And whoso shall receive one such little child in my name receiveth me.

But whoso shall offend one of these little ones which believe in me, it were better for him that a millstone were hanged about his neck, and that he were drowned in the depth of the sea. —Matthew 18: 1-6.

Take heed that ye despise not one of these little ones; for I say unto you, That in heaven their angels do always behold the face of my Father which is in heaven. —Matthew 18:10.

Whosoever shall receive one of such children in my name, receiveth me: and whosoever shall receive me, receiveth not me, but him that sent me. —Mark 9:37.

And they brought young children to him, that he should touch them: and his disciples rebuked those that brought them.

But when Jesus saw it, he was much displeased, and said unto them, Suffer the little children to come unto me, and forbid them not: for of such is the kingdom of God.

Verily I say unto you, Whosoever shall not receive the kingdom of God as a little child, he shall not enter therein.

And he took them up in his arms, put his hands upon them, and blessed them. —Mark 10: 13-16.

585 PARABLE: THE VIRGINS

Then shall the kingdom of heaven be likened unto ten virgins, which took their lamps, and went forth to meet the bridegroom.

And five of them were wise, and five were foolish.

They that were foolish took their lamps, and took no oil with them: But the wise took oil in their vessels with their lamps.

While the bridegroom tarried, they all slumbered and slept.

And at midnight there was a cry made, Behold, the bridegroom cometh; go ye out to meet him.

Then all those virgins arose, and trimmed their lamps.

And the foolish said unto the wise, Give us of your oil; for our lamps are gone out.

But the wise answered, saying, Not so; lest there be not enough for us and you: but go ye rather to them that sell, and buy for yourselves.

And while they went to buy, the bridegroom came; And they that were ready went in with him to the marriage and the door was shut.

Afterward came also the other virgins, saying, Lord, Lord, open to us.

But he answered and said, Verily I say unto you, I know you not.

Watch therefore, for ye know neither the day nor the hour wherein the Son of man cometh.
—Matthew 25: 1-13.

586 PARABLE: THE TALENTS

For the kingdom of heaven is as a man traveling into a far country, who called his own servants, and delivered unto them his goods.

And unto one he gave five talents, to another two, and to another one; to every man according to his several ability; and straitway took his journey.

Then he that had received the five talents went and traded with the same, and made them other five talents.

And likewise he that had received two, he also gained other two.

But he that had received one went and digged in the earth, and hid his lord's money.

After a long time the lord of those servants cometh, and reckoneth with them. (over)

And so he that had received five talents came and brought other five talents, saying, Lord, thou deliveredst unto me five talents: behold, I have gained beside them five talents more.

His lord said unto him, Well done, thou good and faithful servant: thou hast been faithful over a few things, I will make thee ruler over many things: enter thou into the joy of thy lord.

He also that had received two talents came and said, Lord, thou deliveredst unto me two talents: behold, I have gained two other talents beside them.

His lord said unto him, Well done, good and faithful servant; thou hast been faithful over a few things, I will make thee ruler over many things: enter thou into the joy of thy lord.

Then he which had received the one talent came and said, Lord, I knew thee that thou art an hard man, reaping where thou hast not sown, and gathering where thou hast not strawed:

And I was afraid, and went and hid thy talent in the earth: lo, there thou hast that is thine.

His lord answered and said unto him, Thou wicked and slothful servant, thou knewest that I reap where I sowed not, and gather where I have not strawed:

Thou oughtest therefore to have put my money to the exchangers, and then at my coming I should have received mine own with usury.

Take therefore the talent from him, and give it unto him which hath ten talents.

For unto every one that hath shall be given, and he shall have abundance: but from him that hath not shall be taken away even that which he hath. —Matthew 25: 14-29.

587 JUDGMENT AND REWARD

When the Son of man shall come in his glory, and all the holy angels with him, then shall he sit upon the throne of his glory:

And before him shall be gathered all nations: and he shall separate them one from another, as a shepherd divideth his sheep from the goats:

And he shall set the sheep on his right hand, but the goats on the left.

Then shall the King say unto them on his right hand, Come, ye blessed of my Father, inherit the kingdom prepared for you from the foundation of the world:

For I was an hungred, and ye gave me meat: I was thirsty, and ye gave me drink: I was a stranger, and ye took me in:

Naked, and ye clothed me: I was sick, and ye visited me: I was in prison, and ye came unto me.

Then shall the righteous answer him, saying, Lord, when saw we thee an hungred, and fed thee? or thirsty, and gave thee drink?

When saw we thee a stranger, and took thee in? or naked, and clothed thee?

Or when saw we thee sick, or in prison, and came unto thee?

And the King shall answer and say unto them, Verily I say unto you, Inasmuch as ye have done it unto one of the least of these my brethren, ye have done it unto me.

Then shall he say also unto them on the left hand, Depart from me, ye cursed, into everlasting fire, prepared for the devil and his angels:

For I was an hungred, and ye gave me no meat: I was thirsty, and ye gave me no drink:

I was a stranger, and ye took me not in; naked, and ye clothed me not: sick, and in prison, and ye visited me not.

Then shall they also answer him, saying, Lord, when saw we thee an hungred, or athirst, or a stranger, or naked, or sick, or in prison, and did not minister unto thee?

Then shall he answer them, saying, Verily I say unto you, Inasmuch as ye did it not to one of the least of these, ye did it not unto me.

And these shall go away into everlasting punishment: but the righteous into life eternal. —Matthew 25: 31-46.

588   THE LAST SUPPER

Now the first day of the feast of unleavened bread the disciples came to Jesus, saying unto him, Where wilt thou that we prepare for thee to eat the passover?

And he said, Go into the city to such a man, and say unto him, The Master saith, My time is at hand; I will keep the passover at thy house with my disciples.

And the disciples did as Jesus had appointed them; and they made ready the passover.

Now when the even was come, he sat down with the twelve.

And as they did eat, he said, Verily I say unto you, that one of you shall betray me.

And they were exceeding sorrowful, and began every one of them to say unto him, Lord, is it I?

And he answered and said, He that dippeth his hand with me in the dish, the same shall betray me.

The Son of man goeth as it is written of him: but woe unto that man by whom the Son of man is betrayed! it had been good for that man if he had not been born.

Then Judas, which betrayed him, answered and said, Master, is it I? He said unto him, Thou hast said.

And as they were eating, Jesus took bread, and blessed it, and brake it, and gave it to the disciples, and said, Take, eat; this is my body.

And he took the cup, and gave thanks, and gave it to them, saying, Drink ye all of it; For this is my blood of the new testament, which is shed for many for the remission of sins.

But I say unto you, I will not drink henceforth of this fruit of the vine, until that day when I drink it new with you in my Father's kingdom.
—Matthew 26: 17-29.

589   THE RISEN LORD

In the end of the sabbath, as it began to dawn toward the first day of the week, came Mary Magdalene and the other Mary to see the sepulchre.

And, behold, there was a great earthquake; for the angel of the Lord descended from heaven, and came and rolled back the stone from the door, and sat upon it.

His countenance was like lightning, and his raiment white as snow:

And for fear of him the keepers did shake, and became as dead men.

And the angel answered and said unto the women, Fear not ye: for I know that ye seek Jesus, which was crucified.

He is not here; for he is risen, as he said. Come, see the place where the Lord lay.

And go quickly, and tell his disciples that he is risen from the dead; and, behold, he goeth before you into Galilee; there shall ye see him: lo, I have told you.

And they departed quickly from the sepulchre with fear and great joy; and did run to bring his disciples word.

And as they went to tell his disciples, behold, Jesus met them, saying, All hail. And they came and held him by the feet, and worshipped him.

Then said Jesus unto them, Be not afraid: go tell my brethren that they go into Galilee, and there shall they see me. —Matthew 28: 1-10.

590 THE GREAT COMMISSION

Then the eleven disciples went away into Galilee, into a mountain where Jesus had appointed them.

And when they saw him, they worshipped him: but some doubted.

And Jesus came and spake unto them, saying, All power is given unto me in heaven and in earth.

Go ye therefore, and teach all nations, baptizing them in the name of the Father, and of the Son, and of the Holy Ghost:

Teaching them to observe all things whatsoever I have commanded you: and, lo, I am with you alway, even unto the end of the world.
—Matthew 28: 16-20.

Jesus said unto them, Thus it is written, and thus it behoved Christ to suffer, and to rise from the dead the third day:

And that repentance and remission of sins should be preached in his name among all nations, beginning at Jerusalem.

And ye are witnesses of these things.

And, behold, I send the promise of my Father upon you: but tarry ye in the city of Jerusalem, until ye be endued with power from on high.
—Luke 24: 46-49.

They asked of him, saying, Lord, wilt thou at this time restore again the kingdom to Israel?

And he said unto them, It is not for you to know the times or the seasons, which the Father hath put in his own power.

But ye shall receive power, after that the Holy Ghost is come upon you:

And ye shall be witnesses unto me both in Jerusalem, and in all Judaea, and in Samaria, and unto the uttermost part of the earth.

And when he had spoken these things, while they beheld, he was taken up; and a cloud received him out of their sight. —Acts 1: 6-9.

591 THE TRIUMPHAL ENTRY

And when they came nigh to Jerusalem, unto Bethphage and Bethany, at the mount of Olives, he sendeth forth two of his disciples, and saith unto them,

Go your way into the village over against you: and as soon as ye be entered into it, ye shall find a colt tied, whereon never man sat; loose him, and bring him.

And if any man say unto you, Why do ye this? say ye that the Lord hath need of him; and straightway he will send him hither.

And they went their way, and found the colt tied by the door without in a place where two ways met; and they loose him.

And certain of them that stood there said unto them, What do ye, loosing the colt?

And they said unto them even as Jesus had commanded: and they let them go.

And they brought the colt to Jesus, and cast their garments on him; and he sat upon him.

And many spread their garments in the way; and others cut down branches off the trees, and strawed them in the way.

And they that went before, and they that followed, cried, saying, Hosanna; Blessed is he that cometh in the name of the Lord:

Blessed be the kingdom of our father David, that cometh in the name of the Lord: Hosanna in the highest. And Jesus entered into Jerusalem, and into the temple.
—Mark 11: 1-11.

And when he was come into Jerusalem, all the city was moved, saying, Who is this?

And the multitude said, This is Jesus the prophet of Nazareth of Galilee. —Matthew 21: 10, 11.

592 THE SAVIOUR'S ADVENT

And there were in the same country shepherds abiding in the field, keeping watch over their flock by night.

And, lo, the angel of the Lord came upon them, and the glory of the Lord shone round about them: and they were sore afraid.

And the angel said unto them, Fear not: for, behold, I bring you good tidings of great joy, which shall be to all people.

For unto you is born this day in the city of David a Saviour, which is Christ the Lord.

And this shall be a sign unto you; Ye shall find the babe wrapped in swaddling clothes, lying in a manger.

And suddenly there was with the angel a multitude of the heavenly host praising God, and saying,

Glory to God in the highest, and on earth peace, good will toward men.

And it came to pass, as the angels were gone away from them into heaven, the shepherds said one to another,

Let us now go even unto Bethlehem, and see this thing which is come to pass, which the Lord hath made known unto us.

And they came with haste, and found Mary, and Joseph, and the babe lying in a manger.

And when they had seen it, they made known abroad the saying which was told them concerning this child.

And all they that heard it wondered at those things which were told them by the shepherds.

But Mary kept all these things, and pondered them in her heart.

And the shepherds returned, glorifying and praising God for all the things that they had heard and seen, as it was told unto them.—Luke 2: 8-20.

593 THE CHILD JESUS

The child grew, and waxed strong in spirit, filled with wisdom: and the grace of God was upon him.

Now his parents went to Jerusalem every year at the feast of the passover.

And when he was twelve years old, they went up to Jerusalem after the custom of the feast.

And when they had fulfilled the days, as they returned, the child Jesus tarried behind in Jerusalem; and Joseph and his mother knew not of it.

But they, supposing him to have been in the company, went a day's journey; and they sought him among their kinsfolk and acquaintance.

And when they found him not, they turned back again to Jerusalem, seeking him.

And it came to pass, that after three days they found him in the temple, sitting in the midst of the doctors, both hearing them, and asking them questions.

And all that heard him were astonished at his understanding and answers.

And when they saw him, they were amazed: and his mother said unto him, Son, why hast thou thus dealt with us? behold, thy father and I have sought thee sorrowing.

And he said unto them, How is it that ye sought me? wist ye not that I must be about my Father's business?

And they understood not the saying which he spake unto them.

And he went down with them, and came to Nazareth, and was subject unto them:

But his mother kept all these sayings in her heart.

And Jesus increased in wisdom and stature, and in favor with God and man.—Luke 2: 40-52.

594 THE GOOD SAMARITAN

And, behold, a certain lawyer stood up, and tempted him, saying, Master, what shall I do to inherit eternal life?

He said unto him, What is written in the law? how readest thou?

And he answering said, Thou shalt love the Lord thy God with all thy heart, and with all thy soul, and with all thy strength, and with all thy mind; and thy neighbour as thyself.

And he said unto him, Thou hast answered right: this do, and thou shalt live.

But he, willing to justify himself, said unto Jesus, And who is my neighbour?

And Jesus answering said, A certain man went down from Jerusalem to Jericho, and fell among thieves, which stripped him of his raiment, and wounded him, and departed, leaving him half dead.

And by chance there came down a certain priest that way: and when he saw him, he passed by on the other side.

And likewise a Levite, when he was at the place, came and looked on him, and passed by on the other side.

But a certain Samaritan, as he journeyed, came where he was: and when he saw him, he had compassion on him,

And went to him, and bound up his wounds, pouring in oil and wine, and set him on his own beast, and brought him to an inn, and took care of him.

And on the morrow when he departed, he took out two pence, and gave them to the host, and said unto him, Take care of him; and whatsoever thou spendest more, when I come again, I will repay thee.

Which now of these three, thinkest thou, was neighbour unto him that fell among the thieves?

And he said, He that showed mercy on him.

Then said Jesus unto him, Go, and do thou likewise. —Luke 10: 25-37.

595 CHRIST TEACHES PRAYER

And it came to pass, that, as he was praying in a certain place, when he ceased, one of his disciples said unto him, Lord, teach us to pray, as John also taught his disciples.

And he said unto them, When ye pray, say, Our Father which art in heaven, Hallowed be thy name. Thy kingdom come. Thy will be done, as in heaven, so in earth.

Give us day by day our daily bread.

And forgive us our sins; for we also forgive every one that is indebted to us.

And lead us not into temptation; but deliver us from evil.

And he said unto them, Which of you shall have a friend, and shall go unto him at midnight, and say unto him, Friend, lend me three loaves;

For a friend of mine in his journey is come to me, and I have nothing to set before him?

And he from within shall answer and say, Trouble me not: the door is now shut, and my children are with me in bed; I cannot rise and give thee.

I say unto you, Though he will not rise and give him because he is his friend, yet because of his importunity he will rise and give him as many as he needeth.

And I say unto you, Ask, and it shall be given you; seek, and ye shall find; knock, and it shall be opened unto you.

For every one that asketh receiveth; and he that seeketh findeth; and to him that knocketh it shall be opened.

If a son shall ask bread of any of you that is a father, will he give him a stone? or if he ask a fish, will he for a fish give him a serpent?

Or if he shall ask an egg, will he offer him a scorpion?

If ye then, being evil, know how to give good gifts unto your children: how much more shall your heavenly Father give the Holy Spirit to them that ask him? —Luke 11: 1-13.

596 THE INCARNATE CHRIST

In the beginning was the Word, and the Word was with God, and the Word was God.

The same was in the beginning with God.

All things were made by him; and without him was not anything made that was made.

In him was life; and the life was the light of men.

And the light shineth in darkness; and the darkness comprehended it not.

There was a man sent from God, whose name was John.

The same came for a witness, to bear witness of the Light, that all men through him might believe.

He was not that Light, but was sent to bear witness of that Light.

That was the true Light, which lighteth every man that cometh into the world.

He was in the world, and the world was made by him, and the world knew him not.

He came unto his own, and his own received him not.

But as many as received him, to them gave he power to become the sons of God, even to them that believe on his name:

Which were born, not of blood, nor of the will of the flesh, nor of the will of man, but of God.

And the Word was made flesh, and dwelt among us, and we beheld his glory, the glory as of the only begotten of the Father, full of grace and truth. —John 1: 1-14.

597 GOD'S REDEEMING LOVE

As Moses lifted up the serpent in the wilderness, even so must the Son of man be lifted up: that whosoever believeth in him should not perish, but have eternal life.

For God so loved the world, that he gave his only begotten Son, that whosoever believeth in him should not perish, but have everlasting life.

For God sent not his Son into the world to condemn the world; but that the world through him might be saved.

He that believeth on him is not condemned: but he that believeth not is condemned already, because he hath not believed in the name of the only begotten Son of God.

And this is the condemnation, that light is come into the world, and men loved darkness rather than light, because their deeds were evil.

For every one that doeth evil hateth the light, neither cometh to the light, lest his deeds should be reproved.

But he that doeth truth cometh to the light, that his deeds may be made manifest, that they are wrought in God.

He that believeth on the Son hath everlasting life: and he that believeth not the Son shall not see life; but the wrath of God abideth on him.
—John 3: 14–21, 36.

Beloved, let us love one another: for love is of God; and every one that loveth is born of God, and knoweth God.

He that loveth not knoweth not God; for God is love.

In this was manifested the love of God toward us, because that God sent his only begotten Son into the world, that we might live through him.

Herein is love, not that we loved God, but that he loved us, and sent his Son to be the propitiation for our sins. —I John 4: 7-10.

598 THE GOOD SHEPHERD

Verily, verily, I say unto you, He that entereth not by the door into the sheepfold, but climbeth up some other way, the same is a thief and a robber.

But he that entereth in by the door is the shepherd of the sheep.

To him the porter openeth; and the sheep hear his voice: and he calleth his own sheep by name, and leadeth them out.

And when he putteth forth his own sheep, he goeth before them, and the sheep follow him: for they know his voice.

And a stranger will they not follow, but will flee from him: for they know not the voice of strangers.

Then said Jesus unto them again, Verily, verily, I say unto you, I am the door of the sheep.

All that ever came before me are thieves and robbers: but the sheep did not hear them.

I am the door: by me if any man enter in, he shall be saved, and shall go in and out, and find pasture.

The thief cometh not, but for to steal, and to kill, and to destroy: **I am come that they might have life, and that they might have it more abundantly.**

I am the good shepherd: the good shepherd giveth his life for the sheep.

But he that is an hireling, and not the shepherd, whose own the sheep are not, seeth the wolf coming, and leaveth the sheep, and fleeth: and the wolf catcheth them, and scattereth the sheep.

The hireling fleeth, because he is an hireling, and careth not for the sheep.

I am the good shepherd, and know my sheep, and am known of mine.

As the Father knoweth me, even so know I the Father: and I lay down my life for the sheep.

And other sheep I have, which are not of this fold: them also I must bring, and they shall hear my voice; and there shall be one fold, and one shepherd.

My sheep hear my voice, and I know them, and they follow me:

And I give unto them eternal life; and they shall never perish, neither shall any man pluck them out of my hand. —John 10: 1-5, 7-16, 27, 28.

599 THE NEW COMMANDMENT

Jesus said, A new commandment I give unto you, That ye love one another; as I have loved you, that ye also love one another.

By this shall all men know that ye are my disciples, if ye have love one to another. —John 13: 34, 35.

My little children, these things write I unto you, that ye sin not. And if any man sin, we have an advocate with the Father, Jesus Christ the righteous:

And he is the propitiation for our sins: and not for ours only, but also for the sins of the whole world.

And hereby we do know that we know him, if we keep his commandments.

He that saith, I know him, and keepeth not his commandments, is a liar, and the truth is not in him.

But whoso keepeth his word, in him verily is the love of God perfected: hereby know we that we are in him.

He that saith he abideth in him ought himself also so to walk, even as he walked.

Brethren, I write no new commandment unto you, but an old commandment which ye had from the beginning.

The old commandment is the word which ye have heard from the beginning.

He that saith he is in the light, and hateth his brother, is in darkness even until now.

He that loveth his brother abideth in the light, and there is none occasion of stumbling in him.

But he that hateth his brother is in darkness, and walketh in darkness, and knoweth not whither he goeth, because that darkness hath blinded his eyes.

Love not the world, neither the things that are in the world. If any man love the world, the love of the Father is not in him.

For all that is in the world, the lust of the flesh, and the lust of the eyes, and the pride of life, is not of the Father, but is of the world.

And the world passeth away, and the lust thereof: but he that doeth the will of God abideth for ever.
—I John 2: 1-7, 9-11, 15-17.

600 COMFORT FROM CHRIST

Let not your heart be troubled: ye believe in God, believe also in me.

In my Father's house are many mansions: if it were not so, I would have told you. I go to prepare a place for you.

And if I go and prepare a place for you, I will come again, and receive you unto myself; that where I am, there ye may be also.

And whither I go ye know, and the way ye know.

Thomas saith unto him, Lord, we know not whither thou goest; and how can we know the way?

Jesus saith unto him, I am the way, the truth, and the life: no man cometh unto the Father, but by me.

If ye had known me, ye should have known my Father also: and from henceforth ye know him, and have seen him.

Philip saith unto him, Lord, show us the Father, and it sufficeth us.

Jesus saith unto him, Have I been so long time with you, and yet hast thou not known me, Philip? he that hath seen me hath seen the Father; and how sayest thou then, Show us the Father?

Believest thou not that I am in the Father, and the Father in me? the words that I speak unto you I speak not of myself: but the Father that dwelleth in me, he doeth the works.

Believe me that I am in the Father, and the Father in me: or else believe me for the very works' sake.

Verily, verily, I say unto you, He that believeth on me, the works that I do shall he do also; and greater works than these shall he do; because I go unto my Father.

And whatsoever ye shall ask in my name, that will I do, that the Father may be glorified in the Son.

Peace I leave with you, my peace I give unto you: not as the world giveth, give I unto you. Let not your heart be troubled, neither let it be afraid.
—John 14: 1-13, 27.

601   THE HOLY SPIRIT

Verily, verily, I say unto you, He that believeth on me, the works that I do shall he do also; and greater works than these shall he do; because I go unto my Father.

And I will pray the Father, and he shall give you another Comforter, that he may abide with you for ever;

Even the Spirit of truth; whom the world cannot receive, because it seeth him not, neither knoweth him:

But ye know him; for he dwelleth with you, and shall be in you.

I will not leave you comfortless: I will come to you.

Yet a little while, and the world seeth me no more; but ye see me: because I live, ye shall live also.

(over)

At that day ye shall know that I am in my Father, and ye in me, and I in you. —John 14:12, 16–20.

But now I go my way to him that sent me; and none of you asketh me, Whither goest thou?

But because I have said these things unto you, sorrow hath filled your heart.

Nevertheless I tell you the truth; It is expedient for you that I go away:

For if I go not away, the Comforter will not come unto you; but if I depart, I will send him unto you.

And when he is come, he will reprove the world of sin, and of righteousness, and of judgment:

Of sin, because they believe not on me;

Of righteousness, because I go to my Father, and ye see me no more;

Of judgment, because the prince of this world is judged.

I have yet many things to say unto you, but ye cannot bear them now.

Howbeit when he, the Spirit of truth, is come, he will guide you into all truth:

For he shall not speak of himself; but whatsoever he shall hear, that shall he speak: and he will show you things to come.

He shall glorify me: for he shall receive of mine, and shall show it unto you.

These things I have spoken unto you, that in me ye might have peace. In the world ye shall have tribulation: but be of good cheer; I have overcome the world. —John 16: 5-14, 33.

602 THE VINE AND BRANCHES

I am the true vine, and my Father is the husbandman.

Every branch in me that beareth not fruit he taketh away: and every branch that beareth fruit, he purgeth it, that it may bring forth more fruit.

Now ye are clean through the word which I have spoken unto you.

Abide in me, and I in you. As the branch cannot bear fruit of itself, except it abide in the vine; no more can ye, except ye abide in me.

I am the vine, ye are the branches: He that abideth in me, and I in him, the same bringeth forth much fruit: for without me ye can do nothing.

If a man abide not in me, he is cast forth as a branch, and is withered; and men gather them, and cast them into the fire, and they are burned.

If ye abide in me, and my words abide in you, ye shall ask what ye will, and it shall be done unto you.

Herein is my Father glorified, that ye bear much fruit; so shall ye be my disciples.

As the Father hath loved me, so have I loved you: continue ye in my love.

If ye keep my commandments, ye shall abide in my love; even as I have kept my Father's commandments, and abide in his love.

These things have I spoken unto you, that my joy might remain in you, and that your joy might be full.

This is my commandment, That ye love one another, as I have loved you.

Greater love hath no man than this, that a man lay down his life for his friends.

Ye are my friends, if ye do whatsoever I command you.

Henceforth I call you not servants; for the servant knoweth not what his lord doeth: but I have called you friends; for all things that I have heard of my Father I have made known unto you.

Ye have not chosen me, but I have chosen you, and ordained you, that ye should go and bring forth fruit, and that your fruit should remain: that whatsoever ye shall ask of the Father in my name, he may give it you. —John 15: 1-16.

603 CRUCIFIXION OF CHRIST

Then delivered he him therefore unto them to be crucified. And they took Jesus, and led him away.

And he bearing his cross went forth into a place called the place of a skull, which is called in the Hebrew Golgotha:

Where they crucified him, and two other with him, on either side one, and Jesus in the midst.

And Pilate wrote a title, and put it on the cross. And the writing was, Jesus of Nazareth the King of the Jews.

Then the soldiers, when they had crucified Jesus, took his garments, and made four parts, to every soldier a part; and also his coat: now the coat was without seam, woven from the top throughout.

They said therefore among themselves, Let us not rend it, but cast lots for it, whose it shall be: these things therefore the soldiers did.

Now there stood by the cross of Jesus his mother, and his mother's sister, Mary the wife of Cleophas, and Mary Magdalene.

When Jesus therefore saw his mother, and the disciple standing by, whom he loved, he saith unto his mother, Woman, behold thy son!

Then saith he to the disciple, Behold thy mother! And from that hour that disciple took her unto his own home.

After this, Jesus knowing that all things were now accomplished, that the scripture might be fulfilled, saith, I thirst.

Now there was set a vessel full of vinegar: and they filled a sponge with vinegar, and put it upon hyssop, and put it to his mouth.

When Jesus therefore had received the vinegar, he said, It is finished: and he bowed his head, and gave up the ghost. –John 19: 16-19, 23-30.

604 THE HOLY SPIRIT GIVEN

And when the day of Pentecost was fully come, they were all with one accord in one place.

And suddenly there came a sound from heaven as of a rushing mighty wind, and it filled all the house where they were sitting.

And there appeared unto them cloven tongues like as of fire, and it sat upon each of them.

And they were all filled with the Holy Ghost, and began to speak with other tongues, as the Spirit gave them utterance.

And there were dwelling at Jerusalem Jews, devout men, out of every nation under heaven.

Now when this was noised abroad, the multitude came together, and were confounded, because that every man heard them speak in his own language.

And they were all amazed and marvelled, saying one to another, Behold, are not all these which speak Galilaeans?

And how hear we every man in our own tongue, wherein we were born?

We do hear them speak in our tongues the wonderful works of God.

And they were all amazed, and were in doubt, saying one to another, What meaneth this?

Others mocking said, These men are full of new wine.

But Peter, standing up with the eleven, lifted up his voice, and said unto them, Ye men of Judaea, and all ye that dwell at Jerusalem, be this known unto you, and hearken to my words:

For these are not drunken, as ye suppose, seeing it is but the third hour of the day.

But this is that which was spoken by the prophet Joel: (over)

And it shall come to pass in the last days, saith God, I will pour out of my Spirit upon all flesh:

And your sons and your daughters shall prophesy, and your young men shall see visions, and your old men shall dream dreams:

And on my servants and on my handmaidens I will pour out in those days of my Spirit; and they shall prophesy:

And I will show wonders in heaven above, and signs in the earth beneath; blood, and fire, and vapour of smoke:

The sun shall be turned into darkness, and the moon into blood, before that great and notable day of the Lord come:

And it shall come to pass, that whosoever shall call on the name of the Lord shall be saved.
—Acts 2: 1-8, 11-21.

605 REDEMPTION IN CHRIST

Therefore being justified by faith, we have peace with God through our Lord Jesus Christ:

By whom also we have access by faith into this grace wherein we stand, and rejoice in hope of the glory of God.

And not only so, but we glory in tribulations also: knowing that tribulation worketh patience;

And patience, experience; and experience, hope:

And hope maketh not ashamed; because the love of God is shed abroad in our hearts by the Holy Ghost which is given unto us.

For when we were yet without strength, in due time Christ died for the ungodly.

For scarcely for a righteous man will one die: yet peradventure for a good man some would even dare to die.

But God commendeth his love toward us, in that, while we were yet sinners, Christ died for us.

Much more then, being now justified by his blood, we shall be saved from wrath through him.

For if, when we were enemies, we were reconciled to God by the death of his Son, much more, being reconciled, we shall be saved by his life.

And not only so, but we also joy in God through our Lord Jesus Christ, by whom we have now received the atonement.

Wherefore, as by one man sin entered into the world, and death by sin; and so death passed upon all men, for that all have sinned:

Therefore as by the offence of one judgment came upon all men to condemnation;

Even so by the righteousness of one the free gift came upon all men unto justification of life.

For as by one man's disobedience many were made sinners, so by the obedience of one shall many be made righteous.

There is therefore now no condemnation to them which are in Christ Jesus, who walk not after the flesh, but after the Spirit.
—Romans 5: 1-12, 18, 19; 8: 1.

606 CHRISTIAN ASSURANCE

As many as are led by the Spirit of God, they are the sons of God.

For ye have not received the spirit of bondage again to fear; but ye have received the Spirit of adoption, whereby we cry, Abba, Father.

The Spirit itself beareth witness with our spirit, that we are the children of God:

And if children, then heirs; heirs of God, and joint-heirs with Christ; if so be that we suffer with him, that we may be also glorified together.

For I reckon that the sufferings of this present time are not worthy to be compared with the glory which shall be revealed in us.

And we know that all things work together for good to them that love God, to them who are the called according to his purpose.

What shall we then say to these things? If God be for us, who can be against us?

He that spared not his own Son, but delivered him up for us all, how shall he not with him also freely give us all things?

Who shall separate us from the love of Christ? shall tribulation, or distress, or persecution, or famine, or nakedness, or peril, or sword?

Nay, in all these things we are more than conquerors through him that loved us.

For I am persuaded, that neither death, nor life, nor angels, nor principalities, nor powers, nor things present, nor things to come,

Nor height, nor depth, nor any other creature, shall be able to separate us from the love of God, which is in Christ Jesus our Lord.
—Romans 8: 14-18, 28, 31, 32, 35, 37-39.

607 CALL TO CONSECRATION

I beseech you therefore, brethren, by the mercies of God, that ye present your bodies a living sacrifice, holy, acceptable unto God, which is your reasonable service.

And be not conformed to this world: but be ye transformed by the renewing of your mind, that ye may prove what is that good, and acceptable, and perfect, will of God.

For I say, through the grace given unto me, to every man that is among you, not to think of himself more highly than he ought to think;

But to think soberly, according as God hath dealt to every man the measure of faith.

For as we have many members in one body, and all members have not the same office:

So we, being many, are one body in Christ, and every one members one of another.

Having then gifts differing according to the grace that is given to us, whether prophecy, let us prophesy according to the proportion of faith;

Or ministry, let us wait on our ministering; or he that teacheth, on teaching; Or he that exhorteth, on exhortation:

He that giveth, let him do it with simplicity; he that ruleth, with diligence; he that showeth mercy, with cheerfulness.

Let love be without dissimulation. Abhor that which is evil; cleave to that which is good.

Be kindly affectioned one to another with brotherly love; in honour preferring one another;

Not slothful in business; fervent in spirit; serving the Lord;

Rejoicing in hope; patient in tribulation; continuing instant in prayer;

Distributing to the necessity of saints; given to hospitality.

Bless them which persecute you: bless, and curse not.

Rejoice with them that do rejoice, and weep with them that weep.

Be of the same mind one toward another. Mind not high things, but condescend to men of low estate. Be not wise in your own conceits.

Recompense to no man evil for evil. Provide things honest in the sight of all men.

If it be possible, as much as lieth in you, live peaceably with all men.

Dearly beloved, avenge not yourselves, but rather give place unto wrath: for it is written, Vengeance is mine; I will repay, saith the Lord.

Therefore if thine enemy hunger, feed him; if he thirst, give him drink: for in so doing thou shalt heap coals of fire on his head.

Be not overcome of evil, but overcome evil with good.   —Romans 12.

608 THE LOVE CHAPTER

Though I speak with the tongues of men and of angels, and have not love, I am become as sounding brass, or a tinkling cymbal.

And though I have the gift of prophecy, and understand all mysteries, and all knowledge; and though I have all faith, so that I could remove mountains, and have not love, I am nothing.

And though I bestow all my goods to feed the poor, and though I give my body to be burned, and have not love, it profiteth me nothing.

Love suffereth long, and is kind; love envieth not; love vaunteth not itself, is not puffed up.

Doth not behave itself unseemly, seeketh not her own, is not easily provoked, thinketh no evil;

Rejoiceth not in iniquity, but rejoiceth in the truth;

Beareth all things, believeth all things, hopeth all things, endureth all things.

Love never faileth: but whether there be prophecies, they shall fail; whether there be tongues, they shall cease; whether there be knowledge, it shall vanish away.

For we know in part, and we prophesy in part.

But when that which is perfect is come, then that which is in part shall be done away.

When I was a child, I spake as a child, I understood as a child, I thought as a child: but when I became a man, I put away childish things.

For now we see through a glass, darkly; but then face to face:

Now I know in part; but then shall I know even as also I am known.

And now abideth faith, hope, love, these three; but the greatest of these is love. —I Corinthians 13.

609 CHRIST & IMMORTALITY

Now is Christ risen from the dead, and become the firstfruits of them that slept.

For since by man came death, by man came also the resurrection of the dead.

For as in Adam all die, even so in Christ shall all be made alive.

But every man in his own order: Christ the firstfruits; afterward they that are Christ's at his coming.

Then cometh the end, when he shall have delivered up the kingdom to God, even the Father; when he shall have put down all rule and all authority and power.

For he must reign, till he hath put all enemies under his feet.

The last enemy that shall be destroyed is death.

There is one glory of the sun, and another glory of the moon, and another glory of the stars: for one star differeth from another star in glory.

So also is the resurrection of the dead. It is sown in corruption; it is raised in incorruption:

It is sown in dishonour; it is raised in glory: it is sown in weakness; it is raised in power:

It is sown a natural body; it is raised a spiritual body. There is a natural body, and there is a spiritual body.

And so it is written, The first man Adam was made a living soul; the last Adam was made a quickening spirit.

The first man is of the earth, earthy: the second man is the Lord from heaven.

As is the earthy, such are they also that are earthy: and as is the heavenly, such are they also that are heavenly.

And as we have borne the image of the earthy, we shall also bear the image of the heavenly.

For this corruptible must put on incorruption, and this mortal must put on immortality.

So when this corruptible shall have put on incorruption, and this mortal shall have put on immortality, then shall be brought to pass the saying that is written, Death is swallowed up in victory.

O death, where is thy sting? O grave, where is thy victory?

The sting of death is sin; and the strength of sin is the law.

But thanks be to God, which giveth us the victory through our Lord Jesus Christ.

—I Corinthians 15: 20-26, 41-45, 47-49, 53-57.

610   CHRISTIAN CONDUCT

The fruit of the Spirit is love, joy, peace, longsuffering, gentleness, goodness, faith, meekness, temperance: against such there is no law.

And they that are Christ's have crucified the flesh with the affections and lusts.

If we live in the Spirit, let us also walk in the Spirit.

Let us not be desirous of vainglory, provoking one another, envying one another.

Brethren, if a man be overtaken in a fault, ye which are spiritual, restore such an one in the spirit of meekness; considering thyself, lest thou also be tempted.

Bear ye one another's burdens, and so fulfill the law of Christ.

For if a man think himself to be something, when he is nothing, he deceiveth himself.

Let every man prove his own work, and then shall he have rejoicing in himself alone, and not in another: for every man shall bear his own burden.

Let him that is taught in the word communicate unto him that teacheth in all good things.

Be not deceived; God is not mocked: for whatsoever a man soweth, that shall he also reap.

For he that soweth to his flesh shall of the flesh reap corruption;

But he that soweth to the Spirit shall of the Spirit reap life everlasting.

Let us not be weary in well doing: for in due season we shall reap, if we faint not.

As we have therefore opportunity, let us do good unto all men, especially unto them who are of the household of faith.

As many as walk according to this rule, peace be on them, and mercy, and upon the Israel of God.

The grace of our Lord Jesus Christ be with your spirit. Amen.

—Galatians 5: 22-26; 6: 1-10, 16, 18.

611   SPIRITUAL WARFARE

Finally, my brethren, be strong in the Lord, and in the power of his might.

Put on the whole armour of God, that ye may be able to stand against the wiles of the devil.

For we wrestle not against flesh and blood, but against principalities, against powers, against the rulers of the darkness of this world, against spiritual wickedness in high places.

Wherefore take unto you the whole armour of God, that ye may be able to withstand in the evil day, and having done all, to stand.

Stand therefore, having your loins girt about with truth, and having on the breastplate of righteousness;

And your feet shod with the preparation of the gospel of peace;

Above all, taking the shield of faith, wherewith ye shall be able to quench all the fiery darts of the wicked.

And take the helmet of salvation, and the sword of the Spirit, which is the word of God: (over)

Praying always with all prayer and supplication in the Spirit, and watching thereunto with all perseverance and supplication for all saints.
—Ephesians 6: 10-18.

The night is far spent, the day is at hand: let us therefore cast off the works of darkness, and let us put on the armour of light.

Let us walk honestly, as in the day; not in rioting and drunkenness, not in chambering and wantoness, not in strife and envying.

But put ye on the Lord Jesus Christ, and make not provision for the flesh, to fulfil the lusts thereof.
—Romans 13: 12-14.

612 THE MIND OF CHRIST

If there be therefore any consolation in Christ, if any comfort of love, if any fellowship of the Spirit, if any tender mercies and compassions,

Fulfil ye my joy, that ye be like-minded, having the same love, being of one accord, of one mind.

Let nothing be done through strife or vainglory; but in lowliness of mind let each esteem other better than themselves.

Look not every man on his own things, but every man also on the things of others.

Let this mind be in you, which was also in Christ Jesus:

Who, being in the form of God, thought it not robbery to be equal with God:

But made himself of no reputation, and took upon him the form of a servant, and was made in the likeness of men:

And being found in fashion as a man, he humbled himself, and became obedient unto death, even the death of the cross.

Wherefore God also hath highly exalted him, and given him a name which is above every name:

That at the name of Jesus every knee should bow, of things in heaven, and things in earth, and things under the earth;

And that every tongue should confess that Jesus Christ is Lord, to the glory of God the Father.

It is God which worketh in you both to will and to do of his good pleasure.

Do all things without murmurings and disputings: that ye may be blameless and harmless, the sons of God, without rebuke, in the midst of a crooked and perverse nation,

Among whom ye shine as lights in the world; holding forth the word of life.
—Philippians 2: 1-11, 13-16.

613 THE RETURN OF CHRIST

But I would not have you to be ignorant, brethren, concerning them which are asleep, that ye sorrow not, even as others which have no hope.

For if we believe that Jesus died and rose again, even so them also which sleep in Jesus will God bring with him.

For this we say unto you by the word of the Lord, that we which are alive and remain unto the coming of the Lord shall not precede them which are asleep.

For the Lord himself shall descend from heaven with a shout, with the voice of the archangel, and with the trump of God: and the dead in Christ shall rise first.

Then we which are alive and remain shall be caught up together with them in the clouds, to meet the Lord in the air: and so shall we ever be with the Lord.

Wherefore comfort one another with these words.

But of the times and the seasons, brethren, ye have no need that I write unto you.

For yourselves know perfectly that the day of the Lord so cometh as a thief in the night.

For when they shall say, Peace and safety; then sudden destruction cometh upon them, as travail upon a woman with child; and they shall not escape.

But ye, brethren, are not in darkness, that that day should overtake you as a thief.

Ye are all the children of light, and the children of the day: we are not of the night, nor of darkness.

Therefore let us not sleep, as do others; but let us watch and be sober.

For they that sleep sleep in the night; and they that be drunken are drunken in the night.

But let us, who are of the day, be sober, putting on the breastplate of faith and love; and for an helmet, the hope of salvation.

For God hath not appointed us to wrath, but to obtain salvation by our Lord Jesus Christ,

Who died for us, that, whether we wake or sleep, we should live together with him. —I Thessalonians 4: 13-18; 5: 1-10.

614 A CHALLENGE TO FAITH

Now faith is the substance of things hoped for, the evidence of things not seen.

For by it the elders obtained a good report.

By faith Abel offered unto God a more excellent sacrifice than Cain,

By which he obtained witness that he was righteous, and by it he being dead yet speaketh.

By faith Enoch was translated that he should not see death; and was not found, because God had translated him:

For before his translation he had this testimony, that he pleased God.

By faith Noah, being warned of God of things not seen as yet, moved with fear, prepared an ark to the saving of his house;

By the which he condemned the world, and became heir of the righteousness which is by faith.

By faith Abraham, when he was called to go out into a place which he should after receive for an inheritance, obeyed; and he went out, not knowing whither he went.

For he looked for a city which hath foundations, whose builder and maker is God.

These all died in faith, not having received the promises, but having seen them afar off, and were persuaded of them, and embraced them, and confessed that they were strangers and pilgrims on the earth.

Wherefore God is not ashamed to be called their God: for he hath prepared for them a city.

And what shall I more say? for the time would fail me to tell of Gideon, and of Barak, and of Samson, and of Jephthah; of David also, and Samuel, and of the prophets: Of whom the world was not worthy:

Who through faith subdued kingdoms, wrought righteousness, obtained promises, stopped the mouths of lions, quenched the violence of fire, escaped the edge of the sword, out of weakness were made strong, waxed valiant in fight, turned to flight the armies of aliens.

Wherefore seeing we also are compassed about with so great a cloud of witnesses, let us lay aside every weight, and the sin which doth so easily beset us, and let us run with patience the race that is set before us,

Looking unto Jesus the author and finisher of our faith; who for the joy that was set before him endured the cross, despising the shame, and is set down at the right hand of the throne of God. —From Hebrews 11; 12.

615 THE HOLY SCRIPTURES

Knowing this first, that no prophecy of the scripture is of any private interpretation.

For the prophecy came not in old time by the will of man: but holy men of God spake as they were moved by the Holy Ghost.
—II Peter 1:20, 21.

All scripture is given by inspiration of God, and is profitable for doctrine, for reproof, for correction, for instruction in righteousness:

That the man of God may be perfect, thoroughly furnished unto all good works. —II Timothy 3:16, 17.

Study to show thyself approved unto God, a workman that needeth not to be ashamed, rightly dividing the word of truth. —II Timothy 2:15.

For the word of God is quick, and powerful, and sharper than any two-edged sword, piercing even to the dividing asunder of soul and spirit, and of the joints and marrow, and is a discerner of the thoughts and intents of the heart. —Hebrews 4:12.

But these are written, that ye might believe that Jesus is the Christ, the Son of God; and that believing ye might have life through his name.
—John 20:31.

For whatsoever things were written aforetime were written for our learning, that we through patience and comfort of the scriptures might have hope. —Romans 15: 4.

Teach me, O Lord, the way of thy statutes; and I shall keep it unto the end.

Give me understanding, and I shall keep thy law; yea, I shall observe it with my whole heart.

For ever, O Lord, thy word is settled in heaven.

Thy word is a lamp unto my feet, and a light unto my path.

The entrance of thy words giveth light; it giveth understanding unto the simple.

Great peace have they which love thy law: and nothing shall offend them. —Psalm 119: 33, 34, 89, 105, 130, 165.

616 THE NEW CREATION

And I saw a new heaven and a new earth: for the first heaven and the first earth were passed away; and there was no more sea.

And I John saw the holy city, new Jerusalem, coming down from God out of heaven, prepared as a bride adorned for her husband.

And I heard a great voice out of heaven saying, Behold, the tabernacle of God is with men, and he will dwell with them, and they shall be his people, and God himself shall be with them, and be their God.

And God shall wipe away all tears from their eyes; and there shall be no more death, neither sorrow, nor crying, neither shall there be any more pain: for the former things are passed away.

And he that sat upon the throne said, Behold, I make all things new. And he said unto me, Write: for these words are true and faithful.

And he said unto me, It is done. I am Alpha and Omega, the beginning and the end. I will give unto him that is athirst of the fountain of the water of life freely.

He that overcometh shall inherit all things; and I will be his God, and he shall be my son.

But the fearful, and unbelieving, and the abominable, and murderers, and whoremongers, and sorcerers, and idolaters, and all liars, shall have their part in the lake which burneth with fire and brimstone: which is the second death.

And there came unto me one of the seven angels which had the seven vials full of the seven last plagues, and talked with me, saying, Come hither, I will show thee the bride, the Lamb's wife.

And he carried me away in the spirit to a great and high mountain, and showed me that great city, the holy Jerusalem, descending out of heaven from God,

Having the glory of God: and her light was like unto a stone most precious, even like a jasper stone, clear as crystal.

And I saw no temple therein: for the Lord God Almighty and the Lamb are the temple of it.

And the city had no need of the sun, neither of the moon, to shine in it: for the glory of God did lighten it, and the Lamb is the light thereof.

And the nations of them which are saved shall walk in the light of it: and the kings of the earth do bring their glory and honour into it.

And the gates of it shall not be shut at all by day: for there shall be no night there.

And they shall bring the glory and honour of the nations into it.

And there shall in no wise enter into it any thing that defileth,

Neither whatsoever worketh abomination, or maketh a lie: but they which are written in the Lamb's book of life.

—Revelation 21: 1-11, 22-27.

617 CALLS TO WORSHIP

1—The earth is the Lord's, and the fullness thereof; the world, and they that dwell therein. Lift up your heads, O ye gates; even lift them up, ye everlasting doors; and the King of glory shall come in. Who is this King of glory? The Lord of hosts, he is the King of glory.
(Psalm 24:1, 9, 10)

2—Rejoice in the Lord, O ye righteous: for praise is comely for the upright. The counsel of the Lord standeth forever, the thoughts of his heart to all generations. Blessed is the nation whose God is the Lord; and the people whom he hath chosen for his own inheritance.
(Psalm 33:1, 11, 12)

3—How amiable are thy tabernacles, O Lord of hosts! My soul longeth, yea, even fainteth for the courts of the Lord: my heart and my flesh crieth out for the living God. For the Lord God is a sun and shield: the Lord will give grace and glory: no good thing will he withhold from them that walk uprightly.
(Psalm 84:1, 2, 11)

4—O sing unto the Lord a new song: sing unto the Lord, all the earth. Declare his glory among the heathen, his wonders among all people. Give unto the Lord the glory due unto his name; bring an offering and come into his courts. O worship the Lord in the beauty of holiness: fear before him all the earth.
(Psalm 96:1, 3, 8, 9)

5—Make a joyful noise unto the Lord, all ye lands. Serve the Lord with gladness: come before his presence with singing. Enter into his gates with thanksgiving, and into his courts with praise; be thankful unto him, and bless his name.

For the Lord is good; his mercy is everlasting; and his truth endureth to all generations.
(Psalm 100:1, 2, 4, 5)

6—O give thanks unto the Lord; call upon his name: make known his deeds among the people. Sing unto him, sing psalms unto him: talk ye of all his wondrous works. Glory ye in his holy name: let the heart of them rejoice that seek the Lord.
(Psalm 105:1-3)

7—O give thanks unto the Lord for he is good: for his mercy endureth forever. Let the redeemed of the Lord say so, whom he hath redeemed out of the hand of the enemy. For he satisfieth the longing soul, and filleth the hungry soul with goodness.
(Psalm 107:1, 2, 9)

8—O praise the Lord, all ye nations: praise him, all ye people. For his merciful kindness is great toward us: and the truth of the Lord endureth forever. Praise ye the Lord.
(Psalm 117)

9—Great is the Lord and greatly to be praised; and his greatness is unsearchable. The Lord is righteous in all his ways, and holy in all his works. The Lord is nigh unto all them that call upon him, to all that call upon him in truth.
(Psalm 145:3, 17, 18)

10—Praise ye the Lord: for it is good to sing praises unto our God; for it is pleasant; and praise is comely. Great is our Lord, and of great power: his understanding is infinite. The Lord taketh pleasure in them that fear him, in those that hope in his mercy. Praise the Lord, O Jerusalem; praise thy God, O Zion.
(Psalm 147:1, 5, 11, 12) **(over)**

11—Praise ye the Lord. Sing unto the Lord a new song, and his praise in the congregation of saints. Let Israel rejoice in him that made him: let the children of Zion be joyful in their King. For the Lord taketh pleasure in his people: He will beautify the meek with salvation.
(Psalm 149:1, 2, 4)

12—Praise ye the Lord. Praise God in his sanctuary: Praise him in the firmament of his power. Praise him for His mighty acts: Praise him according to his excellent greatness. Let every thing that hath breath praise the Lord. Praise ye the Lord. (Psalm 150:1, 2, 6)

13—The Lord is in his holy temple: let all the earth keep silence before him. Surely the Lord is in this place. This is none other but the house of God, and this is the gate of heaven. God is a spirit; and they that worship him must worship him in spirit and in truth.
(Habakkuk 2:20; Genesis 28:17; John 4:24)

14—Come unto me, all ye that labour and are heavy laden, and I will give you rest. Take my yoke upon you, and learn of me: for I am meek and lowly in heart; and ye shall find rest unto your souls. For my yoke is easy, and my burden is light. (Matthew 11:28-30)

15—If ye then be risen with Christ, seek those things which are above, where Christ sitteth on the right hand of God. Set your affection on things above, not on things on the earth. For ye are dead, and your life is hid with Christ in God. Let the word of God dwell in you richly in all wisdom; teaching and admonishing one another in psalms and hymns and spiritual songs, singing with grace in your hearts to the Lord. (Colossians 3:1-3, 16)

618   BENEDICTIONS

1—The Lord bless thee, and keep thee: the Lord make his face to shine upon thee, and be gracious unto thee: the Lord lift up his countenance upon thee, and give thee peace. Amen. (Numbers 6:24-26)

2—Let the words of my mouth, and the meditation of my heart, be acceptable in thy sight, O Lord, my strength and my redeemer. Amen. (Psalm 19:14)

3—God be merciful unto us, and bless us, and cause his face to shine upon us; that thy way may be known upon earth thy saving health among all nations. Amen. (Psalm 67:1, 2)

4—Now unto the King eternal, immortal, invisible, the only wise God, be honour and glory for ever and ever. Amen.
(I Timothy 1:17)

5—And the very God of peace sanctify you wholly; and I pray God your whole spirit and soul and body be preserved blameless unto the coming of our Lord Jesus Christ. The grace of our Lord Jesus Christ be with you. Amen.
(I Thessalonians 5:23, 28)

6—Now our Lord Jesus Christ himself, and God, even our Father, which hath loved us, and hath given us everlasting consolation and good hope through grace, Comfort your hearts, and stablish you in every good word and work. Amen.
(II Thessalonians 2:16, 17)

7—Now unto him that is able to do exceeding abundantly above all that we ask or think, according to the power that worketh in us, Unto him be glory in the church by Christ Jesus throughout all ages, world without end. Amen.
(Ephesians 3:20, 21)

8—And the peace of God, which passeth all understanding, shall keep your hearts and minds through Jesus Christ. Amen.
(Philippians 4:7)

9—Be perfect, be of good comfort, be of one mind, live in peace; and the God of love and peace shall be with you. The grace of the Lord Jesus Christ, and the love of God, and the communion of the Holy Ghost, be with you all. Amen.
(II Corinthians 13:11, 14)

10—Now the God of peace, that brought again from the dead our Lord Jesus, that great shepherd of the sheep, through the blood of the everlasting covenant, Make you perfect in every good work to do his will, working in you that which is well pleasing in his sight, through Jesus Christ; to whom be glory for ever and ever. Amen. (Hebrews 13:20, 21)

11—Now unto him that is able to keep you from falling, and to present you faultless before the presence of his glory with exceeding joy, to the only wise God our Saviour, be glory and majesty, dominion and power, both now and ever. Amen.
(Jude 24, 25)

12—The grace of our Lord Jesus Christ be with your spirit. Amen. (Philemon 25)

ALPHABETICAL INDEX OF SCRIPTURE READINGS

SUBJECT INDEX OF SCRIPTURE READINGS

This Index follows the same general order of classification as the hymns, and the Readings are listed under each subject by title and number in the order in which they appear in the section.

page 487

ALPHABETICAL INDEX OF TUNES

ALPHABETICAL INDEX OF TUNES

METRICAL INDEX OF TUNES

METRICAL INDEX OF TUNES

INDEX OF AUTHORS, COMPOSERS, & SOURCES

NOTATION: w following a name signifies the author or translator of hymn or song poem; m following a name signifies the composer or arranger of music; c signifies circa (around).

INDEX OF AUTHORS, COMPOSERS, AND SOURCES

INDEX OF AUTHORS, COMPOSERS, AND SOURCES

TOPICAL INDEX

TOPICAL INDEX

TOPICAL INDEX

TOPICAL INDEX

TOPICAL INDEX

SERVICE MUSIC SECTION INDEX

GENERAL INDEX

Titles are in small CAPS; first lines in lower case type

GENERAL INDEX

GENERAL INDEX

2396